Regulatory Encounters

Multinational Corporations
and American Adversarial Legalism

D0054698

EDITED BY

Robert A. Kagan and Lee Axelrad

UNIVERSITY OF CALIFORNIA PRESS
Berkeley   Los Angeles   London

University of California Press
Berkeley and Los Angeles, California

University of California Press, Ltd.
London, England

© 2000 by the Regents of the University of California

Library of Congress Cataloging-in-Publication Data

Regulatory encounters : multinational corporations and American adversarial legalism /
edited by Robert Allen Kagan and Lee Axelrad
   p.   cm.—(The California series in law, politics, and society; no. 1)
Includes bibliographical references and index.
ISBN 0-520-22287-3 (alk. paper).—ISBN 0-520-22288-1 (pbk. : alk paper)
1. International business enterprises—Law and legislation—United States. 2. International
business enterprises—Law and legislation.   3. Adversarial system (Law) I. Axelrad, Lee,
1963– II. Kagan, Robert Allen, 1938– III. Series.
KF1419.R44   2000
346.73'066—dc21   99-057669

Manufactured in the United States of America

09 08 07 06 05 04 03 02 01 00

10 9 8 7 6 5 4 3 2 1

The paper used in this publication is both acid-free and totally chlorine-free. It meets the
minimum requirements of ANSI/NISO Z39.48–1992 (R 1997) (*Permanence of Paper*).

CONTENTS

Regulatory Encounters

THE CALIFORNIA SERIES IN LAW, POLITICS, AND SOCIETY
Robert A. Kagan and Malcolm Freeley, General Editors

1. Regulatory Encounters: Multinational Corporations and American Adversarial Legalism, *edited by Robert A. Kagan and Lee Axelrad*

ACKNOWLEDGMENTS

This is a many-authored book, and there are many more contributors whose names are not included in the table of contents. Most important are the corporate officials who gave generously of their time to describe and document their interactions with regulatory and legal systems in the United States and other countries. These officials—regulatory affairs officers, environmental managers, attorneys, risk managers, human relations officers, plant managers, and others—are vital cogs in the regulatory process, working regulatory and legal norms into the everyday activities of business enterprises; drawing on their experience, they provided specific insights into the distinctive qualities and effectiveness of national regulatory and legal systems. We were consistently impressed by their candor and by the seriousness with which they took their responsibilities.

We are also grateful to the many corporate and trade association officials, lawyers, regulatory officials, business consultants, and academic colleagues—too numerous to catalog here—who granted us exploratory interviews, guided us to cooperating companies, and provided additional perspective on the issues and findings in each case study in this book. The premise for the informal conversations and formal interviews that led to this volume was a pledge of confidentiality that now constrains us, and the authors of the chapters, from adequately naming many of the subjects of our gratitude.

We extend special thanks to Edward Rubin, Marc Galanter, and Erhard Blankenburg, who provided encouragement and advice in the formulation of the research project as a whole; to the colleagues, lawyers, consultants, and corporate officials who participated in an exploratory workshop at the University of California, Berkeley, in May 1994; and to the colleagues who offered useful comments during the presentation of particular chapters at the Brookings Institution, the University of Wisconsin, Madison, annual meetings of the Law and Society Association, and at Center for the Study of Law and Society, the Department of Political Science, and the School of Law, University of California, Berkeley.

Valuable insights and suggestions were provided by colleagues who read and commented on all or part of the manuscript, including Eugene Bardach, Bridget Hutter, R. Shep Melnick, Pietro Nivola, Roger Noll, Robert Post, David Vogel, and numerous others. Nobu Kitamura provided expert advice and perspective with respect to regulatory enforcement in Japan.

Institutional support for the Comparative Legal Systems Project was steadfastly provided by Rod Watanabe and Margo Rodriguez of UC Berkeley's Center for the Study of Law and Society, an ideal setting for collaboration across disciplinary and national boundaries. Finally, the editors of this volume count themselves fortunate to have had the opportunity to work with a remarkably energetic, cooperative, congenial, and dedicated group of authors, and even more fortunate to have had, throughout the long days and evenings of this project, the love and support of their spouses, Betsy Kagan and Jackie Hausman.

Robert A. Kagan
Lee Axelrad

CHAPTER ONE

How Much Do National Styles of Law Matter?

Robert A. Kagan

This is a book about differences in national legal and regulatory systems—not merely differences in the law on books but differences in the law in action—and about how much those differences really matter. It focuses particularly on the practical consequences of "adversarial legalism," a style of policy implementation and dispute resolution that is especially prevalent in the United States. To highlight the impact of American adversarial legalism, the book presents ten case studies. Each uses a multinational enterprise as a "research site." Each enterprise engages in similar business activities in the United States and in at least one other economically advanced democracy, encountering parallel regulatory regimes and legal institutions. Comparing the company's "regulatory encounters" in the United States and in other countries reveals how national methods of regulation differ in practice and how the companies are compelled to adapt. With some exceptions, the research indicates that adversarial legalism imposes much higher costs and delays on the American operations of multinational corporations. More tentatively, and again with some exceptions, these case studies suggest that American adversarial legalism, despite its more threatening character, often does not generate higher levels of protection for the public than do the less legalistic regulatory regimes of other developed countries—at least in the sector of the economy occupied by large corporations.

I. THE ISSUES IN BRIEF

In a global economy, in which businesses can more easily choose which country to invest or expand in, the costs of doing business imposed by a nation's domestic legal system—its tax law, labor law, environmental law, and so on—take on greater economic significance.[1] In European welfare states, policy analysts argue that generous worker-protection laws are responsible for high unemployment and sluggish economic growth.[2] In Japan, a government report expressed concern that legal restrictions on land use, contrasted to those in Germany and the United States, are "holding back Japan's future development and progress."[3] These statements are part of a domestic political struggle about law and regulation that recurs in all trading nations. In one camp are proponents of security, social justice, and environmental protection; they demand legal rights and governmental regulations to prevent or offset the economic losses and social disruptions, the chemical hazards and environmental degradation that flow from what Joseph Schumpeter called the "creative destruction" of capitalism. In the opposing camp are advocates of laws, legal institutions, and regulatory regimes that above all promote competition and economic efficiency, that limit taxes and restrictions on entrepreneurial activity.

It is risky, of course, to make sweeping generalizations about entire national legal systems, with all their internal complexity and variation. Still, it is probably true that in comparison with most other economically advanced democracies, the legal order of the United States generally has been more supportive of the "economic efficiency" camp. Most European nations levy heavier taxes. Their laws and regulations impose tighter restrictions on business activities such as dismissing unneeded or undesirable workers, starting certain ventures (such as large discount stores), and acquiring and developing property. American corporation law, antitrust law, securities law, and banking regulations all have contributed to a uniquely fluid and competitive system of corporate finance and governance, a high rate of new business formation, and a flexible and mobile labor market. But, again, generalizations are risky. It is not difficult to point out American laws that mandate economically inefficient and wasteful methods of achieving regulatory goals, such as the federal rules for promoting motor vehicle fuel economy or the "Superfund" program for cleaning up contaminated waste disposal sites.[4]

Generalizations also are risky because national legal systems, spurred by sensitivity to the mobility of goods, jobs, and capital in a more competitive global economy, are constantly changing. Both in the United States and abroad, domestic economic and political forces hammer away at obviously inefficient laws and regulations.[5] Moreover, the European Union and a growing array of worldwide treaties demand cross-national *harmonization* of domestic laws on a variety of subjects, from pollution control and protection of intellectual property to the testing and licensing of new pharmaceutical drugs. In consequence, some observers speak of a relentless trend toward convergence of national legal systems.[6]

Both the rate of convergence and the ultimate validity of this "competitive convergence" hypothesis, however, remain uncertain. In every nation, there are political factions and legal traditions that do not worship at the shrine of economic efficiency. Moreover, powerful organizations and interest groups fight to retain laws that buffer them from the rigors of the market. One topic addressed in this volume, therefore, is the degree to which legal rules in the United States, as actually applied, make significantly greater or lesser demands on business enterprises than do comparable legal rules in other economically advanced democracies.

Particularly resistant to transnational harmonization, it appears, are *procedural* and *institutional* aspects of national legal systems: their methods of adjudication and public administration, their modes of drafting statutes, penalizing illegal behavior, and managing relations between regulatory agencies and regulated firms. In this realm—the sphere of "legal and regulatory style"—deeply ingrained national legal and political cultures still seem to govern. That is the message of a substantial body of comparative research, which shows that even when basic substantive legal norms in the United States are similar to those in other countries, the American "legal and regulatory style"—its way of implementing regulations and resolving disputes—is uniquely legalistic, adversarial, and expensive.[7]

Of course, adversarial legalism, as I label this legal style,[8] does not pervade the American legal order uniformly or completely. Indeed, legal contestation in the United States is so cumbersome, costly, and frightening that disputants resolve most conflicts and litigated disputes by informal negotiation. The comparative literature, however, suggests that adversarial legalism is far more common in the United States than elsewhere, and that it is the distinguishing feature of the basic structures of American law and regulation.

In addition to the "competitive convergence" hypothesis concerning basic national legal norms, therefore, this book addresses the "American adversarial legalism" hypothesis: to the direct costs of complying with national laws and regulations, American adversarial legalism adds "friction costs"—expenditures on lawyers, studies, litigation, liability insurance, legally imposed delays and distractions—that are considerably larger than those imposed by other economically advanced democracies.

Like the "competitive convergence" hypothesis, the "American adversarial legalism" hypothesis raises many unanswered questions. How *large*, and how *significant*, are the friction costs that stem from American adversarial legalism? How do the additional expenditures imposed on the American economy by the United States' more fearsome liability law system compare with the higher taxes European nations extract to provide economic security for similar accident victims? How *pervasive* is American adversarial legalism across different sectors of law and different sectors of the economy, particularly as business enterprises and regulatory agencies alike, repelled by the economic and relational costs of litigation, proclaim their preference for nonlegalistic modes of regulation and "alternative dispute resolution"? Is adversarial legalism, as some European observers claim, becoming equally prominent in other economically advanced democracies? How much do the procedural friction costs associated with American adversarial legalism matter in comparison with the direct costs of compliance with different substantive environmental, consumer protection, or labor law rules? Finally, what of the social and economic benefits of adversarial legalism? Does it make the law more effective and responsive to public concerns than the regulatory methods of other countries? Does American adversarial legalism produce norms and added social protections that outweigh its immediate costs?

The answers, not surprisingly, are elusive. Anecdotes and assertions abound, but rarely have they been verified or put into perspective. Scholars have tried to calculate cross-national differences in costs of complying with environmental regulations,[9] but the studies generally are cast at a very high level of aggregation, masking differences in the impact of particular kinds of environmental rules. Moreover, there is almost no serious, systematic research that examines the salience, pervasiveness, and consequences of American adversarial legalism per se, partly because there are no readily available statistical data on the subject.[10]

In the absence of relevant aggregate statistical information, one research approach is to undertake detailed case studies that compare the demands that the American and other national regulatory systems, as they actually operate, make on the governed, and compare how those subject to the law respond to it.[11] This book presents ten such case studies. Each chapter reports on the experience of a specific multinational corporation that conducts parallel business operations, subject to similar national legal or regulatory norms, in the United States and in at least one other economically advanced democracy. Each of the companies studied interacts repeatedly, with respect to the same issues, with two or more national legal and regulatory systems. Thus each multinational corporation is used as an observation post, as it were, for viewing the routine operations and characteristic demands of the different national regimes. By holding constant the business activity and the sphere of legal control—such as environmental regulation, regulation of consumer debt collection, or patent law—the case studies graphically illuminate the extent and the concrete impacts of cross-national differences in national regulatory and legal practices.

II. EXTENDING SOCIOLEGAL RESEARCH ON REGULATION

In adopting a comparative case study method, this volume both draws upon and seeks to contribute to the field of sociolegal studies. Scholars in this intellectual tradition emphasize empirical analysis of the ways in which legal rules, ideas, and practices actually function in legal decision making and how they affect social life. One premise of the field is that the implementation of law is shaped by social, economic, and political factors. The actions and responses of law enforcement officials and of those subject to legal controls cannot be deduced from the text of statutes and high court opinions. Nor can the actions of legal officials or legal subjects be deduced from what an observer might believe to be their economic or political interests, since law-related behavior is affected by people's ideas and attitudes concerning law and legal obligation.[12] The law's salience and meaning to legal decision makers and legal subjects, therefore, must be gleaned from systematic empirical study of the ways in which they attend to, understand, or redefine legal rules, rights, and liabilities.

This maxim has been validated repeatedly in sociolegal research concerning the implementation of regulatory statutes, particularly in the field of "social regulation"—that is, regulations that seek to advance safety and health, environmental protection, nondiscrimination in employment, consumer protection, and so on. Yet even empirical assessments of regulatory implementation have resulted in conflicting generalizations. One extreme position, which can be labeled "legal skepticism," is that most regulatory laws do not have much of an effect at all. One such view reflects the dictum of the late-nineteenth-century sociologist William Graham Sumner: "Law ways cannot change folkways,"[13] including the profit-driven "folkways" of business firms in competitive capitalist systems. Similarly, proponents of a "symbolic politics" theory of regulation point out that politicians often seek to appease the electorate by enacting highly publicized regulatory statutes but then fail to give enforcement agencies the resources needed for thorough monitoring and forceful implementation.[14]

Most empirical studies of regulation, however, suggest that generalizations based on undiluted legal skepticism vastly overstate the case. Many regulatory programs have been extremely effective, even if relatively little is spent on enforcement. Regulations to prevent anthrax in cattle herds virtually eradicated that deadly disease.[15] In the United States, at least, regulations forbidding smoking in restaurants and workplaces have met with surprisingly little resistance.[16] Safety regulations have sharply reduced deaths in coal mines.[17] Environmental regulations have compelled manufacturing companies to spend billions of dollars on pollution control equipment, eliminated lead from gasoline, and sharply reduced particulate matter and chlorofluorocarbons in the air of economically advanced democracies.[18] To prevent burns to small children, the State of Washington passed a law in 1983 requiring new water heaters to be set at a lower temperature; five years later, more than 80 percent of homes (old and new) were in compliance with the level set as safe, compared with some 20 percent before the law, and hospital admissions for tap water burns had declined sharply.[19]

But the legal skeptics are far from completely wrong. Banking regulations did not prevent disastrously large numbers of overly risky loans by American savings and loan organizations in the 1980s or by their Japanese equivalents half a decade later.[20] An example of widespread noncompliance or wholly inadequate enforcement can be found to match almost every regulatory success story. Consequently, most students of regulation regard the degree of regulatory effectiveness (compared with the degree of mere symbolism) as a *variable* phenomenon. And they find that the variation is determined by a wide array of factors—from the level of political consensus surrounding the regulatory norms, to how costly and disruptive it is to comply with them, to kinds of legal powers granted regulatory officials.

Regulatory variability also stems from the divergent enforcement practices of regulatory agencies. Empirical studies have demonstrated, for example, that regulatory enforcement offices differ markedly in the degree to which they "go by the book" in citing rule violations and imposing penalties; some do it, some do not. To understand this variability in regulatory enforcement style, it is helpful to recognize the ineluctable tension between two politically salient visions of the regulatory process. One image, often emphasized by political leaders and interests who advocate forceful regulation, conceives of regulation as an exercise in law enforcement: regulation is viewed as a matter of imposing authoritative legal standards on inherently recalcitrant business enterprises and of promptly levying legal sanctions against violators. The competing image conceives of regulation as a process of social engineering and normative guidance. In this image, regulated businesses have mixed motives and varying capacities, while centrally formulated regulatory rules frequently are ill adapted to the wide range of particular circumstances to which they ostensibly apply. Hence, effective regulation requires whatever blend of rules and exhortation, threat and education, will best induce particular companies to advance the values embodied in the regulatory legislation.[21] The goal is cooperative government-business problem solving and a remediative regulatory response to violations.

Proponents of the more legalistic approach understandably fear that regulatory cooperation will lapse into regulatory capture, as a result of the political leverage of regulated industries and their control of crucial technical and financial information. Some sociolegal studies have described regulator-regulated business relationships that play out that "capture scenario" all too vividly.[22] Other studies, however, have shown that "capture" is far from inevitable and that legalistic enforcement styles can generate pathologies of their own, such as engendering unproductive legalistic defensiveness or cutting off the cooperation that is essential to the institutionalization of regulatory values in technologically changing business firms.[23] Again, the central finding of the cumulative body of sociolegal case studies is that agencies' "regulatory styles" are variable. They evolve in response to a number of factors. Some determinative influences arise from the agency's "political environment"—such as the relative capacity of regulated industries (and of pro-regulation political factions and advocacy organizations) to challenge agency officials effectively in court, or their capacity to generate political pressure on regulatory agencies to be either "tougher" or "more reasonable," or the relative capacity of those contending forces to increase or decrease regulatory enforcement budgets.[24] But researchers have noted that enforcement style just as often is shaped by intrinsic features of an agency's "task environment"—such as whether violations are readily visible to regulatory inspectorates, the economic resilience of regulated firms, the seriousness of the harms threatened by regulatory violations, and whether a highly publicized catastrophe attributable to inadequate regulation has occurred in the recent past.[25]

While most sociolegal studies of regulatory enforcement have sought to *explain why* implementation style varies, there has been less research concerning the *consequences* of variation in enforcement methods—that is, how regulatory style affects the day-to-day responses of regulated entities. The relative infrequency of that kind of research is understandable. It is far easier to interview or observe public officials in regulatory agencies than to interview or observe regulated businesses that are widely scattered and induce them to disclose how they adapt to the regulatory laws and agencies that they encounter. Thus there has been little systematic research on whether more legalistic modes of enforcement actually generate significantly higher levels of deterrence or elicit more thoroughgoing compliance than do more flexible enforcement methods.[26]

This book seeks to make a contribution to that line of sociolegal research, while extending it in two ways. First, our research method is comparative, examining how the same multinational company responds to contrasting national regulatory regimes and methods of regulatory implementation. Second, in focusing on multinational corporations, the research necessarily focuses on very large companies. This is significant not only because very large corporations are immensely important actors in contemporary economies but also because their regulatory compliance activities and interactions with regulators rarely have been studied in intimate detail. Moreover, research has suggested that large corporations generally have a strong pragmatic interest in developing a reputation for compliance with regulations.[27] Consequently, they can be viewed as sensitive receptors and reflectors of differences in the demands actually made by different regulatory and legal regimes. In short, large multinational companies provide a unique perspective on some ways in which differences in law and regulatory practices really matter.

III. WHAT IS ADVERSARIAL LEGALISM?

After comparing corporate governance in the United States, the United Kingdom, France, Japan, and Germany, Jonathan Charkham wrote, "Litigation only figures in one of the countries studied. . . . The unheavenly trio of derivative suits, class actions, and contingency fees is unique to the USA."[28] Thomas Church, Robert Nakamura, and Christopher McMahon studied cleanup of toxic waste sites in the United States, Denmark, and the Netherlands. They found that under the American regulatory regime, governed by the federal "Superfund" statute, the Environmental Protection Agency (EPA) regularly instituted legal action demanding payment for cleanup costs from companies whose chemical wastes had ended up in a site. The result has been constant and expensive legal conflict surrounding each site, which ends up delaying cleanup efforts. "[C]leanup of hazardous waste sites in The Netherlands and Denmark," the researchers conclude, "almost certainly operates with less acrimony . . . and more cooperation than in the United States."[29] In the 1970s and 1980s, the rate of asbestos-related diseases among Dutch workers was five to ten times higher than in the United States. Although Dutch law permitted tort suits against employers, fewer than ten asbestos-related tort cases were filed in the Netherlands between 1981 and 1991; diseased workers relied instead on a publicly funded compensation program.[30] In the United States, in contrast, an estimated two hundred thousand asbestos-related tort claims had been filed by 1992, as claimants circumvented the administratively based workers' compensation system.[31]

The contrasting images conveyed by these studies are not idiosyncratic. In the past two decades, social scientists and legal scholars have conducted numerous studies that compare particular legal and regulatory processes in the United States and in other economically advanced democracies. The studies cover such social functions as adjudicating civil lawsuits;[32] compensating individuals injured in motor vehicle accidents,[33] or those hurt by dangerous products or medical malpractice;[34] and regulating pollution,[35] workplace safety,[36] and exposure to toxic chemicals.[37] Repeatedly, these studies found that the relevant *American* legal or regulatory process tends to be characterized by (1) more complex and detailed bodies of rules; (2) more frequent recourse to formal legal methods of implementing policy and resolving disputes; (3) more adversarial and expensive forms of legal contestation; (4) more punitive legal sanctions (including larger civil damage awards); (5) more frequent judicial review, revision, and delay of administrative decision making; and (6) more legal uncertainty, malleability, and unpredictability.

I use the term *adversarial legalism* to help summarize those features of the American legal and regulatory style. Table 1.1 helps distinguish adversarial legalism from other modes of governance. As the table suggests, adversarial legalism, by emphasizing formal legal governance and contestation, differs from *informal* methods of implementing public policy and resolving disputes—such as mediation, reliance on expert professional judgment, or "corporatist" bargaining among political and business elites. But formal legal methods are not all the same. In adversarial legalism, private interest groups, business firms, litigants, and lawyers play active roles in the policy implementation and decision-making process; hence, adversarial legalism differs from governance and conflict resolution that is legally formal but more hierarchically organized. In systems characterized by *bureaucratic legalism,* legal and regulatory authority is concentrated in a single (often nationwide) judicial or administrative bureaucracy; decision makers are relatively insulated from local pressures and aggressive lawyers, for they are expected above all to adhere closely to centrally formulated, uniformly applicable legal rules. In adversarial legalism, in contrast, legal and regulatory authority is fragmented; administrative and legal bodies compete for control and are deliberately made more open to local and litigant influence. In short, adversarial legalism can be defined as a method of policy making and dispute resolution characterized by the following:

- formal legal contestation—competing interests and disputants readily invoke legal rights, duties, and procedural requirements, backed by recourse to formal law enforcement, strong legal penalties, litigation, and/or judicial review;
- litigant activism—formal legal contestation is of a particular kind: the assertion of claims and the gathering and submission of evidence are dominated not by judges or governmental officials but by disputing parties or interests, acting primarily through lawyers.

Organizationally, adversarial legalism typically is associated with and is embedded in decision-making institutions in which authority is fragmented and hierarchical control is relatively weak.

As a consequence of these defining features, adversarial legalism also entails two further characteristics noted in the comparative studies:

- costliness—litigant-controlled, adversarial legal decision making tends to be particularly complex, protracted, and costly;
- legal uncertainty—both the fragmentation of political and legal authority and adversarial advocacy render official legal norms and decisions relatively malleable and variable.

TABLE 1.1. Modes of Policy Implementation and Dispute Resolution

	Informal	↔	*Formal*
Hierarchical	Expert or political judgment		Bureaucratic legalism
Party-influenced	Negotiation		
	Mediation		Adversarial legalism

Thus the American tort law system for compensating victims of highway, medical, and product-related accidents is more decentralized and adversarial, more driven by litigant activism and energetic lawyering, than European methods, which operate primarily through hierarchically organized national benefit-paying bureaucracies. Similarly, in Western European courts, bureaucratically organized judges dominate fact-finding and selection of expert witnesses. In American adversarial legalism, attorneys for the parties dominate those processes.[38] The American judiciary is not organized in a neat nationwide hierarchy; politically selected American judges are less bureaucratically oriented than European judges, more venturesome in reinterpreting legal rules and making new law.[39] Even when compared with the British "adversarial system," American adjudication is more party-influenced. American judges are more diverse and autonomous than British judges, more open to novel legal and policy arguments put forth by parties and their lawyers; their decisions are less uniform and predictable.[40] In the United States, judges in civil cases share power with lay jurors, which magnifies the importance of skillful legal advocacy by the parties and reduces legal certainty.[41]

Similarly, while the parliamentary democracies of Western Europe and Japan arm governmental environmental and safety regulators with strong hierarchical authority, regulatory policy making and implementation in the United States reflects an abiding distrust of hierarchical authority. American regulatory policy making entails many more legal formalities that are designed to facilitate interest group participation and party-triggered judicial review of administrative decisions. These formalities include public notice and comment on proposed rules; open hearings; restrictions on informal contacts between regulators and regulated groups; legalistically specified evidentiary and scientific standards; and mandatory official "findings" and responses to interest group arguments. In Western European and Japanese regulatory policy making, by contrast, a combination of "expert and political judgment" prevails, checked by corporatist arrangements in which business leaders (and, in some countries, labor leaders) play a strong consultative role; lawyers rarely participate, and appeals to the courts are even rarer.[42]

At the level of regulatory policy implementation, governmental authority in the United States tends to be institutionally fragmented and subject to legal challenge, both by regulated companies and by pro-regulation advocacy groups. In consequence, American regulatory implementation often has been described as legalistic and adversarial. In this regulatory style, regulated entities are treated with mistrust; desired behaviors are closely specified in detailed regulations; detected violations are often penalized; recourse to courts, by both the regulators and the regulated, is common; and a spirit of adversarial gamesmanship often prevails.

In other economically advanced democracies, where hierarchical authority is less aggressively questioned, regulatory agencies tend to employ a more informal, cooperation-seeking, or "educational" implementation style. Disputes between regulators and regulated industries are resolved through negotiation or via informal appeal to higher political authorities. Recourse to courts and to formal legal conflict is infrequent. As summarized by Daniel Okimoto, whereas government-business relations in Japan are "informal, close, cooperative, flexible, reciprocal, non-litigious, and long-term in orientation," in the United States most business-government relations "can be characterized as formal, distant, rigid, suspicious, legalistic, narrow, and short-term oriented."[43]

A. *The Political Sources of Adversarial Legalism*

Adversarial legalism characterizes many (although not all) spheres of law and regulatory policy in the United States because of distinctive features of American politics. It reflects a political tradition pervaded by mistrust of both concentrated governmental power and concentrated economic power. The federal and state constitutions are designed to fragment governmental authority and to constrain it by law. American antitrust and banking laws fostered the development of a system of corporate ownership and finance that, viewed comparatively, is particularly disaggregated and competitive. In contrast to many Western European countries and Japan, the United States never developed hierarchical instruments of economic governance—such as powerful central banks and finance ministries, strong business associations, cartels, closely linked families of interlocked corporations—which give central governments informal, nonlegalistic ways of restraining corporate misbehavior and influencing industrial structure. The American business community, David Vogel has argued, is less deferential to government than its counterparts in England and Western Europe and is far more inclined to battle government regulation in the courts.[44] Markets and contracts, structured by lawyers and judges and enforced through litigation, have always played a more prominent role in economic governance in the United States than in other capitalist systems.

Contemporary American adversarial legalism, however, has been intensified by more recent changes in political culture. At least since the 1960s, political movements and advocacy groups have demanded increasingly comprehensive governmental protections from a variety of harms—racial discrimination, gender inequality, environmental degradation, hazardous products and technologies, sudden economic loss, arbitrary treatment by police and other governmental bodies, and so on. These political demands, in effect, have called for a more powerful, more *activist* government. The United States is not alone in this regard, of course. In the last few decades, similar political demands have been made in other rich democracies. But in the United States, political demands for a more powerful and active government have been shaped and channeled by the distinctive political legacies mentioned previously: (1) a political culture that continues to reflect deep mistrust of governmental and business power, and (2) political structures—separation of powers, politically divided government, loosely disciplined political parties—that fragment governmental power. The result has been a style of regulation that is more adversarial and legalistic than the regulation in other countries.

For example, in the 1964–72 period, Congress enacted a wave of ambitious environmental, consumer protection, and antidiscrimination laws, mandating significant changes in business behavior. But at the same time, American regulatory reformers were preoccupied by fears of regulatory "capture"—the notion that in the permeable American political and administrative system, regulated businesses would corrupt and distort regulatory policy making and enforcement. Conversely, business interests feared that newly empowered federal bureaucracies would be hostile to capitalism and insensitive to economic needs and technological limits. For all factions, adversarial legalism provided the tools for guarding against the feared abuses of power. Thus Congress increased governmental regulatory authority dramatically but fragmented that authority among many agencies and subjected it to the checks of detailed laws and privately activated adversarial procedures.

Moreover, because of the political legacy of fragmenting governmental authority, the new regulatory powers often were divided among a welter of cross-checking federal, state, and local agencies.[45] But again, pro-regulation interests and politicians were concerned that these far-flung, politically responsive regulatory officials would be unduly lenient, while pro-business interest groups and politicians were concerned that regulators appointed by pro-regulation politicians would be unreasonably strict. Hence, the new federal regulatory statutes, shaped by the clash of competing interest groups, restricted administrators' discretion, spelling out in extraordinary detail the rules, procedures, deadlines, and analytic standards that regulatory agencies must follow. Regulatory advocacy groups and regulated businesses obtained expanded legal rights to participate in regulatory deliberations and appeal regulatory decisions to the judiciary. To counteract the prospect of evasion by regulated entities, the new statutes and regulations tended to be unusually detailed and prescriptive (compared with regulations in other countries); they also prescribed substantial monetary fines and criminal penalties for violators, and empowered citizens and advocacy groups to bring lawsuits against noncompliant companies and governmental bodies.[46]

In sum, fueled by mistrust of concentrated governmental power and mistrust of business, lawsuits, rights, legal penalties, lawyers, and courts—the building blocks of adversarial legalism—have been the American substitutes for the powerful bureaucracies, corporatist bodies, central banks, and industrial groups that dominate the regulatory state in other economically advanced democracies.

B. *The Consequences of Adversarial Legalism*

By exalting formal legal procedures, lawyers, and courts, adversarial legalism gives ordinary citizens, businesses, and activist organizations a greater voice in regulatory processes and empowers them to challenge governmental arbitrariness and corporate heedlessness. It makes public policy more responsive to new ideas, local conditions, and the interests of political minorities. Using the sword of adversarial legalism, the National Association for the Advancement of Colored People (NAACP) mounted a surprisingly successful attack on official racial discrimination, disabled children won rights to better education, and innovative companies cracked open telecommunications and financial monopolies. By enabling plaintiffs' lawyers to uncover evidence of negligence or fraud, adversarial legalism probably plays a role in encouraging safer technologies and more trustworthy financial markets. By putting real teeth into environmental law, adversarial legalism has pushed private enterprise to take environmental problems seriously, thereby reducing harmful pollution. In a political culture that mistrusts governmental and corporate power, adversarial legalism, with its emphasis on legal rights and legal challenge, may lend a valuable dose of legitimacy to the regime as a whole.

On the other hand, adversarial legalism is an extraordinarily costly, divisive, and often ineffective way of making and implementing public policy. Similarly, in compensating victims of negligently inflicted injuries, the adversarial and legalistic American tort law system is far more wasteful, erratic, and ineffective than the social insurance plans and more predictable tort law of other economically advanced democracies. And despite years of welfare rights litigation, the United States lags well behind other rich nations in social provision for the poor.

Broad generalizations about adversarial legalism's virtues and limits, however, obscure the rich variability of outcomes. Whether adversarial legalism is "better" or "worse" than other approaches depends on detailed assessment of particular legal, regulatory, and social contexts. From a public policy perspective, the most relevant issues are these: Under what circumstances and for what social problems do adversarial legalism's virtues outweigh its social and economic costs? Precisely when and where would alternative legal and regulatory methods be more effective and fair? Before addressing such normative or policy questions, however, it would be helpful to consider some relevant comparative information. That more limited goal is the purpose of the research presented in this volume.

IV. SPECIFYING THE RESEARCH QUESTIONS

Within the United States, as noted earlier, adversarial legalism is by no means omnipresent. Some policy arenas, administrative systems, communities, and business sectors are relatively free of it.[47] The costs and uncertainties of litigation impel *most* disputants to negotiate an informal settlement or to structure their conduct to avoid even a hint of a regulatory violation or cause for a lawsuit. In recent years, state legislatures have enacted dozens of laws designed to restrict tort litigation and to encourage streamlined permitting systems for new businesses.[48] Businesses have scrambled to build "alternative dispute resolution" procedures into their contracts and personnel management systems. Some American regulatory agencies emphasize flexible rather than legalistic and punitive modes of enforcement.[49] Regulatory officials recurrently announce less legalistic, "cooperative" strategies of implementation. Some state environmental protection agencies routinely fail to penalize violations at all, even when a legalistic approach seems quite warranted.[50] Adversarial legalism, in short, is under attack, raising questions about whether it is actually on the wane.

At the same time, some legal scholars have suggested that American-style adversarial legalism is on the rise in other countries, diminishing the uniqueness of the United States in this respect. Privatization of government-owned monopolies, the crumbling of tight industrial-banking cartels, and the declining power of labor unions have made European capitalist systems look a bit more like the competitive, legal-conflict-generating American model. As regulatory authority in Europe has shifted to European Union bureaucracies in Brussels, European business executives have begun to complain about encountering more formalistic and procedurally complex modes of regulation.[51] Some legal scholars now speak of the "Americanization" of European commercial law.[52] Disputes over land use projects in France and Germany, one study suggests, end up in court as often as in the United States.[53] One set of questions that animates this study, therefore, asks the following:

• Viewed in comparative perspective, to what extent does adversarial legalism remain *distinctive* to the United States?
• How *pervasive* is adversarial legalism across areas of American law and regulation?

Even if differences in national legal and regulatory style persist, it is not clear how important they are in terms of either economic or environmental *outcomes*. Nationwide or sectoral studies of national environmental compliance costs and of their effects on corporate production decisions tend to show either no significant effects or effects that are rather small.[54] Factors other than regulatory experience (such as labor costs, human capital, locational advantages, tax laws) are far more important than environmental regulation in shaping corporate strategy and national competitiveness.

Moreover, many multinational corporations claim to implement identical standards of pollution control in all their facilities, regardless of differences in national regulations and implementation methods. A pollution control consultant who has had broad international experience told us that in 1996 that "probably 75 percent of big firms" based in the United States had required their overseas subsidiaries to achieve the same level of environmental performance as their American operations. Whether this policy is adopted for economic reasons or as part of a political or public relations strategy, multinational *corporate-level* "harmonization" may be making national differences in law and regulation less important. These trends raise a second set of questions:

• Do regulated enterprises regard differences among national legal standards and regulatory methods as important factors or as minor factors in their business operations?
• Do national differences in law and regulation result in large or small differences in corporate compliance measures, compliance costs, transaction costs, and effective protections for the public?
• Compared with cross-national differences in *substantive law,* how important to business operations are cross-national differences in *styles* of litigation and regulation?

V. THE COMPARATIVE LEGAL SYSTEMS PROJECT

To take some steps toward addressing these broad questions, in 1995 the Center for Law and Society at the University of California, Berkeley, initiated a Comparative Legal Systems Project. The project's method has been to explore the legal experience of multinational corporations that conduct "parallel" business operations in the United States and in at least one other economically advanced democracy. By holding constant the business activity, we sought to discern the extent and the actual impact of differences in national legal and regulatory rules and methods.

Project researchers first conducted exploratory interviews with more than one hundred corporate executives and lawyers, as well as with over forty experienced consultants, independent attorneys, trade association officers, and governmental officials. In the case of nine corporations, initial interviews developed into intensive case studies; in each, a multinational company agreed to provide detailed information concerning its legal and regulatory experience in the United States and another country concerning a particular sphere of law or regulation. One additional case study (Johnson, Fujie, and Aalders, chapter 11) is based on in-depth interviews with officials from *several* multinational chemical companies. Since the requested information is often competitively or legally sensitive, the researchers in all but one study (in which the company asserted its indifference to being identified) agreed not to disclose the identities of cooperating companies and officials.[55] Table 1.2 lists the nature and location of the enterprises that participated in detailed case studies, the type of business activity that the studies focus on, and the relevant sphere of law and regulation. For company officials, cooperating in a case study is far more demanding than filling out a questionnaire or agreeing to a single, relatively short interview. As researchers, the primary problem we faced was persuading busy company executives and lawyers not only to take the time to engage in extended interviews but also to commit other company officials to provide supporting information through interviews and corporate records. Each case study emerged only after a rather extended courtship.

The companies interviewed and the case studies, therefore, do not represent a statistically representative sample of business firms. The selection of respondents can best be described as opportunistic. We approached most cooperating companies through chains of personal contact, referring to an intermediary who could vouch for the researchers' commitment to objectivity. Not infrequently, even this method was unsuccessful, as corporate officials knowledgeable enough to compare their company's experience across nations were difficult to locate or said they lacked time to cooperate.[56]

Many kinds of companies and issues we would have wished to study, therefore, eluded our courtship efforts, sometimes declining even a second date. Our list of case studies, it turned out, is weighted more heavily toward environmental regulation than we originally expected. The list does not include any multinational investment banking firms, which could provide insight into the significance, in their experience, of national differences in

TABLE 1.2.   Case Studies

Authors	Industry	Countries	Legal Policy/ Functional Activity
Aoki and Cioffi	Metals fabrication	U.S., Japan	Regulation of industrial waste disposal
Aoki, Axelrad, and Kagan	Manufacture of electronic parts	U.S., Japan	Regulation of industrial effluent
Axelrad	Chemicals	U.S., U.K., and Netherlands	Remediation of contaminated factory sites
Welles and Engel	Solid waste disposal	U.S., U.K., and Netherlands	Siting and design of waste disposal facilities
Dwyer, Brooks, and Marco	Motor vehicle manufacturing	U.S., Germany	Regulation of air pollution
Nielsen	Pharmaceuticals	U.S., Canada	Dismissal of employees
Ruhlin	Banking	U.S, Germany	Collecting consumer debt
Somaya	Chemicals	U.S., EU, Japan	Obtaining and defending patents
Kraus	Biotech bio-logical products	U.S., EU	Licensing of production facilities
Johnson Fujie, and Aalders	Chemicals	U.S., EU, Japan	Regulation of new chemical products

securities regulation. Nor does it include a car rental, package delivery, or insurance company, which could illuminate the significance of national differences in the law of motor vehicle accidents; or food processors and toy manufacturers, which could speak to the significance of national differences in product liability law; or producers of motion pictures, recorded music, or computer software, who could inform us about the practical impact of national differences in law and enforcement practices related to copyright protection. The list of omissions obviously could be extended considerably. It would take at least one more wave of case studies to provide even a partially rounded picture of industrial sectors and spheres of law.

In most of the case studies, the *researchers* chose the particular line of business and regulatory law that would be studied. Thus Welles and Engel (chapter 5) approached Waste Corp. (a pseudonym) directly about its experience in dealing with different national and local regulatory regimes in the siting and design of its municipal waste disposal facilities. Ruhlin (chapter 8) asked Credit Co. (also a pseudonym) about its experience in collecting credit card debt in the United States and Europe. However, in some case studies, when choosing which line of business activity and sphere of law to concentrate on, we were guided in part by corporate officials' opinions regarding which of their business activities are most sensitive to differences in national legal rules and practices, and which particular aspects of those activities were most amenable to our research strategy. For example, our discussions with motor vehicle manufacturers led from our initial broad queries about national differences in regulation to a more manageable focus on differences in the regulation of changes in emissions from paint shops in motor vehicle assembly plants. But, as a practical matter, a focus on this area, however significant to the regulated company, precluded our exploring multinational motor vehicle corporations' experience with national differences in labor law, tax law, and safety regulations.

More generally, when we relied on company officials to suggest the policy area to be studied, one might argue that we overemphasized regulatory areas in which American adversarial legalism is more salient and problematic, while underemphasizing areas of regulation where the opposite is true. Thus in Axelrad's initial contacts with "B Corporation" (chapter 4), corporate regulatory affairs officers suggested that it would be most illuminating to discuss their cross-national experience concerning the regulation of industrial sites that had been found to be chemically contaminated—and in which the American regulatory regime had been experienced as more adversarial, legalistic, and costly. PREMCO, the manufacturing company discussed in chapter 2, suggested we focus on industrial waste disposal regulation, rather than their air pollution control program, because they did not regard the latter as problematic.

This volume of case studies, therefore, cannot support unqualified generalizations about any of the national legal systems as a whole or about the across-the-board economic impact of national styles of law and regulation. But research must begin somewhere. Subfields of sociolegal knowledge often have developed from initial case studies that illuminated in a few settings the dynamic relationship between law and those it seeks to influence. The case studies led to insights or tentative generalizations that subsequently could be tested more systematically. Similarly, because there are few scholarly investigations of the "on the ground" impact of national differences in legal and regulatory processes, the necessarily selective case-study approach used in this project makes methodological sense.

Although the detailed cases center on the experience of business firms, this research project is not so much a study of business as a study of governmental regulatory and legal practices. The business firms are used as vantage points for viewing the character and impact of particular legal and regulatory regimes in the United States and abroad. We interviewed business executives and lawyers who could serve as *knowledgeable informants* about cross-national differences in legal practices—the methodological equivalent of the village elders interviewed by anthropologists who seek to ascertain the routine norms and practices of a particular community. Or, to use another analogy, our respondents are the equivalent of experienced travelers whom one interviews to learn how border crossing officials, drinking water safety, and taxi driver customs in Country A differ from those of Country B. The primary methodological concern is whether the "knowledgeable informant" has an accurate or a skewed perspective on the customs and practices in question.

Our focus on multinational companies has certain advantages in this regard, along with certain limitations. Large companies represent a significant proportion of the economy and hence a significant portion of the "regulatory problem" in all economically advanced nations. They typically have repeated interactions with national legal and regulatory systems. They have offices that specialize in keeping abreast of the relevant law and in working with regulators, lawyers, and courts. Large companies often have some executives or lawyers who are extremely knowledgeable and capable of making solid generalizations about the day-to-day operation of domestic legal and regulatory systems, for they can go beyond basing their observations on infrequent and perhaps atypical legal encounters.

Large multinational corporations also tend to be visible regulatory targets, both economically and politically. They usually are concerned about their reputation with regulators and political officials, as well as their reputation in consumer and financial markets. Hence sociolegal researchers repeatedly have found that large companies, while they may attempt to influence the development of the law on the books, typically adopt a strategy of full compliance with existing legal and regulatory demands.[57] There are always exceptions to be noted, of course. Managers of corporate subunits, pushed to maximize profits, sometimes cut corners. Corporate operatives can get careless: notwithstanding company policy, the many applicable regulations, and the threat of massive civil liability, the captain of the *Exxon Valdez* was asleep in his bunk below when the ship ground onto the rocks in Prince William Sound. But by and large, the experience of large companies provides a reasonably good indicator of the compliance measures and other kinds of adaptations that legal and regulatory systems actually demand or induce.

Perhaps most important, multinational companies are an invaluable repository of cross-national comparative information. Even so, one might wonder, will corporate officials report their knowledge completely accurately? Perhaps they would be inclined to exaggerate the costs and minimize the social benefits of the legal and regulatory controls they must cope with; one often hears regulated company officials say, "The regulations don't really help, because we would have invested in similar precautionary measures anyway." In conducting this research, however, we assumed that company officials would not be inclined to overstate the costs or understate the benefits of regulation *in different degrees* when describing their experience with legal controls in the United States as compared with their experience in Canada, Germany, or Japan.

But here, too, one might imagine an exception: company officials might be more critical of American adversarial legalism than of other countries' regulatory styles, and hence might be inclined to exaggerate its pervasiveness and costliness relative to the regulatory regimes of other countries. Believing in their own corporate virtue, they might dismiss the more detailed demands of American regulators as unnecessary extra and costly precautions. We cannot dismiss that possibility out of hand, and indeed suspected it in a few case studies. But for several reasons, we are inclined to believe that any possible anti-American-adversarial-legalism bias on the part of corporate officials had at most a minimal impact on our research.

First, many of the corporate officials whom case study researchers interviewed had worked in only one country. They professed little knowledge of their company's regulatory experience in other countries. They reported their own experiences directly and had little opportunity or incentive to know about or address the *relative* merits or demerits of U.S. regulation. If they believed their firm was "doing the right thing" without the need for regulators' prodding, there was no reason to believe that corporate officials in *American* subsidiaries would have a higher opinion of their company in that regard (and hence a more jaundiced view of regulators' demands) than the same company's officials in subsidiaries abroad. For the most part, moreover, researchers interviewed corporate specialists in regulatory and legal compliance, who generally seem personally committed to the objectives of the regulations and laws they deal with every day and seem to have a dispassionate view of the governmental regulators with whom they repeatedly interact.

Second, to a large extent our research focused on companies' regulatory compliance–related *behavior,* as opposed to corporate officials' evaluative *opinions.* When corporate officials offered generalizations, we asked for and usually received corroborative evidence. Thus, in many cases the researchers examined the corporate files that recorded interactions between the company and governmental officials—applications, government communications concerning the results or inspections or permit application reviews, permits specifying required measures, and, in some cases, litigation records. For example, Nielsen (chapter 7) examined a large sample of corporate personnel files in cases involving termination of employment. Ruhlin (chapter 8) obtained from Credit Co. special quantitative analyses of company debt collection efforts in both the United States and Germany. In two cases (Welles and Engel [chapter 5] and Dwyer, Brooks, and Marco [chapter 6]) researchers' analysis of regulatory permits led them to an independent conclusion that the U.S. legal regime had resulted in some protections, and hence possibly some social benefits, that were more extensive than those provided by parallel European regulatory systems—a difference that some corporate officials themselves had not been aware of. In general, therefore, we believe that the factual record has been sufficient to negate the risk of deliberate or negligent misreporting by company officials.

Third, in a number of case studies—such as Kraus (chapter 10), Somaya (chapter 9), and Johnson, Fujie, and Aalders (chapter 11)—company officials were in many respects *less* critical of the U.S. legal regime than of its foreign counterpart. This suggests the absence of any general disposition to the contrary. In sum, therefore, multinational companies should provide a reasonably reliable perspective on how national legal systems differ in their impacts on the sector of economy and society occupied by large companies.

That said, it is important to recognize some significant limits associated with our research strategy. First, the corporate-focused case study method often proved to be an imperfect mechanism for assessing the social benefits that flow from differences in regulation. In some cases, company records showed precisely what public-regarding compliance measures it had taken in the two countries—such as installation of particular pollution abatement or prevention systems, or safety precautions, or the like; those chapters provide useful information for assessing the differences in social benefits, if any. In other cases, however, only qualitative estimates could be attempted, and in others the researchers felt they could not make such judgments. As noted earlier, to obtain access to corporate compliance-related information, ordinarily regarded as a carefully protected trade secret, we usually pledged not to disclose the cooperating company's identity. In consequence, we often were not able to interview relevant regulatory or governmental officials about specific interactions with the company studied.

In some cases, the governmental perspective on particular regulatory encounters might have cast further light on the reasons for the agency's behavior and on the social benefits of the regulatory system.

A second limitation is that the legal experience of the large companies we studied may differ from that of small companies, which are less frequently targeted by regulators and plaintiffs, less likely to have routinized compliance systems, and less able to afford the costs of compliance. The legal measures that are effective in controlling big companies may be less adequate for small companies. For example, Richard Wokutch studied workplace safety regulation in the American and Japanese factories of Japanese motor vehicle manufacturers. He found that although Japan's workplace safety regulators were far less likely than American offices of the Occupational Safety and Health Administration (OSHA) to issue legal citations and impose fines, the workplace safety record in Japanese auto assembly plants was better than in those companies' comparable facilities in the United States. On the other hand, Wokutch found that the occupational safety record in the small Japanese motor vehicle parts manufacturers was inferior to that of the smaller American companies covered by OSHA.[58]

Recognizing these limitations, it seemed that the gains in knowledge from studying large multinational companies, across a variety of industries and policy areas, justify our research strategy. The picture these case studies allow us to paint is an incomplete one. The parts of the canvas that would depict how differences in legal style affect the small business sector remain unpainted, as does the space that would be occupied by the many industries and legal policy areas that we did not study. Some of the chapters paint their section of the picture in greater depth than others, providing more background detail concerning the institutional and political sources of national differences in regulation. The picture necessarily deals with regulatory laws and interactions during one particular period of time. But the canvas is no longer blank. Some knowledge, I would argue, is a lot better than none.

VI. A BRIEF SUMMARY OF FINDINGS

At the risk of some oversimplification, the results can be briefly summarized. The case studies in this volume, along with more than one hundred additional exploratory interviews that Lee Axelrad and other project members conducted with business executives, lawyers, and consultants who have had cross-national experience, tend to confirm the "American adversarial legalism" hypothesis. In the experience of large multinational companies, American legal and regulatory rules, processes, and permits in the 1990s usually were more prescriptive and detailed than those of other countries.

The American regimes were more legally complex, more punitive, more unpredictable, and more costly to comply with than their counterparts in other economically advanced democracies. In many fields of regulation studied, the company had to respond to a more institutionally fragmented system of regulation in the United States—one that included courts as well as federal, state, and local regulatory agencies. American citizens and advocacy groups, the case studies indicate, generally have more access to regulatory processes and information and broader opportunities to make legal challenges to regulatory and corporate decisions. Those procedural and institutional differences, moreover, generally were far more salient to the companies than were cross-national differences in substantive legal norms, which usually differed, if at all, only slightly.

The "extra" costs attributed to American adversarial legalism include not only direct expenditures on lawyers and legal processes but also opportunity costs that stem from legal and regulatory delays, and "accountability costs"—the costs of determining one's legal obligations and proving that one has complied with them. To the companies studied, all the extra legal process costs they absorb in the United States, while difficult to quantify, are both salient and troublesome. In some cases, adversarial legalism has had demonstrable counterproductive consequences, pushing companies toward a more defensive, legalistic relationship with American regulatory officials, consumers, and employees than with their counterparts in other countries.

Moreover, and although our conclusions necessarily must be more tentative on this point, many of the case studies suggest that, viewed in comparative perspective, American adversarial legalism often does not generate offsetting social benefits, at least with respect to governance of large corporations of the kind studied in this project. Despite the greater detail and punitiveness of American law, the multinational corporations in our case studies—with a few exceptions—did not provide demonstrably higher levels of protection for customers, workers, or neighbors than they did in their operations in other rich democracies, where regulators employed less legalistic and adversarial methods.

On the other hand, the case studies provide some interesting exceptions to or qualifications of these general patterns. Researchers found significant differences in the nature and level of adversarial legalism across American states, as in the case studies of regulation of new municipal waste disposal sites (chapter 5) and of air pollution controls on automobile assembly plants (chapter 6). In some spheres of law and regulation, particularly the protection of intellectual property (chapter 9), the multinational company studied encountered significant levels of legal contestation not only in the United States but also in Europe and even in Japan. Most strikingly, within the United States, the incidence of adversarial legalism was much lower in regulatory programs that (in contrast to the American norm) are centralized in Washington—such as licensing of genetically engineered biological products (chapter 10) and premarketing review of new chemical substances (chapter 11); indeed, in these policy arenas, the multinational companies experienced the U.S. regime as equally efficient or in some respects more efficient than its counterpart abroad.

Some other interesting exceptions and complications emerge from the studies. In some fields of legal governance, such as consumer debt collection, cross-national differences in *substantive law*—particularly U.S. restrictions on aggressive dunning by creditors and the ready availability of individual bankruptcy—mattered as much as the cumbersome and costly American court process, and also presumably provide American credit card debtors with more protections than the stricter German rules about debtor's obligations (chapter 8). In two other case studies—one concerning the siting and design of municipal garbage dumps (chapter 5), the other concerning air pollution controls on motor vehicle manufacturing (chapter 6)—American substantive regulations, together with adversarial legalism, apparently yielded somewhat higher levels of public protection. The multinational waste disposal company studied by Welles and Engel was compelled by law to install a thicker liner at its new sites in California and Pennsylvania than at its British site, and it was compelled to make much larger "side payments"—providing environmental amenities unconnected with the waste disposal process—in California. Although Ford Motor Company (chapter 6) was compelled by U.S. and German regulatory regimes to adopt similar pollution and odor reduction technologies, the controls in the American permits appear to be slightly more stringent. The U.S. patent protection regime (chapter 9) provides patent holders with more powerful court-based legal remedies against infringers, although the American courts are particularly costly and erratic in this regard, and the system as a whole, while providing more protection for patent holders, also may be less friendly to the diffusion of innovations than the patent regimes of Japan and Europe, as actually administered.

This research is far from the last word on the subject. It reflects the insights provided by the experience of large companies, in some industries, with respect to some spheres of law and regulation. The cases do not deal with some spheres of law—such as certain aspects of labor relations, banking regulation, and competition in retailing—in which cross-national differences in *substantive* legal norms probably would have loomed larger. Comparative studies of other industries and areas of law, and studies of smaller, more financially pressed companies might reveal that in some settings American-style adversarial legalism is less inefficient and more socially beneficial than our case studies generally suggest.

Moreover, this research often did not result in precise estimates of *mag-*

nitude of the "extra" costs attributable to adversarial legalism, viewed in relation to a company's total costs or sales volume. Most corporate accounting systems, it turns out, typically do not identify and isolate even the direct costs of adversarial legalism, much less the indirect opportunity costs.

The costs of adversarial legalism, while substantial, obviously have not been so high as to drive the companies we studied completely out of the large and lucrative American market. These multinationals view adversarial legalism, in effect, as a tariff they must pay to do business in the United States, just as they may choose to do business in Western Europe despite the higher payroll taxes and legal restrictions on personnel policy they encounter there. But even if the additional costs attributable to adversarial legalism are not so large as to paralyze the dynamic American economy, the studies in this volume suggest that those costs are very substantial, very alienating, and often counterproductive. Understanding why these consequences occur and learning that in some policy spheres competitor nations employ effective alternatives—as revealed in some of these studies—may be a first step toward constructive change.

NOTES

1. Sylvia Ostry, *Governments and Corporations in a Shrinking World: Trade and Innovation Policies in the United States, Europe and Japan* (New York: Council on Foreign Relations Press, 1990); Pietro Nivola, "American Social Regulation Meets the Global Economy" in *Comparative Disadvantages? Social Regulations and the Global Economy,* edited by Pietro Nivola (Washington, D.C.: Brookings Institution, 1997).

2. Union of Industrial and Employers' Confederations of Europe, *Releasing Europe's Potential through Targeted Regulatory Reform* (Brussels: UNICE, 1995), 43; Organisation for Economic Co-operation and Development, *The OECD Jobs Study: Unemployment in the OECD Area 1950–1995* (Paris: OECD, 1994); David Coe and Dennis Snower, "Policy Complementarities: The Case for Fundamental Labour Market Reform," *IMF Staff Papers* 44 (1997).

3. Economic Planning Agency, Government of Japan, *Economic Survey of Japan (1993–1994)* 336, 354.

4. See Pietro Nivola, "American Social Regulation Meets the Global Economy," David Vogel, "Trouble for Us and Trouble for Them: Social Regulations as Trade Barriers," and Marc Landy and Loren Cass, "U.S. Environmental Regulation in a More Competitive World," all in *Comparative Disadvantages? Social Regulations and the Global Economy,* edited by Pietro S. Nivola (Washington, D.C.: Brookings Institution, 1997); Thomas Church and Robert Nakamura, "Beyond Superfund: Hazardous Waste Cleanup in Europe and the United States," *Georgetown International Law Review* 7 (1994): 56.

5. Martin Shapiro, "The Globalization of Law," *Indiana Journal of Global Legal Studies* 1 (1993): 37. Brigitte Unger and Frans van Waarden, eds., *Convergence or Diversity? Internationalization and Economic Policy Response* (Avebury: Aldershot, 1995).

6. See generally Robert A. Kagan, "Should Europe Worry about Adversarial Legalism?" *Oxford Journal of Legal Studies* 17 (1997): 166–83.

7. See notes 28, 29, 32–37.

8. Robert A. Kagan, "Adversarial Legalism and American Government," in *The New Politics of Public Policy,* edited by Mark Landy and Martin Levin (Baltimore: Johns Hopkins University Press, 1995), also published in *Journal of Policy Analysis and Management* 10 (1991): 369–406.

9. See, e.g., Karen Palmer, Wallace E. Oates, and Paul R. Portney, "Tightening Environmental Standards: The Benefit-Cost or the No-Cost Paradigm?" *Journal of Economic Perspectives* 9, no. 4 (fall 1995): 119–32; Adam Jaffe, Steven Peterson, Paul Portney, and Robert Stavins, "Environmental Regulation and the Competitiveness of U.S. Manufacturing: What Does the Evidence Tell Us?" *Journal of Economic Literature* 33 (1995): 132–63; Congressional Budget Office, *Environmental Regulation and Economic Efficiency* (Washington, D.C.: Congressional Budget Office, 1985); Michael Porter and Class van der Linde, "Toward a New Conception of the Environment-Competitiveness Relationship," *Journal of Economic Perspectives* 9 (fall 1995): 97–118.

10. For some preliminary efforts, see Leigh Anderson and Robert A. Kagan, "Adversarial Legalism and Transactions Costs: The Industrial Flight Hypothesis Revisited," *International Journal of Law and Economics* 20 (March 2000).

11. For other examples of this strategy, see John Braithwaite, *To Punish or Persuade: Enforcement of Coal Mine Safety* (Albany: State University of New York Press, 1985); Braithwaite, "The Nursing Home Industry," in *Beyond the Law: Crime in Complex Organizations,* vol. 18, *Crime and Justice,* edited by Michael Tonry and Alberg J. Reiss Jr. (Chicago: University of Chicago Press, 1993), 11–54; Richard Wokutch, *Worker Protection, Japanese Style* (Ithaca, N.Y.: ILR Press); John T. Scholz and Wayne Gray, "OSHA Enforcement and Workplace Injuries: A Behavioral Approach to Risk Assessment," *Journal of Risk and Uncertainty* 3 (1990): 283–305; Robert A. Kagan, "How Much Does Law Matter? Labor Law, Competition, and Waterfront Labor Relations in Rotterdam and U.S. Ports," *Law and Society Review* 24 (1990): 35.

12. See Tom Tyler, *Why People Obey the Law* (New Haven, Conn.: Yale University Press, 1990); Patricia Ewick and Susan Silbey, *The Common Place of Law* (Chicago: University of Chicago Press, 1998).

13. William Graham Sumner, *Folkways* (Boston: Ginn and Company, 1907).

14. See Murray Edelman, *The Symbolic Uses of Politics* (Urbana: University of Illinois Press, 1964). Even if this view is overstated, it is true that whereas American antipollution laws have required industry to spend billions of dollars each year on abatement equipment, Congress has appropriated less than 1 percent of those amounts for governmental monitoring of air and water quality. Bruce Ackerman and Richard Stewart, "Comment: Enforcing Environmental Law," *Stanford Law Review* 37 (1985): 1333; C. S. Russell, "Monitoring and Enforcement," in *Public Policies for Environmental Protection,* edited by Paul Portney (Washington, D.C.: Resources for the Future, 1990).

15. Gerald Nash, *State Government and Economic Development: A History of Administrative Policies in California, 1849–1933* (Berkeley: Institute of Governmental Studies, 1964).

16. Robert A. Kagan and Jerome Skolnick, "Banning Smoking: Compliance

without Enforcement," in *Smoking Policy: Law, Policy, and Politics,* edited by Robert Rabin and Stephen Sugarman (New York: Oxford University Press, 1993).

17. Michael Lewis-Beck and John Alford, "Can Government Regulate Safety? The Coal Mine Example," *American Political Science Review* 74 (1980): 745.

18. Organisation for Economic Co-operation and Development, *The State of the Environment* (Paris: OECD, 1985).

19. Thomas Erdmann, Kenneth Feldman, Frederick Rivara, David Heimbach, and Harry Wall, "Tap Water Burn Prevention: The Effect of Legislation," *Pediatrics* 88 (September 1991): 572.

20. Curtis Milhaupt and Geoffrey Miller, "Regulatory Failure and the Collapse of Japan's Home Mortgage Lending Industry: A Legal and Economic Analysis," *Law and Policy in International Business* 29 (1997): 1.

21. See Ian Ayres and John Braithwaite, *Responsive Regulation* (New York: Oxford University Press, 1992); Robert A. Kagan and John T. Scholz, "The 'Criminology of the Corporation' and Regulatory Enforcement Strategies," in *Enforcing Regulation,* edited by Keith Hawkins and John Thomas (Boston: Kluwer-Nijhoff, 1984).

22. See, e.g., Neil Gunningham, "Negotiated Non-compliance: A Case Study of Regulatory Failure," *Law and Policy* 9 (1987): 69.

23. Braithwaite, *To Punish or Persuade;* Braithwaite, "The Nursing Home Industry"; Eugene Bardach and Robert A. Kagan, *Going by the Book: The Problem of Regulatory Unreasonableness* (Philadelphia: Temple University Press, 1982).

24. See, e.g., John T. Scholz and Feng Heng Wei, "Regulatory Enforcement in a Federalist System," *American Political Science Review* 80 (1986): 1249; Robert A. Kagan, "Regulatory Enforcement," in *Handbook of Regulation and Administrative Law,* edited by David Rosenbloom and Richard D. Schwartz (New York: Marcel Dekker, 1994).

25. See, e.g., Neil Shover, John Lynxweiler, Stephen Groce, and Donald Clelland, "Regional Variation in Regulatory Law Enforcement: The Surface Mining Control and Reclamation Act," in *Enforcing Regulation,* edited by Keith Hawkins and John Thomas (Boston: Kluwer-Nijhoff, 1984); Bridget Hutter, *The Reasonable Arm of the Law? The Law Enforcement Procedures of Environmental Health Officials* (Oxford: Clarendon Press, 1988); Kagan, "Regulatory Enforcement."

26. Among the studies that do probe this issue are Braithwaite, *To Punish or Persuade,* and "The Nursing Home Industry"; Bardach and Kagan, *Going by the Book;* Katherine Harrison, "Is Cooperation the Answer? Canadian Environmental Enforcement in Comparative Context," *Policy Analysis and Management* 14 (1995): 221; and John Scholz and Wayne Gray, "OSHA Enforcement and Workplace Injuries: A Behavioral Approach to Risk Assessment," *Journal of Risk and Uncertainty* 3 (1990): 283. See also Bridget Hutter, *Compliance: Regulation and Environment* (Oxford: Clarendon Press, 1997); and Alex Mehta and Keith Hawkins, "Integrated Pollution Control and Its Impact: Perspective from Industry," *Journal of Environmental Law* 10 (1998): 61.

27. Mehta and Hawkins, "Integrated Pollution Control."

28. Jonathan P. Charkham, *Keeping Good Company: A Study of Corporate Governance in Five Countries* (Oxford: Clarendon Press, 1994), 357.

29. Thomas Church, Robert Nakamura, and Christopher McMahon, *Cooperative*

and Adversary Regimes in Environmental Policy, report prepared for the 1993 Conference of the Association of Public Policy Analysis and Management (Albany: State University of New York, 1993), 9, 19; Andrew Lohof, *The Cleanup of Inactive Hazardous Waste Sites in Selected Industrialized Countries* (Washington, D.C.: American Petroleum Institute, 1991); R. Kopp, Paul R. Portney, and D. DeWitt, *International Comparisons of Environmental Regulation,* Discussion Paper QE90–22-REV (Washington, D.C.: Resources for the Future, 1990); Marc Landy and Mary Hague, "The Coalition for Waste: Private Interests and the Superfund," in *Environmental Politics: Public Costs, Private Rewards,* edited by M. Greve and F. Smith (New York: Greenwood, 1992); Thomas Church and Robert Nakamura, *Cleaning Up the Mess: Implementation Strategies in Superfund* (Washington, D.C.: Brookings Institution, 1993). Litigation and related transaction costs, governmental and private, add up to at least one-third of the funds actually expended on cleanup. Timothy Noah, "Clinton, Facing Conflicting Advice on Superfund, May Attempt to Ease the Burden of Business," *Wall Street Journal,* December 2, 1993, A16; Peter Menell, "The Limitations of Legal Institutions for Addressing Environmental Risks," *Journal of Economic Perspectives* 6 (1991): 93.

30. Harriet Vinke and Ton Wilthagen, *The Non-mobilization of Law by Asbestos Victims in the Netherlands: Social Insurance versus Tort-Based Compensation* (Amsterdam: Hugo Sinzheimer Institute, University of Amsterdam, 1992).

31. Deborah Hensler and Mark Peterson, "Understanding Mass Personal Injury Litigation: A Socio-Legal Analysis," *Brooklyn Law Review* 59 (1993): 962, 1004; John C. Coffee Jr., "Class Wars: The Dilemma of the Mass Tort Action," *Columbia Law Review* 95 (1995): 1343.

32. John Langbein, "The German Advantage in Civil Procedure," *University of Chicago Law Review* 52 (1985): 823–66.

33. Takao Tanase, "The Management of Disputes: Automobile Accident Compensation in Japan," *Law and Society Review* 24 (1990): 651–74.

34. Gary Schwartz, "Product Liability and Medical Malpractice in Comparative Context," in *The Liability Maze,* edited by Peter Huber and Robert Litan (Washington, D.C.: Brookings Institution, 1991).

35. David Vogel, *National Styles of Regulation* (Ithaca, N.Y.: Cornell University Press, 1986); Lennart Lundqvist, *The Hare and the Tortoise: Clean Air Policies in the United States and Sweden* (Ann Arbor: University of Michigan Press, 1980).

36. Steven Kelman, *Regulating America, Regulating Sweden: A Comparative Study of Occupational Safety and Health Policy* (Cambridge, Mass.: MIT Press, 1981).

37. Joseph Badarraco, *Loading the Dice: A Five-Country Study of Vinyl Chloride Regulation* (Cambridge, Mass.: Harvard Business School Press, 1985); Ronald Brickman, Sheila Jasanoff, and Thomas Ilgen, *Controlling Chemicals: The Politics of Regulation in Europe and the United States* (Ithaca, N.Y.: Cornell University Press, 1985).

38. Langbein, "The German Advantage in Civil Procedure," 823.

39. Mirjan Damaska, *The Faces of Justice and State Authority: A Comparative Approach to the Legal Process* (New Haven, Conn.: Yale University Press, 1986).

40. P. S. Atiyah and R. Summers, *Form and Substance in Anglo-American Law: A Comparative Study of Legal Reasoning, Legal Theory, and Legal Institutions* (Oxford: Clarendon Press, 1987).

41. Surveys and experiments have shown that attorneys and insurance claims

managers assign widely different settlement values to the same or similar civil cases. See Marc Galanter, "The Quality of Settlements," *Journal of Dispute Resolution* (1988) 55; Gerald Williams, *Legal Negotiation and Settlement*, vol. 6 (St. Paul, Minn.: West Publishing, 1983), 111–14; Douglas Rosenthal, *Lawyer and Client: Who's in Charge?* 202–7 (New York: Russell Sage Foundation, 1974); Michael Saks, "Do We Really Know Anything about the Behavior of the Tort Litigation System—And Why Not?" *Pennsylvania Law Review* 140 (1992): 1215, 1223.

42. See Badaracco, *Loading the Dice;* Brickman, Jasanoff, and Ilgen, *Controlling Chemicals;* Vogel, *National Styles of Regulation;* Harvey Teff, "Drug Approval in England and the United States," *American Journal of Comparative Law* 33 (1985): 567.

43. Daniel Okimoto, *Between MITI and the Market: Japanese Industrial Policy for High Technology* (Stanford, Calif.: Stanford University Press, 1989), 158. See also David Wallace, *Environmental Policy and Industrial Innovation: Strategies in Europe, the U.S. and Japan* (London: Royal Institute of International Affairs, 1995).

44. Vogel, *National Styles of Regulation.*

45. See Terry Moe, "The Politics of the Bureaucratic State," in *Can the Government Govern?* edited by John Chubb and Paul Peterson (Washington, D.C.: Brookings Institution, 1989); Kagan, "Adversarial Legalism and American Government," 369.

46. Bardach and Kagan, *Going by the Book;* Robert A. Kagan, "The Political Construction of Adversarial Legalism," in *Courts and the Political Process: Jack W. Peltason's Contributions to Political Science,* edited by Austin Ranney (Berkeley: Institute of Governmental Studies, 1996); George Hoberg, *Pluralism by Design* (New York: Praeger, 1992); Martin Shapiro, *Who Guards the Guardians? Judicial Control of Administration* (Athens: University of Georgia Press, 1988); Michael McCann, *Taking Reform Seriously: Perspectives on Public Interest Liberalism* (Ithaca, N.Y.: Cornell University Press); R. Shep Melnick, "Pollution Deadlines and the Coalition for Failure," in *Environmental Politics: Public Costs, Private Rewards,* edited by M. Greve and F. Smith (New York: Greenwood, 1992).

47. Carol Greenhouse, *Praying for Justice: Faith, Order and Community in an American Town* (Ithaca, N.Y.: Cornell University Press, 1986); Robert C. Ellickson, "Of Coase and Cattle: Dispute Resolution among Neighbors in Shasta County," *Stanford Law Review* 38 (1986): 623; Stewart Macaulay, "Non-contractual Relations in Business: A Preliminary Study," *American Sociological Review* 28 (1963): 55; Robert A. Kagan, "The Routinization of Debt Collection," *Law and Society Review* 18 (1984): 323. See, generally, Richard Miller and Austin Sarat, "Grievances, Claims and Disputes: Assessing the Adversary Culture," *Law and Society Review* 15 (1981): 525; Marc Galanter, "Reading the Landscape of Disputes: What We Know and Don't Know (and Think We Know) about Our Allegedly Contentious and Litigious Society," *UCLA Law Review* 31 (1983): 4; Deborah Hensler et al., *Compensation for Accidental Injuries in the United States* (Santa Monica, Calif.: Rand Institute for Civil Justice, 1991).

48. Joseph Sanders and Craig Joyce, "Off to the Races: The 1980s Tort Crisis and the Law Reform Process," *Houston Law Review* 27 (1990): 207–96; John H. Cushman Jr., "Many States Give Polluting Firms New Protections," *New York Times,* April 7, 1996, A1, A12.

49. Joseph Rees, *Reforming the Workplace: A Study of Self-Regulation in Occupational*

Safety (Philadelphia: University of Pennsylvania Press, 1988); studies cited in Kagan, "Regulatory Enforcement."

50. See John Cushman Jr., "EPA and States Found to be Lax on Pollution Law," *New York Times,* June 7, 1998, 1.

51. Kagan, "Should Europe Worry about Adversarial Legalism?"

52. Wolfgang Wiegand, "Americanization of Law: Reception or Convergence?" in *Legal Culture and the Legal Profession,* edited by Lawrence M. Friedman and Harry N. Scheiber (Boulder, Colo.: Westview Press, 1996); Yves Dezelay and Bryant Garth, "Merchants of Law as Moral Entrepreneurs: Constructing International Justice from Competition for Transnational Business Disputes," *Law and Society Review* 29 (1995): 27–64.

53. Jeffrey Sellers, "Litigation as a Local Political Resource: Courts in Controversies over Land Use in France, Germany, and the United States," *Law and Society Review* 29 (1995): 475–516.

54. See studies cited in notes 9 and 10.

55. In one case the company, Ford Motor Company, did not express any desire to maintain its identity secret. See chapter 6 of the current volume.

56. We have no reason to suspect that there are systematic differences between cooperating companies and those that declined; that is, differences that would be reflected in or that arose from their legal experience. We got the strong impression that corporate officials who declined to agree to a full case study did so not because of greater sensitivity concerning what might be found or disclosed, but because they were less interested in the project intellectually or feared that the research would make disruptive time demands on company officials.

57. See Bardach and Kagan, *Going by the Book;* Mehta and Hawkins, "Integrated Pollution Control and Its Impact," 61.

58. Wokutch, *Worker Protection, Japanese Style.*

PART I

Environmental Regulation

CHAPTER TWO

Poles Apart

Industrial Waste Management Regulation and Enforcement in the United States and Japan

Kazumasu Aoki and John W. Cioffi

Comparative research has shown that the implementation of regulatory programs in the United States is more likely to be legalistic and adversarial than in other advanced industrial nations. Regulation tends to rely on formal rules; enforcement is prone to contentious and expensive legal disputation.[1] At the opposite pole, regulation in Japan is generally, and correctly, characterized as informal and cooperative. Less research has been done, however, detailing the consequences of different "national regulatory styles" at the level of the firm, the manufacturing plant, and the shop floor. This chapter addresses these issues by examining a multinational corporation that conducts similar manufacturing operations in the United States and Japan but is subject to divergent regulatory regimes.

In this chapter we explore the formation of attitudes toward regulation and compliance strategies in the Precision Metalworking Company (PREMCO).[2] PREMCO, a multinational corporation specializing in the manufacture of precision metal parts, encounters governmental waste management regulation in its plant in Japan and two plants in the northeastern United States. In the United States, PREMCO is subject to the prescriptive regulatory demands of the Resource Conservation and Recovery Act (RCRA)[3] and its state-level equivalents, and in Japan, to the Waste Disposal and Cleanup Law (*Haikibutsu no shori oyobi seisō ni kansuru hōritsu;* JWDCL).[4] Our research involved intensive interviewing of over two dozen firm personnel, attorneys, regulators, and business association officials in the United States and Japan from late 1995 to early 1997. In addition, we visited PREMCO's manufacturing plant facilities in both countries for extended periods of time. Our account of PREMCO's regulatory experience necessarily relies heavily on interviews with company personnel. This research focus reflects our interest in discovering how divergent regulatory regimes affect corporate attitudes and responses to regulation. We sought to verify company officials' reports of regulatory disputes and compliance efforts by interviewing regulatory officials in Japan. Because we pledged to maintain the American respondents' confidentiality, we could not interview U.S. regulatory officials about their relationship with PREMCO. But we did examine regulatory records and litigation files of PREMCO's U.S. subsidiaries and interviewed their outside environmental counsel, who is the former chief of the Environmental Enforcement Bureau in the state where the company's plants are located. Overall, we are confident that our findings are reliable.

Our primary findings can be summarized briefly. Viewed through the lenses of PREMCO's comparative experience, American environmental regulations are more detailed and prescriptive, and American enforcement processes, in contrast with Japan's, emphasize the legalistic interpretation of formal regulations and the imposition of sanctions to modify economic behavior. In contrast to Japanese waste management regulation, the complex American regulatory scheme poses more difficulties in compliance, imposes substantial additional economic costs on regulated entities, and engenders antagonism and defensiveness on the part of firm personnel.

The Japanese mode of environmental regulation is far more cooperative and nonadversarial. "Administrative guidance" *(gyōsei shidō)* reduces the Japanese regulatory system's reliance on formal legal rules, sanction-based enforcement, and litigious relations.[5] In addition, the Japanese regulatory framework tends to emphasize (1) "performance standards," rather than specific, mandatory methods of waste control, and (2) informal regulatory initiatives formulated and implemented jointly by industry associations and government ministries and agencies. In comparison with the United States, corporate antagonism toward regulators in Japan is extremely low, as the system appears to facilitate corporate acceptance of regulatory norms. Shop-floor environmental practices in PREMCO's Japanese plant are equal or superior to those imposed on the U.S. factories by prescriptive American regulations.[6]

Sharp economic differences between the American and Japanese operations also played a significant role in shaping plant-level responses to regulatory styles. First, the Japanese plant is engaged in substantial export-oriented production, which makes the Japanese managers highly sensitive to international and foreign environmental standards that might have a bearing on the plant's export markets. The American plants produce almost exclusively for the domestic market, and their managers therefore have been less sensitive to such regulatory issues. Second, the Japanese plant is a highly profitable operation, while the American plants are, at best, marginally profitable. The Japanese plant therefore can afford more easily to improve environmental performance and management practices, and thus regulatory compliance. The American operations remain hard-pressed to devote resources to environmental matters. Finally, one of the American plants has absorbed very substantial Comprehensive Environmental Response, Compensation, and Liability Act (CERCLA or "Superfund") environmental cleanup liabilities resulting from plant site contamination caused by the property's prior owner. These liabilities have caused a further deterioration in the American operation's finances and, to some extent, its relations with regulators.

Although each of these economic and regulatory factors has influenced the attitudinal and performance outcomes described in this chapter, we conclude that differences in regulatory structures and styles are substantial independent forces. PREMCO's comparative experience suggests that Japan's more cooperative mode of regulation reduces both the economic costs of regulation and formal and informal resistance to regulation. The American system's legalistic enforcement mechanisms appear to produce adversarial relations with regulators, more negative attitudes among company personnel toward regulatory norms, and more frequent and costly legal disputation.

I. THE COMPANY

PREMCO is one of the preeminent producers of precision metal products in the world, with global revenues of approximately $2.6 billion and total American sales of $500 million in 1994. The bulk of its worldwide production capacity is now located in a number of huge state-of-the-art computer-automated facilities in developing countries. The company's older American and Japanese production operations are much smaller. The American plants manufacture precision custom parts for the United States' defense and aerospace industries and satisfy the "buy American" policies of some American customers.

In the United States, PREMCO's operations are split between (1) supervisory and administrative functions performed by PREMCO-USA, an American holding company wholly owned by the Japanese parent, and (2) production operations performed by AMERCO, a subsidiary wholly owned by PREMCO-USA. AMERCO is separated into divisions composed of individual production facilities with substantial autonomy. Until recently, AMERCO's environmental management has been decentralized among these divisions and almost completely autonomous from the Japanese parent. PREMCO management in Japan, however, decides production specifications and capital investments in new plant equipment almost exclusively, and its representatives are sent to oversee production in the American plants. PREMCO exercises little direct influence over AMERCO's environmental practices or its responses to regulatory requirements.

Each of the plants examined generates similar amounts and types of wastes. The manufacture of precision metal parts involves high-speed cutting, grinding, polishing, and finishing operations that require intensive lubrication and cooling with oil and with oil-and-water solutions. At various stages of fabrication, the parts must be thoroughly cleaned by using various solvents. Oil, water, and solvents must be filtered and, in time, disposed. In the American plants, the stainless steel finishing process, called *passivation,* produces chromium-tainted acid wastes. Chromium is not generated by the Japanese plant's waste stream because of stringent regulations concerning toxic metals. In both Japan and the United States, the disposal of these wastes is regulated to protect the environment.

One distinctive and costly difference between the Japanese and American operations stems from the environmental contamination of one of the American plant sites and adjacent properties, resulting in huge cleanup costs under CERCLA.[7] The contamination originated between 1960 and 1967, long before the plant was acquired by PREMCO. Solvents and other chemicals leaked from the plant into the underlying soil and aquifer, spread over several adjacent properties, and contaminated and forced the closure of a local municipal water supply well. In 1985 the site was placed on the Superfund cleanup list; later that year, the Japanese parent bought the American company without performing an adequate environmental review.[8]

The Superfund cleanup process is technically complex, time-consuming, cumbersome, and litigious, partly because of the law's imposition of retroactive, absolute liability, and partly because of its extremely demanding cleanup standards.[9] For all these reasons, it is also extremely expensive. Over the last five years, AMERCO has spent $14 million on CERCLA-related cleanup costs and fees for the previously mentioned site—an average expenditure of $2.8 million per year. Engineering consultants alone have consumed $5 to $6 million of the total, and over $1 million more has been paid for attorneys' fees. The company had to accrue $600,000 per month for several years to establish reserves for CERCLA liabilities and will continue to spend approximately $200,000 per year on the site for the foreseeable future. The average $2.8 million annual CERCLA expense represents 7 percent of the division's maximum annual revenues ($40 million), virtually wiping out its profits.[10]

The CERCLA site's contamination of a local municipal water supply well was also a political and public relations disaster for AMERCO. Although AMERCO's present owners and managers had nothing to do with the twenty-year-old site contamination, adversarial negotiations over the immensely costly CERCLA cleanup plan produced profound misunderstandings on both sides. PREMCO retained a prominent Washington, D.C., law firm to represent AMERCO and endorsed aggressive negotiating and litigation tactics. The state regulators interpreted these moves as evincing corporate hostility and resistance to environmental obligations.[11] The attitudes of AMERCO personnel do not appear to have been shaped by the ongoing CERCLA cleanup. By the early 1990s, the cleanup was fairly self-contained, handled by outside consultants, and overseen by several managers. This disjuncture between how the regulators viewed the company and how AMERCO personnel viewed it led to future conflict over the company's regulatory performance.

Senior PREMCO-USA and AMERCO managers whom we interviewed left no doubt that environmental regulation is a legal and financial problem of the first order. Environmental matters constitute the American operations' single largest law-related cost. PREMCO-USA requires two attorneys and a substantial support staff, including an environmental manager and paralegals, to deal with legal matters in the United States *alone*—and this staffing level, the lawyers insist, remains inadequate. The American operations have had to spend additional substantial sums on outside counsel for compliance counseling, negotiations with regulators, and litigation of matters that cannot be resolved. According to PREMCO-USA's general counsel, the volume of legal matters requiring outside counsel in the United States far exceeds the total for the rest of PREMCO's global operations. Over the past several years, AMERCO has spent millions of dollars in legal and related consulting fees dealing with disputes with state and federal environmental regulators, hundreds of thousands of dollars in regulatory fines under the RCRA, and millions of dollars in cleanup costs under CERCLA. Nowhere else in the world have PREMCO's legal costs approached this total.[12]

In contrast to its experience in the United States, company officials assert that environmental regulation in Japan is a relatively minor issue in terms of fiscal impact and managerial burdens. This reflects the absence of site contamination or related cleanup problems in Japan. But it is also attributable to the distinctively nonadversarial approach to environmental regulation adopted by Japanese agencies and companies alike. The Japanese parent and its subsidiaries operate in twenty-nine countries worldwide. Two attorneys on staff in Japan, only one of whom is admitted to the Japanese bar, are able to handle legal and regulatory problems in Japan and oversee legal matters in the other twenty-eight nations in which PREMCO operates. Much of the work performed by the three nonlawyer staff members of PREMCO's legal department in Japan is devoted to patent and commercial law issues. The Japanese operations have never paid a regulatory fine or needed outside environmental counsel or consultants.

The difference also stems from PREMCO's reliance on international trade. PREMCO's management decided that uniform and stringent environmental management, policies, and practices are economically prudent for the protection of its global export trade and production. First, senior management perceives a general global trend toward more stringent environmental regulations and believes that investment in pollution control methods will give PREMCO an eventual edge over competitors. Second, Thailand and China (major locations of PREMCO's direct foreign investment) recently have imposed environmental standards that are more stringent than those of Japan, the United States, or Europe.[13] Third, an increasing number of PREMCO's customers in Europe and the United States ask whether PREMCO uses certain substances or generates certain wastes and imply that they will purchase parts elsewhere if environmental performance is found inadequate. Moreover, PREMCO's Japanese customers include prominent Japanese export-oriented firms; concerned with their own foreign markets, a significant number have submitted questionnaires to the company to confirm or press for PREMCO's compliance with foreign environmental standards. In order to preserve both its export markets and its domestic customer base, the company adheres to customer-imposed standards derived from the terms of foreign environmental laws. Finally, PREMCO officials have concluded that uniform company-wide environmental practices allow for economies of scale with respect to investment in new technology, facilities maintenance, and training of managers and workers. By hosting engineers from its foreign subsidiaries, the Japanese plant acts as a "mother factory" for the dissemination of environmental technology and technical expertise to all PREMCO plants around the world—*except* those in the United States.

The Montreal Protocol banning the use of ozone-depleting substances (ODSs) also influenced PREMCO to adopt common environmental policies and practices worldwide.[14] The company, which had used ODS solvents extensively to clean parts, moved swiftly to modify its production processes in all its plants and eliminated the use of these substances two years before the 1995 deadline set by the protocol. PREMCO's rush to comply partly reflected the impact of post-Montreal rules in the United States that required *labeling* of products produced by ODS-generating processes.[15] Moreover, numerous customers in Japan and abroad sent PREMCO questionnaires inquiring whether the company was using ODSs in production. PREMCO officials told us that Japanese law implementing the protocol[16] played virtually no role in prompting the company to accelerate its replacement of ODSs with new cleaning methods.[17]

PREMCO also has given high priority to obtaining International Standards Organization (ISO) 14000 certification. The draft ISO 14000 standards for environmental management systems require precise allocation of managerial authority and responsibility for environmental matters, audit and training procedures, and the formal adoption of a general management philosophy favoring improved environmental performance.[18] The standards are an attempt to create an international framework for firm-level environmental self-management. Heightened environmental concerns and customer inquiries have convinced PREMCO that meeting ISO 14000 environmental standards will become essential for maintaining the company's global customer base.

In several respects, however, PREMCO-USA and AMERCO have operated somewhat independently from PREMCO's uniform corporate environmental policy. In addition, unlike PREMCO's other operations, AMERCO exports less than 20 percent of its output and has fewer export-oriented customers.[19] Environmental questionnaires from customers have played, at most, a minor role in the American operations. The technical, prescriptive character of American environmental law requires substantial technical *legal* expertise and prompts responses to regulatory demands that may not be generally applicable on a global basis. Hence, PREMCO's Japanese management generally has allowed PREMCO-USA and AMERCO to handle their own environmental regulatory affairs.

II. WASTE MANAGEMENT REGULATION IN THE UNITED STATES: ADVERSARIALISM BY PRESCRIPTION

A. The American RCRA Regime: Prescriptive Rules and the Micromanagement of Complexity

The Resource Conservation and Recovery Act (RCRA), was enacted in 1976 to prevent environmental pollution from improper disposal and to encourage increased recycling. RCRA mandated a multifaceted system to identify and list regulated substances; an invoice system to track wastes from generation to disposal; standards governing the conduct of generators and haulers of hazardous wastes and of "treatment, storage, and disposal" (TSD) facilities; and a permit system to ensure compliance with the program. RCRA authorized the Environmental Protection Agency (EPA) to relinquish program administration to state governments if they qualified for delegation. Even among American environmental statutes, renowned for their complexity and prescriptive detail, RCRA is notoriously intricate. One court of appeals called the attempt to comprehend RCRA a "mind-numbing journey."[20] Understanding the rules and keeping abreast of regulatory requirements, as well as compliance, have become significant challenges under RCRA. The facilities managers at AMERCO's plants estimated that they spend approximately 15 to 20 percent of their time on RCRA issues.

The state in which the AMERCO plants are located has been delegated authority to implement RCRA, but under federal delegation criteria state RCRA rules must adopt *each individual provision* of the federal RCRA and must be *at least* as stringent and as strictly enforced as the federal analogue.[21] Thus, the detailed and prescriptive character of federal law devolves to the state level. State regulators' compliance with these delegation standards is enforced by federal oversight and the threat of withheld funding. The regional EPA office monitors state RCRA enforcement regarding the number of violations found and penalties imposed—a process disparaged by company officials as "bean counting."

As one example of the prescriptive character of RCRA, the state program governing AMERCO contains "the twelve-hour rule," which provides, inter alia, that hazardous wastes must be moved from shop-floor collection containers to a "satellite" or "main" storage area once every shift or every twelve hours. If these criteria are not met, the collection containers are subject to numerous additional labeling, sealing, and placement requirements. In addition, the state program has classified waste oil as a hazardous waste under RCRA. Since the manufacture of metal products uses lubricating and coolant oils intensively, this regulation has had an enormous impact on the company. This legal classification of oil as a RCRA hazardous waste brought much of AMERCO's production process within the ambit of RCRA regulations.

B. Enforcement American-Style: The RCRA Inspections and Enforcement Dispute

Beginning in 1992, three AMERCO plants went through a series of RCRA inspections that led to an enforcement dispute over civil penalties with state regulators. This narrative highlights many of the features often said to typify the American style of environmental regulation: infrequent inspections, legalistic application of the law, sanction-driven enforcement, and adversarial relations between regulators and the regulated community. It also reveals the importance of managerial structures and professional training in dealing effectively with regulatory matters.

1. THE RCRA INSPECTIONS

In October 1992, state RCRA inspectors visited an AMERCO plant scheduled to close two weeks later. The inspectors found a number of violations, including failures to properly collect, label, and store waste oil under the twelve-hour rule. According to AMERCO's current management officials, these violations resulted in neither environmental contamination nor any significant environmental risks, and the regulators alleged neither. The violations did indicate, however, that environmental management and regulatory compliance programs were inadequate. No fines were assessed at this time; the state authorities simply sent the plant a list of citations and an administrative order to correct them. The plant managers told the inspector, "We'll go ahead and fix these problems, but we're not going to send you documentation that we have fixed the problem or that there is no ongoing problem, since in two weeks this plant is not going to even exist." In light of the contamination emanating from the company's CER-CLA site (at another plant) and the difficult negotiations over its cleanup, the regulators perceived this response as evidence that AMERCO was indifferent or resistant to environmental regulation.

In April 1993, state regulatory officials simultaneously inspected the two remaining AMERCO plants, indicating that they had been "targeted." These plants were cited for numerous violations similar to those found in the 1992 inspection. Regulators also cited the plants for some potentially serious violations not found in their first inspection, such as improper maintenance and layout of the main hazardous waste storage facility and inadequate environmental training programs.

Regulators appeared most concerned by the continuity of violations across plants. A manager at the closing plant had sent the 1992 administrative order to managers at the other two plants, but they failed to correct identical violations. At that time, communication between the facilities was minimal, and each facility regarded itself as autonomous in production, management, and regulatory affairs. The regulators, in contrast, regarded the company as a single integrated entity and expected all plants to respond uniformly to regulatory violations cited in any particular plant.[22] They saw the company's failure to respond to the first warning as symptomatic either of persistently disorganized, haphazard waste management practices or of outright defiance.

The state regulators thus sanctioned AMERCO by interpreting regulatory provisions legalistically in order to multiply the cited violations. For each violation of the twelve-hour rule, regulators cited the company not merely for violating the rule but also for violating labeling, sealing, and storage requirements. A single violation immediately mushroomed into four or five; and with each violation cited, the company's liability for regulatory fines increased. Two-thirds of the approximately 150 citations issued following the 1993 inspections derived from violations of the twelve-hour rule. After the initial *1992* inspection, regulators had simply noted *single* violations of the twelve-hour rule. Only when confronted with additional violations in the other plants did the regulators use this legalistic "multiplication technique."

2. LEGALISTIC ENFORCEMENT: THE PETITION FOR SANCTIONS

The state environmental agency did not immediately fine the company. As in 1992, after regulators in 1993 issued a list of cited violations (this time much longer) and an administrative order to correct them. After AMERCO submitted two status reports and additional correspondence confirming rectification of all violations, the state agency issued a notice of compliance to both plants in late March 1994. But in May 1994 the company received a draft Petition for Civil Penalties demanding $495,000 in fines for violations found during *both* inspections at *all three* plants. Thus, rectification of the cited violations was clearly not the agency's motivation in assessing what was then the largest RCRA fine in state history. In the Petition for Civil Penalties state regulators and the state attorney general's office referred disparagingly to the firm's environmental ethics, citing the firm's involvement in Superfund sites (despite the historical and legal irrelevance of the CERCLA issues to the RCRA violations). The petition explicitly alleged that the company had willfully and repeatedly violated waste management regulations, thus posing significant risks to the environment. Both these allegations served to increase the amount of the fine.

Company officials, including those who are very much in favor of environmental protection, regard the fine as gratuitously punitive and the petition's rhetoric as unjust. The company's errors, they argue, were not willful but stemmed primarily from decentralization and lack of coordination in corporate regulatory affairs. Moreover, they insist that none of the alleged RCRA violations resulted in any environmental contamination or posed a substantial risk to the environment. The company and its attorneys argued that regulators had grossly inflated the environmental risk factor and thus the size of the fine. Indeed, a thorough review of the litigation file, including the inspection citations, the regulators' charges and petition, and the substantial amount of correspondence that followed supported the managers' position. Indeed, the state agency's chief of environmental enforcement later apologized in private to company officials for what he conceded was unfairly harsh treatment.

3. LEGALISTIC DISPUTATION, ADVERSARIALISM, AND MISTRUST

AMERCO disputed the $495,000 fine and ultimately settled the matter for approximately $200,000—$100,000 cash, a $10,000 donation to a local environmental group, and a credit of $92,500 in return for $185,000 in capital expenditures for new pollution controls. The expenditures on pollution controls were made pursuant to the state's Supplemental Environmental Program (SEP), adopted by the state under EPA guidelines. AMERCO's SEP investments addressed issues that had not constituted violations and required the company to undertake waste reduction measures not mandated by RCRA.[23] The fine and SEP investment thus cost AMERCO $295,000.

The negotiations took six months as the opposing attorneys, hobbled by mutual mistrust and antagonism, haggled over changes in language that did not significantly alter the substantive terms of the settlement agreement. These negotiations alone cost the company over $50,000 in attorneys fees—far more than the cost of remedying the original violations—and engendered continuing bitterness. Current company managers still believe that the regulators were inappropriately punitive and antagonistic, and they still assume the very worst of agency motivations. Regulatory officials, for their part, saw legalistic enforcement as their only effective tool for remedying what they saw as AMERCO's ineffective environmental management. AMERCO's outside counsel—a former chief of the Environmental Enforcement Bureau of the state attorney general's office who is personally familiar with agency policy and all the principal actors in the dispute—believes that the persistence of similar RCRA violations across plants over time and the company's failure to act like a single integrated entity explain the regulators' punitive approach. AMERCO's attorney agreed that the state's assistant attorney general in charge of the RCRA enforcement action was personally hostile to the company because of its CERCLA sites. However, both he and AMERCO's environmental manager regard the state's concerns as legitimate even if the rhetoric and sanctions were unduly harsh.

The regulators' legalistic and punitive response was also reinforced by institutional structures. The agency's enforcement officials, from the inspectors to the lawyers, are drawn from law enforcement and litigation attorneys, and their training emphasizes adversarial and legalistic processes. The agency's Waste Management Division has few technical specialists trained for and suited to counseling and consulting. This legalistic and adversarial approach to regulation, however, is not institutionally overdetermined. The state agency's Clean Air Division is run by technical specialists in environmental engineering and maintains more cooperative relations with the regulated community, with no appreciable loss in regulatory effectiveness. Similarly, the state's Occupational Health and Safety Administration (OSHA) officials have adopted a more cooperative approach to regulation by focusing on the facilities with the most work-related accidents and conducting regular inspections devoted to improving performance through counseling. Legalistic enforcement and sanctions are held in reserve to ensure that advice is heeded.

There is another possible explanation for the state agency's legalistic stance. Since the mid-1980s, efforts to induce companies to undertake SEPs have been part of the agency's standard operating procedure. Because RCRA does not directly confer regulatory authority to compel alteration of production processes to *reduce* wastes, the agency has some incentive to use adversarial legalism to extract SEP concessions. At least in the AMERCO case, prescriptive rules, legalistic enforcement, and punitive sanctions were used to secure waste reduction measures otherwise unobtainable under the law. Regulators may actually be manipulating an adversarial system and legalistic means to reach (potentially) rational, performance-based ends. If this was their agenda, however, it remains somewhat opaque to the company and is tainted by the adversarial means of its implementation. Company officials view environmental regulation as highly technical, somewhat trivial, and fiercely adversarial. This has led to a general sentiment that the environmental problems facing the company are not in fact substantial and has given rise to defensive and fatalistic attitudes among management regarding environmental regulation. The facilities managers still "dread" the arrival of inspectors. They believe that if the regulators are inclined to issue citations, they will always be able to find violations.

Moreover, RCRA's highly prescriptive regulatory framework and the regulators' legalistic mode of enforcement have induced a political backlash. The classification of waste oil as hazardous under the state RCRA program has been substantially amended and weakened, in the wake of intense criticism of the regulatory burdens caused by subjecting such a ubiquitous staple of industrial processes to the full range and stringency of RCRA hazardous waste regulation. But the amendment of the waste oil regulation arguably leaves underregulated a toxic substance that has caused widespread and serious environmental damage.[24] The cumbersome effects of the regulation and its subsequent demise tell a cautionary tale about how legalistic environmental regulation and adversarial enforcement methods can contribute to reactive antiregulation politics.[25]

III. WASTE MANAGEMENT REGULATION IN JAPAN

A. The Structure of Japanese Waste Management Regulation

"Co-regulation" is the governing philosophy of the Japanese system of environmental regulation, in which administrative officials view extensive consultation with regulated industries and entities as an important means of formulating and achieving policy goals. Prefectures and municipal agencies, which are responsible for most regulatory enforcement, vary in the extent to which they resort to formal legal enforcement proceedings and administrative orders, but they do so very rarely in comparison with regulatory practices in the United States. In general, regulatory officials strongly prefer informal enforcement mechanisms; some officials regard formal action as an admission of regulatory failure.[26] The most common enforcement mechanism is "administrative guidance": regulators confer with corporate managers and issue informal instructions to undertake measures necessary for regulatory compliance or the improvement of environmental performance.[27] Although administrative guidance can be challenged in court under some circumstances, formal legal disputes with regulators are extremely unusual. This nonadversarial approach typifies regulation of industrial wastes under the JWDCL.[28] According to a report issued by the Ministry of Health and Welfare, in 1990 administrative guidance under the JWDCL was used 629 times, seventy administrative orders were issued, and judicial prosecution was resorted to only once.[29]

A formal framework of statutes and regulatory rules guides the conduct of Japanese waste management regulators, but the regulatory regime eschews the detailed, prescriptive regulations that characterize the American system.[30] Japan has no direct analogue of RCRA; no single program or body of statutory law or regulatory rules governs the handling of wastes from generation to disposal. Waste management regulation in Japan is governed, at the formal level, by the provisions of the JWDCL, and groundwater contamination is governed under recent amendments to the Water Pollution Prevention Law (*Suishitsu odaku bōshi hō;* JWPPL).[31] Japanese regulators implement the formal provisions of these statutes through informal and discretionary interactions with regulated entities, and local regulatory officials enjoy more enforcement-level discretion than American state regulators who enforce state-level RCRA regulations.

Japanese environmental statutes and regulations impose *performance-based* standards on industrial waste generators rather than prescribing, as RCRA does, the *means* for achieving regulatory goals. For example, the JWDCL distinguishes between "special-control industrial wastes" (*Tokubetsu kanri sangyō haikibutsu*), analogous to hazardous wastes under RCRA, and ordinary "industrial wastes."[32] Section 12–2(2) of the JWDCL requires waste generators to store special control industrial wastes in an environmentally safe manner, in accordance with standards prescribed by the Ministry of Health and Welfare. The ministry's storage rules for such wastes are phrased in similarly general, performance-based terms. The rules simply require industrial companies to employ any necessary measures to prevent the industrial wastes from scattering, flowing away, seeping into the ground, or emitting an offensive odor.[33] The rules' sole prescriptive provisions require generators to enclose the waste storage areas, to post signs identifying them as such, and to store wastes in sealed containers using any necessary measures to ensure that the wastes do not become volatilized or exposed to high temperatures.[34]

When violations of these provisions are found, the JWDCL requires that regulators first issue an "improvement order" containing no financial penalties.[35] Indeed, the JWDCL contains *no* provisions authorizing the administrative imposition of civil sanctions. Only if an improvement order is ignored are regulators allowed to seek *criminal* sanctions.[36] Resort to formal enforcement mechanisms is thus discouraged and typically extremely rare. Thus, in the municipality in which PREMCO's Japanese plant is located, regulators told us that formal sanctions have never been imposed for violation of storage standards, and, in contrast with AMERCO's experience, regulators inspecting the Japanese plant have never formally found a violation of waste management regulations. Regulators instead focus on monitoring the firm's waste manifests and on waste reduction as their primary regulatory goals.

Because Japanese waste management regulations tend to set technical goals concerning reduction of environmental risks and damage, the rules are more comprehensible to company engineers and production personnel than RCRA's lengthy, complex, and prescriptive regulations. Companies therefore have less need to concentrate responsibility for environmental matters in highly trained *legal* specialists. In contrast with AMERCO, PREMCO has taken advantage of the performance-based character of the Japanese waste storage standards by diffusing environmental knowledge, training, and responsibility throughout the firm, including to shop floor workers and supervisors. Performance-based regulation also allows greater flexibility in compliance efforts. Perhaps as a consequence, PREMCO's Japanese managers display none of the negative attitudes toward environmental regulation and regulators detected among AMERCO's managers.

Japanese environmental policy directly seeks to reshape corporate environmental management. Under the Law for Establishment of Organization for Pollution Control in Specialized Factories (*Tokutei kōjō ni okenu kōgai bōshi soshiki no seibi ni kansuru hōritsu;* LEOPC),[37] Japanese companies are obligated to designate one senior plant official as the "pollution control supervisor" and designate an additional "pollution control manager."[38] These officials are legally responsible for the corporation's compliance with, or violations of, environmental laws or regulations.[39] Pollution control managers must be certified by the government after either passing a qualifying examination or, in certain cases, attending a series of seminars.[40] Their training ensures that the responsible managers are knowledgeable about pollution control systems, waste disposal methods, and the chemical and environmental characteristics of industrial wastes. In turn, regulators can use these environmental managers to communicate regulatory demands to the firm.

B. Informal and Cooperative Institutional Dynamics

Japanese environmental regulation is shaped by the interplay of national political and economic institutions, particularly industry and trade associations, the Environmental Agency, and the Ministry of International Trade and Industry (MITI), which regularly bargain over environmental policy initiatives.[41] In the context of waste management, national political and economic actors have developed a plan to improve environmental performance by means of voluntary self-regulation without resort to formal regulation.[42] In 1991 the Environmental Agency proposed the enactment of the Basic Environmental Law *(Kankyō kihon hō),*[43] broadly defining Japan's medium- and long-term environmental protection goals. Manufacturing industry association representatives and MITI officials criticized a draft provision that authorized the Environmental Agency to impose "economic surcharges"—a form of environmental taxes—to improve firms' environmental performance.[44] According to industry association officials, MITI informally urged industry associations to preempt the proposed tax measures and stricter formal regulation by adopting *voluntary* "green" measures.[45] On April 23, 1991, the Federation of Economic Organizations (the Keidanren)—Japan's premier industrial association—released its "Global Environmental Charter" (*Keidanren chikyū kankyō kenshō*), which presented guidelines for the development of corporate environmental management policies and the appointment of internal environmental managers.[46]

MITI officials, along with Japanese exporters like PREMCO, see the global tendency toward more stringent environmental regulation as a potential opportunity: technical and managerial superiority in dealing with environmental problems may provide Japanese industry with an advantage in global markets. On October 12, 1992, MITI issued its own "voluntary plan," which it sent to eighty-seven major industry associations.[47] The MITI plan was more specific than the Keidanren charter and provided corporations with a general model of the managerial structures, policies, and practices, including energy conservation, recycling, and reduced generation of industrial wastes. The MITI plan did not set any quantitative waste reduction targets or recycling rates. MITI left the task of developing and disseminating concrete standards to sectoral industry associations and firms familiar with the technical issues facing each industry.[48] Both industry association officials and MITI believed that individual firms, by and large, were ready to improve their environmental performance if assured that less-willing competitors would not undercut them as free riders. The MITI voluntary plan instructed the industry associations to issue and urge compliance with numerical performance-based standards and thus give firms some assurance that each company's efforts would be matched by its competitors. According to industry association officials, many firms also saw the MITI plan as forestalling potentially costly legal changes.

PREMCO was informed of the Keidanren charter and MITI's voluntary plan by its sectoral industry association.[49] These initiatives mobilized PREMCO's senior management to monitor and address environmental issues more systematically. But this increased attention to environmental concerns emerged, according to one senior PREMCO official, against a broader backdrop of perceived "global trends in public opinion" supporting greater corporate responsiveness to environmental concerns and the emergence of international environmental regulation. This official described the Montreal Protocol, the American EPA labeling regulations, and the resultant customer pressures on PREMCO to phase out the use of ODSs as a "watershed event." It signaled to PREMCO's management a coming era of intensifying environmental regulation and *global* environmental concerns. In July 1991, before the MITI voluntary plan was announced,

PREMCO had established an ODS committee to phase out the use of ODSs such as the chloroflurocarbon CFC-113 and 1.1.1.-trichloroethane. The success of this effort resulted in substantial positive publicity, underscoring for PREMCO's management the potential economic utility of imaginative, high-level environmental management and the aggressive introduction of environmentally friendly policies and practices.

C. Japanese Regulation in Practice

Rather than resisting regulatory demands for improved environmental performance, PREMCO's Japanese plant consciously seeks *overcompliance* with waste management regulation. Its managers appear open to requests and suggestions from regulators to adopt practices and performance standards in excess of codified law. PREMCO's Japanese plant, for example, voluntarily adopted a far more complete manifest reporting program (almost identical to the method mandated under RCRA) than the JWDCL required, one in which all industrial wastes are tracked from generation to final disposal. This practice was prompted, in part, by local regulators' administrative guidance following a Ministry of Health and Welfare initiative advocating a more extensive manifest system.[50] The plant also voluntarily adopted an *internal* waste-tracking system not formally required by law; no administrative guidance impelled its development. Rather, the system of full manifest tracking aids the company in preparing legally required reports on volume, types, and disposal of industrial wastes, and in ensuring proper disposal of its industrial wastes by waste-hauling firms.

The regular use of administrative guidance and informal, voluntary self-regulation in Japan has blurred the distinction between what is required by law and what is simply a policy or practice advocated by regulators. For example, PREMCO plant officials conduct annual inspections of waste disposal facilities operated by companies that handle the plant's wastes. This practice was instituted partly in response to administrative guidance, but it also accords with the company's interest in ensuring that it is not subject to public criticism for improper disposal methods that might be used by third parties.[51] Only when reminded that the inspections are not legally required did company officials recall that the inspection practice was adopted pursuant to administrative guidance as a sensible way of protecting the company against allegations of illegal dumping. In contrast, although the environmental manager for AMERCO and PREMCO-USA has realized the wisdom of an annual inspection of outside waste disposal facilities, AMERCO still has not instituted an inspection program—despite having been impleaded into several minor lawsuits as a result of its waste haulers' alleged improper disposal methods.

Perhaps the more important point, however, is that PREMCO managers appear unconcerned with the distinction between "legally required" and "discretionary" acts, as indicated by the fact that they typically do not check which portions of the notices relate to formal legal rules and which simply constitute administrative guidance. PREMCO managers tend to regard administrative guidance as predictive of future trends in formal regulation. For example, local regulators suggested that the plant dig wells on its property to monitor groundwater quality. At the time, prefectural and municipal officials had little legal authority to enforce groundwater purity standards, and there was no legal basis to require such prophylactic behavior. Yet PREMCO dug four wells and instituted quarterly groundwater testing at considerable expense to ensure that its waste management practices are effective and that no environmental contamination has been caused by its operations.[52] PREMCO managers believed, correctly, that the administrative guidance indicated the future direction of regulation. Indeed, the 1996 amendment to the JWPPL has empowered governors to issue administrative orders requiring firms to remedy any leakage of toxic substances into the groundwater.[53] Further, PREMCO officials said that testing records prepared in advance by a third party are an effective defense against regulatory actions.[54] Because the prior administrative guidance led PREMCO to monitor its groundwater, the firm has been able to demonstrate to the local regulators the sufficiency of the firm's waste management practices and the absence of any groundwater contamination.

Relationships between managers and regulators in Japan also have a more personal character than they do in the United States. Local environmental regulators rotate every two to three years. Each time a new one is assigned to the local public health center (*Hokensho*), PREMCO managers are sure to establish personal contacts with him. PREMCO can also rely on its unblemished record of regulatory compliance, stretching back for over a decade, to cultivate the regulators' confidence. The Japanese managers welcome regulators into the plant and seek out administrative guidance as potentially valuable information. These relations appear to reflect mutual trust, not regulatory laxity or agency capture. In sharp contrast, AMERCO's management resents and dreads the arrival of anonymous and legalistic regulators with whom they have no personal relationships of trust or respect.

IV. ADVERSARIAL AND COOPERATIVE REGULATORY REGIMES COMPARED

Significantly, many similarities exist between waste management practices in PREMCO and AMERCO. The Japanese operations employ a waste manifest system and have implemented waste separation, storage, recycling, and disposal practices that are very similar to, and in some respects superior to, those employed in the American facilities.[55] Yet the Japanese plant has undertaken these measures in the absence of prescriptive rules and formal enforcement methods. The prescriptive rules, legalistic enforcement, and harsh penalties of the American regulatory approach have imposed much larger transaction costs but have not yielded commensurately higher levels of environmental protection. Further, the American system's legalistic regulation and enforcement have produced, at least in AMERCO's case, a residue of antiregulation sentiments and suspicion of regulatory authority. These attitudes impede the acceptance of regulatory norms and perpetuate the system's reliance on legalistic regulation and punitive enforcement.

Why, despite the apparent gentility of Japanese regulation, are waste control practices in PREMCO's Japanese factory equal to or better than those at AMERCO? First, economic factors provide part of the answer. Despite the operational similarities between Japanese and American facilities, the Japanese plant reflects the position of a financially strong, competitive multinational corporation with a global outlook, long-term planning horizons, and the money to satisfy greater regulatory demands at home and abroad. The American plants operate as cash-strapped, smaller companies focusing on short-term profitability within a single domestic market. PREMCO is extremely sensitive to the environmental regulations and regulatory trends in countries receiving its exports and foreign direct investment because it seeks to ensure penetration of foreign markets. Indeed, PREMCO officials concede that in the absence of international trade pressures, including their interest in ISO 14000 certification, current Japanese environmental law alone would be relatively ineffective in ensuring adequate environmental performance.

Second, PREMCO's regulatory compliance reflects the political and social history of Japanese environmental law.[56] In the 1960s and 1970s, Japanese society and politics were shaken by the numerous deaths, painful and debilitating diseases, and birth defects that resulted from decades of indiscriminate dumping of toxic chemical wastes and heavy metals in waterways. The severity of the environmental tragedies and persistent government inaction sparked lawsuits and a traumatic political crisis that resulted in strict environmental regulations,[57] the criminal convictions of some prominent industrialists, and the disgrace of many others. The backlash against corporate polluters and their managers left an indelible imprint on Japanese management. Managers believe pollution of the environment carries enormous risks to corporate existence and personal reputation.[58] PREMCO officials believe that Japanese society's sensitivity to water pollution means that a mere *accusation* of groundwater contamination would be extremely damaging to the firm's reputation. Compliance with regulators' administrative guidance thus reflects the interplay of social, political, and legal environments.

Likewise, regulatory compliance is encouraged by the apparent Japanese preference for consensual social and political relations, although some argue that this is primarily the result of institutions that constrain dissent.[59] As noted earlier, Japanese manufacturers are bound in strong trade associations, which bargain with governmental agencies in formulating regulatory policies. In addition, business interests are advanced within the government by MITI. These mechanisms ensure that the economic costs and repercussions of proposed environmental regulations do not outweigh the benefits. Once this consultative process has run its course and regulations are approved with industry participation, the consensual character of this bargaining process and of Japanese regulatory institutions discourages noncompliance by major firms and tends to secure incremental compliance by less wealthy, lower-tier firms.[60]

In the United States, environmental regulation was ushered in by an equally traumatic social and political upheaval in the late 1960s and early 1970s. However, the regulation developed during this era emphasized the role of rights, specific legal obligations, penalties, and formal legal procedures. Agency discretion was minimized by generous opportunities for judicial review of agency rule making and enforcement actions. Regulatory relations were structured by formal legal channels in which lawyers are the intermediaries, adversarial relations are common, and legal conflict often engenders resistance to regulatory demands.[61] This institutional framework has produced a paradoxical situation in which environmentalism is a far more powerful and politicized movement in the United States than in Japan, but the laws it has helped generate often provoke political, legal, and managerial opposition. Without exception, every American manager we interviewed expressed support for regulation *in principle* and did not wish to see less effective environmental laws. Yet the peculiarly legalistic and adversarial nature of American regulatory enforcement *in practice* has produced the ironic result of reinforcing a corporate culture of antagonism and suspicion toward regulators and regulation.

A third influence on PREMCO's environmental performance is the difference between environmental management in the United States and Japan, a contrast that reflects differences in governmental regulation. The RCRA penalties dispute was a watershed for AMERCO. The company hired a full-time environmental manager to coordinate environmental practices, ensure legal compliance, and deal with ever-changing complexities of American environmental regulation. This manager does not exert day-to-day control over AMERCO's production divisions, and he has little direct power and authority over local managers. But he does conduct compliance reviews of plant practices and receives warning of forthcoming environmental regulations and policies, coordinates environmental and regulatory practices throughout the firm, and provides a stable source of institutional learning and expert knowledge. No significant environmental decisions or actions concerning RCRA, OSHA, waste disposal, stormwater permitting, and budgeting for some environmental matters now occur without consultation among the environmental manager and the facilities managers. Finally, the environmental manager has been charged with imposing greater centralization and uniformity on environmental policies, practices, and regulatory compliance auditing within AMERCO and PREMCO-USA. The ISO 14000 certification process requires that AMERCO adopt a more centralized, uniform, and coordinated company-wide environmental policy. The environmental manager was charged with drafting this policy, which has been completed and approved by senior PREMCO and PREMCO-USA management.

Whereas improved environmental management in AMERCO was triggered by legalistic regulatory enforcement, in Japan environmental management is the joint product of legal requirements and economic incentives. As described earlier, Japanese law and regulatory policy push responsibility upward in the corporate hierarchy by providing for the appointment of a trained pollution control manager and supervisor, and of a permanent headquarters Environmental Committee. Internal company policy—partially in response to ISO 14000 environmental management requirements—devolves responsibility downward to shop-floor managers and workers. PREMCO's Environmental Committee has taken an informal environmental management system and begun the internal *formalization* of waste management responsibilities and practices, and is thus becoming more "legalistic" in its embrace of rule-defined roles and responsibilities. A plant-level Environmental and Safety Committee, composed of the facilities and production managers and the representatives of the different production lines, translates policy directives of the headquarters Environmental Committee into concrete measures and procedures to carry them out in shop-floor practice. Working groups of approximately five members each perform monthly audits, inspecting each production line for pollution, waste management, and safety problems; they submit written reports to the plant committee covering environmental risks, fire safety, noise, and odor. Regulatory violations are not the primary focus of these regular reviews. In contrast with the AMERCO environmental manager, the PREMCO pollution control manager's training and expertise are predominantly technical rather than legal; he is also responsible for the education of subordinates regarding environmental matters.

The handling of waste management within the Japanese plant reveals how this formalization and devolution of managerial responsibility operates at the shop-floor level. Wastes are tracked from their source of generation on the shop floor, to their movement to a storage facility within the plant building (analogous to RCRA's satellite storage area), to their storage in a facility outside the production building yet still on the facility grounds. Finally, another supervisor tracks the plant's wastes as they are conveyed to waste haulers, intermediate disposal facilities, and then to final disposal sites. This takes the tracking process further than RCRA and practices adopted in the American plants.

This involvement of Japanese workers in environmental affairs is in marked contrast to American patterns of work and authority. Japanese officials in residence at the American plants remarked to us about the lack of communication and interaction between managers and workers. In their view, the Japanese plant is less hierarchical than the American counterparts. As they see it, the relative passivity of American workers in shop-floor environmental matters has inhibited regulatory compliance in the American plants, while communication, collaboration, and cooperation between management and workers has facilitated improved environmental performance in Japan.[62] Hence, AMERCO's regulatory performance is impaired by problematic authority relationships on two levels: first, by the antagonistic relations and attitudes between managers and regulators, and second, by the lack of close coordination among managers and shop-floor workers.

Finally, it should be emphasized that whereas the informal Japanese regulatory system appears to have been quite effective in the case of sophisticated, well-staffed companies like PREMCO,[63] environmental contamination remains a serious problem in Japan. The Japanese regulatory system affords major industrial corporations and industry associations far greater access and influence in the regulatory process than it does smaller firms, environmentalists, and consumers.[64] The imbalance in power between small and large firms is addressed in part by the flexibility adopted by regulators in enforcing regulations against smaller and financially weak companies, but this has led to ineffective environmental regulation of these firms.[65] The political impotence and exclusion of environmental interests may present a more serious problem for the effectiveness and stability of the Japanese system. In contrast to the United States, where environmental groups influence agencies and use the courts to accomplish policy goals,[66] Japanese administrative law limits participation by environmentalists. The Japanese system is only now beginning to confront this problem.[67] Japanese environmental regulation also falters when private actors refuse or resist voluntary compliance or when proposed regulations meet with industry opposition.[68] Recent evidence, generated by the cleanup and remedial requirements of the 1996 JWPPL amendments, has disclosed substantial environmental contamination problems in Japan that had been concealed by the cooperative but opaque regulatory regime.[69] These revelations have led to calls for more stringent regulations and enforcement.[70] For all the antagonism and expense generated by the RCRA's legalism, it worked: the regulators forced AMERCO to comply and to adopt improved management systems.

V. CONCLUSION

In the United States, regulatory power over private economic activities has been simultaneously defined and constrained by (1) a legalistic framework of procedures, duties, and rights-based relationships; (2) budgetary limitations affecting number and quality of agency personnel; and (3) the prominent role of attorneys on both sides of the regulatory system. RCRA's environmental goals are surely desirable, yet its minutely detailed rules severely constrain enforcement officials' discretion to tailor regulatory requirements to the specific risks posed by different wastes in particular sites. Nor are these officials adequately trained or funded to do so. Rather, RCRA's legal structure encourages rigidly legalistic enforcement that increases legal disputation and generates further legal complexity. The prescriptive American regime, as the RCRA case study indicates, encourages legalistic enforcement techniques by regulators and legal disputation of regulations and sanctions by industry. This structure, viewed comparatively, is costly, complex, and cumbersome. Further, the political costs to the regulatory agenda have been substantial. The system generates mutual resentment and distrust of regulatory authority that fuels its contentious character.

The cooperative and pragmatic features of the Japanese regulatory model may be distinctive, but they are not wholly foreign to American practices in certain regulatory programs.[71] This study suggests that decreased reliance on the adversarial and prescriptive enforcement processes that characterize American environmental regulation may be a practical and fruitful starting point for regulatory and legal reform. Prescriptive rules might be partially replaced or tempered by performance-based standards. Reliance on legal sanctions might be diluted by greater utilization of inspection, consultation, and technical expertise by both regulatory agencies and firms, with the state's formal coercive powers held in reserve to prevent cheating within a cooperative program of environmental regulation.[72] Regulation can also promote the creation of a system of environmental management, rather than focus solely on specific conduct to be prescribed or prohibited. Managers with requisite expertise and authority can introduce the technical knowledge and the sensitivity to environmental and legal norms necessary for regulatory compliance within a profit-driven enterprise. Adoption of such a model in the United States would require a profound transformation of the institutional and ideological foundations of the administrative state. Implausible? Perhaps. However, today's unsettled domestic politics and the ferment of discontent rumbling beneath it may contain the seeds of transformation that would surprise us as we peer forward but may appear inevitable when we look back.

NOTES

1. Robert A. Kagan and Lee Axelrad, "Adversarial Legalism: An International Perspective," in *Comparative Disadvantages? Social Regulations and the Global Economy*, edited by Pietro S. Nivola (Washington, D.C.: Brookings Institution, 1997), 146–202; Robert A. Kagan, "Regulatory Enforcement," in *Handbook of Regulation and Administrative Law*, edited by David H. Rosenbloom and Richard D. Schwartz (New York: Marcel Dekker, 1994), chap. 14; David Vogel, *National Styles of Regulation: Environmental Policy in Great Britain and the United States* (Ithaca, N.Y.: Cornell University Press, 1986). Eugene Bardach and Robert A. Kagan, *Going by the Book: The Problem of Regulatory Unreasonableness* (Philadelphia: Temple University Press, 1982).

2. The name of the firm and other identifying details have been altered or omitted to preserve the anonymity of the company. All information contained in this chapter was gleaned from company documents and interviews with company employees, trade and industry association officials, and regulatory officials.

3. 42 U.S.C. §§ 6901–6992k, as amended by the Hazardous and Solid Waste Amendments (HSWA) of 1984, 42 U.S.C. §§ 6921–6939a. RCRA's regulatory provisions covering hazardous wastes are codified at 40 C.F.R. pts. 260–272.

4. See *Haikibutsu no shori oyobi seisō ni kansuru hōritsu* (Waste Disposal and Cleanup Law), Law No. 137, 1970, as amended by Law No. 95, 1991. For a thorough and comprehensive review of the 1991 amendments, see Yasutaka Abe, "Haikibutsu shori hō no kaisei to nokosareta hōteki mondai" (1)–(7) (On the Amendments to the Waste Disposal Act and Its Unresolved Legal Problems, parts 1–7), published in *Jichikenkyū* 69, no. 6 (1993): 3–23, *Jichikenkyū* 69, no. 8 (1993): 3–20, *Jichikenkyū* 69, no. 9 (1993): 3–18, *Jichikenkyū* 69, no. 10 (1993): 16–37, *Jichikenkyū* 69, no. 11 (1993): 24–38, *Jichikenkyū* 70, no. 1 (1994): 3–24, *Jichikenkyū* 70, no. 2 (1994): 3–21.

5. This distinctive characteristic of Japanese regulation has been analyzed by scholars in the United States and Japan. See, e.g., Frank K. Upham, "Privatizing Regulation: The Implementation of the Large-Scale Retail Stores Law," in *Political Dynamics in Contemporary Japan*, edited by Gary D. Allinson and Yasunori Sone (Ithaca, N.Y.: Cornell University Press, 1993); Yoshinobu Kitamura, "Gyōsei teki taiō no genkai to shihō teki shikkō" (1)–(4) (On the Limits of Administrative and Judicial Enforcement: Activities of Local Environmental Offices and Police toward Illegal Dumping of Industrial Wastes), parts (1)–(4), published in *Jichikenkyū* 69, no. 7 (1993): 53–66, *Jichikenkyū* 69–92, no. 8 (1993): 67–89, *Jichikenkyū* 69, no. 9 (1993): 44–62, *Jichikenkyū* 69, no. 10 (1993): 69, Yoshinobu Kitamura, "Kankyō gyōsei hō to kankyō kēhō no kōsaku" (2) (Interplay between Environmental Administrative Law and Environmental Criminal Law, Part 2), *Jichikenkyū* 67, no. 8 (1993): 90–112; John O. Haley, *Authority without Power: Law and the Japanese Paradox* (New York: Oxford University Press, 1991); John O. Haley, "Administrative Guidance versus Formal Regulation: Resolving the Paradox of Industrial Policy," in *Law*

and Trade Issues of the Japanese Economy, edited by Gary R. Saxonhouse and Kozo Yamamura (Seattle: University of Washington Press, 1986); Michael K. Young, "Judicial Review of Administrative Guidance: Governmentally Encouraged Consensual Dispute Resolution in Japan," *Columbia Law Review* 84 (1984): 923–83; Kazuo Yamanouchi, "Administrative Guidance and the Rule of Law," *Law in Japan* 7 (1974): 22–33.

6. This conclusion is based on waste-stream documentation supplied to us in Japan and the United States that indicates that the waste streams are similar in content. On-site inspection, admittedly yielding a rather rough and subjective assessment, showed the Japanese plant to be significantly cleaner and attentive to shop-floor waste management issues.

7. Actually, two statutes constitute CERCLA, the Comprehensive Environmental Response, Compensation, and Liability Act of 1980, and the Superfund Amendments and Reauthorization Act of 1986. They are collectively referred to and cited as CERCLA, 42 U.S.C. §§ 9661–9675.

8. At the time of purchase the estimate of cleanup liabilities transferred to the purchaser was around $750,000—a vast underestimate of the ultimate liabilities. The company did not perform a thorough environmental inspection of the property before its purchase largely because it did not realize the potential enormity of liabilities under CERCLA and thus the risks to which it was exposing itself.

9. Thomas W. Church and Robert T. Nakamura, *Cleaning Up the Mess: Implementation Strategies in Superfund* (Washington, D.C.: Brookings Institution, 1993).

10. Another substantial impediment to the company's profitability is the debt service on the Japanese parent's leveraged buyout of the firm in 1985. The company is responsible for this debt repayment. No exact figures were available, but the monthly sums are in the range of peak CERCLA accruals (i.e., $600,000 per month).

11. The Japanese management reacted to initial, and virtually arbitrary, EPA estimates of cleanup costs exceeding $100 million. In a move that casts doubt on cultural theories asserting that Japanese management and regulatory styles are determined by cultural norms of cohesion and hierarchy, the Japanese management appeared to adapt to American adversarial legal regulatory relations without qualm. On the propensity toward this downward spiral of mutual mistrust in legalistic regulatory regimes, see Bardach and Kagan, *Going by the Book,* chaps. 3 and 4, esp. pp. 7–82, 104–7, 109–16. For a game-theoretical account of the same phenomenon, see John T. Scholz, "Cooperation, Deterrence, and the Ecology of Regulatory Enforcement," *Law and Society Review* 18 (1984): 179–224.

12. Senior company officials in Japan understand the high legal costs of doing business in the United States but expect AMERCO officials to drive the best bargain possible with regulators before going to the parent in Japan for money to pay for regulatory requirements and liabilities. Responsibility for earnings, losses, and expenses—including those for legal matters—is devolved to the division heads in charge of each plant. If a division cannot cover its environmental liabilities and costs from its own revenues, the Japanese parent will pay for them in the form of a loan that must be paid back eventually. Accordingly, the division heads have powerful incentives to reduce legal and environmental costs to improve their divisions' short-term financial performance.

13. For example, China conditioned the granting of a building permit on PREMCO's designing its new plant so that no oil whatsoever would be released outside the plant. This required the company to develop extremely expensive on-site waste treatment facilities. According to PREMCO officials, China and Thailand have set significantly more stringent regulatory standards on waste oil and grease effluents, hydrochloric acid, and biological oxygen demand (BOD) than has Japan. These nations tend to enforce their strict environmental standards selectively against foreign-owned companies and plants. PREMCO accepts this as a cost of doing business in these countries.

14. See Protocol on Substances That Deplete the Ozone Layer, September 16, 1987 (Montreal Protocol), 26 International Legal Materials 1550; Section 611 of the Clean Air Act, P.L. 101–549 (Nov. 15, 1990); 104 Stat. 2399; 42 U.S.C. §§ 7671, et seq. (Clean Air Amendments of 1990).

15. 42 U.S.C. § 7671j.

16. *Tokutei bushitsu no kisei tō niyoru ozonsō no hogo ni kansuru hōritsu* (The law for protection of the ozone layer by regulating certain substances), Law No. 53, 1988.

17. By developing ODS-free metal-cleaning processes, the company also garnered considerable prestige with regulators around the world and within its industry. Indeed, PREMCO won an EPA award for these pioneering efforts and its public disclosure of the cleaning technology. In Japan, Thailand, and Singapore, the company made the process available to other manufacturers free of charge. PREMCO managers explained this technology-sharing decision as an attempt to generate goodwill and publicity in the marketplace—although it also helped maintain good relations with regulators.

18. See International Standards Organization, "Environmental Management Systems: Specification with Guidance for Use," Committee Draft ISO/CD 14001.2, February 17, 1995, ref. no. ISO/TC 207/SC1 n60; "Environmental Auditing and Related Environmental Investigations," Committee Draft ISO/CD 14011/1–2, January 1, 1995, ref. no. ISO/TC 207/SC2 n64; "Environmental Management Systems—General Guidelines on Principles, Systems and Supporting Techniques," Committee Draft ISO/CD 14000.2, February 17, 1995, ref. no. ISO/TC 207/SC1 n.59. For a view that the development of ISO 14000 standards have been driven by firms' need to achieve and maintain regulatory compliance, see Brian Rothery, *ISO 14000 and ISO 9000* (Hampshire, United Kingdom: Gower, 1995), 8–9.

19. In contrast, PREMCO's Thai plants export approximately 35 percent of their product to Japan, 30 to 40 percent to elsewhere in South East Asia, and 30 percent to the United States and Europe. Similarly, the Japanese plant sells a significant percentage of its output to Japanese firms heavily reliant on exports.

20. *American Mining Congress v. EPA*, 824 F.2d 1177, 1189 (D.C. Cir. 1987).

21. See RCRA, § 1002(a)(4) (control of wastes should remain "primarily the function of State, regional, and local agencies"); subchapter III, §§ 3006, 3009; subchapter IV, §§ 4001–4010 (delegation provisions); 42 U.S.C. §§ 6901(a)(4), 6926, 6929, 6941–6949a.

22. Company managers who recognize that serious problems resulted from the company's decentralized approach to environmental compliance largely accepted the regulators' judgment later. First, the company had no system in place for disseminating regulatory or inspection information among its own plants. Second,

managers primarily concerned with production issues lacked the technical expertise needed to deal effectively with technically complex bodies of environmental regulation and often gave inadequate attention to environmental compliance. Moreover, cost-cutting and employee turnover had impaired efforts to educate and enculturate managers to understand and accept regulatory norms by destroying institutional knowledge of regulatory requirements and organizational approaches to compliance issues.

23. It is significant that the SEPs were designed and proposed by AMERCO itself. Based on a review of the litigation record, the regulators did not appear to possess the technical knowledge to perform a more active role. The SEPs required the company to do the following:

> (1) Recycle aqueous wash bath water to remove detritus and oils through ultrafiltration using diatomaceous earth filters—a large capital expenditure, but one that recouped its cost within one year by dramatically decreasing the volume of oily wastewater that previously entailed costly disposal by waste haulers.
> (2) Recycle nitric acid in the passivation process wastes through diffusion dialysis so that the only remaining toxic waste by-product is chrome-tainted water that is then precipitated into a chrome sludge;
> (3) Install centrifugal devices to separate "tramp oils" (hydraulic and machine lubricant oils that leak into coolant mixtures) in emulsified oil-water based coolant to reuse emulsified coolants and extend coolant life between "batch-outs."

24. For discussion of the RCRA mandate to regulate waste oils, see Richard C. Fortuna and David J. Lennett, *Hazardous Waste Regulation—The New Era: An Analysis and Guide to RCRA and the 1984 Amendments* (New York: McGraw-Hill, 1987), 36–37, 93–96.

25. See, e.g., Eckard Rehbinder, "Reflexive Law and Practice: The Corporate Officer for Environmental Protection as an Example," in *State, Law, and Economy as Autopoietic Systems: Regulation and Autonomy in a New Perspective,* edited by Gunther Teubner and Alberto Febbrajo (Milan: Dott A. Giuffre Editore, 1992).

26. Yoshinobu Kitamura, "Gyōsei teki taiō no genkai to shihō teki shikkō" (2), 77–79; Young, "Judicial Review of Administrative Guidance," 950–53.

27. Kahei Rokumoto, "Kisei katei to hō bunka: Haisui kisei ni kansuru nichibei no jittai kenkyū wo tegakarini," (Regulatory Process and Legal Culture: Empirical Studies of Japanese and British Effluent Regulation), in *Hirano Ryūichi sensei koki shukuga ronbun shū gekan,* edited by Naitō, et al. (Tokyo: Yūhikaku, 1991), 25–53; see also Yoriaki Narita, "Gyōsei shidō no kinō to kōzai" (The Merits and Demerits of Administrative Guidance), *Jurisuto* 741 (1981): 39–44. Young asserts that administrative guidance may account for over 80 percent of Japanese regulatory activity ("Judicial Review of Administrative Guidance," 935, 954). Administrative guidance is not by any means a practice unique to Japanese bureaucracies, but it is common to all other advanced industrial democracies. Frank K. Upham (translated by Yoshiko Terao), "Nihonteki gyōsei kisei sutairu no shiron teki moderu" (A Tentative Model for Regulatory Style of the Japanese Bureaucracy) in *Soto kara mita nihon hō* (The Japanese Law Viewed from the Outside), edited by Shiro Ishii and Norio Higuchi (Tokyo: Tōdaishuppankai, 1992), 49–84; Haley, *Authority without Power;* Haley, "Administrative Guidance versus Formal Regulation." The legal formalism of much American regulation is the exception, not the rule.

28. Kitamura, "Kankyō gyōsei hō to kankyō kēhō no kōsaku" (2); Young, "Judicial Review of Administrative Guidance," 923; J. Mark Ramseyer, "On the Non-reviewability of Administrative Guidance, and Other Myths" (paper presented at the Sho Sato Conference on Sociological Perspectives on Governmental Regulation in Japan and the U.S., Center for the Study of Law and Society, University of California, Berkeley, May 10, 1997). The doctrinal bases for challenging agency actions in court remain far narrower than those in the United States. Tanase argues that Japanese legal institutions have been carefully and deliberately structured to discourage legal disputation. Takao Tanase, "The Management of Automobile Disputes: Automobile Accident Compensation in Japan," *Law and Society Review* 24 (1990): 679–82. Moreover, deliberate governmental policy keeps the Japanese private bar tiny in comparison with the per capita number of American attorneys. This keeps the market price of lawyering artificially high and the amount of formal litigation artificially low. See John O. Haley, "The Myth of the Reluctant Litigant," *Journal of Japanese Studies* 4 (1978): 359–89.

29. Kitamura, "Gyōsei teki taiō no genkai to shihō teki shikkō" (2), 73.

30. Japanese waste management regulations do impose prescriptive command and control regulations on waste *disposal* facilities to prevent improper disposal or dumping of hazardous wastes. The scope of this study, however, is limited to waste generators and does not extend to the regulation of disposal facilities.

31. *Suishitsu odaku bōshi hō* (Water Pollution Prevention Law), Law No. 137, 1970; as amended by Law No. 34, 1989, and Law No. 58, 1996.

32. See JWDCL §§ 2(4) and (5).

33. Ministry Implementation Rules (*Shikō kisoku*) § 8–13(1).

34. Ministry Implementation Rules, §§ 8–13(2)-(5).

35. See JWDCL § 19–3.

36. See JWDCL § 26(2).

37. *Tokutei kōjyō ni okeru kōgai bōshi soshihi no seibi ni kansuru hōritsu* (Law for Establishment of Organization for Pollution Control in Specialized Factories), Law No. 107, 1971.

38. See LEOPC § 1.

39. Section 10(1) of the LEOPC empowers prefectural governors to issue administrative orders to companies relieving these officials of their posts if they fail to secure corporate compliance with environmental laws. Should a company fail to relieve a pollution control supervisor or manager of statutory duties after issuance of such an administrative order, it is subject to a fine of up to 500,000 yen; see LEOPC § 16(1). In addition, Section 9(2) of the LEOPC provides that plant employees must follow the directives of the pollution control supervisor and manager with respect to pollution prevention. This provision, however, contains no enforcement provisions and, instead, acts merely as a normative statement. For a commentary on the LEOPC, see, generally, MITI, ed., *Sangyō to kōgai* (Industry and pollution) (Tokyo: Tsūsanshiryōchōsakai, 1989).

40. See LEOPC § 12. In addition, the JWDCL requires firms generating "special control industrial wastes" to appoint a "special control industrial waste manager" (SCIWM) responsible for monitoring the handling of such wastes; see JWDCL §§ 12–2(4) and (5); Ministry Implementation Rules § 8–17.

41. David Wallace, *Environmental Policy and Industrial Innovation: Strategies in*

Europe, the U.S. and Japan (London: Royal Institute of International Affairs, Earthscan Publications, 1995).

42. Mitsutsune Yamaguchi, "Planning and Implementing Environmental Policy and the Role of Industry: The Relationship between Government and Industry—The Situation in Japan" (paper prepared for the U.S.–Japan Conference on Environmental Policy: Lessons of U.S. and Japanese Environmental Policy for Industrialized and Developing Countries, Center for Global Change, University of Maryland, December 1, 1994); Wallace, *Environmental Policy and Industrial Innovation.*

43. *Kankyō kihon hō* (Basic Environmental Law), Law No. 91, 1993. For a commentary on the significance of the Basic Environmental Law, see Naoto Asano, "Nihon no kankyō hō no tenkai to kankyō kihon hō no ronten" (The development of Japanese environmental law and issues of basic environmental law), *Kankyōkenkyū* 93 (1994): 26–38.

44. See Kōya Ishino, "Kankyō kihon hō no seitei keii to gaiyō" (Summary of the Legislative History of the Basic Environmental Law), *Jurisuto* 1041 (1994): 46–87; *Nihon Kōgyō Shimbun*, "Policy Consultative Committee Calls for Comprehensive Environmental Policy: Recommendations for the Basic Environmental Law," March 10, 1993, 2 (discussing the Keidanren's concern over economic incentives proposals and its support for voluntary self-regulation); *Asahi Shimbun*, "Call for Comprehensive Environmental Policy: Use of Tax Measures Emphasized," October 21, 1992, 1 (discussing the opposition of MITI and industry to the use of tax incentives for regulatory ends).

45. Ultimately, the Basic Environmental Law was passed in a form that contained rather weak provisions that tentatively endorsed the principles of economic incentives and environmental taxes. See Basic Environmental Law § 22 (containing the weakened remnants of the incentive program); see also "Government Bill for the Basic Environmental Law Put Together by the Environmental Agency," *Tokyo Yomiuri Shimbun* (yūkan), November 12, 1993, 1 (discussing the weakening of the Environmental Agency's proposed economic incentives programs in the face of MITI and industry opposition).

46. Id., "Basic Principles and Guidelines."

47. See MITI, ed., *Kigyō ni okeru kankyō kōdō keikaku* (Action plans for corporate environmental activities) (Tokyo: Nihonkōgyōshimbunsha, 1994), MITI, ed., *Sangyō kankyō bijyon* (Industrial vision for the environment) (Tokyo: Tsūsanshiryōchōsakai, 1994); *Kankyō ni kansuru borantarī puran sakutei ni kakawaru kyōryoku yōsei nitsuite* (Request for cooperation in making voluntary plans for the environment), October 12, 1992, document found in PREMCO files; see also MITI, *Kankyō ni kansuru borantarī puran no sakutei jyōkyō ni tsuite* (On the development of corporate voluntary environmental plans) (1993) (unpublished MITI document).

48. For scholarly treatment of the structure and operation of the hierarchy of business associations within the Japanese political economy, see, e.g., Kosuke Oyama, *Gyōsei shidō no seiji keizai gaku* (The political economy of administrative guidance) (Tokyo: Yūhikaku, 1996), esp. chap. 3; Gregory Noble, "The Japanese Industrial Policy Debate," in *Pacific Dynamism,* edited by Stephen Haggard and Chung-in Moon (Boulder, Colo.: Westview Press, 1989), 54; Richard Boyd, "Government-Industry Relations in Japan: Access, Communication, and Competitive Collaboration," in *Comparative Government-Industry Relations: Western Europe, the United*

States, and Japan, edited by Stephen Wills and Maurice Wright (Oxford: Clarendon Press, 1987), 63; Takashi Wakiyama, "The Implementation and Effectiveness of MITI's Administrative Guidance," in *Comparative Government-Industry Relations: Western Europe, the United States, and Japan,* edited by Stephen Wills and Maurice Wright (Oxford: Claredon Press, 1987), 211; Richard J. Samuels, *The Business of the Japanese State* (Ithaca, N.Y.: Cornell University Press, 1987); Chalmers Johnson, *MITI and the Japanese Miracle: The Growth of Industrial Policy* (Stanford, Calif.: Stanford University Press, 1982); Chalmers Johnson, "The Institutional Foundations of Japanese Industrial Policy," *California Management Review* 27 (1985): 59.

49. PREMCO is not a member of the Keidanren and was not afforded an opportunity to participate in its policy discussions about the voluntary plan or even in the discussions within its own industry association. PREMCO managers were not perturbed by this lack of input, for the voluntary plan initially appeared to be truly voluntary. However, in November 1995, MITI began advocating greater efforts in (1) implementing environmental management systems, (2) waste reduction, (3) waste recycling, (4) energy conservation, and (5) cooperating with foreign regulatory bodies and business communities in nations where Japanese firms have invested in production facilities. These "suggestions" have significantly increased the substantive demands and the scope of the MITI voluntary plan. These changes have surprised and angered some firms; see "First Report," *Shūkan enerugī to kankyō* (Energy and Environment), November 16, 1995, 2–4. As noted so often in the scholarly literature, administrative guidance is not as "voluntary" as it may at first appear.

50. See Tsūchi (Notification) by the Ministry of Health and Welfare, issued to prefectural governors and designated mayors on June 26, 1990. See Yukichi Suzuki, "Haishutsu kigyō to shorigyō no jittai" (Current conditions of waste generators and the waste disposal industry), *Jurisuto* 1055 (1994): 63–67.

51. Legal liability is not a concern; so long as a company has complied with regulations requiring the proper identification of wastes, it cannot be held liable for misdeeds of legally qualified waste haulers and disposal facilities. See JWDCL, §§ 12(3), 12–2(3) (setting forth standards for entrusting industrial wastes to waste haulers and disposal facilities). These legal rules have been criticized as too lax and have inspired calls for the imposition of strict liability on generators whose wastes have been improperly disposed. See Yoshinobu Kitamura, "Haishutsu jigyōsha no gyōsei sekinin" (Regulatory responsibilities of industrial waste generators), *Jurisuto* 1055 (1994): 9–16; Yasutaka Abe, "Haikibutsu hōsei no kadai" (Remaining issues concerning legal regulation of waste), *Jurisuto* 946 (1989): 107–15.

52. Groundwater testing costs $24,000 per year ($1,500 per well, per fiscal quarter). The firm itself determined the frequency of monitoring, not by regulators.

53. See JWPPL § 14–3.

54. In the United States, prior testing analyses would likely become another issue in litigation. In Japan, such reports prepared by a well-reputed lab are usually dispositive without the need for formal proceedings in a system that does not otherwise favor legalistic defenses to regulatory enforcement actions.

55. For example, the Japanese plant's internal waste-tracking system, groundwater monitoring program, and waste disposal facility review practices all exceed AMERCO's procedures and the requirements of American law.

56. Nobuko Iijima, ed., *Pollution in Japan: Historical Chronology* (Tokyo: Asahi Evening News, 1979).

57. See Hideyuki Kawana, *Dokyumento nihon no kōgai dai ni kan: Kankyōchō* (Document on pollution in Japan, vol. 2, The Environmental Agency) (Tokyo: Ryokuhūshuppan, 1988); Margaret McKean, *Environmental Protest and Citizen Politics in Japan* (Berkeley: University of California Press, 1981). In 1970, a special session of the Japanese parliament (the Diet) was held to enact comprehensive environmental laws, including the JWPPL and JWDCL. This session became known as "the Pollution Diet" (Kōgai kokkai). Frank K. Upham, *Law and Social Change in Postwar Japan* (Cambridge, Mass.: Harvard University Press, 1987).

58. See Upham, *Law and Social Change in Postwar Japan.*

59. Ibid., 211; Haley, "The Myth of the Reluctant Litigant."

60. Yasunori Sone, "Structuring Political Bargains: Government, Gyōkai, and Markets," in *Political Dynamics in Contemporary Japan,* edited by Gary D. Allinson and Yasunori Sone (Ithaca, N.Y.: Cornell University Press, 1993); Yamaguchi, "Planning and Implementing Environmental Policy and the Role of Industry."

61. See, e.g., Cass R. Sunstein, *After the Rights Revolution: Reconceiving the Regulatory State* (Cambridge, Mass.: Harvard University Press, 1990); Martin M. Shapiro, *Who Guards the Guardians? Judicial Control of Administration* (Athens: University of Georgia Press, 1988); Michael W. McCann, *Taking Reform Seriously* (Ithaca, N.Y.: Cornell University Press, 1986). The mistrust of autonomous government regulatory power by both business interests and environmental activists, and the resistance of business to environmental regulation produced a distinctively legalistic mode of regulation in which formal rules and legal proceedings assure accountability and constrain the exercise of state power. Eugene Bardach and Robert A. Kagan, *Going by the Book: The Problem of Regulatory Unreasonableness* (Philadelphia: Temple University Press, 1982); Robert A. Kagan, "Adversarial Legalism and American Government," *Journal of Policy Analysis and Management* 10 (1991): 369–406.

62. The significance of worker incorporation into workplace waste management practices is apparent in differences between AMERCO plants as well. In one plant, the workers are unionized, and the local steward has prevailed upon them to maintain a noticeably cleaner—and thus safer—workplace than the second, nonunionized plant, where worker involvement in safety and environmental issues has not been as successfully implemented.

63. The Environmental Agency in Japan reported that by 1995, 74.5 percent of companies listed on the stock exchange had instituted environmental management bodies, and 48.3 percent had adopted company environmental policies; see Environmental Agency, ed., *Kankyō hakusho (sōsetsu)* (White Paper on the environment: General edition) (Tokyo: Ministry of Finance, 1996); see also Yamaguchi, "Planning and Implementing Environmental Policy and the Role of Industry"; MITI, ed., *Kigyō ni okeru kankyō kōdō keikaku.* The very substantial flaw in the voluntary framework remains the inability to ensure compliance by smaller firms. A MITI official told us that small firms are financially unable to comply with calls for "greener" practices and will need tax breaks or subsidies to improve environmental performance.

64. See, e.g., Laura D'Andrea Tyson and John Zysman, *Politics and Productivity:*

Developmental Strategy and Production Innovation in Japan (Berkeley: Berkeley Round-table on the International Economy, 1987).

65. According to Kitamura ("Kankyō gyōsei hō to kankyō kēhō no kōsaku") and Rokumoto ("Kisei katei to hō bunka"), Japanese regulators are acutely attuned to the cost-benefit ratio of regulatory demands and the financial condition of firms when enforcing regulations or engaging in administrative guidance. Regulators tend to relax demands for strict compliance with regulations that will not result in appreciable improvements in environmental quality or reduction of environmental risks, and they rarely demand immediate compliance where the expense will bankrupt an enterprise or where compliance is impracticable.

66. McCann, *Taking Reform Seriously;* Vogel, *National Styles of Regulation.*

67. Takao Tanase, "Hōka shakai to saiban" (Legalized Society and the Courts), *Jurisuto* 971 (1991): 68–78; Lorenz Kodderitsch, "Japan's New Administrative Procedure Law: Reasons for Its Enactment and Likely Implications," *Law in Japan* 24 (1994): 105–37; Gregory Noble, "Japan in 1993: Humpty-Dumpty Had a Great Fall," *Asian Survey* 34 (1994): 19.

68. Yamaguchi, "Planning and Implementing Environmental Policy and the Role of Industry."

69. "The Burning Issue: Toxic Waste in Japan," *The Economist,* July 25, 1998, 60–61.

70. Id.

71. See, e.g., Kagan, "Regulatory Enforcement," 387–90.

72. Bardach and Kagan, *Going by the Book,* chap. 5; see also Ian Ayers and John Braithwaite, *Responsive Regulation* (New York: Oxford University Press, 1992); John Braithwaite, "Enforced Self-Regulation: A New Strategy for Corporate Crime Control," *Michigan Law Review* 80 (June 1982): 1466–1507.

CHAPTER THREE

Industrial Effluent Control
in the United States and Japan

Kazumasu Aoki, Lee Axelrad, and Robert A. Kagan

Responding to political pressures for environmental protection, governments in many countries have adopted increasingly stringent water pollution control standards and regulatory methods. Multinational manufacturing companies, in consequence, face an array of national regulatory regimes. Some multinationals have adopted a strategy of staying ahead of the regulatory curve—and of their competitors—by implementing similar, technologically advanced environmental management systems in all their installations, endeavoring to reduce pollutants to levels that satisfy the most demanding current national standards. Q Corp, a large Japan-based manufacturer of electronic parts, is one such company. In view of Q Corp's commitment to company-wide harmonization, its experience with contrasting industrial effluent control regimes in Japan and the United States suggests how differences in national regulatory regimes affect corporate incentives, costs, and regulatory performance. That is the subject of this chapter.

Because Q Corp has sought to be a corporate leader in environmental management systems, its regulatory experience, in both Japan and the United States, may not be completely representative of the style or the consequences of regulation with respect to smaller or less ambitious companies. Moreover, although Q Corp officials have been cooperative, it has proved difficult to obtain quantitative comparisons of the company's effluents. On the other hand, there has been little prior research concerning the actual operation of Japanese methods of regulation at the specific site level, or about the experience of similar factories in two different regulatory regimes. Hence this qualitative account of Q Corp's contrasting experiences in the two countries provides new insights into the character and the consequences of Japanese and American regulatory styles.

To conduct this research, we visited Q Corp headquarters and two similar Q Corp factories, one in Japan and one in California. All three authors visited the American plant, for a total of five visits; Aoki visited the Japanese plant on three occasions. At these plants and at Q Corp's headquarters, we interviewed sixteen Q Corp officials responsible for effluent control and regulatory compliance. In Japan, Aoki interviewed senior officials in the corporate Environmental Management Division, the Environmental Preservation Programs, Facilities Division, and their counterparts at the factory level. In the United States we interviewed senior environmental managers at the site level and frequently asked them further questions by telephone. Most officials interviewed had experience only with U.S. or Japanese regulatory regimes, but we interviewed three Q Corp officials who have had experience in both countries. In the United States we examined regulatory permits and supporting documents that describe Q Corp effluent controls and their capacities, and obtained information on actual effluent levels. In Japan we examined documents reflecting the factory's internal effluent limits, its pollution control agreement with municipal regulatory officials, notifications the company sent to regulatory officials, and notices regulators sent to the company. In addition, we interviewed a private attorney who represents Q USA (a Q Corp subsidiary) in regulatory matters, a U.S.-based environmental compliance consultant with experience in the United States and Japan, and two Japanese industry association representatives in Japan. We interviewed ten Japanese regulatory officials (at the national, prefectural, and municipal levels of government). We interviewed officials from three relevant regulatory offices in the United States—the Environmental Protection Agency (EPA), the state regional water quality control board, and the local water treatment district. However, because (as a condition of cooperation) we agreed to keep Q Corp's identity confidential, we did not interview regulatory officials in either country about specific interactions with Q Corp.

I. OVERVIEW

Q Corp's subsidiaries, Q Japan and Q USA, operate factories that manufacture the same kinds of electronic parts. In both the Japanese and the American facility, water is used to cool equipment and clean the product. The wastewater contains potentially harmful pollutants that in both countries are subject to stringent regulatory controls, especially because in both Q Corp locations the wastewater, after treatment, is discharged into sewer systems and into surface waters that are linked to local water supplies. Both Q Japan and Q USA, their officials insist, have installed systems that *overcomply* with the end-of-pipe effluent quality standards embodied in Japanese and American law. Nevertheless, Q Corp has experienced the U.S. regulatory regime as strikingly different from Japan's:

- Japan's regulatory system, as implemented, grants regulated manufacturers considerable discretion in choosing which methods to use to meet water quality standards. American regulation, as implemented, is much more prescriptive, legalistic, and confusing.
- Although Q USA's environmental engineers see actual environmental protection as their ultimate objective, their activities are shaped to a great extent by legal rules, official regulatory demands, and concern about avoiding regulatory sanctions. In Japan the legal rules and potential sanctions are far less salient to company officials. Relatively speaking, their pollution control efforts are driven more by quasi-regulatory considerations, which include (1) domestic reputational concerns; (2) an agreement entered into with the municipal government; (3) customers' specifications; and (4) company officials' belief that their firm's long-term economic interests will be served by staying ahead of increasingly stringent regulatory standards.
- Although Q USA's relationships with water quality regulators generally have not entailed high levels of legal contestation,[1] Q USA has experienced more delay and more conflict than Q Japan in obtaining regulatory permits and approvals. On a day-to-day basis, Q USA environmental compliance officials are far more preoccupied with the threat of substantial monetary fines and civil liability claims for inadvertent regulatory violations. Unlike Q Japan, Q USA feels compelled to spend money on frequent legal advice.
- Despite the greater legal specificity and potential punitiveness of the American regulatory system, it does not appear to us that Q USA has achieved better environmental protection than Q Japan. Whereas Q Japan has never been cited for an environmental violation, Q USA has twice received substantial fines for unpermitted discharges. Across a range of pollutants, the end-of-pipe effluent quality standards achieved by the Japanese plant on average are as good as those achieved by Q USA, and Q Japan seems to achieve its water quality goals more consistently. Q USA officials apparently have made less progress than their Q Japan counterparts in implementing Q Corp's plans for obtaining ISO 14000 certification for advanced environmental management,[2] in formalizing the waste-reduction planning process, and in providing a margin of error against violation of regulatory standards.
- Confronted with a more complex, fragmented, and confusing legal environment, Q USA officials seem to have a more legalistic and skeptical attitude toward regulatory demands than do Q Japan officials. Q USA officials regard keeping up with and complying with American regula-

tions as burdensome. Q Japan officials regard the straightforward end-of-pipe effluent quality standards embodied in Japanese law not only as reasonable but also as a minimum standard that they should continually attempt to exceed.

Despite the lower levels of legitimacy U.S. officials accord environmental regulations, it would be misleading to suggest that Q USA does not have a generally good environmental record. Nevertheless, Q Corp's experience suggests that at least for the sector of the economy represented by large industrial firms, the American style of water pollution regulation, in conjunction with the entire array of state and federal regulatory regimes those firms face, tends to alienate corporate compliance officials and to undermine incentives for the most pro-active and creative kinds of corporate pollution control efforts.

II. THE COMPANY

Q Corp is headquartered in Japan but manufactures electronic parts and components in more than twenty countries. Its annual sales exceed approximately $10 billion. A leading company in its primary product markets, Q Corp is generally regarded as having a strong record in terms of technological innovation, financial strength, and environmental consciousness.

Like Q Corp's other subsidiaries, the two that are the focus of this study—Q USA and Q Japan—are expected to compete against one another in terms of product quality, productivity, and profitability. Consequently, whereas Q Corp allocates to both subsidiaries a substantial environmental budget, Q USA and Q Japan are under identical pressures to implement their local effluent control measures in a cost-effective way. At both companies, wastewater treatment is the largest item in their environmental budget. According to corporate officials, headquarters monitors each subsidiary's environmental performance.

Q Corp's company-wide environmental business plan, corporate officials tell us, reflects the heightened environmental consciousness and product specifications of Q Corp's primary customers, which include multinational business firms and both domestic and foreign governments. A reputation for environmental leadership (and avoidance of negative publicity concerning environmental matters) is regarded as a positive business asset. Although Q Corp officials in Japan view Japanese environmental regulation as less stringent than that of some European Union countries and the United States, they anticipate a continuous global trend toward more stringent environmental regulation. Hence, they decided to internalize future costs of compliance as early and as efficiently as possible, expecting that this would provide a competitive edge against slower-to-respond competitors.

One element in Q Corp's worldwide environmental business plan is its effort to obtain ISO 14000 certification for all its manufacturing sites. Q Corp's environmental plan also demands that regardless of domestic governments' regulatory standards, each Q Corp factory should comply voluntarily with *corporate* environmental standards, which meet or exceed the most stringent governmental standards. In relation to effluent control, Q Corp's plan also calls for pollution prevention, by phasing out or reducing use of certain chemicals in production processes.[3]

The plants operated by Q Japan and Q USA are very similar in terms of product line, production capacity, and production technologies. Q Japan's plant has thirty-six hundred employees, Q USA, eighteen hundred. The kinds of pollutants generated by the production process are similar but not identical. Both plants generate process wastewater, used to clean the product during manufacturing, and nonprocess wastewater, used to cool production equipment. At Q USA, process wastewater is discharged to a sewer leading to a municipal wastewater treatment plant, while nonprocess wastewater (which contains no chemical additives) is discharged to a system leading to a stream without treatment by others. Both the stream and the municipal treatment plant's discharges make their way to waters used to supply potable water to nearby communities.

At Q Japan, both process and nonprocess wastewater have been discharged to surface waters; with the recent extension of a public sewer line to its plant, however, some process wastewater is now discharged to the sewer system, and eventually all the plant's wastewater will be.[4] But insofar as surface waters have been used, rather than a sewer line/treatment plant system as in the American case, the environmental risks posed by Q Japan's operations may be somewhat greater and may help explain Q Japan's vigilant concern about "overcompliance." Moreover, in the municipal area in which Q Japan is located, residential drinking water is supplied almost exclusively from groundwater, and residents are said to be very vigilant concerning groundwater quality.

Both Q USA and Q Japan have invested heavily in treatment programs for a variety of contaminants in the wastewater, each of which requires different techniques, including scrubbing, aerobic biological treatment, precipitation, filtration, and chemical neutralization. Q USA performs effluent treatment only on the process wastewater before discharging it to a sewer and ultimately to a municipal treatment plant; its nonprocess effluent is discharged directly to surface waters. Q Japan, in addition to treating process wastewater (until recently discharged to surface water), treats nonprocess wastewater for pH as well. Both subsidiaries have engineered a considerable amount of redundancy (or extra capacity) into their treatment systems for process wastewater, so that in the event of system malfunction the inadequately treated water can be retained in holding tanks (rather than discharged) and treated subsequently.

III. TWO APPROACHES TO REGULATION

In both Japan and the United States, water pollution control is effectuated by both national and subnational governments (state and municipal governments in the United States, prefectural and municipal governments in Japan). The two countries have adopted sharply different approaches to regulation, however. In the United States, regulation is generally conceived of as a matter of carefully prescribed legal mandates, backed by the threat of legal sanctions. In Japan, legal mandates are far less salient. Advanced firms, such as Q Japan, are subject not only to "mandatory" regulatory standards and procedures but also to government and industry peer pressure to "voluntarily" achieve regulatory policy goals that have been established by political negotiation between government and industry. Those cross-national differences in regulatory approach reflect sharply different forms of industrial organization and governmental structures.

A. Industrial Organization and Business-State Relations

As noted by David Wallace, the author of a comparative study of environmental policy, the distinctive organizational structure of the Japanese business community has made an important contribution to the relatively effective implementation of environmental norms.[5] Groupings of companies in tightly knit keiretsu (companies closely linked by ownership and business relationships) and in industry associations (e.g., Keidanren) facilitate reciprocal interaction between business and government. Through these groupings, industry can influence national ministries that are responsible for formulating regulatory policy. Hence Q Corp officials express confidence that environmental regulations and administrative guidance promulgated by the Japanese government will not impose requirements more burdensome than industry generally regards as acceptable. In return, regulatory authorities can expect that their informal administrative guidance, disseminated through industry groupings, will reliably influence individual firm behavior. And individual firms can count on the industrial organizations to ensure that there are no free riders, that is, that all members will move together in adopting more costly environmental controls.

Japan's new Basic Environmental Law, enacted in 1993, specifically calls for voluntary corporate efforts to reduce pollution.[6] The influential governmental Ministry for International Trade and Industry (MITI) explicitly took the lead in coordinating voluntary measures by corporations, often working through sectoral industry associations.[7] Q Corp, like several other major firms, had *already* instituted company-wide environmental management and pollution prevention programs. MITI issued "administrative guidance" designed to extend the formation and implementation of similar advanced corporate plans to other firms. By October 1994, 362 firms, including 60 percent of all manufacturing companies with more than three hundred employees, had submitted their plans.[8] Q Corp officials told us that administrative guidance from MITI often can be used by firms to glimpse the seeds of future environmental regulations.[9] MITI's Corporate Voluntary Plan did push Q Corp further, inducing the company (1) to specify precise pollution reduction goals and timetables for objectives that had previously been articulated narratively and (2) to release its action plans to the public. The burden of finding specific ways to meet precise numerical conservation targets under the corporate-wide plan falls upon Q Corp's subsidiaries, compelling them to compete in seeking to lower material input, disposal, and treatment costs.

Business organization and business-government communications in the United States contrast dramatically with the Japanese model. Viewed in comparative perspective, American industrial structure has long been unusually competitive and fragmented. Since the late nineteenth century, antitrust laws, a politically fragmented banking system, reliance on private financial markets, and the absence of a powerful national ministry of trade and industry combined to preclude or minimize interlocking directorates and cartels of the kind that spearheaded industrial development in Germany, France, and Japan. The late arrival and comparatively decentralized nature of collective bargaining in the United States inhibited the development of employers' associations with control over their members.

Thus in the 1960s and 1970s, when the federal government of the United States enacted environmental laws, there were few powerful trade associations with whom regulators could negotiate and implement compliance plans. Even if they had existed, the populist strain in American political culture, deeply distrustful of backroom deals between government and business, would have precluded such negotiations.[10] Interaction between business and government, in consequence, is highly formal and legalistic, at least when viewed in comparative perspective. Instead of the informal interaction between business associations and government agencies that shapes Japanese regulatory policies, the formulation of American regulatory rules is often described as judicialized.[11] American environmental statutes are legalistically drafted and enforced, so as to lessen any suspicion of unwarranted favoritism, leniency, or corruption on the part of governmental officials.

American business organizations, in turn, are likely to conceive of their relations with government in legal terms. Since they are not nested in industrial groupings that enable them to count on coordinated action by their competitors, American companies often see strict legal enforcement as a way of ensuring that they are not being put at a disadvantage by corner-cutting competitors. Whereas Q Corp officials in Japan could recount how their corporate plans helped shape and mobilize MITI's voluntary plan initiative, Q USA environmental officials did not tell us of any similar high-level interactions they had with federal or state environmental policy makers. The complex regulations they must cope with emerge, often unpredictably (for them), from a politically variable array of state and federal agencies, legislators, and courts.

B. Governmental Structure and Regulatory Style

1. HIERARCHICAL VERSUS FRAGMENTED GOVERNMENT

In comparison with the United States, governmental power in Japan is more hierarchically organized. Prefectural and municipal governments operate within spheres of governance delegated by the central government,[12] which also exerts great influence on their finances. The national Water Pollution Prevention Law (JWPPL)[13] establishes specific, nationwide, generally applicable end-of-pipe standards for a variety of pollutants,[14] but it delegates implementing authority to prefectural governors and certain designated mayors, who act largely as agents of the national government.[15] The national Environmental Agency does not exercise direct enforcement authority vis-à-vis regulatees. Similarly, Japanese municipal governments are delegated authority for enforcing national legal provisions concerning sewer discharges under the national Sewer Law (JSL).[16] To respond to local environmental needs, however, local governments are permitted to promulgate ordinances (*uwanose jyōrei*) establishing effluent limits that are more stringent than the minimum standards established by the national government.[17] In Japan, therefore, the national, prefectural, and municipal governments act in a coordinated way, with each level undertaking implementing actions not duplicated by the others.

In contrast, the legalistic approach to regulation in the United States arises in large measure from a much more fragmented governmental structure. The federal government, acting through the EPA, retains direct enforcement authority under the Clean Water Act (CWA).[18] Individual state governments are authorized by the EPA on a state-by-state basis to implement the state industrial effluent permitting regime "in lieu" of the federal program, provided that the state initially and continually satisfies federal authorities that the regime and its implementation satisfy federal requirements. In many instances, regulated entities are subject to both state and federal regulatory laws and requirements. Because state governments are largely autonomous from the federal government, an important part of the

EPA's role is regulating state environmental agencies, which gives rise to the possibility that it will seek to override state permit or enforcement decisions.[19]

Finally, American environmental activists and their allies in Congress trusted neither the state governments nor the federal bureaucracy (which often has been controlled by Republican presidents) to implement the national standards rigorously. Therefore, they fought for and obtained CWA provisions that authorize private lawsuits against both state and federal agencies for failing to meet the law's requirements, as well as against business enterprises that violate regulatory standards.[20] Private environmental advocacy organizations and courts thus were invited to serve as mechanisms of legal accountability. Conversely, because regulated enterprises in the United States mistrusted both federal and state environmental agencies, the governing laws allow businesses to appeal agency decisions to the courts. This political mistrust of administrative discretion and accountability through judicial review helps explain why American environmental statutes and regulations tend to be far more detailed, lengthy, and complex than those that the Japanese governmental structure has produced.[21]

The complex U.S. governmental structure for water pollution control also provides interest groups who are unhappy with regulatory decisions and policies—environmentalists, fishermen, business firms, or municipalities—many more points of bureaucratic and political access to demand policy change or more vigorous (or more relaxed) enforcement decisions. At both the state and national levels of government, shifts in power between political parties often lead to changes in policy and in regulations, as well as to conflict between state and federal officials. Many of the effluent standards and other requirements applicable to Q USA have been embroiled in legal or political challenges that throw into doubt whether or when particular proposed requirements will become applicable to the company, or how those requirements will be changed by the conflict, or even, once promulgated, whether their legality will be later overturned in court.[22]

This level of doubt is far less likely to be generated under Japan's more stable set of political authority arrangements (even though conflicts between local governments and the national government sometimes occur in Japanese environmental policy) and under Japan's tradition of minimizing judicial review of administrative decisions.[23] Japanese environmentalists did not have to worry about a "race to the bottom" among the local governments because it was the local governments, faced with public dissatisfaction concerning the severe industrial effluent pollution problems during the late 1960s and 1970s, that took the initiative by enacting stringent local ordinances and entering into contractual agreements with individual firms. The politically conservative national government, which was widely understood to be intimate with industry, followed the locals by enacting JWPPL in 1970.[24] Hence the Japanese national government, compared with the federal government in Washington, is much less concerned about monitoring local regulators with regard to proper implementation of environmental policies. Q Japan officials do not perceive their regulatory legal environment to be shifting and difficult to predict. In national legislation, effluent controls are stated in the form of straightforward numerical standards; this also is true of those prefectural ordinances and local agreements that articulate more stringent standards. The numerical standards do not change frequently and are easy to comprehend. The interrelationships among national, prefectural, and municipal regulations in Japan are not nearly as complicated as the overlapping matrix of U.S. national, state, and local regulations. The administrative guidance system and avenues for consultation with regulators, Q Corp officials say, ensure early warning of significant regulatory changes.

2. COMPLEX VERSUS SIMPLE LAW

The upshot is that Q USA officials experience the governing law as complex, changeable, and difficult to keep up with and comprehend. Q Japan officials do not. Q USA officials regard their legal obligations as uncertain. They feel compelled to consult attorneys frequently. Q Japan officials do not. According to the plant's compliance official at Q Japan, compliance for them is a matter of engineering. Compliance for Q USA officials is also a matter of legal interpretation and attentiveness to various sources of legal change.

Q Japan's discharges, as noted earlier, are governed solely by numerical end-of-pipe effluent limits stated in the national law and local ordinances (which are somewhat stricter than the national minimum standards). For Q USA, however, numerical end-of-pipe effluent limits are supplemented by legal requirements concerning the impact of Q USA's effluent on the ambient quality of receiving waters, by narrative standards, and by bioassay testing requirements. Thus Q USA's state permit stipulates that receiving waters beyond the area where Q Corp's discharges mix with natural waters must not have less than 5 mg/l dissolved oxygen; that 70 percent of test fish must survive a bioassay after swimming in Q USA's effluent for ninety-six hours; and that Q USA's effluent must not cause aesthetically undesirable discoloration in receiving waters.[25] This does not necessarily mean that Q Japan's effluents are less clean or that they would not pass the more detailed U.S. requirements (although they conceivably would not for some contaminants). It does mean that Q Japan's environmental planners can concentrate on achieving and surpassing a single set of effluent standards that are simple to understand and monitor.

3. TAILORING REGULATION TO INDIVIDUAL SITES: PERMITS VERSUS MUNICIPAL AGREEMENTS

Under federal and state law in the United States, governmental permits for individual point sources are the primary tool for tailoring general regulatory requirements to the environmental risks posed by particular sources to particular local conditions. Q USA has had to obtain three permits: one applies to discharges of nonprocess wastewater into local surface waters; two apply to discharges of process wastewater to the sewer leading to the municipal water treatment plant. The municipal water authority, a publicly owned treatment works (POTW), in establishing Q USA's permit for sewer discharges, seeks to establish standards for each pollutant that will provide "a margin of safety" for the POTW, which itself must meet complex federal and state water quality standards. The procedure leading to grant of the permits is rather complicated and slow and, as Q USA learned, often entails regulatory review of and suggested revisions of the applicant's particular abatement technology. This creates considerable uncertainty for the permit applicant.

In Japan, some degree of tailoring to local conditions, as noted earlier, is provided by prefectural authority to promulgate end-of-pipe effluent standards that are more stringent than the generally applicable national standards. Further specification of treatment standards to the individual plant level is often provided by voluntary agreements between factories and municipal governments.[26] Q Japan first entered into such an agreement in the mid-1980s, and into a revised agreement a decade later, expressly committing to pollution controls (for air and noise as well as water) and accountability measures that exceed those required by the national law and prefectural ordinances.[27]

According to a Q Japan official, the municipal regulators began the negotiations with the company in an adversarial fashion, seeking very stringent measures from the firm.[28] However, after the municipal regulators were made aware of the firm's extensive efforts to exceed legally mandated requirements, they seemed reassured, and further negotiations went reasonably smoothly.

The final agreement set forth standards that were stricter than those of the national laws and prefectural ordinances but more lenient than those of the company's internal code.[29] Environmental officials at Q Japan gave us the impression that in the day-to-day operation of the factory they accord as much importance to the municipal agreement, in terms of its normative gravity and binding effect, as they do to the national laws and prefectural ordinances, even though the agreement specifies no monetary sanctions for violations of the agreed-upon standards.

We have been unable to determine definitively whether the effluent standards specified in Q Japan's municipal agreement are less stringent than those in U.S. regulations and Q USA's permit, although we believe that Q Japan's internal operating standards are roughly equivalent, at the very least, to the U.S. permit standards. Q Corp headquarters officials assure us that the actual treatment systems in the two factories are basically similar and produce similar levels of pollution abatement.[30] But it has been difficult for us to make an independent comparison in this regard. While Q Japan officials provided us with the company's internal operating limits for effluents, they did not provide us with actual effluent data, citing confidentiality concerns. Comparing Q Japan effluent limits with Q USA effluent permits and reports is complicated. For some of the numerous contaminants in Q Corp's effluent, the Japanese regulatory regime (including the municipal agreement) appears to impose stricter limits than the United States; for others, the American regime appears to be more stringent. The Japanese regime requires treatment of some contaminants not mentioned in the American standards, and vice versa.[31] And for some contaminants, the two regulatory regimes specify the pollutants in different ways or employ somewhat different terminology.

IV. INTERACTION BETWEEN FIRMS AND REGULATORS

The impact of regulatory programs depends not only on the general structure of regulatory institutions and the language of regulatory rules but also on the character of day-to-day interaction between regulators and regulated entities.[32] For Q Corp, the American regulatory style in the realm of effluent control has been experienced as somewhat punitive and always potentially so. Second, in at least one instance, U.S. regulatory permitting officials have been more intrusive than their Japanese counterparts, using their legal leverage to demand process changes that the company found unacceptable.

A. Permits and Notifications

In Japan, firms that wish to install or modify certain types of facilities that result in discharges must obtain preconstruction approval from the prefectural governor or from the local mayor (in case of discharges to the public sewer); these officials are responsible for ensuring compliance with legally prescribed numerical effluent limits.[33] In obtaining approvals, Q Japan has experienced less delay and less second-guessing by regulatory officials than has Q USA.

According to Q Corp officials, prompt governmental response to requests for approvals is important because of the frequency with which production process changes are necessary. Q Japan's notifications (*todokede*) have always been approved in sixty days or less, as required by JWPPL, although notifications may have been preceded by prefiling discussions. For Q USA, formal permit approvals from the California state agency (for discharges to surface waters) have taken seven months, and permits from the local municipal sewer system have taken from one and a half to three and a half years. On the other hand, in none of these cases was Q USA forbidden to operate pending approval. Hence in neither country has Q Corp experienced significant production losses due to regulatory delays.

In the course of the notification and approval process, Q Japan has never received a regulatory order or informal request to modify its plans.[34] The prefectural government regulators themselves told us that they always try to be flexible and accommodative to business concerns. The agreement between Q Japan and the municipal government gives the municipal agency some authority to ensure that the firm's equipment is appropriate for achieving the agreed-upon effluent standards, but the officials, apparently influenced by Q Japan's excellent compliance record, have not used that authority. Q USA's experience has been somewhat different.

In California, where Q USA is located, state agency officials in charge of permitting, while responsible for insisting on compliance with end-of-pipe water quality standards, are not legally authorized to specify particular technologies or directly regulate the degree of redundancy (or excess capacity) in the firm's effluent control system. However, in discussing Q USA's proposed discharge of process wastewater to surface waters, state regulators called for a higher level of redundancy than company engineers had planned. The added costs were so high that the firm chose instead to discharge its process wastewater to the sewer system, even though doing so has required a substantial fee to the municipal water treatment authority. Q USA environmental managers assume that it would have been very difficult to reach agreement with state agency officials concerning the appropriate level of redundancy.

B. Accountability: Monitoring, Reporting, Inspections

Contemporary regulatory regimes typically require enterprises not merely to comply with the law but also to provide evidence of their compliance. These mandatory accountability measures include such actions as monitoring effluents and emissions, maintaining records of compliance-related activities (such as equipment maintenance and employee training), reporting to governmental officials, providing certifications by third parties, and allowing governmental officials to inspect company facilities and files. In the realm of effluent control, both Q USA and Q Japan must monitor and maintain records regarding their effluents. But U.S. law imposes more demanding sampling, testing, and reporting requirements, and in the United States, reports are made available to the public.

In the United States, effluent self-monitoring data, whether voluntary or required by law, must be reported to government officials.[35] Q USA reports to federal authorities two times per year, to state authorities four times per year, and to municipal authorities twelve times per year for the firm's older production line and four times per year for the newer production line. Significantly, citizens have statutorily guaranteed access to this effluent data. Whereas citizens in both countries can sue for damages if they are injured by a company's discharge, only in the United States can citizens sue to enforce regulatory requirements directly against dischargers even in the absence of proof of individual harm. Public access to effluent monitoring data is indispensable to this citizen enforcement device, and, although invoked in only a small percentage of cases, private enforcement suits always remain a possibility under the U.S. regime, where numerous organized environmental advocacy groups are ready to go to court and are experienced in doing so.[36] In Japan, Q Corp officials told us that litigation by advocacy groups is not a salient threat.

For Q Japan, the law does not require reporting of self-monitoring data to government officials. However, Q Japan does so pursuant to its municipal agreement, for those pollutants covered by the agreement. Environmental officials at Q Japan are confident that the municipality does not and will not disclose the information in those reports without prior consent from the company, and they do not envision any circumstances in which they will agree to release the data. In addition, prefectural regulatory officials told us that in considering whether to make any company effluent data public, they would strive to avoid causing public panic. In contrast to the U.S. regime, therefore, Japanese regulators adopt a paternalistic stance toward the public, as if skeptical about its ability to react to pollution information in a sensible, balanced manner.[37]

Q USA does not regard its effluent reporting requirements as particularly burdensome, partly because they are so much less burdensome than the record-keeping and reporting requirements under the U.S. waste management regime, established under the Resource Conservation and Recovery Act (RCRA). Comparatively speaking, according to Q USA's outside counsel for environmental matters, the sampling, sample-analysis, record-keeping, and reporting requirements under the effluent control regime make sense, do not cost very much, and do not engender many complaints from industry.

Although Q Japan's legally prescribed reporting requirements are less demanding and less open to public scrutiny, Q Japan appears to undergo more frequent governmental inspections of company facilities. Whereas Q USA typically undergoes just one water pollution inspection per year, Q Japan has five, conducted by municipal officials. Japanese inspectors, however, limit their inquiry to company records and sampling, and each inspection typically is limited in scope, focusing on particular pollutants.[38] Moreover, a Q Corp official told us that a Japanese regulatory official, at the conclusion of an inspection, generally gives Q Japan at most only informal, quite general administrative guidance—partly because the governing rules are straightforward effluent standards and because the plant, well endowed with appropriate treatment technologies, has always been in full compliance.

By contrast, Q USA's environmental manager complains that the various American rules are so detailed and complex that a regulator can almost always find the company out of compliance with some provision, although that concern is less salient for water pollution than for RCRA rules.[39] Nonetheless, the applicable rules in the United States consist of more than merely numerical end-of-pipe limits, including some qualitative water quality standards. Q USA's permit from the municipal water district says that the firm must comply with all applicable federal requirements, present and future. Hence Q USA officials seem to lack confidence that they are in compliance; they feel more vulnerable about what inspectors may point out and cite or penalize them for.

C. Legal Penalties for Violations

Regulatory enforcement in the United States is often said to be more punitive than in other countries;[40] this legalistic image, however, has only intermittently described Q USA's experience with respect to effluent control. Federal and state law empower water pollution control agencies to brandish a formidable arsenal of administrative, civil, and criminal penalties—including large criminal fines even for negligent violations.[41] But in Q USA's experience, American officials have exercised discretion in dealing with effluent violations. Q USA periodically has exceeded the ammonia limit in its sewer discharge permit and the pH limit for surface water discharges, and it has had two operational upsets that resulted in violations of surface water discharge standards. Only in the latter cases have agencies responded by imposing fines. Nevertheless, Q USA officials see regulatory officials as somewhat unpredictable and view legal action as an ever-present threat.

Q Japan, on the other hand, has never been cited for committing any violations and does not fear legalistic action. In part, this reflects differences in law. The JWPPL links legal penalties to demonstrable, health-threatening environmental harm. If a company causes harm to human health through discharges of designated toxic substances, it is strictly liable, under the JWPPL, to pay compensatory damages, regardless of whether it can be shown to have been negligent.[42] Q Corp officials believe that law will be strictly enforced. However, Q Japan is less likely than Q USA to be formally cited and penalized for regulatory violations that do *not* result in harm to human health.

In addition, Q Japan faces a different regulatory enforcement style. Unlike in the United States, there is no provision in the Japanese regime for administratively issued civil penalties. According to field research by Kitamura, unless clear risk to public health is posed, Japanese regulators typically respond to detected violations by providing violators with administrative guidance concerning remediation and improvement. If regulators subsequently are not satisfied with a company's response to administrative guidance, they may refer the case to the police or government prosecutors to seek penalties in court.[43]

The closest encounter to an enforcement story for Q Japan involved an alleged violation in which the regulators ultimately backed down. Government effluent samples indicated that Q Japan was violating the 3-mg/l limit for n-hexane in the municipal agreement. When confronted with this charge, Q Japan officials produced their own self-monitoring data, which showed no violation. To resolve the conflict, government and company officials held an informal meeting, to which a qualified third party was invited to assist in working through the issues. All participants were engineers or management generalists; none were lawyers. Since the case involved alleged violation of the agreement only, no regulatory punishment was at stake. It emerged that the government took samples downstream from the company's sampling point and also used a different sampling method. The participants concluded that machine oil from the government officials' pumps had contaminated the samples. Monitoring is now done only at the location that the firm argued would provide a more accurate sample, using a sampling device that the company had argued was more appropriate.

In Q USA's experience, in the case of violations that entail no environmental harm, the relevant state agency has often been rather flexible. (It is almost surely significant in this regard that Q USA's discharges of process wastewater go to the municipal sewer/treatment plant system, and only uncontaminated nonprocess water is discharged to the surface waters, which are policed by the state agency.) In policing Q USA discharges to the municipal waste treatment plant, the officials have been consistently nonlegalistic. For example, when the aerators in the bottom of Q USA's biological treatment equipment periodically (perhaps twice a year) become plugged, the company violates its end-of-pipe numerical effluent limit for sewer discharges of ammonia. POTW officials seem to take this in stride, presumably because the POTW system can manage minor exceedances with respect to ammonia. Hence when such an exceedance occurs, a Q USA official calls up the POTW official, who responds, "OK, let us know when you're back in spec."[44] Yet, Q USA's outside attorney told us, there is always some possibility that state regulatory officials who monitor the POTW will cite the POTW and Q USA for violation of state water quality standards.

Q USA's surface water discharges are directly regulated by a regional water board, a State of California agency. Q USA's discharge to surface waters periodically exceeds regulatory limits for pH because the company's *influent* from the stream in question during certain seasons exceeds the regulatory limit for pH. Upon receiving monitoring reports from the firm self-reporting this violation, a responsible state enforcement official telephoned one of the company's engineers and left a voice mail message saying, in essence, "You are in violation of your permit limits and must cease and desist." After this legalistic opening salvo from regulators, however, company officials had an opportunity to speak with regulators about the situation, and the regulators told the firm, in essence, "You're not immediately impacting water quality. We'll negotiate and resolve it over time."[45] Such a response cannot be guaranteed, however. Company officials believe that the outcome for the firm in situations such as these is highly dependent on the personalities of the particular regulators involved and on whether the federal officials who review state agency enforcement are currently supportive of a nonlegalistic approach.[46]

One of Q USA's operational upsets occurred when a contractor improperly plumbed a new production line, causing process wastewater to be mistakenly discharged to surface waters. The factory's process wastewater is treated so as to meet applicable surface water standards; therefore, according to Q USA environmental officials, no harm was caused to human health or the environment. Nonetheless, in legal terms, this constituted an unpermitted discharge. Q USA voluntarily reported the spill as soon as it was discovered and took prompt action to fix the problem. Nevertheless, the state agency imposed a fine of $25,000. Regulators told the company that this was the minimum fine allowable under the circumstances. (The statutory scheme provides for increasing fines according to the severity of the environmental harm that stems from a violation, which in this instance could have amounted to as much as $167 million.)[47]

Q USA's more serious operational upset involved an accidental spill of sodium hydroxide, which is used in the plant's effluent treatment system, into nearby surface waters. This spill violated the Clean Water Act and increased the stream's pH, killing fish and frogs. The company reported the violation and responded quickly, plugging the creek temporarily to pump out the contaminated water. The firm also responded to the long-term operational problem by installing, at a cost of around $100,000, a cutoff switch that can stop any future similar spills before they progressed too far. Again, state officials issued the minimum fine allowable under the circumstances: $25,000. In calculating this fine, state regulators chose to consider this a second violation (warranting a fine of that magnitude)—with the first violation being the aforementioned nonharmful unpermitted discharge of process wastewater.[48] Thus, while this operational upset caused environmental harm and merited a response from regulators—as even Q Japan officials agree—that response was issued within a legalistic framework for calculating penalties.[49]

V. THE CONSEQUENCES OF DIFFERENT REGULATORY STYLES: CORPORATE INCENTIVES, ATTITUDES, AND COSTS

Q Corp, as noted at the outset of this chapter, has for a variety of reasons developed a corporate environmental business plan that calls on all its subsidiaries to adopt internal standards that exceed national regulatory standards, to institute positive environmental management systems, and to adopt specific commitments with respect to recycling and waste reduction. Individual corporate subsidiaries, however, respond to signals and threats from their immediate economic, political, and legal environment, as well as to policies that emanate from corporate headquarters. Q USA environmental management officials are intensely attentive to formal legal requirements and the threat of legal sanctions that lie behind them. Their incentives seem to be to keep their company out of trouble with the law—a demanding task because the law is much more detailed, complex, and subject to uncertainty. In consequence, Q USA has been reluctant to initiate formal commitments with respect to internal effluent limits or adherence to ISO 14000 management systems and auditing requirements.

To Q Japan officials, in contrast, the law on the books is both far less salient and far less complicated. The law is regarded as powerful, for serious violations entail strict liability. Moreover, Q Japan's "pollution control supervisor" and "pollution control manager"—positions made mandatory by Japanese environmental law—are subject to sanctions in the event of violations that cause serious environmental damage.[50] But regulators are not regarded as potentially unreasonable, and the threat of legal sanctions seems rather remote as long as the company vigilantly maintains an adequate control system. Staying abreast of and complying with the law is not regarded as burdensome or preoccupying. To Q Japan officials, incentives to meet and exceed regulatory standards stem not so much from legal threat as from political and societal pressure.

If the Q USA environmental manager's nightmare is an untoward effluent spill that results in large civil penalties or a class action lawsuit, the Q Japan environmental manager's nightmare is an untoward effluent spill that results in widespread negative publicity, local political responses, and public disapproval—all of which would have real and adverse economic consequences. In Japan, a reputation for progressive environmental concern is regarded as a significant business asset. The incentives facing Q Japan officials, therefore, are to adopt highly visible policies that signal the company's continuous efforts to exceed legal standards and demonstrate its good citizenship. Hence whereas Q USA officials have been reluctant to establish explicit internal effluent limits and ISO 14000 measures, perhaps out of concerns that they could be used against the company in an adversarial legal proceeding, Q Japan has been eager to establish such norms.

The two regulatory regimes also have differential effects on Q Corp headquarters' ability to monitor and control its subsidiaries. In Japan, the law's emphasis on clear, end-of-pipe effluent standards that are not too difficult to achieve tends to provide a benchmark for judging the subsidiary and measuring its pollution reduction achievement (but without risking legal sanctions for falling a little short). In the United States the greater detail, complexity, and stringency built into the law result in a tendency to evaluate the subsidiary solely on its ability to avoid legal trouble.

A. *Responses to Legal Complexity and Uncertainty*

The book of effluent control regulations in Japan is "this thin," a Q USA environmental manager told us, holding two fingers an inch apart. The material she had to master in the United States, in contrast, filled a four-foot bookshelf in her office. It held, among other items, loose-leaf binders containing relevant federal and state agency regulations and updates; summaries of effluent control law and judicial decisions; a file of trade magazine articles on regulatory requirements and compliance; and binders containing Q USA's permits and supporting documents. Thus, Q USA environmental managers spend much more time than their Q Japan counterparts striving to assimilate and reconcile regulatory requirements that are promulgated—separately and not always consistently—by federal agencies, state agencies, municipal agencies, and courts. Q USA officials spend much more time attending meetings, communicating with regulatory enforcement officials, and going to private workshops aimed at clarifying the law and ascertaining how it applies to particular industrial operations. Q USA officials spend more time communicating with environmental lawyers retained by the company, from whom they seek a second opinion in an effort to reduce the legal uncertainty that they regularly experience.

Even so, legal uncertainty remains. U.S. regulatory law is often in flux. Recently, certain California water pollution rules were rejected by the EPA for being too lenient. Local governments attacked the same rules for being too strict, and they were invalidated by a California court. Meanwhile, a federal court ordered the EPA to promulgate new rules on the same subject, in a lawsuit filed by an environmental advocacy organization.[51] In a published interview, Q USA's environmental lawyer said that it is practically impossible for businesses to figure out the rules by themselves.[52] When he conducted a detailed compliance audit of Q USA, he issued a thick report designating areas in the firm's practices that were out of compliance or ought to be improved. Q USA environmental officials dismissed the company's previous outside attorney because he was unable to go beyond analyzing the uncertainties and provide affirmative guidance regarding what course of action would be advisable under the circumstances.

For Q USA, legal complexity, uncertainty, and the potential legal sanctions attached to any action found to be in violation entail a range of costs that are not borne by Q Japan. Most obvious are the ongoing direct costs of paying for legal advice and outside audits and workshops.[53] Just as important are the opportunity costs incurred when the company's staff of environmental managers spend time trying to keep up with, clarify, and respond to legal developments rather than working more directly on pollution control or reduction itself. One can think of them as playing legal defense instead of playing environmental offense. Q Japan officials have more time to do the latter.

A more intangible cost of the U.S. regulatory system's complexity and punitiveness, however, is its impact on the attitudes of Q USA officials. In their conversations with us, Q USA environmental officials seemed, if not overwhelmed, at least preoccupied by the task of regulatory compliance in a legally uncertain environment.[54] They repeatedly characterized the regulatory system as burdensome and troublesome. Q Japan officials said the opposite. Whereas Q Japan environmental officials express dismay that Q USA has actually violated the law on occasion, Q USA officials, while clearly committed to the goals of environmental protection, seem to regard occasional violations of particular regulatory rules as something close to inevitable and less than shameful. In the United States, where legal penalties often are imposed for unintentional violations that do not entail serious harm, the social stigma attached to a regulatory "violation" seems less severe than in Japan, where sanctions are reserved for serious violations.

In Japan, we conclude, the regulatory regime appears to have gathered greater "normative gravity," partly because Q Japan officials view it as comprehensible, reasonable, and predictable. This appears to facilitate the internalization of regulatory norms by operating managers and workers. The fluctuating, polycentric character of the American regime, in contrast, appears to *impair* the law's normative gravity (although not its threat) and to make it more difficult for regulatory norms and the idea of perfect compliance to permeate the corporate culture and the planning process.

B. Responses to Corporate Environmental Policy: Voluntary Overcompliance with Regulatory Standards.

Q Corp's headquarters in Japan has promulgated a formal company-wide policy instructing subsidiaries to overcomply with regulatory effluent limits by at least 10 percent. Because they operate in different regulatory regimes, Q USA and Q Japan respond differently to this corporate policy.

1. OVERCOMPLIANCE AND CHANGING REGULATORY STANDARDS

Both Q Japan and Q USA overcomply with numerical end-of- pipe effluent limits. Some degree of overcompliance must be built into a control system if a factory, with its normal fluctuations, is to achieve compliance consistently.[55] In addition, overcompliance buys insurance against tightening regulatory standards. For example, when the nitrogen and phosphorous standards applicable to Q Japan changed in 1993, company officials, having engineered into their operation a margin of overcompliance, could meet the new standard without modifying their technologies and thus triggering preconstruction notification requirements. In this regard, voluntary overcompliance in part means early compliance.

Q USA, however, is less able than Q Japan to foresee new regulatory developments, partly because the firm's Japanese headquarters and its industry association participate actively in the policy formation process. But Q USA officials also feel disadvantaged by the legal and political uncertainties endemic to the U.S. environmental regulatory process. For instance, the EPA and the states are subject to numerous statutory deadlines for implementing new regulations. These deadlines often are not met, for the relevant government officials fear that they will be entangled in litigation concerning the scientific or economic assumptions in the new regulation.[56] Thus, American firms cannot regard those statutory deadlines as an accurate gauge of their own deadlines. Moreover, federal oversight of state and municipal regulatory actions, and state oversight of municipal actions means that any decision by frontline regulators is realistically subject to reversal. Uncertainty makes it somewhat riskier for firms to install new pollution reduction measures, since it is not clear if they will end up meeting future legal standards.

2. DIFFERENT INCENTIVES AND INTERNAL CORPORATE EFFLUENT STANDARDS

Q Japan officials are convinced that violation of regulatory standards would have negative reputational consequences, whereas voluntary commitment to overcompliance has positive reputational consequences. Q USA officials do not fully share those attitudes.

The anxiety Japanese firms feel regarding revelation of regulatory violations stems partly from the fact that no firm in the country has ever fully revealed its pollution performance to the public. In the United States, firms know that environmental watchdogs have statutorily guaranteed access to all effluent data. This allows citizens to identify problematic dischargers, but it also creates a context in which to identify and ignore nonproblematic dischargers. Japan officials note that Japanese citizens, in their relative information vacuum, could easily react strongly to news that any single large firm had violated a regulatory limit.

In Japan, the perceived reputational damage that could result from a violation is amplified by memories of a series of notorious water pollution disasters, such as the mercury poisoning caused by Chisso Corporation in Minamata. The first Minamata mercury poisoning victim was recognized in 1956. Chisso has lost money every year since 1973, posting losses of about 10 million yen per year, because of the financial burden of compensating pollution victims.[57] In the wake of pollution in Minamata and other locales throughout Japan, many major corporations, including Q Corp, were sued in court. The national news media adopted the environment as a cause. Today, according to Q Japan's officials, violation of an effluent law by a major Japanese corporation could be a leading story in the Japanese media.

Conversely, Q Japan officials also believe that overcompliance with the regulatory standards creates positive reputational consequences for the firm in the eyes of local Japanese environmental regulators. They believe it helps local regulators handle citizen concerns and complaints, and may induce local authorities to treat the firm's proposals for expansion or process change favorably.

In consequence, Q Japan voluntarily promulgates stringent internal standards as an added precaution to help prevent any regulatory violations. Based on data on fluctuation in actual effluent discharge concentrations, the firm identifies the highest concentration level that occurs under normal circumstances, and then sets an internal limit more stringent than that level. A violation of the internal standard signifies a deterioration in the treatment system. If Q Japan's environmental engineers, who continually consult current monitoring data, detect a violation of the firm's internal standard, a report is to be made to senior workers, and company officials would seek to identify and solve the effluent quality problem before a legal violation or environmental harm could occur.

Q USA, on the other hand, does not promulgate internal standards. Q USA officials feel that the firm is overregulated and are reluctant to create an additional layer of norms to comply with. They also believe that if Q USA promulgated voluntary internal standards, any possible reputational gains would be unlikely to lead to more benign treatment from regulators. Although Q USA officials do take proactive steps to build good relationships with regulators, both company officials and the regulators themselves believe that such relationships are not likely to result in significant softening of regulatory enforcement. As one Q USA official put it, "No matter how good a relationship we've got with regulators, things still move slowly." The reason is that regulators themselves operate within a generally legalistic regime.[58]

C. ISO 14000 and Environmental Management Systems

In accordance with the company-wide plan, Q Japan has pursued third-party certification of plant compliance with the ISO 14000 series of environmental management standards, which require documented plans to audit environmental problems, solve them, and actually improve environmental performance.[59] Q Japan's officials report that codifying their environmental management activities has generated a much greater (and quite beneficial) level of specificity and detail regarding what managers and workers must do at their shop floor. Since the Japanese national regulations are neither as demanding nor as prescriptively detailed as U.S. regulation, officials feel that ISO 14000 generates a set of shop-floor-level instructions that are in some ways comparable to the standards U.S. governmental regulations impose on American plants.

The conventional wisdom for American firms, according to Q USA officials, has been to adopt a wait-and-see attitude regarding ISO 14000 certification, while progressively improving environmental management operations to facilitate such certification quickly should it become necessary and desirable.[60] However, Q USA officials are reluctant to promulgate self-imposed standards if compliance with ISO 14000 is not accompanied by any relief from regulatory requirements.

The difference in response to ISO 14000 is paralleled by differences in the integration of environmental officials in production decisions. Senior managers in Q Japan consider it legitimate for the environmental staff to participate in decisions about production equipment. Q USA's Environmental Department, by contrast, has had a more difficult time persuading senior company officials that achievement of company environmental goals requires an expanded role for environmental staff in decisions regarding *production*. This contrast is a matter of degree, not absolutes. Nevertheless, Q USA officials can recall only one instance in which possible environmental problems became a topic of discussion regarding a proposed production equipment decision. At Q Japan, environmental considerations are taken into account in many such decisions.

VI. CONCLUSION

Both Q Japan and Q USA comply—indeed overcomply—with their nations' effluent control regulations. However, in light of Q Japan's system of self-imposed internal standards and environmental management, it is fair to say that Q Japan's compliance is more systematic and institutionalized than Q USA's. Thus, it appears that although U.S. effluent control limits for some pollutants are more stringent than Japan's, the added measure of legalism characteristic of the U.S. effluent control regime has not led to superior environmental performance for Q USA and its neighboring communities.

Paradoxically, Q Japan officials express admiration for some features of the American regulatory regime for industrial effluent control, with its more detailed specification of rules and its commitment to positive action against violators. Legal specificity, they suggest, provides definitive guidance to firms, and legalistic enforcement contributes to fair and equal imposition of regulatory burdens. They criticize the Japanese system for its lack of transparency, and they are concerned that "administrative guidance" leads to unequal outcomes. Some Q Japan officials, confident of their own firm's full compliance, think that regulatory officials should more often "go by the book" and impose penalties on violations by firms, usually smaller ones, that are less committed to aggressive environmental management.

The paradox, we learn from Q USA's experience, is that greater legal formality does not necessarily produce legal certainty and equal compliance. The deepest concern of Q USA's environmental managers is legal uncertainty—a sense of insecurity about whether they are in full compliance with a complex, malleable, polycentric body of regulations, which generates uncertainty about their ability to avoid legal penalties. This contrasts with Q Japan's sense of certainty and stability concerning its obligations in a regulatory regime that is less "transparent" to outsiders but that conveys clear messages to company officials, at least in large, highly visible companies such as Q Corp.

The greater legal formality and specificity of the U.S. regime does not produce legal certainty (1) because of the inherent difficulty of spelling out all requirements fully in a world of diverse technologies and conditions; (2) because the greater legal complexity generated by the effort to do so leads to difficulties in interpreting and reconciling different provisions; and (3) because errors in legal understanding and compliance by a regulated enterprise can often—but not always—result in a legal penalty. These problems are exacerbated by the jurisdictional complexity of the American regime, in which a regulated entity such as Q USA must deal with regulatory demands from imperfectly coordinated federal and state and municipal officials, whose decisions sometimes clash and sometimes are challenged by courts, and which are subject to change following shifts in political party dominance at each level and branch of government. Regulatory uncertainty is thus intensified by legal malleability. Not surprisingly, one of the most striking differences we observed is that Q USA officials, unlike their Q Japan counterparts, spend a good deal of time and money consulting thick regulatory rule books, meeting with attorneys, attending legal workshops, employing consultants, and taking other measures simply to try to ensure that they understand what is legally required.

The greater legal complexity and uncertainty of the American regulatory regime reflects basic features of the American political system, which tends to mistrust and fragment governmental authority and encourage formal legal challenge. Q Japan's parent company is embedded in an industry association that *regularly* engages in *informal* dialogue with Japanese regulatory policy makers; there is no equivalent informal, regularized consultative relationship between most American trade associations and federal regulatory policy makers. Thus, Q Japan enjoys greater security that regulatory requirements will not come as surprises and will be crafted in ways that regulated enterprises find acceptable.

Perhaps in consequence, Japanese effluent regulations seem to carry a normative gravity in Q Japan that American regulations do not produce in Q USA. Q Japan officials appear more systematically committed to corporate environmental management and goals of gradual pollution reduction. In Q USA, environmental compliance officials, while attentive to corporate environmental policy, are cast in a more defensive role, assigned to keep their company "out of trouble" with a complex and unpredictable regulatory regime whose rules and behavior are regarded as potentially arbitrary. Q USA has a generally fine record of regulatory compliance, but it has not complied quite as consistently as Q Japan and seems less fully engaged in forward-looking efforts to improve environmental performance beyond what is legally required.

NOTES

1. According to a U.S. EPA engineer, among all U.S. environmental programs, the Clean Water Act achieves "the most compliance with the least amount of rancor, the least amount of lawsuits, the least amount of haggling over how to comply."

2. ISO 14000 is a new series of private standards, promulgated by the International Standards Organization, that call for active corporate environmental management structures, procedures, and audits. Its principal compliance-forcing mechanism is the specification by customers that the selling company's products be made in ISO 14000–certified facilities. Some businesspeople anticipate that ISO 14000 certification will become a virtual requirement for exporting products to Western Europe and for selling to some governments.

3. Pollution prevention measures, Q Corp officials have told us, are seen as financially beneficial for the company, reducing chemical use and lowering purchasing costs. The company may be able to make money by licensing its new treatment technologies or providing know-how to other firms.

4. The Japanese Sewer Law provides that all industrial effluent must be discharged to a sewer/treatment plant system, if connections are possible. See *Gesui dō hō* (Sewer Law), Law No. 79, 1958, § 10 (1).

5. David Wallace, *Environmental Policy and Industrial Innovation: Strategies in Europe, the U.S. and Japan* (London: Royal Institute of International Affairs, 1995), 107.

6. See *Kankyō kihon hō* (Basic Environmental Law), Law No. 91, 1993, §§ 4 and 8 (advocating more corporate voluntarism).

7. On MITI's Corporate Voluntary Plan initiatives and corresponding reactions from the industry, see Mitsutsune Yamaguchi, "Planning and Implementing Environmental Policy and the Role of Industry: The Relationship between Government and Industry—The Situation in Japan" (paper prepared for the U.S.-Japan Conference on Environmental Policy in the United States and Japan for Industrialized and Developing Countries, Center for Global Change, University of Maryland, December 1, 1994).

8. Wallace, *Environmental Policy and Industrial Innovation*, 104. See also MITI, ed., *Kigyō ni okeru kankyō kōdō keikaku* (Action plans for corporate environmental activities), (Tokyo: Nihonkōgyōshimbunsha, 1994); and MITI, *Kankyō ni kansuru borantarī puran no sakutei jyōkyō ni tsuite* (On the development of corporate voluntary environmental plans), December 8, 1993 (unpublished MITI document). For detailed arguments concerning MITI's administrative guidance and its influence, see Kosuke Oyama, *Gyōsei shidō no seiji keizai gaku* (The political economy of administrative guidance) (Tokyo: Yūhikaku, 1996); and Gregory W. Noble, "The Japanese Industrial Policy Debate," in *Pacific Dynamics: The International Politics of Industrial Change*, edited by Stephan Haggard and Chung-in Moon (Boulder, Colo.: Westview Press, 1989), 53–95.

9. Partly this is due to the particularly influential role MITI plays in the preregulation consultation that takes place between government and industry for environmental matters. According to a Q Corp official, when consultative committees (*shingikai*) recommend new environment-related policies, the relevant ministry and agency (usually the Ministry of Health and Welfare or the Environmental Agency) come to Keidanren to explain their content. MITI also comes to Keidanren to listen to manufacturing industries' reactions to the new proposals. Generally, the Environmental Agency needs MITI's support for particular proposals. According to company officials, when both the Keidanren and MITI say yes to a policy proposal relevant to manufacturers, it means the measure will become law.

10. See David Vogel, *National Styles of Regulation* (Ithaca, N.Y.: Cornell University Press, 1986).

11. See Martin Shapiro, *Who Guards the Guardians? Judicial Control of Administration* (Athens: University of Georgia Press, 1988); Joseph L. Badaracco Jr., *Loading the Dice: Five-Country Study of Vinyl Chloride Regulation* (Boston: Harvard Business School Press, 1985).

12. The scope of local regulatory power is defined and constrained by *Nihon*

koku kenpō (Japanese Constitution) Article 94 and *Chihō jichi hō* (Local Autonomy Law), §§ 2(2)(3) and 14(1).

13. *Suishitsu odaku bōshi hō* (Water Pollution Prevention Law), Law No. 138, 1970, as amended by Law No. 34, 1989, and Law No. 58, 1996. For a comprehensive annotation, see Kankyōchō (Environmental Agency), editorial supervision, *Chikujyō kaisetsu: Suisitsu odaku bōshi hō* (Annotations; Water Pollution Prevention Law) (Tokyo: Chūōhōkishuppan, 1996).

14. JWPPL § 3 and *Sōrihurei* (Order of the Prime Minister's Office) § 1, Tables 1 and 2.

15. JWPPL § 28(1) and *Shikōrei* (Cabinet Order) § 10.

16. See note 4, JSL § 3(1).

17. JWPPL § 3(3) and Cabinet Order § 4; JSL §§ 8 and 12–2(3) and *Shikōrei* (Cabinet Order) §§ 6(2), 9–4(3), and 9–5.

18. Water Pollution Control Act Amendments of 1972, 33 U.S.C. §§ 1251, et seq. These amendments are collectively referred to as the Clean Water Act.

19. Thus if a federal EPA official disagrees with a state water quality board's handling of a particular discharger's permit application or regulatory violation, the EPA may take action under federal law against both the state agency and the discharger. The same overlapping of authority occurs at the state and local levels of government. If a discharger into a local sewer system (such as Q USA) violates its "indirect discharge permit," and the local water treatment authority (POTW) treats the discharger leniently, state environmental officials could charge the POTW and the discharger with violating state law. And if the state fails to do so, the EPA could take legal action against the discharger, the POTW, and the state for violating the federal Clean Water Act.

20. 33 U.S.C. § 1365.

21. See Robert A. Kagan, "Adversarial Legalism and American Government," in *The New Politics of Public Policy,* edited by Marc Landy and Martin Levin (Baltimore: Johns Hopkins University Press, 1996).

22. For example, in 1991 California responded to a federal mandate by issuing water quality standards under the California Inland Surface Waters Plan. Those standards were challenged in court and in 1994 were rescinded by the state agency that promulgated them. State Water Resources Control Board, State of California, California Inland Surface Waters Plan, 91–12 WQ (April 11, 1991); Water Quality Control Cases, Judicial Counsel Proc. No. JC2160, California Superior Court, Sacramento County, March 25, 1994; State Water Resources Control Board, Resolution 94–87.

23. See Frank Upham, "After Minamata: Current Prospects and Problems in Japanese Environmental Litigation," *Ecology Law Quarterly* 8 (1979): 225–48. For more general perspectives on the courts' decisions on environmental litigation, see Naohiko Harada, *Kankyō hō* (Environmental law) (Tokyo: Kōbundō, 1994), chap. 5.

24. Margaret A. McKean, "Pollution and Policymaking," in *Policymaking in Contemporary Japan,* edited by T. J. Pempel (Ithaca, N.Y.: Cornell University Press, 1977), 201–38.

25. The JWPPL does authorize regulation of contamination of surface water and groundwater in terms of color and temperature. See JWPPL §§ 1, 2(2), and 3. But

these two measures have not yet been promulgated as regulatory standards. As of 1996, at the local levels, one prefecture (Fukushima Prefecture) and two cities (Kawasaki City and Wakayama City) have in fact promulgated water quality standards in terms of colors of effluent.

26. First triggered in 1964 by local concerns about unregulated pollution, over 37,000 agreements have now been negotiated between companies and municipalities, including (as of 1994) 220 by firms in Q Corp's industry. For general reviews of municipal agreements; societal background, and function, see Naoto Asano, "Kyōtei" (Agreements), published as chap. 2, sec. 3, in "Kōgai bōshi kyōtei oyobi kankyō hozen ni kakawaru kisoku, yōkō, kyōtei tō no hogaku teki kenkyū" (Legal studies on regulations, guidelines, and agreements concerning pollution control and environmental protection), *Kankyōhōkenkyū* 14 (1981): 32–42.

27. In the case of Q Japan, the municipal agreement was entered into after Q Japan's plant had already started production. Usually, however, such agreements are made in advance of construction; companies are compelled to enter into the agreements in exchange for approval of construction and other permits. Thus, in Japan, municipal agreements actually function like legally mandated permit systems in the United States. In the process, local governments often make substantial and intrusive demands.

28. The municipal regulators' initial "toughness" may have occurred because the municipality is almost 100 percent dependent on groundwater for its potable water supply; or because officials believe that the residents worry about how the plant handles its chemical-intensive operations; or because this particular locality has had a troublesome history of industrial water pollution; or because, due to the prominence of Q Japan, municipal officials perceived that in this agreement they would be setting a precedent for interactions with other firms. Company officials report feeling as if, at the beginning, the attitude of municipal officials was, "If you do not make an agreement with us, you can just get out of our town." Ultimately the agreement between the firm and municipality helped municipal regulators signal residents that they were effectively controlling Q Corp, while enabling Q Corp to develop a favorable image in a community that harbored deep ambivalence about the risks of industrial pollution.

29. For example, for arsenic, national law calls for a limit of 0.1 mg/l, the prefectural ordinance calls for a limit of 0.05 mg/l, the municipal agreement sets an arsenic limit of 0.03 mg/l, and the company's internal standards call for a limit of 0.02 mg/l.

30. Q Corp's corporate policy instructs all its factories to construct and operate effluent treatment facilities that exceed government standards by a margin of error, and their environmental managers and engineers take pride in their successes. Hence, Q Corp officials conceivably might consider it embarrassing to reveal information suggesting that Q USA and Q Japan effluent levels did not reach an equivalent level of stringency. On the other hand, Q Corp does have the financial resources and expertise to implement its corporate policy, and its commitment to successful company-wide environmental management seems quite genuine. Hence, we came to regard as quite credible Q Corp environmental managers' statements that the two factories' posttreatment effluents are basically equivalent with respect to average level of contaminants.

31. Whereas Q USA's permit for discharge to the sewer plant requires treatment of fluoride, ammonia, pH, and solids, Q Japan is required to treat phenol, nitrogen, and phosphorus as well. According to a Q Japan official, the U.S. standard for fluoride is more lenient than the standard that Q Japan must meet. Whereas Q Japan does not face a specific standard for ammonia, Q USA does, and Q Japan officials regard that standard as very stringent. On the other hand, Q Japan faces a specific standard for nitrogen.

32. Robert A. Kagan, "Regulatory Enforcement," in *Handbook of Regulation and Administrative Law,* edited by David Rosenbloom and Richard Schwartz (New York: Marcel Dekker, 1994).

33. See JWPPL §§ 5, 7, and 8; JSL §§ 12–3 (1), 12–4, and 12–5.

34. Although the local regulators sometimes called for explanations of parts of the applications, in Q Japan's experience, the regulators would never step into complex technological issues that might be posed by the changes in the specified facilities in question.

35. In the past, criminal prosecution and civil penalty practices of the EPA provided no incentive for self-auditing. Effective January 22, 1996, a new EPA policy entitled "Incentives for Self-Policing: Discovery, Disclosure, Correction and Prevention of Violations" (60 FR 66706 [December 22, 1995]) provides, in essence, that the EPA will not seek criminal prosecution or gravity-based civil penalties for a violation of environmental requirements if that violation was detected through a voluntary environmental audit, was promptly disclosed to the EPA independent of action by government or third-party plaintiffs (e.g., citizen suit), was corrected within sixty days, was not a repeat violation, and resulted in no harm to human health or the environment.

36. In the United States, Section 308 of Clean Water Act expressly provides that "[a]ny records, reports, or information obtained under [the act] shall be available to the public" except for company "trade secrets." Section 308 also expressly states that "effluent data" is never a trade secret. Under Section 505 of the Clean Water Act, any citizen with standing may commence a civil action on his own behalf against any person violating an effluent standard or order issued under the act, or against the government for failing to perform a nondiscretionary duty. Also, Section 505 allows the courts to award "costs of litigation" to any "substantially prevailing party." On the frequency of such suits by organized environmental advocacy organizations, see Jeffrey G. Miller and Environmental Law Institute, *Citizen Suits: Private Enforcement of Federal Pollution Control Laws* (New York: Wiley Law Publications, 1987); Michael Greve, "Environmentalism and Bounty Hunting," *The Public Interest,* fall 1989, 15–29. Even if a regulatory agency and a regulated company reach a settlement regarding a remedy for a particular violation, citizens are free to sue for penalties. Unocal, for example, agreed with regulators in 1993 to pay $780,000 for discharging selenium into San Francisco Bay in excess of applicable standards. In 1997 the federal courts agreed with citizen groups that the citizens could nevertheless sue Unocal for those same violations, resulting in penalties against the company that possibly will exceed $50 million.

37. On Japanese regulators' paternalistic stance, see Yoshinobu Kitamura, *Jichitai kankyō gyōsei hō* (The local governments and environmental administrative laws) (Tokyo: Ryōshohukyūkai, 1997), chap. 4.

38. Government inspectors who visit Q Japan do not sample every pollutant or inspect all records each time they visit the company. Rather, they inspect for each particular pollutant at least once per year, on average. On the other hand, Q Japan never knows which pollutant will be examined at which visit, and regulators sometimes visit the plant at midnight.

39. For the effluent control regime, on-site regulatory inspections are not the principal vehicle for governmental compliance oversight, since dischargers must report their discharge data to the government; absent employee malfeasance or neglect, it would be unusual for a violation of numerical end-of-pipe effluent standards to first come to a U.S. company's attention by means of a governmental on-site inspection.

40. See Kagan, "Regulatory Enforcement"; and Eugene Bardach and Robert A. Kagan, *Going by the Book: The Problem of Regulatory Unreasonableness* (Philadelphia: Temple University Press, 1982).

41. Under both federal and California law, courts can impose civil penalties of up to $25,000 per day of violation; criminal fines of the same magnitude for negligent violations; and for violations that "knowingly endanger another person," a criminal fine of up to $1 million for an organization and up to $250,000 for individuals, plus up to fifteen years in prison. 33 U.S.C. § 1319 (c) (d); Cal. Water Code, §§ 13385–86.

42. JWPPL § 19(1).

43. Yoshinobu Kitamura, *Gyōsei shikkō katei to jichitai* (Regulatory enforcement and local government) (Tokyo: Nihonhyōronsha, 1997), chap. 2.

44. If Q USA instead discharged treated process water to the surface and exceeded NPDES (National Pollutant Discharge Elimination System) permit limits for ammonia in the same way, a company official says, it would likely result in a formal cease and desist order and fine, partly because an exceedance in that situation would have a direct environmental impact.

45. Possible approaches being discussed include the company installing technology to move the pH level downward or the agency modifying the firm's permit limit for pH.

46. At Q Japan, since the company treats nonprocess water for pH as well as process water by neutralization, influent that is in violation of regulatory limit leaves the plant in compliance with it.

47. The penalty level imposed in this case is not atypical. In fiscal 1989, the EPA concluded 166 administrative penalty orders for NPDES and pretreatment violations. The average penalty imposed for pretreatment violations was $24,056; the average for effluent violations was $16,696; the average for reporting rule violations was $12,882. The amount of the fine in the case described supports the assertion by Q USA environmental officials that no environmental harm had resulted from the discharge. It is also notable, in assessing their credibility in this regard, that the same officials were quite willing to tell us about a violation that had indeed resulted in environmental harm.

48. The California State Water Board's guidance to regional boards, referring to administrative civil penalties (ACL), states, "If the Regional Water Board has already imposed ACL for past violations, then ACL for additional violations of the same type should be substantially higher." State Water Resources Control Board,

California Environmental Protection Agency, Guidance to Implement the Water Quality Enforcement Policy (April 1996), 19.

49. Q Japan officials told us that Q USA got what it deserved from the regulators, that Japanese regulators should and would impose fines for causing such an incident, and that even the Japanese regulators probably would not be able to handle such a case only by giving administrative guidance.

50. See *Tokutei kōjyō ni okeru kōgai bōshi soshiki no seibi ni kansuru hōritsu* (Law for Establishment of Organization for Pollution Control in Specialized Factories), Law No. 107, 1971, §§ 3, 4, 10, and 16 (2).

51. In 1987, Congress directed the states to adopt by 1990 numerical ambient water quality objectives for priority toxic pollutants. As of April 1990, twenty-two states, including California, still had not fully adopted the required objectives. States were reluctant to embrace these objectives for fear that they would be subject to legal challenges. In 1991, California promulgated the Inland Surface Water Plan (ISWP), which partly complied with the federal mandate but omitted objectives for some bodies of water and for thirty-seven of the pollutants it was supposed to cover. Consequently, the EPA disapproved the ISWP. Around the same time, several cities and counties sued the state because the ISWP would compel them to build new or renovated POTWs. Faced with state inaction and partial action, the EPA was required by law to issue the required standards. When the EPA delayed doing so, it was sued by the Natural Resources Defense Council. The agency issued some of the required standards in 1992, in the so-called National Toxics Rule. In 1991 a California Superior Court invalidated the standards in the ISWP, based on purely procedural legal mistakes made by the state agency issuing the plan.

52. This attorney said, "I do a lot of environmental audits for companies. I promise that if I spend a day reviewing the company and don't find any [violations], it's free. So far, I have always been paid."

53. In addition, Q USA, as noted earlier, has had to pay more than $50,000 in civil penalties.

54. Overall, one gets the sense from the Q USA environmental manager that she must be very cautious with U.S. regulators (1) because the regulations are so detailed and complex that a regulator can almost always find the company "out of compliance"; (2) because of the consequent ever-present possibility of a large fine, which is financially troublesome; and (3) because of the sense that U.S. regulators are compelled to (or believe they should) respond to violations legalistically. She agreed with the formulation that she is always "walking on eggs" in her relations with U.S. (i.e., California state) regulatory officials.

55. Pollutant levels coming off any piece of production equipment vary over time. Removal efficiencies for any piece of treatment technology also vary over time. Consequently, end-of-pipe effluent characteristics will always fluctuate, but this fluctuation is usually within a range that is predictable using historical performance data. The company officials face the task of engineering their technology so that (1) the worst performance of the plant under normal operating conditions will at least meet the regulatory limit; and (2) under unusual operating conditions (called breakdowns, upsets, or excursions), the plant either is prepared to shut down operations or has some sort of auxiliary or redundant treatment capacity to avoid exceeding the regulatory limit. This is an inherent feature of the technology and,

therefore, of the problem of regulating effluent. The statement "If you do not overcomply sometimes, you cannot comply all the time" applies to both Q USA and Q Japan.

56. For more general analysis of the interaction of statutory deadlines, litigation, and rule-making delays, see R. Shep Melnick, "Pollution Deadlines and the Coalition for Failure," in *Environmental Politics: Public Costs, Private Rewards*, edited by Michael S. Greve and Fred S. Smith (New York: Praeger, 1992); and John Dwyer, "The Pathology of Symbolic Legislation," *Ecology Law Quarterly* 17 (1990): 233–316.

57. For a historical overview of Japanese industrial pollution, see Hideyuki Kawana, *Dokyumento: Nihon no kōgai dai yon kan* (Document: Pollution in Japan), vol. 4 (Tokyo: Ryokuhūshuppan, 1989), chaps. 2 and 3.

58. In 1996, Q USA installed a scrubber for treating air emissions, at a cost of around $1 million, that it was not required to install until 1999. The firm acted early because it made economic sense to do so. The firm obtained no regulatory relief or benefit for being early. On the contrary, even though the equipment was optional at the time it was installed, once it was installed, regulators required (1) that the equipment be fully permitted; (2) that the plant report any upset conditions; (3) that the plant operate the equipment as if it were regulated; and (4) that the plant have an outside party certify its efficiency. According to one of Q USA's environmental engineers, there is no provision in the law for the regulator to say, "For the time being, you're doing us a favor." He adds, "I don't feel that there is any relief for taking an early step toward compliance." Permitting, for example, would not occur faster in the United States as a result of early installation of this equipment.

59. Among other things, ISO 14001, at § 4.1, requires "[t]op management [to] define the organization's environmental policy and ensure that it . . . includes a commitment to continual improvement and prevention of pollution [and] is available to the public." After a plant brings its operations into compliance with the ISO 14000 series, the plant has the option of self-declaring that it has complied or of obtaining a third-party audit and certification that it has complied. Once certified, a firm is "registered" under ISO 14000.

60. Firms are motivated to pursue certification under the ISO 14000 series chiefly if they anticipate that purchasers of their products are interested in the firm possessing this certification. Q Japan, like many Japanese manufacturing firms, is export-oriented. *The Economist* reported, "Half of the Japanese plants that have complied with the new ISO standard are in the electronics sector. Being top exporters, Japanese electronics firms have been understandably nervous about having their goods barred from countries that are signatories to the ISO 14000 agreement. To be awarded the ISO seal of approval means making fundamental changes in the way a plant is managed, with strict planning, implementing, checking and reporting systems put in place." "Toxic Waste in Japan: The Burning Issue," *The Economist*, July 25, 1998, 61. Q USA, on the other hand, is not export-oriented. Typically, Q USA's products do not cross borders.

CHAPTER FOUR

Investigation and Remediation of Contaminated Manufacturing Sites in the United States, the United Kingdom, and the Netherlands

Lee Axelrad

I. INTRODUCTION

When factories cause contamination of land or groundwater, national governments in economically developed democracies respond, but each does so in a different manner. This chapter compares governmental responses to site contamination at four manufacturing sites operated by B Corporation, a U.S.-based multinational maker of chemicals. Two of these facilities are located in the United States, one in the United Kingdom, and one in the Netherlands. The comparison reveals striking contrasts among national styles of regulation in this policy area.

Contamination is a significant problem in all three of these countries. Although precise numbers are unavailable, the Netherlands may have 110,000 contaminated sites, the United Kingdom may have between 50,000 and 100,000, and the United States may have between 400,000 and 600,000.[1] Each of these countries has enacted laws that define firms' responsibilities for investigation, assessment, and remediation of contaminated sites. The relevant U.S. regulatory regime is called Resource Conservation and Recovery Act (RCRA) Corrective Action.[2] The Dutch regime is currently implemented under the Soil Protection Act.[3] The U.K. regime is contained in the Water Resources Act and the Environmental Protection Act.[4]

Land and groundwater contamination is also a significant concern for B Corporation, which currently is investigating and remediating contamination caused by its past manufacturing activities at numerous sites. Total direct expenditures for remediation of environmental contamination resulting from past industrial activity at B Corporation manufacturing sites are projected to be more than $250 million.[5] For each of the sites discussed in this chapter, contamination occurred on B Corporation's property and involved leaks of solvents from underground storage tanks or sewer lines. Some of the solvents were suspect carcinogens; these account for an extremely small share of the total volume of leakage, but B Corporation officials characterize them as the "risk-drivers" at all of the sites.[6]

Interviews with officials from B Corporation revealed marked differences among these countries' regimes for shaping company investigation of contamination. B Corporation's experience indicates that, compared with the corresponding regimes of the United Kingdom and the Netherlands, RCRA Corrective Action is more prescriptive, more costly, and slower. In the view of B Corporation environmental experts, moreover, the added costs and delays that the firm experienced in the United States were not accompanied by commensurate increases in protections for the public or benefits to the firm.

II. RESEARCH METHOD

We began the research for this chapter by conducting one daylong interview with B Corporation officials responsible for the company's environmental performance, including both legal and technical experts. We invited these professionals to compare national methods of environmental regulation, both in general and within their individual areas of specialization. These officials had grappled with problems of compliance in a number of environmental regimes. Although they disagreed among themselves on some points, at the end of the day they were in general agreement about which of their regulatory encounters they considered to be not only the most typical of their U.S. experiences generally but also the most distinct from their experiences in other countries. Although they indicated that adversarial legalism was a notable feature of the U.S. system across numerous areas of environmental regulation, they considered the RCRA Corrective Action regime to be the area most illustrative of the contrasts they had found between B Corporation's experiences in the United States and elsewhere.

Subsequent to this initial roundtable discussion, we conducted more focused interviews with several B Corporation officials principally about investigation and remediation activities at contaminated industrial sites. B Corporation personnel play an active role in investigation and remediation at all company sites worldwide, periodically visiting each location and often personally attending important meetings with regulators. The interviews were numerous and lengthy. The officials interviewed had obviously devoted considerable time to preparing for the discussion. For example, they had gathered information on the chronology of investigation and remediation activities, the technical aspects of each investigation, and the costs incurred by the company. In successive sessions, interviewees provided additional details that had not been at their fingertips during previous interviews, clarified unresolved factual issues, and provided their views on conclusions that the interviewer had drawn from preceding discussions.

We began the focused series of interviews by asking B Corporation officials to suggest contaminated manufacturing sites in different countries that we might be able to discuss in parallel terms. Although B Corporation officials were ready with examples, we initially devoted considerable time to exploring the similarities and dissimilarities among the proposed sites. We attempted to identify—and have noted in this chapter—any nonregulatory factor affecting the various sites that, in our judgment, might have shaped the contrasting costs and delays experienced by B Corporation. We have not noted here every point of similarity or dissimilarity between the sites.

We then asked B Corporation officials to elaborate on some of the generalizations that they had made earlier, during our initial group discussion, contrasting the RCRA Corrective Action regime with its counterparts in other countries. For example, we asked interviewees to characterize regulatory personnel in each country, to give us their impressions of the regulators' level of technical or legal expertise, or of how formal or bureaucratic their mode of interaction was with the regulated company's environmental experts. Throughout the series of interviews that focused on site investigation and remediation, B Corporation officials continued to clarify—and, in a few instances, to qualify—the contrasts they had articulated concerning the regulatory style found in the United States and those found elsewhere.

The interviews then continued, with B Corporation officials providing a narrative account of investigation and remediation activities at each of the four sites. In order to discuss the sites in more parallel terms, we then identified the key milestones in the investigatory process that were common to all the regulatory regimes. For example, we drew a parallel between the point at which the RCRA Facilities Assessments began in the United States and the point at which B Corporation officials first held substantive discussions with government officials in the Netherlands, finding that these events marked the point at which regulators became actively involved in the investigatory process. We then used these milestones to discuss particular topics comparatively, such as issues of cost and time. Overall, we felt that B Corporation officials provided us with sufficient detailed information for each site to support their broader narratives and judgments.

Ideally, we also would have interviewed the regulatory officials responsible for overseeing B Corporation's investigation and remediation efforts at each of the four sites. We could not do so, however, because its cooperation in the research was conditioned on maintenance of confidentiality regarding the company's identity, particularly because the firm has ongoing relationships with regulators at each site.

III. REGULATION OF CONTAMINATION IN THREE COUNTRIES: AN OVERVIEW

Certain events are common to every company investigation of a contaminated manufacturing site. There is an occasion upon which contamination is first detected. After detection, but prior to a full-scale systematic investigation, B Corporation always conducts an early and fast, but less thorough, investigation to promptly determine whether the detected contamination poses any immediate risk to human health or the natural environment near its factories. Any suspected risks discovered in this *preliminary investigation* are then *mitigated*. For example, at one site in the United States where B Corporation discovered contamination, the firm immediately supplied neighboring residents with bottled water to replace the suspect groundwater supply and later connected those residents to the firm's own potable supply.

Then comes the moment at which the manufacturing firm begins a systematic investigation to ascertain the extent and character of the contamination. Another step is when regulators begin to engage actively with the investigatory procedures of the firm. Another key event occurs when regulators approve (or select) a specific plan for cleaning up the site. Finally, a point is reached at which an approved remedial design has been fully installed. At any one site, those milestones may occur seriatim or, for some milestones, almost simultaneously. At any two sites such milestones may occur in different orders.

A. Comparative Regulatory Style

B Corporation officials have found the U.S. RCRA Corrective Action regime to be more *prescriptive* than its overseas analogues in two respects. In the United States, investigation and remediation activities are governed by highly detailed, generally applicable guidance documents specifying what should be done to investigate and remediate sites.[7] Agency officials use the guidance documents to impose site-level work plans that specify detailed tasks, schedules, and stipulated penalties for noncompletion.[8] The greater specificity of U.S. regulations, the B Corporation case indicates, sometimes leads to more stringent environmental investigation and remediation standards at U.S. sites than at those abroad.

B Corporation has found U.S. cleanup regulation to be *slower* as well, *because it is prescriptive* and *because it is implemented legalistically*. The company must wait for regulators to prescribe and approve a particular course of investigatory or remedial action, and the company must accomplish and document a larger number of site-specific tasks than in other countries. In addition, B Corporation officials have found that U.S. site-level regulators are slow to accept new ideas, such as risk-based remedy selection and natural attenuation, even after these ideas have been accepted and articulated in newer guidance promulgated by upper levels of the U.S. Environmental Protection Agency (EPA).[9]

In the Netherlands, the firm's investigation of site contamination was neither prompted nor shaped by a detailed, prescriptive regime. At first, the pertinent Dutch law entailed only a general prohibition against contamination. There were no highly detailed guidance documents governing firms' responsibilities for investigation of potential contamination. Site-level regulators did not wield their discretion in a legalistic or prescriptive manner, but rather adopted a cooperative, receptive attitude toward company investigation and remediation activities. More recently, Dutch law has changed. Now, detailed guidance documents and best-practice manuals are applicable to the firm's activities. However, according to B Corporation officials, the degree of detail remains far less than that in corresponding U.S. documents, and the approach of Dutch regulators remains nonadversarial and less prescriptive than that of their U.S. counterparts.

In the United Kingdom, in contrast with both the United States and the Netherlands at the time of the events described in this chapter, investigation and remediation were not governed by official guidance documents. Rather, in interacting with the company's investigation and remediation process, U.K. regulators invoked and implemented only a general prohibition against contaminating groundwater. As with Dutch regulators, company officials found U.K. regulators to have a cooperative, receptive, nonlegalistic attitude toward the company's investigation and remediation activities.

These contrasts are summarized in Figure 4.1. Although the regimes of the United Kingdom and the Netherlands were not free of problems, B Corporation officials say, navigating those regimes entailed lower costs for the firm and less delay in the important process of initiating remediation.

B. Comparing Regulatory Costs and Delays

Table 4.1 presents estimated time and costs for investigation of four B Corporation sites in the United States, the United Kingdom, and the Netherlands.[10] B Corporation started operating at all of these sites in the 1950s, and contamination of soil and groundwater occurred at each site during the ensuing thirty to forty years.[11] B Corporation officials took approximately the same approach with its proposals to regulators in all three coun-

	Detailed Guidance Documents or Regulations Governing Remediation	No Detailed Guidance Documents, Regulations, or Statutes Governing Remediation
Prescriptive approach to investigatory work plan	U.S.	
Flexible, receptive approach to investigatory work plan	Netherlands (documents less detailed than in U.S.)	U.K.

Figure 4.1. Summary Comparison of U.S., U.K., and Dutch Investigation and Remediation Regimes

tries. In formulating investigatory work plans, they say, the firm attempted to determine the most technically valid and scientific approach. Where guidance documents did not accommodate what it believed to be the most technically valid approach, the firm negotiated with agency officials. Thus, the contrasting costs and delays are not the result of contrasting company strategies for each site.

As Table 4.1 indicates, B Corporation experienced greater regulation-related costs and delays in the United States than in the other regimes. The length of the *regulatory* obstacle course for site investigation in the United States has so far been approximately fifteen years at one site and approximately eleven years at another.[12] In the Netherlands it was approximately five years, and in the U.K., approximately one year.

The firm's activities in the Netherlands began on a voluntary basis and have continued under cooperative government oversight. Total systematic investigation time for the Dutch site (i.e., including the period prior to regulator involvement) was approximately seven years, roughly the same magnitude as the total investigation time in the United Kingdom.

B Corporation's experience does not prove that voluntary site investigation—or investigation conducted under cooperative government oversight—will always proceed faster than investigation conducted under adversarial, legalistic, and prescriptive government oversight. Yet B Corporation's experience suggests that investigations conducted under a flexible and cooperative style of oversight at least *can* proceed efficiently. B Corporation's experience does not imply that every site investigation conducted in the United States goes slower than every site investigation conducted elsewhere. Rather, as described in greater detail in the following, B Corporation's experience supports the conclusion that the manner in

TABLE 4.1.   Estimated Time and Cost to Achieve Installation of Approved Remedy at Four B Corporation Manufacturing Sites

Facility	Time (in years)		Cost (in millions of $U.S.)	
	Since Investigation Began[a]	Since Regulators Became Involved[b]	Since Investigation Began[c]	Due to Regulator Involvement[d]
U.S. "One"[e]	16+	15+	$22+	$10+
U.S. "Two"[e]	11+	11+	$22+	$ 8+
Netherlands	7	5	$4	Negligible
U.K.	6	1	$8	Negligible

SOURCE: B Corporation estimates.

[a]As measured from the date at which systematic company investigation of contamination began. In all cases, that date occurred after contamination had been detected. In the Netherlands, the seven-year milestone denotes the point at which the company's ongoing but less methodical investigation of that site shifted to a systematic approach comparable to that employed at the U.S. and U.K. sites. The hallmark of that shift was an increase in the number of wells installed to delineate the extent of contamination and to more precisely define the risk that resulted from that contamination.

[b]As measured from the date at which regulators became actively involved in the investigatory process. In the United States, that date was the date regulators began an RCRA Facilities Assessment. In the United Kingdom and the Netherlands, that date was the date of the first substantive meeting between company and government officials.

[c]Estimated total investigation and remediation costs.

[d]A subset of cost "since investigation began." Figures in this column are necessarily based, in part, on B Corporation's informed judgment regarding which investigatory tasks served only a regulatory rather than a scientific purpose.

[e]As of the date of our most recent interview with B Corporation officials, regulators had yet to approve a remedial design for either of the U.S. sites. Consequently, installation of a full approved remedial design had been achieved at neither of the U.S. sites. Figures for the two U.S. sites, therefore, represent the time and cost "so far," as denoted by the symbol "+."

which the RCRA Corrective Action regime is implemented *tends to preclude* exploitation of opportunities to accelerate the investigatory process. In other words, in the United States, investigations are typically thorough but not likely to be fast. Some U.S. investigations could go fast but do not. In that lost opportunity lies the time-related cost of the U.S. regulatory style: human health and the environment stand by, biding their time, until the regulatory analysis is completed.

Total costs for each of the U.S. sites, according to B Corporation estimates, are more than double the costs for the U.K. and Dutch sites. As this research ended, investigatory costs at the U.S. sites are still mounting. In the Netherlands, the process was four times less expensive for the firm than in the United States.

The U.K. data, as described in greater detail later, indicate the pace and cost of investigation when B Corporation pursues site remediation entirely voluntarily and endeavors to proceed as quickly and effectively as possible. Thus, it provides a reference point for formulating a sense of the added burdens of regulation elsewhere. The U.K. experience also helps us distinguish between (1) the costs of investigating a site in a scientific manner and (2) the added costs when regulatory officials ask for investigatory measures beyond what B Corporation officials considered necessary to formulate a sound remedial design. We asked B Corporation officials to use their U.K. experience in this way in formulating the figures depicted in the last column of Table 4.1: cost due to regulator involvement. Formulating the figures in this column entailed an exercise of judgment based on experience; although they cannot be considered precise or wholly reliable, these figures do convey numerically the contrasting orders of magnitude. In contrast with B Corporation's experience in the United Kingdom and the Netherlands, regulatory oversight in the United States was responsible for more than one-third of the total cost to the firm.

C. Comparative Benefits

Although the U.S. regulatory regime proved more costly and time-consuming for B Corporation, those added costs do not appear to have been accompanied by commensurate added benefits to the firm or the public. For example, even though the U.S. regime is highly prescriptive, B Corporation officials indicated that it does not provide regulated companies a high level of *legal predictability*. In the firm's experience, even if state or federal regulators initially agree to a particular investigatory or remedial approach, regulators may change policy course abruptly, thereby imposing added costs and delays on firms.

The principal benefits sought by the public from an investigation and remediation program are (1) information (i.e., speedy, thorough, and reliable identification of risks) and (2) protection of human health and the natural environment (i.e., speedy, thorough, and reliable cleanup). B Corporation officials acknowledge that the U.S. regime generates more thorough information on risks than the Dutch and British systems, but they point out that the added increment of information is obtained slowly and at significant cost. Also, much of the additional information obtained as a result of regulatory oversight in the United States, B Corporation officials say, has turned out not to have been especially revealing and often has been of relatively low practical usefulness for these remediations.[13] Their detailed analysis of types of regulatory demands lends plausibility to this assertion.

Elaborating on the meaning of "usefulness," B Corporation officials draw a distinction between (1) information that enhances one's *understanding* of a contaminated site, and (2) a subset of the first category, information that is "useful" in shaping one's approach to *remediating* the site. B Corporation officials emphasize that whereas much, or even most, information demanded by U.S. regulators fits into both categories, the company has often been compelled to pay for enhanced understanding of matters that have no practical import for remediation. For example, a firm may be compelled to install and operate costly investigatory wells in every subarea of a site long after everyone has acknowledged that remediating the site will require the most extreme measures technically available (i.e., where it is impossible for the additional wells to alter the remediation strategy). Regulators in the United States want to understand *everything*, say B Corporation officials, even when EPA guidance documents call for a more practical approach.[14] As a result, the typical U.S. approach shunts investigations onto the slow but excruciatingly thorough track, thereby delaying approval of remedial designs and postponing some of the protections that cleanup is meant to achieve.[15]

Thoroughness of remediation at the four sites is difficult to compare, partly because much of the *remediation,* as opposed to the *investigation,* is still to come. At all the sites, however, B Corporation experts insist that the company did whatever remediation was needed to ensure that human health and environmental receptors were not at risk.

The balance of this chapter focuses on B Corporation's experience with regulatory shaping of *investigation*—not remediation—because investigations at the firm's U.S. sites have taken so long to wend their way through the regulatory process that, at the time of our field research, virtually no *regulation-driven* remediation (as opposed to early voluntary remediation) has occurred at those sites. Meanwhile, investigation has been completed, and remediation is already under way or almost under way at the two European sites discussed in this chapter.

IV. THE CASE STUDIES

A. *The United States*

B Corporation officials described their experiences with two U.S. sites, one in a state where the federal government has primary responsibility for overseeing investigation and remediation, and one where the state government has primacy.[16]

1. THE FEDERALLY REGULATED SITE

a. Detection of Contamination and Systematic Company Investigation

In the 1980s, B Corporation officials discovered a leak in one of the underground storage tanks at a U.S. chemical manufacturing facility ("Facility

1'') and contamination in the groundwater supply serving nearby homes. The firm responded by supplying clean water to those homes, installing wells on the factory site to address major sources of groundwater contamination, and formally agreeing with the state environmental agency (acting under state law) to study the site to characterize where the contaminants were coming from and to begin remediation. All this was accomplished prior to the advent of the federal RCRA Corrective Action program in 1984.

b. Active Federal Government Involvement and Further Investigation

Unrelated to the contamination, Facility 1 had submitted to the U.S. EPA an application to modify an existing RCRA permit to handle hazardous wastes on-site. Pursuant to RCRA section 3004(u), corrective action is required for *all* releases of hazardous wastes or constituents at *any* facility seeking *any* RCRA permit.[17] U.S. EPA officials conducted an on-site preliminary inquiry into the need for a more thorough investigation. As a result of this inquiry, known as a RCRA Facilities Assessment (RFA), the EPA directed the firm to conduct a RCRA Facilities Investigation (RFI). In conducting an RFI, companies (1) submit a description of current conditions and of the state of knowledge regarding the factory's current and past waste management practices; (2) submit a work plan delineating what will be done to investigate the site; (3) identify all parts of the facility that have ever received any hazardous wastes or hazardous constituents;[18] (4) determine whether each solid waste management unit (SWMU) on the site could have released contaminants; (5) determine which SWMUs, if any, did release contaminants; (6) determine the extent of the releases; and (7) determine the extent of the effect of these releases on the environment.[19]

To begin the RFI, B Corporation officials submitted a proposed investigatory work plan to the agency for approval. Such a work plan must systematically address a long checklist of potential risks, regardless of each risk's plausibility or seriousness. In practice, firms typically are not permitted to eliminate minor sources of risk from consideration early on. Company officials point out that, for the most part, in considering the site-wide investigatory approach, "It's a very controlled program. There's no sitting down with the agency and saying, 'Let's focus on risk.' "

The RFI work plan was ultimately approved by the agency. B Corporation investigated the contamination (which, it should be remembered, it had already addressed under the consent order with the state) by means of groundwater wells. While implementing the work plan, the firm submitted numerous reports to agency officials; when the plan had been fully implemented, the company submitted a Draft Final RFI, which concluded that the site presented no risk to any receptors. The RFI itself was about 1.5 inches thick, accompanied by attachments adding about another inch. An

RFI, however, is only one of the items that a firm must submit in the United States. Adding the RFI to the other documents submitted in connection with a typical U.S. site, a complete set of submittals for a single site typically occupies a four-drawer filing cabinet, according to B Corporation officials. They also say that a typical collection of submittals for a comparable site in another country would occupy only one foot of depth in a single file drawer.

c. Remedial Design Approved? Approved Design Installed?

After submitting the Draft Final RFI to federal officials, B Corporation waited approximately two years before receiving a response—which turned to be not approval but critical comments. The firm then responded to those comments but, as of this writing, is waiting for agency approval and permission to move on to the next step in the Corrective Action process, remedial design. The contamination, according to B Corporation environmental officials, poses no unacceptable risk to any potential off-site receptor. Nonetheless, the firm is preparing to propose remediation strategies for reducing the mass of contamination on the site, although, because of the low current risk, firm officials will emphasize strategies that are cost-effective.

2. THE STATE-REGULATED SITE

a. Active Government Involvement and Systematic Investigation

In the mid-1980s, after the enactment of RCRA's Corrective Action requirements, one of B Corporation's U.S. chemical manufacturing facilities ("Facility 2") finished a period of "interim status" under RCRA and was issued a RCRA permit,[20] which was needed in order to store hazardous waste on-site. As with Facility 1, the permit requirement triggered RCRA's Corrective Action provisions.

B Corporation was aware that releases, involving at least some contamination, had occurred at the site. However, the company had not yet scientifically delineated the extent or impact of that contamination.

After the RCRA permit was issued, the state environmental agency conducted an RFA (facility assessment) over a three-year period and then instructed the firm to perform an RFI (facility investigation). B Corporation submitted its RFI work plan to the agency, and the plan was approved. As in the case of Facility 1, B Corporation carefully consulted available guidance documents in formulating its proposal. Nevertheless, after the RFI was approved, the state agency reevaluated its general approach to investigations and ordered B Corporation to gather sampling information well beyond what had originally been approved in the RFI work plan. The agency's policy shift indicates that regulatory prescriptiveness is not necessarily accompanied by added certainty.

B Corporation's Facility 2 site investigation disclosed that the contamination within the site was more extensive than the firm had previously believed, but that it did not extend beyond the site and was having no impact on off-site receptors. Thus, the regulatory process prompted collection of substantial beneficial information regarding contamination at Facility 2. Left to its own motivations, B Corporation eventually would have obtained this information and addressed this site's impacts anyway, according to company officials, since, as explained later in regard to the Dutch and U.K. sites, B Corporation has voluntarily undertaken to investigate and remediate all its sites worldwide, even absent prescriptive regulatory requirements. Nevertheless, at Facility 2, RCRA's Corrective Action regime triggered full-scale scientific investigation before this particular site became one of the firm's top priorities.

b. Remedial Design Approved? Approved Design Installed?

B Corporation submitted the Draft Final RFI to the agency in the mid-1990s. As of the most recent interview with B Corporation in 1998, the firm was still awaiting a response. Thus, although the regulatory regime is to be credited with prompting an earlier start to full investigation than otherwise would have occurred, it also appears that the regime has substantially delayed completion of the investigation and, more important, implementation of a full remedial design.

B. The Netherlands

1. DETECTION OF CONTAMINATION AND SYSTEMATIC INVESTIGATION

In the early 1980s, employees noticed chemical odors emanating from soil at B Corporation's manufacturing facility in the Netherlands. Company officials began an investigation, establishing wells and taking soil samples, yet this investigation was relatively unsystematic and provided only limited data. In the late 1980s, B Corporation expanded its investigation of this Dutch site in order to plan for remediation should it prove necessary. The facility in question is in a "polder area"—reclaimed land in an area that once was part of the sea. The water table is about one foot below the surface. Thus, according to B Corporation officials, the ultimate need for groundwater protection and remediation at the site was clear.

2. ACTIVE GOVERNMENT INVOLVEMENT

As in the United States, company officials consulted government guidance documents in an effort to understand the requirements governing investigation in the Netherlands. Whereas in the United States the firm also engaged in immediate consultation with regulators,[21] in the Netherlands the firm was not required to present its investigatory work plan to regulators for prior approval. Rather, B Corporation's first in-person interaction with Dutch regulators occurred after the firm had conducted significant investigation, when the firm was prepared to present a fairly full assessment of the contamination and a "first-order remediation plan."

Dutch regulators reacted to the company's assessment by requesting additional groundwater wells designed to obtain more information about the spread of the contamination. However, in asking for "more wells," regulators did not specify a deadline by which this had to be accomplished. Company officials describe the attitude of regulators at this meeting as "accepting of being informed of the situation. But it was upon us to really continue with the program. They agreed that we were addressing the situation and we were headed in the right direction, and they wanted more information. They were happy with what we were doing."

3. REMEDIAL DESIGN APPROVED AND INSTALLED

At the initial meeting with regulators, B Corporation outlined a "spectrum of alternatives" for remediation ranging from "isolating and monitoring the site"[22] to "completely digging up the site and removing all of the contamination." Attached to the plan were cost estimates for each alternative, pursuant to the detailed procedures for calculating such financial impacts set forth in the Dutch guidance documents. B Corporation's report also identified the remedial option that its officials felt was appropriate: groundwater containment, extraction, treatment, and recharge by injection. The Dutch regulators approved the company's remediation plan as proposed.

Under Dutch law, cleanup is supposed to achieve "multifunctionality"— a standard comparable to what would be called "background level" in the United States; in both cases it represents "pollution levels that will support the widest possible range of subsequent land use."[23] In other words, the standards in both countries envision cleanup to levels that would allow the sites to be used for purposes other than manufacturing, even though no one actually anticipates such uses in the near term.[24] As in the United States, regulators in the Netherlands are instructed by guidance documents to take cost-effectiveness into account when approving remedial measures.[25] According to B Corporation officials, in the United States the agency itself selects the remedial option that will be employed and "tends to select the option with the most cleanup."[26] By contrast, Dutch regulators actually did consider cost-effectiveness in approving the firm's proposal.[27] Perhaps the most notable features of B Corporation's experience with the Dutch regime are that the firm faced no unaccountable regulatory delays, and company officials view the Dutch regulators as having been reasonable.

C. The United Kingdom

1. DETECTION OF CONTAMINATION AND SYSTEMATIC INVESTIGATION

In the late 1980s, while voluntarily installing new sewer lines with "secondary containment" at a U.K. chemical manufacturing facility, B Corporation sampled groundwater, found some contamination, and initiated a further investigation. Unlike in the United States, there was "no regulatory driver" for the firm's U.K. investigation and remediation. That is, the relevant British law, according to B Corporation officials, did not *explicitly* require B Corporation to perform remediation or provide standards for it to meet in doing so. Nevertheless, company officials, soon after discovering the contamination, notified officials at the National Rivers Authority.[28] The government acknowledged notification but, beyond that, provided no guidance, advice, suggestions, consultations, or information regarding the firm's investigation.

In designing its approach to the U.K. site, the firm referred principally to its own past experience with other sites worldwide. According to B Corporation officials, few remediations were under way in the United Kingdom at that time; some multinational firms had begun remediation projects, but no local firms had done so. There had been one or two cases where drinking water wells had been contaminated by factories, and polluters in those cases had done remediation once the serious risks and harms came to light. However, there was virtually no baseline in the experience of other companies for B Corporation officials to refer to in charting their own course. Hence, the investigatory procedure that corporate environmental officials followed in the United Kingdom was similar to the procedure they follow in the United States. The difference, say company officials, was that in the United Kingdom the firm did not perform tasks that made no sense scientifically and that only had regulatory purposes. Since most of what the firm does in the United States has *some* scientific purpose, most of what it did in the United Kingdom was similar, but still, the cost savings were considerable. For example, according to company officials, the reports prepared by the company for the U.K. site consumed about one-tenth the volume of paper the firm generates for a typical U.S. site—and behind every ten additional pages of documentation lie scores of hours B Corporation personnel have to devote to research, testing, measurement, analysis, and preparation and checking of draft reports.

First, the firm ensured "that there were no off-site receptors at risk." As always, the first concern was evaluating risk to the potable water supply, which they ruled out "in a matter of days." Next, the company began to install wells to ascertain the direction and rate of groundwater flow, the concentration at which contaminants were leaving the property, and the areas with the highest mass of contaminants. From the outset, however, company officials knew that the highest mass of contaminants would most likely turn out to be associated with the sewer lines and underground storage tanks. Hence, in this investigation, B Corporation officials did not seek to investigate and rule out all possible sources of contamination but instead sought confirmation of educated hypotheses regarding the most likely causes of the problem. Company officials say, "We eliminated all potential minor sources right off the bat. We didn't even inquire. We said, 'Where were the underground tanks stored?' " This approach would not have been allowed in the United States; even under the guidance of an agency nominally permitting risk-based screening of SWMUs, much more investigation of probable minor sources would have been required.

B Corporation collected and analyzed enough soil samples to characterize the contamination at the U.K. site, but fewer than they would have been compelled to do in the United States. They did no soil gas analysis, since it was possible to understand the technical remediation requirements for the site without doing so. The soil samples revealed that there was no soil contamination distinct from groundwater contamination. Thus, while the firm endeavored to rule out areas of concern and prove some "negatives," the costs of doing so were far less than the firm would have encountered in the United States.

2. ACTIVE GOVERNMENT INVOLVEMENT, REMEDIAL DESIGN APPROVED, REMEDIAL DESIGN INSTALLED

As in the Netherlands, B Corporation's first substantive meeting with regulators occurred *after* significant systematic company investigation of the site had occurred, when the firm was nearly ready to begin remediation. There was no formal requirement that this meeting take place, and there was no formal document for regulators to sign. Rather, company officials took minutes documenting regulators' concurrence with the firm's approach. At this and subsequent meetings, U.K. regulatory officials said to company officials, "This is your program."

With the concurrence of British government officials, B Corporation is remediating the site via wells for containment, pumping, and—after treatment at the facility—injection back into the ground. The "pump" and "treat" aspects of this remediation approach are commonly approved by agencies in the United States. "Reinjection" of the treated water back into the ground, however, would be difficult in the United States, say company officials, since the treatment system removes most, but not all, of the contamination, and hence the water is still minimally contaminated when introduced back into the ground.[29] Both Dutch and U.K. regulators, in accepting this approach, tacitly recognized that the injected water is eventually pumped and treated again, removing further contamination, and that this process is repeated so long as the pumps operate.

Company officials point out that whereas both Dutch and U.K. regulators said that the firm could begin remediation by the means B Corporation suggested, those officials never said definitively when the firm would be allowed to stop.[30] Regulators have indicated that technical capability and risk would be used to determine when the systems could be turned off. As a result, it is unknown how much remediation will cost and how clean the sites will be when remediation is terminated at the U.K. and Dutch sites.

Since the firm investigated and remediated in the U.K. *voluntarily,* B Corporation's U.K. experience is useful as a baseline for measuring what an ostensibly thorough voluntary investigation costs and how long it takes, so that the costs and delays that result from regulation in the United States and the Netherlands can be more easily discerned. Of their investigatory speed in the United Kingdom, officials say, "This is our pace. We went quicker not being controlled by authorities." They assert that there is presently full containment of the site, and that no receptors are exposed to unacceptable risks.

Critics might observe that U.K. regulators "approved" the firm's initial remedial approach even though regulators' *understanding* of the firm's U.K. site was still less than comprehensive. In U.S. EPA parlance, both U.K. agency officials and B Corporation officials still have some uncertainty about whether their current remedy will be adequate as a "final remedy." Meanwhile, however, the community as a whole benefits from the firm having "stabilized" the site and commenced remediation with great speed.[31]

V. CONCLUSION

A. Implications for the U.S. Corrective Action Regime

RCRA Corrective Action may be one of the most expensive environmental regulatory programs in the United States.[32] The experience of B Corporation investigating contaminated manufacturing sites in the United States, the Netherlands, and the United Kingdom is instructive in sorting out the most costly aspects of this program, as well as some of its strengths.

B Corporation's experience indicates that the RCRA Corrective Action regime is more prescriptive than its overseas analogues in the Netherlands and the United Kingdom. By taking a prescriptive approach to investigatory work plans, rather than a more flexible and receptive approach, the RCRA Corrective Action regime adds costs and delays to the investigatory process.[33] The *prescriptive* approach entails (1) mandatory comprehensive investigations (all areas within a site that *may* have been the scene of hazardous waste handling in the past must be investigated); (2) a presumption that each portion of a site is contaminated and poses risks to human health or the environment unless and until investigation proves otherwise; and (3) preinvestigation governmental control over the precise content of the investigations. By contrast, the *flexible and receptive* regulatory approach employed with respect to B Corporation's Dutch and U.K. facilities entails

(1) confirmation of the most likely locations of contamination posing risks, based on well-informed company experience; and (2) end-of-the-investigation governmental review of the adequacy of company-led investigations.

The legalistic, prescriptive, and sometimes adversarial fashion in which U.S. agency officials formulate and implement investigatory work plans is a feature of the law in action, not the law on the books. The U.S. EPA's guidance documents call for reasonableness and site-specific flexibility. But case managers overseeing remediations often do not heed that call.[34] Because flexibility is called for in guidance documents, not in formal regulations, regulated entities cannot insist upon flexibility from agency case managers who are inclined to be legalistic.[35] The governing documents in *all three* of the regimes described in this chapter allow regulators enormous discretion. What principally distinguishes B Corporation's U.S. experience from its experience in the Netherlands is the way frontline regulatory officials interpreted and applied their mandates—in the United States legalistically and in the Netherlands, more flexibly, based on the regulatory officials' informed assessment of the regulated entity's competence and good faith.

In the view of B Corporation environmental officials, the costs of legalistic regulation at the two U.S. sites outweighed the benefits. Their observations in that regard seem plausible. The crucial question is whether site investigations generate any new information that contributes to more effective, more prompt, or better-targeted remediations. At U.S. Facility 1, the investigatory wells installed in response to the RFI did increase the firm's knowledge of "how much" groundwater was flowing beneath the surface and "how fast" it was going. The net environmental and health impacts and the path of the groundwater, however, were already known before the RFI work plan was initiated. Most important, no new risks were identified. "Everything that I said at the beginning should pose no concern eventually got dropped," said one B Corporation official. "All this time and effort really was of little benefit to us." If new risks *had* been identified, B Corporation officials assert, the remediation and mitigation measures installed before the RFI began probably would have been sufficient to address the full extent of the problem. At U.S. Facility 2, RCRA's Corrective Action regime was responsible for putting the scientific investigatory process in motion. On the other hand, delays by regulators overseeing Facility 2 appear to have made the total investigation time longer than would otherwise have been needed.

The relative costs and benefits of the U.S. approach probably differ across firms. A qualitative study of this sort is unable to assess the extent to which RCRA's added prescriptiveness generates new and useful information for a representative sample of sites. Still, it seems clear that the manner in which the U.S. regime is implemented reflects an implicit valuation whereby consistency across sites is considered more important than appropriateness for any one site or firm.[36] If investigations are typically of maximal thoroughness without regard to site-specific or firm-specific conditions, that implies that the *typical* site is likely to experience some degree of investigatory overkill. For RCRA facility owners or operators, this translates into thinner billfolds and distorted markets for real property.[37] For the public, more significantly, this translates into delayed cancer-risk reduction in the near term, as protracted regulatory micromanagement delays stabilization and remediation at sites across the country. As of 1995, more than a decade into the RCRA Corrective Action program, the U.S. EPA reported that only 539 (or 14 percent) of the 3,853 transfer, storage, and disposal facilities then subject to the program had experienced *any* stabilization or cleanup.[38]

Whereas some firms are predisposed to pursue site investigations voluntarily,[39] the RCRA Corrective Action provisions undoubtedly prompt numerous investigations by laggard firms—those that would otherwise avoid confronting the matter altogether. The benefits offered by an inclusive permit-based trigger for prompting investigations seem patent. The advantages of casting a wide net, however, do not affect the weight of criticisms leveled against a costly style of overseeing investigations once they have been initiated.

B. Implications for Environmental Regulation in General

Describing their experiences with environmental regulation in general, B Corporation officials have found the European systems of environmental regulation to be "simpler, not as complicated," and to take a "more common sense approach" than the U.S. system. Regulators in Europe, the company has found, work with the firm, taking more of a team approach. What is the root of such cooperation, flexibility, and perceived reasonableness?

One hypothesis concerns the degree of centralization or decentralization of regulatory decision making. Church and Nakamura conclude that "[d]espite the long-standing Dutch tradition of business-government cooperation in many areas of regulatory policy, relations between government and business seemed to us to be quite adversarial in respect to contaminated soil." Looking further, however, they observed that, since local government officials have authority to issue permits for building on and improving existing industrial sites and unused land,

> Cooperation between business and government resulting in substantial cleanup activity occurs at . . . operating industrial properties on which the proprietors wish to build new, or modify existing, facilities. . . . At such sites, businesses have an interest in obtaining the fruits of commercial

development. This incentive is shared with the local and provincial government authorities responsible for issuing the required permits. Unsurprisingly,
these negotiations are frequently congenial and cooperative.[40]

B Corporation's Dutch facility is indeed an ongoing enterprise that, at
some time in the future, might require permission to construct modifications. Consistent with Church and Nakamura's expectations, B Corporation
experienced a cooperative mode of interaction with Dutch regulators.

In the United States, by contrast, B Corporation did not experience the
same cooperative mode of interaction with state-level regulatory officials.
Compared with their Dutch counterparts, state-level environmental regulatory officials in the United States may have a more attenuated interest in
fostering industrial activity in their local communities. We have no data
addressing this hypothesis, however.

A second hypothesis could be that regulatory flexibility in Europe reflects regulatory officials' weaker legal powers or lack of sophistication. U.S.
regulators overseeing investigation of contaminated manufacturing sites do
have stronger statutory powers at their disposal. At the time of the events
described in this chapter, U.K. regulators lacked the power of their Dutch
and U.S. counterparts to compel investigation and remediation by administrative order or permit.[41] Dutch regulators, absent extreme circumstances,
lack the power of their U.S. counterparts to compel investigation and remediation for pollution that occurred before 1975.[42] B Corporation officials have also observed that U.K. regulators seem less knowledgeable than
their U.S. colleagues about groundwater remediation. Nevertheless, in regard to RCRA Corrective Action, B Corporation officials contended that
frontline regulators in the United States have prescribed investigatory measures that go considerably beyond the point at which human health or the
environment receive added protection, an approach that appears to reflect
a rule-following legalism rather than a greater sophistication or profession-
alism on the part of U.S. regulators. Although it is within the statutory
authority of U.S. regulators to demand maximal investigation and remediation at *any single* RCRA Corrective Action site, the criterion of protectiveness does not mandate a maximal approach at *every* site. Indeed, the
disjuncture between the imperative for protectiveness and the typical manner in which RCRA Corrective Action case managers formulate and implement investigatory work plans has led to the singular sight of U.S. EPA
endeavoring to convince case managers to be more flexible, reasonable,
and amenable to site-specific considerations.

A third hypothesis is that laws and regulations in the United States allow
regulators no discretion to be flexible. Yet, in the RCRA Corrective Action
regime, the nonbinding character of the guidance documents, combined
with the brevity of the statutory provisions and the absence of final rules,
appears to allow case managers considerable discretion to select investi-

gatory and remedial measures, and to approach these tasks in a reasonable fashion. The apparently broad discretion available to Corrective Action case managers is not typical of all U.S. environmental regimes. More often, many final rules apply, as in the rest of the RCRA regime apart from Corrective Action. "American regulation is written to be enforceable," one B Corporation official noted. "It is intentionally not flexible because they do not want people making judgments." However, by looking at a regime such as RCRA Corrective Action, wherein the law on the books affords regulators some discretion, one can dispel the notion that discretion in the law on the books necessarily leads to cooperation and flexibility on the part of regulators.

In the past, one B Corporation official observed, industry itself asked that regulators be denied broad discretion when implementing generally applicable standards.[43] Today, however, B Corporation officials say that they want regulators to have discretion. Yet, although U.S. guidance documents allow discretion and call for reasonableness, B Corporation's experience has been that case managers typically adhere to the other extreme, rendering field-level discretion under RCRA Corrective Action largely illusory. B Corporation officials' primary explanation is this: because of the political consequences associated with exercising discretion, if regulators have it, they are afraid to use it.

A U.S. EPA project manager experienced with the Corrective Action process recounted to us his experience with one site investigation that did move forward efficiently and effectively, a positive appraisal that was shared by the manufacturing firm subject to his oversight. Asked why the Correction Action process went well in this instance, he replied: "It was more pure luck than anything else." The element of luck was especially clear in that instance, he said, considering that the "environmental setting was complicated," featuring complex hydrogeology and high water tables at a site immediately adjacent to a large navigable waterway. He said that, at this particular site, he did not use agency guidance documents in a rote fashion or require that the firm perform every step suggested in the documents. "There are a lot of things in there that don't apply to any one site," he said. Asked why his fellow case managers, working on other sites, might feel a need to regard agency guidance documents as a checklist, implementing the regime more prescriptively, he sympathized: "There's many cases where there are political pressures and industry pressures, where things don't run as smoothly."[44]

Regulators may be afraid that local residents, elected politicians, or community and environmental groups will charge the agency with coddling powerful corporations or with failing to discover the true risks associated with contaminated soil or groundwater. If that is indeed the source of regulatory inflexibility with respect to Corrective Action, then its fuller

diagnosis and ultimate cure would necessarily touch upon a problem identified by B Corporation officials as endemic to U.S. environmental regulation more generally. According to one B Corporation official, regulators
want to issue a permit that is "risk-free to themselves." Said another B
Corporation official, regulators are scared of making a mistake, because
regulators are pilloried and abandoned if they do so.

NOTES

1. These numbers may include both active and inactive sites. Sources consulted
were unclear. Also, "sites" counted in various sources might be of different sizes.
Peter B. Meyer, Richard H. Williams, and Kristen R. Yount, *Contaminated Land:
Reclamation, Redevelopment and Reuse in the United States and the European Union* (Brook-
field, Vt.: Edward Elgar, 1995), 15, 123, and sources cited therein. Thomas W.
Church and Robert T. Nakamura, "Beyond Superfund: Hazardous Waste Cleanup
in Europe and the United States," *Georgetown International Environmental Law Review*.
7 (1994): 30 n. 61. Not every contaminated site in the United States is subject to
RCRA Corrective Action. More than five thousand RCRA facilities are potentially
subject to Corrective Action, over three times the number of sites on the Superfund
National Priorities List. 61 Fed. Reg. 19432, 19440 (May 1, 1996); 55 Fed. Reg.
30798, 30861 (July 27, 1990).

2. Codified at 42 U.S.C. §§ 6924(u) and (v), 6928(h), adopted under the Resource Conservation and Recovery Act (RCRA) Hazardous and Solid Waste Amendments of 1984 (HSWA), Pub. Law No. 98616, effective November 8, 1984. Final
rules implementing RCRA's Corrective Action provisions are found at: 40 C.F.R.
sections 264.90(a)(2), 264.101, 270.60(b), 270.60(c); 52 Fed. Reg. 45788 (Dec.
1, 1987); and 58 Fed. Reg. 8658 (Feb. 16, 1993). Guidance documents used to
implement the program as of May 1994 are listed in Office of Solid Waste and
Emergency Response (OSWER) Directive 9902.3–2A, Final Corrective Action Plan
(May 1994), EPA/520-R-94–004. See, generally, 61 Fed. Reg. 19432 (May 1, 1996);
Karl S. Bourdeau and James T. Price, "Corrective Action Requirements," in *The
RCRA Practice Manual,* edited by Theodore L. Garrett (Chicago: American Bar Association, 1994); Office of Solid Waste and Emergency Response, U.S. EPA, *Intro-
duction to RCRA Corrective Action,* EPA/530-R-96–039 (July 1996).

3. 1982 Interim Soil Cleanup Act, *Interim Wet Bodemsanering;* Soil Protection Act
(a previously existing act), as revised in 1986, and again in 1994, to incorporate
and extend provisions of the 1982 Act. The 1982 Interim Soil Cleanup Act allowed
the government to *recover* the costs of cleaning contaminated land from parties that
caused the contamination. Church and Nakamura, "Beyond Superfund," 30–31
nn. 61, 67. In the 1994 Soil Protection Act, provincial governments were given the
power to issue administrative orders *compelling* current landowners and past polluters to investigate, take interim measures, and remediate "seriously contaminated"
sites. Ibid., 31 and n. 68. Municipal governments, in addition, hold the power to
issue construction permits for occupied or unused land, and typically require that
soil be cleaned up before granting these approvals. Ibid., 33.

4. Stephen Tromans, "Contaminated Land Regime in the United Kingdom,"

Natural Resources and Environment 13, no. 3 (winter 1999): 487–91. As of this writing, a new regime, introduced by the Environment Act 1995 was not yet in force. Ibid.

5. In addition to directly spending money for investigation and remediation, firms owning contaminated property lose money through reduced land values. Meyer et al., *Contaminated Land,* 89 (collecting citations). Furthermore, such firms may experience negative reputational consequences with regulators, customers, or neighbors. Ibid., 63 (collecting citations).

6. At all these facilities, manufacturing is ongoing, and B Corporation readily acknowledged that it was responsible for the contamination. These tanks and sewer lines are all company-owned and within the property lines of the site. The leakage stemmed from the corrosivity of both the soil and water on the outside and the materials stored on the inside of the tanks.

7. One such guidance document is a proposed rule that was never finalized. Proposed Subpart S of 40 C.F.R. part 264, 55 Fed. Reg. 30798 (July 27, 1990); 61 Fed. Reg. 19432, 19434 (May 1, 1996).

8. B Corporation has never paid penalties of this type. However, stipulated penalties were repeatedly pointed to by B Corporation officials as a hallmark of the legalistic *tone* of the interactions between government and industry in the United States in this policy area.

9. 61 Fed. Reg. 19432, 19449, 19452 (May 1, 1996). See also 55 Fed. Reg. 8734 (March 8, 1990); 62 Fed. Reg. 64588–64589 (Dec. 8, 1997).

10. Hydrogeological characteristics and the initial extent of knowledge regarding such characteristics differed from site to site. Distances between the factories and nearby rivers differed also. Furthermore, near some sites residents obtained potable water from groundwater sources, while near others they obtained it from municipal pipes. According to B Corporation officials, none of these factors accounts for the markedly different costs and delays the firm experienced in each country when conducting investigation and remediation activities. Where neighbors consumed groundwater and had no municipal supply, the company incurred the added cost of supplying them with bottled water and hooking them up to the firm's own potable water plant, but this was a *mitigation* cost distinct from the firm's investigation and remediation costs.

11. As noted, the principal contaminants at each site were solvents. Over time, the firm has moved toward use of solvents posing lower health risks, but the composition of the roster of solvents used has been about the same for all plants at any point in time.

12. The U.S. EPA's "hot line" operators are trained to tell callers that the duration of tasks under RCRA Corrective Action will be as follows: three to six months to "identify releases needing further investigation" (the RCRA Facility Assessment); twelve to twenty-four months to "[c]haracterize nature, extent, and rate of contaminant releases" (the RCRA Facility Investigation); six to nine months to "[e]valuate/select remedy" (the Corrective Measures Study); and more than six months for "[d]esign and implementation of chosen remedy" (Corrective Measures Implementation). Office of Solid Waste and Emergency Response, U.S. EPA, Introduction to RCRA Corrective Action, EPA/530-R-96–039 (July 1996), at p. 14.

13. Under the U.S. regime, B Corporation was required to identify and investigate *potential* sources of risk in order to convincingly classify them as *not posing risks.*

Meanwhile, understanding the history of their own facilities, B Corporation officials claim they entered the RCRA Corrective Action process with *what turned out to be* a reliable sense of the true risks posed by those sites. At best, the added information generated under RCRA's Corrective Action authorities resulted in greater assurances to the public regarding the reliability of the investigatory process and the remediation program arising out of it.

14. See also 61 Fed. Reg. 19432, 19444, 19446 (May 1, 1996).

15. Notwithstanding B Corporation's experience and the recognition by the U.S. EPA that the problem is prevalent, local case managers are not *always* legalistic and inflexible. See Testimony of Lisa Nakamura, Manager of Regulatory Compliance, International Technologies, Public Hearing regarding advance notice of proposed rulemaking, 61 Fed. Reg. 19432 (June 3, 1996) (hereafter Testimony of Lisa Nakamura) (describing "success story" wherein EPA Region 9 officials demonstrated a "[r]ecognition of the point at which additional investigations and data would not increase the certainty of decisions, thus allowing the process to move forward").

16. See 42 U.S.C. § 6926(b). As of September 29, 1997, thirty-three states were authorized to run their own Corrective Action programs pursuant to federal requirements. Office of Solid Waste, U.S. EPA, "Waste Cleanup" Web site <http://www.epa.gov/epaoswer/osw/cleanup.htm>.

17. The program casts a wide net due to the broad interpretations that the U.S. EPA affords to key terms in sections 3004(u), 3004(v), and 3005(c)(3). 61 Fed. Reg. 19432, 19443 (May 1, 1996). See also 61 Fed. Reg. 19432, 19442–19443; United States Environmental Protection Agency, EPA/530-R-96–039, Introduction to: RCRA Corrective Action (July 1996) at p. 4, citing 50 Fed. Reg. 28712, 28715 (July 15, 1985).

18. Each part of a facility that has ever handled hazardous wastes is called a Solid Waste Management Unit, or SWMU. The U.S. EPA itself appears none too fond of "the SWMU concept" and has stated that "a holistic approach to corrective action, as opposed to a unit-by-unit approach, could increase cleanup efficiency and reduce transaction costs." 61 Fed. Reg. 19432, 19456 (May 1, 1996).

19. Bourdeau and Price, "Corrective Action Requirements," 178–79.

20. 42 U.S.C. § 6295(e).

21. While early contact with agency officials may be typical in the United States, there may be wide variation among U.S. agency case managers in the degree to which they are willing to consult with facility owners and operators frequently throughout the Corrective Action process, as opposed to sitting back in silence, waiting for submittals to be delivered. See Testimony of Lisa Nakamura.

22. Containment without other remediation is acceptable in some circumstances in the Netherlands. Soil Protection Act § 38(3) (1994), cited in Church and Nakamura, "Beyond Superfund," 38 n. 83.

23. Church and Nakamura, "Beyond Superfund," 21.

24. Ibid., 36. See also 61 Fed. Reg. 19432, 19448–19452 (May 1, 1996) (describing EPA's remedial expectations).

25. 61 Fed. Reg. 19432, 19449 (May 1, 1996).

26. See also 61 Fed. Reg. 19432, 19448, 19450 (May 1, 1996).

27. Company officials attribute the Dutch regulators' choice of remedy to a bona

fide concern for cost-effectiveness. Church and Nakamura report that "there has been erosion over time in cleanup standards" in the Netherlands. "[M]unicipal and provincial governments—the principal implementers of the cleanup program— have tended to compromise on cleanup levels and remediation procedures in order to maximize the number of cleanups supported by limited *public* funds and to encourage private *development* of polluted land." Church and Nakamura, "Beyond Superfund," 37. Yet B Corporation's case involved a privately funded cleanup at an already developed site. Thus, there seems little reason for regulators to compromise cleanup standards at this site. At a minimum, whatever evaluation one makes of the Dutch regulator's concurrence in the *choice of remedy,* it is clear that the mode of interaction between the government and the firm *in arriving at that remedy choice* stands in stark contrast with the mode of interaction found in the United States.

28. Subsequently, this agency merged with others to form the national Environment Agency, but the firm was able to maintain contact with the same government officials throughout that merger and afterward. At first, it was somewhat difficult for company officials to identify the government official who would serve as their main contact. Eventually, they identified someone with responsibility for "groundwater" issues. That person was not a "case manager" such as one would find in the United States, and was not solely specialized in remediation issues. Rather, with the title of "Inspector," he was responsible for groundwater quality in general as well as allocation of groundwater rights.

29. The investigation and remediation process under RCRA Corrective Action is constrained by the Clean Water Act's NPDES permit program and by other statutes. These second-order constraints can pose significant impediments to remediation of individual sites in the United States. 61 Fed. Reg. 19433, 19437–19438 (May 1, 1996); 58 Fed. Reg. 8658 (Feb. 16, 1993); 61 Fed. Reg. 18779 (April 29, 1996). This problem was identified as a possible subject of legislative reform by the Clinton administration. 61 Fed. Reg. 19432, 19438–19439 (May 1, 1996).

30. In regard to *abandoned* contaminated sites, "the U.K. adheres to a 'suitable-for-use' approach to the question of deciding the extent to which contaminated land needs to be treated. The object is to limit the expenditure by not imposing a requirement to improve land beyond the standard necessary for any proposed future land use." Meyer et al., "Contaminated Land," 133, citing U.K., Dept. of Envt. (1994), Framework for Contaminated Land, at paras. 2.5, 2.6. A government report indicates that U.K. policy for contaminated land will feature (1) no promulgation of absolute cleanup standards; and (2) no required remedial action by owners or the state except under conditions of unacceptable risks to health or the environment related to actual or intended land use. Cited in Meyer et al, "Contaminated Land," 143; see also Tromans, "Contaminated Land Regime in the United Kingdom," 490–91 (only "reasonable" remediation, assessed by comparing likely cost of remediation to likely harm from contamination, can be required). The fact that the United Kingdom may nominally ascribe to a different standard than the United States or the Netherlands, is irrelevant to this account of B Corporation's experience, since the firm remediated there voluntarily.

31. The U.S. EPA recognizes that this is a desirable outcome. 61 Fed. Reg. 19342, 19346, 19458 (May 1, 1996). "By focusing on stabilizing many facilities, rather than pursuing a final cleanup at a few facilities, EPA can achieve a greater

overall level of human health and environmental protection in the near-term."
Ibid., 19441.

32. Bourdeau and Price, "Corrective Action Requirements," 171. See also Testimony of Lowell Martin, Morgan, Lewis & Bockius, Public Hearing regarding advance notice of proposed rulemaking, 61 Fed. Reg. 19432 (June 3, 1996) (testifying on behalf of the RCRA Corrective Action Project, an industry group) (hereafter Testimony of Lowell Martin).

33. See also Testimony of Lowell Martin.

34. U.S. EPA and industry officials agree. 61 Fed. Reg. 19432, 19440 (May 1, 1996); Testimony of Peter Day, Senior Environmental Science Specialist, Phillips Petroleum Company, Public Hearing regarding advance notice of proposed rulemaking, 61 Fed. Reg. 19432 (June 3, 1996) (testifying on behalf of the American Petroleum Institute); Testimony of Jim Roewer, Program Manager, Utility Solid Waste Activities Group (an industry group for addressing waste management issues on behalf of the utility industry) Public Hearing regarding advance notice of proposed rulemaking, 61 Fed. Reg. 19432 (June 3, 1996) (hereafter Testimony of Jim Roewer).

35. See also Testimony of Jim Roewer.

36. "[T]he purpose of a standardized cleanup process is to ensure that the program is implemented *consistently* and that *all* facilities appropriately meet cleanup goals." 61 Fed. Reg. 19432, 19456 (May 1, 1996) (emphasis added). See also 19460–19462 (EPA acknowledging the problem by requesting comment on the appropriate balance between site-specific flexibility and national consistency).

37. 61 Fed. Reg. 19432, 19463 (May 1, 1996).

38. Office of Solid Waste, U.S. EPA, *RCRA Environmental Indicators Progress Report: 1995 Update* (June 1996), pp. 4–1 through 4–6 (data from Resource Conservation and Recovery Information System [RCRIS], National Oversight Database, September 19, 1995). See also 61 Fed. Reg. 19432, 19443 (May 1, 1996).

39. 61 Fed. Reg. 19432, 19458 (May 1, 1996).

40. Church and Nakamura, "Beyond Superfund," 36.

41. Under the regime then in place, U.K. regulators could issue an "abatement notice," but if the regulated entity ignored the notice, regulators were left to remediate the contamination themselves and then seek recovery of remediation costs from the polluters in court. Under newer U.K. law, not yet in effect at the time of this research, regulators will be able to issue a "remediation notice," enforceable in court by injunction or monetary penalty, but will first be required to consult with polluters for three months in an effort to agree instead upon a negotiated solution. Tromans, "Contaminated Land Regime in the United Kingdom," 487, 491.

42. Soil Cleanup Act § 75(5), cited in Church and Nakamura, "Beyond Superfund," at 31 n. 67.

43. B Corporation officials pointed out that while it is nice to get the warm fuzzy feeling that regulators listen to you, that flexibility can cut both ways. While it is scary to get "a hard-[nosed] regulator" in the United States, a lack of discretion in frontline staff gives firms better recourse to appeal to EPA supervisors, or ultimately to court, if firms disagree with regulator decisions.

44. See also Testimony of Jim Roewer ("If even a single member of the public expresses an objection to a corrective action, some EPA officials become unwilling

to take any action"). The public can play a prominent role (e.g., reviewing and commenting on the RFI scope, schedules, and conditions such as the number of samples to be collected), as of right, when corrective action is implemented through a permit. Permits Branch, Office of Solid Waste, U.S. EPA, RCRA Public Participation Manual (1996), p. 4–9 (detailing junctures in the Corrective Action process at which the public plays a role).

CHAPTER FIVE

Siting Solid Waste Landfills

The Permit Process in California, Pennsylvania, the United Kingdom, and the Netherlands

Holly Welles and Kirsten Engel

I. INTRODUCTION

The siting and construction of major infrastructure facilities is a frequent source of controversy in economically advanced democracies. Of all facilities, the siting of industrial and municipal landfills is among the most problematic. Even though a landfill provides benefits to the collective population by disposing of its wastes, potential costs and disamenities (truck traffic, odor, ugliness, vermin, fears of contamination of soil and water) may be imposed on neighbors. Commonly, local communities (or factions within them) and environmental groups seek to prevent or redesign landfills they view as unnecessary, unsafe, or environmentally harmful.[1]

Democratic governments respond to these concerns by regulating the siting process and the operation of landfills. Local governments often demand significant side payments from landfill developers to mitigate the local costs of the facility (infrastructure improvements, noise and dust disturbances, additional environmental safeguards) or to compensate generally for disamenities associated with such a facility.

Amid this turmoil, the central dilemma has become whether the regulatory process can successfully resolve environmental controversies, within a reasonable period of time, and without pushing already high waste disposal costs to unsustainably higher levels. This study compares the ways in which four jurisdictions—the United Kingdom, the Netherlands, and the states of California and Pennsylvania in the United States—address this central dilemma. We undertake this comparison through a detailed examination of the experience of a single company that we have labeled Waste Corp., which sought to build and operate solid waste disposal facilities in each of those jurisdictions. Each jurisdiction has an extensive, many-layered regulatory system designed to ensure that landfills meet demanding environmental standards and that the public has a voice in the siting process. In each jurisdiction, environmental activists or neighbors aggressively opposed or criticized the proposed landfill.

Of the four jurisdictions studied, the California permitting process was the most complex, litigious, formal, costly, and time-consuming. The permitting processes in the Netherlands and the United Kingdom were less formal, complex, costly, and time-consuming, and less reliant on the judicial branches for the resolution of permitting disputes. The Pennsylvania case study suggests that adversarial legalism is far from uniform within the United States. Like the United Kingdom and the Netherlands, in Pennsylvania disputes were resolved via administrative appeals, not law courts, and its permitting process was much less complex and time-consuming than California's. Waste Corp. spent a great deal more on attorneys in California than in the less adversarial and legalistic jurisdictions, but significantly more in Pennsylvania than in the U.K. and Dutch cases.

Just as significant as what we did discover, however, is what we have yet to fully understand about the environmental and social consequences of variation in regulatory methods. For example, California's permitting process was the most decentralized, time-consuming, and costly to industry, but it is arguable—although not demonstrable—that it also resulted in greater environmental protections, public education, and public involvement.

II. METHODOLOGY

To explore national styles of regulation in permitting solid waste landfills, we sought to compare (1) the "baseline" environmental safeguards and permitting requirements applicable to solid waste landfills in California and Pennsylvania in the United States, the Netherlands, and the United Kingdom; and (2) a single waste disposal firm's experience in seeking to construct a landfill in each jurisdiction. By comparing the improvements and changes in the firm's proposed facility resulting from the country's regulatory process and the comparative costs of these changes, we sought to gain some sense of the relative costs and environmental benefits of the styles of regulation employed in each jurisdiction.

Based on literature reviews and discussions with several officials from different companies, we entered into agreement with one company, Waste Corp., which constructs waste disposal facilities in the United States and in Europe, and which allowed us access to their documents and staff. The company had recently permitted landfills in California, Pennsylvania, the United Kingdom, and the Netherlands. Several Waste Corp. managers had in-depth experience with permitting or repermitting landfills in these four locations. Both company and government officials considered these land-fills fairly typical for each state or nation, both in physical design and with respect to the permitting processes.[2] Our information was obtained primarily through interviews, either in person or via telephone, fax, or e-mail. In all, we collected information from over eighty contacts, including Waste Corp. officials; local, state, and federal regulators; environmental consultants; and academicians.

Although these four landfills are in many ways similar, no two landfills are exactly alike, and Waste Corp.'s experience at one landfill in each jurisdiction cannot be assumed to represent all companies' experience with that regulatory regime.[3] Further, with respect to one jurisdiction, the Netherlands, we did not have much choice about which facility to study; the corporation had sited only one landfill in that country, and it was smaller than the others studied. However, we were told by the company and local authorities in the Netherlands that the siting and permitting of this facility were typical of solid waste landfills sited and permitted in the country as a whole.

In the different locations, we attempted to identify Waste Corp.'s costs of complying with hearing procedures, environmental impact documentation requirements, litigation before administrative and judicial tribunals, the jurisdiction's requirements in terms of landfill design, and the provision of other environmental benefits, perhaps unrelated to environmental safeguards at the landfill facility itself. The "benefits" we examined included the environmental safeguards required by the jurisdiction at the landfill, as well as other environmental (or even nonenvironmental) improvements made by the firm to the quality of life of the local community as a result of the permitting process. These "benefits" were inherently more difficult to identify or quantify. Since we have conducted only a few interviews with members of the public and community groups to this point, we are not able to draw definitive conclusions about public perceptions of the social costs and benefits or satisfaction with the processes.

III. ENVIRONMENTAL LAWS AND PERMITTING SYSTEMS

A. United States

In the United States, municipal and county governments bear primary responsibility for garbage collection and disposal, and for determining where disposal sites should be located. State and federal laws, however, impose specific environmental restrictions on municipal solid waste landfills (e.g., concerning air pollution, water quality, and habitat conservation).

Since enactment of the 1976 Resource Conservation and Recovery Act

(RCRA), the U.S. Environmental Protection Agency (EPA) has required that states prepare regional solid waste management plans[4] and has imposed minimum technical requirements for the design, operation, and siting of solid waste landfills anywhere in the nation.[5] As a result of the 1991 overhaul of these regulations as they apply to municipal solid waste disposal facilities in particular,[6] the regulatory requirements for municipal solid waste landfills (referred to as the "Subtitle D requirements") are generally considered comprehensive, fairly stringent,[7] and prescriptive.[8] Although states may impose more (but not less) stringent requirements than those contained in the Subtitle D regulations, few actually do.[9] California and Pennsylvania have EPA-approved state municipal solid waste permit programs, and both states have enacted state laws and regulations that are at least as stringent as the EPA's Subtitle D criteria.

In addition to the specific design and operation requirements, solid waste disposal facilities must comply with applicable air and water pollution discharge regulations. Because solid waste landfills emit methane as well as nonmethane organic compounds as a result of the decomposition of waste, landfill operators thus must comply with federal and state air pollution regulations, which, depending on the size and age of the landfill, may require them to obtain a permit and to contain or destroy their gaseous discharges.[10] The landfill operator must treat and obtain a Clean Water Act permit for any contaminated runoff that the operator discharges to surface waters.[11]

Federal and state environmental assessment laws also play an important role in solid waste landfill permitting. The National Environmental Policy Act (NEPA) of 1970 mandates that the federal government prepare comprehensive environmental impact statements (EISs) prior to taking any major federal action having a significant impact on the human environment.[12] When a solid waste landfill requires a federal environmental permit, such as an air emission or water pollutant discharge permit, the landfill operator is usually required to prepare an EIS.[13] Even if all necessary permits are issued by state authorities, the operator will still often be required to prepare an environmental assessment report of some kind, since many states have enacted laws similar to NEPA.

1. CALIFORNIA

California's solid waste management program is highly decentralized. Although the process for obtaining a permit to operate a solid waste facility is nominally overseen by a state agency, the California Integrated Waste Management Board (CIWMB),[14] the CIWMB delegates the actual permitting, inspection, and enforcement of solid waste facilities to agencies of local government, known as local enforcement agencies (LEAs). The LEAs are responsible for issuing solid waste disposal permits under California law, which is even more stringent, specific, and detailed than the RCRA Subtitle D regulations.[15]

In addition to a solid waste permit, a California landfill operator must obtain at least five other approvals from various other units of local, regional, and state governmental units,[16] including a local land use permit, a finding of conformity to a countywide waste management plan,[17] one or more permits from the local air quality management district for air emissions,[18] a permit from a regional water board for discharges of landfill leachate to surface waters,[19] and the certification of compliance under the California Environmental Quality Act (CEQA).[20] This last certification is necessary because California is one of twenty states that has enacted an environmental impact assessment law modeled after NEPA. Any waste disposal firm intending to site or expand a solid waste landfill in California must comply with CEQA, which is widely considered to be broader and more demanding than NEPA.

Under California law, a landfill operator can appeal the denial of each of the permits just described, or any conditions imposed on the permit, first to the issuing agency and then to a higher administrative body such as the State Water Resources Control Board, the State Air Quality Management District, or the CIWMB. The decisions of the higher-level state or regional administrative agency may, in turn, be appealed to California state courts. This chain of appeal also applies to the decisions of the agency designated as the lead agency for CEQA purposes.[21]

2. PENNSYLVANIA

The technical and environmental requirements for municipal solid waste landfills in Pennsylvania are nearly identical to those required by the EPA under Subtitle D of RCRA.[22] In two respects, however, the state's requirements are more stringent: Pennsylvania requires that municipal solid waste landfills have a double liner,[23] and that operators analyze groundwater monitoring samples for a larger number of chemicals.[24] Unlike California, Pennsylvania has not enacted its own state environmental impact assessment law. Nevertheless, Pennsylvania's solid waste disposal law requires that landfill operators perform an environmental impact assessment as part of its application for a solid waste permit.[25] Because the environmental assessment is not a separate requirement in Pennsylvania, the adequacy of the assessment is not subject to administrative or judicial review independently of the operator's solid waste disposal permit.

Pennsylvania's program for permitting solid waste disposal facilities is far more centralized than California's, as a result of a concerted effort by state authorities to coordinate and streamline the varying roles of state and local agencies into one cohesive permit process. In contrast to California's

IWMB, which delegates the task of issuing a solid waste permit to a local lead enforcement agency, the Pennsylvania Department of Environmental Protection (DEP) both issues the facility's solid waste permit and coordinates the issuance of permits by other state agencies. Also unlike the CIWMB, the Pennsylvania DEP helps the applicant determine which permits are required. For instance, the DEP tracks the permit preparation and review so that reviews occur concurrently, and it delays formal issuance of early approvals so that all necessary permits are issued simultaneously.

Moreover, in Pennsylvania a proposed municipal solid waste landfill needs fewer permits and agreements and must withstand a less complex environmental assessment process. In addition to zoning authorization from the local government, a landfill in Pennsylvania will require at most four permits: a solid waste permit, air permit, water discharge permit, and, if the facility construction requires the filling in of wetlands, a dredge and fill permit from the U.S. Army Corps of Engineers. In contrast to the complex hierarchy of local and state regional agencies and boards responsible for permitting in California, all of the permits required in Pennsylvania except Waste Corp.'s dredge and fill permit and land use permits are granted by state-level agencies.[26] In Pennsylvania, an interested party must appeal an adverse permitting decision to the state's Environmental Hearing Board, an "independent quasi-judicial" agency separate from the Pennsylvania DEP.[27]

B. Europe

In April 1999, the European Commission (EC) finalized a directive establishing uniform permitting and technical site design and operational criteria for all classes of new and existing solid waste landfills.[28] Once implemented through national legislation in each of the member countries in the European Union, the solid waste regulations of all nations will be largely similar. In the meantime, while the unifying force of the European Union is manifest in *some* of the policies and trends at work within the United Kingdom and the Netherlands, solid waste regulation in these two European countries still appears largely driven by the countries' unique concerns and specific laws.

1. THE UNITED KINGDOM

Municipal solid waste permitting in the United Kingdom is shared by local and national authorities. Pursuant to the national Town and Country Planning Act of 1990, all private-sector projects and most public-sector development proposals must be approved by a subpart of each county council known as the county planning council.[29] To obtain approval, the operator of a waste disposal facility must demonstrate that the facility is consistent with local land use and waste plans, and that there is both national and local need for the facility. The latter showing is easier when the facility has already been included in the county waste management plan. As part of its planning permit application, a developer must also prepare a detailed environmental assessment.[30]

For projects, such as landfills, that have the potential for significant environmental impact, the county will publicize the application and invite the public to submit written comments. If the planning authority grants the facility operator's application, an interested party (such as a group of neighboring landowners or an environmental organization) may appeal the county's decision to the courts, although this would be unusual. On the other hand, if the planning authority denies the application or grants the application conditioned upon modifications deemed unacceptable to the landfill developer, the developer may appeal to the secretary of state for the environment, who may reverse the county's decision after a public hearing.[31] Officials for one multinational solid waste disposal firm with operations in the United Kingdom claimed that 90 percent of all landfill applications are denied at the county level and then appealed by the company to the central government.[32]

Once a developer appeals a county official's denial of its application, the secretary must decide whether to hold a public inquiry (similar to formal adversarial administrative adjudicatory hearings in the United States)[33] or to instead consider only written statements from interested members of the public.[34] If the secretary upholds the county's denial, the developer may appeal this decision to the courts. Although a community or environmental group can appeal the secretary's decision to reverse the county and grant the application, such appeals are unusual because of the narrow grounds for appeal and the potential liability for the developer's attorney's fees if the community or environmental group loses the appeal.[35]

In addition to the site-related permissions from the applicable land use planning authorities, a developer in the United Kingdom must obtain necessary pollution discharge licenses, demonstrating satisfaction with national technical design standards and the incorporation of required environmental safeguards at the facility.[36] Unlike in the United States, where the developer obtains the environmental permits for a nonhazardous solid waste disposal facility from government agencies at the local or state level, in the United Kingdom the developer must obtain such permits from a national environmental agency. Until recently, a solid waste facility developer had to obtain permissions from three different national environmental agencies.[37] However, since the enactment of the Environmental Act in January 1996, an operator may obtain all necessary licenses from a single national authority, the newly formed central Environmental Agency, which merged the oversight roles of these three entities.

Technical requirements for the design and operation of solid waste landfills in the United Kingdom are governed by national "guidelines" (nonbinding guidance documents), which are the basis for legally binding, site-specific design and operating requirements by the Environment Agency in the facility's license.[38] Thus the U.K. landfill guidelines are both similar and dissimilar to the Subtitle D criteria for solid waste landfills in the United States. Like the Subtitle D criteria, the U.K. guidelines are issued at the national level and tend to require the implementation of similar types of safeguards at a facility (e.g., a liner, leachate collection system, groundwater monitoring). Unlike the United States, the United Kingdom's system of nonbinding technical guidelines allows license writers to specify the exact technical requirements in the license on a case-by-case basis, using site-specific risk assessment to determine the degree of protectiveness necessary.[39] For instance, landfill liners are based on "containment principles" as applied on a case-by-case basis.[40] Despite the flexibility of the guideline approach, Environment Agency license writers routinely require that a waste disposal facility be equipped with a double liner.[41]

2. THE NETHERLANDS

A densely populated country laced with countless waterways, much of the land mass in the Netherlands has been artificially constructed through massive reclamation efforts. As a consequence, land use in the Netherlands has traditionally been tightly controlled, often by high-level governmental entities. Waste management in the Netherlands is governed by the national government, provincial governments (the Netherlands consists of twelve provinces), and the boards of the several water districts.[42] The national Ministry of Housing, Spatial Planning and Environment (referred to simply as the "Ministry of Environment") crafts specific rules on quality and quantity of the waste that may be disposed, landfill design criteria, and the importation and exportation of waste. It is largely up to the provinces, however, to issue licenses for the construction and operation of nonhazardous solid waste landfills. Oversight by the Ministry of Environment is not required for municipal solid waste or construction and demolition of waste landfills, but only for hazardous waste landfills and sorting and recycling facilities.[43]

At the provincial level, the permitting of a landfill is controlled by the Provincial Council and the Water Purification Council, which are responsible for issuing two permits, respectively, a license under the national Environment Management Act (EMA) and a license to discharge pollutants to surface waters.[44] In a manner similar to state and federal regulatory agencies in the United States, provincial authorities initially publish a draft ("concept") license, which is commented on by other agencies and interested parties. The draft is revised as authorities see fit and then published as a final "definitive" license. No specific land use permit is required. Rather, in order to receive a license, a proposed landfill must be detailed in the municipal zoning plan. The detailed municipal plans must comply with the more general provincial plans.[45] Under NEPA of 1989 and the EMA, the Dutch have unified and simplified what was previously a decentralized environmental permitting process by introducing a single environmental permit to cover all potentially environmentally adverse consequences of the operation of a solid waste facility.[46]

Unlike in the United Kingdom, where the county planning authority enjoys some discretion to reject an application, the basis for rejecting a proposed development in the Netherlands is very narrow. If the proposal conforms with an approved development plan, approval of any application for permission to build a project is fairly assured.[47] Hence the critical point of decision making for a project developer is at the time of creation or amendment of the local development plan, as opposed to the individual licensing proceeding.

Like the three other jurisdictions studied, the Dutch require the preparation and circulation of a comprehensive environmental impact report (EIR).[48] What is unique about the Dutch environmental assessment process, however, is the involvement of the Environmental Impact Report Commission, an independent national agency with oversight responsibilities. The process of preparing an EIR begins with the project proponent's drafting of a "starting note" outlining the essence of the project. The provincial authorities send public comments submitted on the "start note" to the national EIR Commission, which then uses the "start note" and any submitted comments to draft guidelines for the preparation of the project EIR and later to review the completed EIR.[49] Neither the jurisdictions we studied in the United States nor the United Kingdom had a national, quasi-governmental body that reviews and provides guidance on every EIR in a manner similar to the Dutch EIR Commission.

The Netherlands' General Administrative Law Act provides an administrative procedure for both the landfill developer seeking an EMA license and for third parties, such as neighbors or environmental groups, objecting to the landfill. Both the developer and opposing organizations may comment on the concept license, and both sides may appeal the final permit decision to the Netherlands' administrative court.[50]

The Netherlands is unique among the jurisdictions we studied in having a special court devoted solely to appeals of administrative agency decisions.[51] Similar to the rules applicable to U.S. administrative and judicial tribunals, according to the Dutch General Administrative Law Act, a party appearing before this administrative court need not be represented by an attorney but may represent herself or may be represented by a nonlawyer, such as a doctor, a social worker, or a student (the latter frequently represent clients who cannot afford a lawyer).[52] Nevertheless, in most important cases—and we can presume that contested actions involving the siting or permitting of a solid waste landfill would qualify as such—the parties hire legal professionals to represent them before the administrative court.[53]

C. Discussion

Across the four jurisdictions studied, the primary differences in the landfill permitting process concern (1) the levels of government issuing permits; (2) the approximate number of permits required for a single facility; (3) the division of regulatory authority among different agencies at the same level of government; (4) the prescriptiveness of national technical landfill regulations and the degree to which local permitting authorities are allowed to stray from the national regulations; (5) whether national or regional governing bodies can overrule local governing bodies concerning necessary permits; (6) whether the adequacy of environmental documentation may be legally challenged independently of the facility's compliance with other environmental or land use regulations; (7) the formality of the primary administrative permitting procedures; and (8) the availability of legal grounds for groups opposing the landfill to appeal the permits to judicial bodies (see Table 5.1). Differences were found not only between the United States and Europe but also between the American jurisdictions of Pennsylvania and California, and between the European jurisdictions of the United Kingdom and the Netherlands.

The landfill permitting process in the United States reflects the peculiar American style of environmental regulation, in which highly prescriptive technical requirements are largely controlled by national government even while administered through permit programs delegated to state officials. At the same time, the location and integration of the facility into land use or waste management plans is generally a matter of wholly state and local control. Nevertheless, differences between California and Pennsylvania demonstrate significant variation within this basic scheme. In California, permitting authority is more fragmented among state, regional, and county agencies. This extreme fragmentation vastly complicates the permitting process and gives parties opposed to a project more opportunities to block or slow it. Pennsylvania differs from California, too, in channeling challenges to permits into a state Environmental Hearing Board, an administrative appeals body whose decisions are entitled to substantial deference in state courts. This board reduces the number of challenges to permit decisions that make their way to state courts.

Compared with the United States, the national governments of the United Kingdom and the Netherlands exert less influence over the technical standards applicable to the design and operation of solid waste landfills. As opposed to the prescriptive Subtitle D RCRA requirements promulgated by the U.S. EPA, the national governments of the United Kingdom and the Netherlands have promulgated guidelines that local permitting officials use in crafting the actual technical requirements applicable to individual facilities. Also in contrast to the United States, the national governments of the United Kingdom and the Netherlands have at least some role in local land use decisions, a critical element in bringing the proposal for a solid waste landfill to fruition. In the United Kingdom, national officials can reverse a county government's refusal to grant a planning permit to a landfill. Although national officials in the Netherlands do not exercise control over individual land use decisions, they are involved in the creation of provincial land use plans, which may dictate the permissibility of a waste disposal facility.

Nevertheless, significant differences mark the two countries' permitting schemes. In the Netherlands, all permitting authority is consolidated at the provincial level, whereas permitting authority in the United Kingdom is divided between the national and county governments. A second difference between the Netherlands and the United Kingdom (and, indeed, between the Netherlands and all three of the other jurisdictions studied) is the controlling nature of the provincial land and waste management plans. Issues concerning the need for more landfill capacity are resolved in the Netherlands as part of the development of land and waste management plans. This up-front planning process reduces controversy at the time a waste disposal project is proposed, since its prior inclusion or exclusion from a provincial plan virtually guarantees or dooms its subsequent permitting. Furthermore, the Netherlands was the only jurisdiction that has a quasi-governmental body that reviews and provides guidance on every EIR. Finally, unlike the United Kingdom and all the other jurisdictions studied, permit appeals in the Netherlands are heard by an administrative court (distinct from an administrative agency adjudicatory body).

The major differences between the four jurisdictions studied are outlined in Table 5.1. The differences observed in the permitting systems in the four jurisdictions studied can affect the relative influence of the interest groups involved in an individual waste facility siting dispute, or at least the manner in which the dispute is resolved. For instance, the prescriptiveness of the American technical requirements may bolster the influence of siting opposition groups, which can invoke specific legal requirements as the basis of a lawsuit challenging the landfill siting. Similarly, landfill siting opponents would appear advantaged by a system such as California's, which requires a multiplicity of permits from several agencies at the local, state, and federal level. The decentralized structure of the various agencies and the lack of coordination or appeal procedures among the agencies provide

TABLE 5.1 Comparison of Solid Waste Landfill Permitting
in California, Pennsylvania, the United Kingdom, and the Netherlands

Criteria of Comparison	California	Pennsylvania	United Kingdom	Netherlands
Level of government authority issuing permits	State, regional, county, and possibly national (if facility requires a Clean Water Act 404 permit for filling of wetlands)	State and possibly national (if facility requires a Clean Water Act 404 permit for filling of wetlands)	County (land use planning permit, possible water discharge and building construction consents) and national (environment/waste permit)	Provincial
Approximate number of different levels of government issuing permits	5 (national, state, regional, county, city)	2 (state and borough)	2 (national and county)	1 (province)
Need company obtain permit from more than one agency at the same level of government?	Yes, because different state, regional, and county permitting authorities	No	No	Yes

TABLE 5.1 (Continued)

Criteria of Comparison	California	Pennsylvania	United Kingdom	Netherlands
Level of government issuing technical requirements for landfill design and environmental safeguards	National minimum standards and more stringent state standards	National minimum standards and more stringent state standards	National minimum standards, but with high county-government discretion	National minimum standards, but with high provincial-government discretion
Technical requirements are nationally uniform or vary by local jurisdiction?	Nationally uniform, though some variation allowed where state has a nationally approved program	Nationally uniform, though some variation allowed where state has a nationally approved program	National guidance standards that provide for local variation	National guidance standards that provide for local variation
Technical requirements are prescriptive or allow for exercise of permit authority discretion?	Highly prescriptive	Highly prescriptive	Allow for exercise of fair amount of discretion	Discretion based on local conditions
Local land use permit	Yes	Yes	Yes	Do not require a specific land use permit, but site must comply with municipal zoning plans

National government override of local land use decisions?	No	No	Yes	The national government does not involve itself with individual land use projects which must conform to the Provincial zoning plan. However, the development of provincial zoning plans is overseen by the national government which may veto such plans in their development stage.
Environmental impact review/statement	Yes	Yes	Yes, depends on size of landfill and/or expansion	Yes, depends on size of landfill and/or expansion
Opportunity to appeal adequacy of EIS/EIR to courts independently of permit decision?	Yes	No	No	No

TABLE 5.1 (Continued)

Criteria of Comparison	California	Pennsylvania	United Kingdom	Netherlands
Formality/informality of industry contacts with permitting authorities	Formal	Formal	Formal and informal	Informal
Requirement that party appeal adverse decision within permitting agency prior to resorting to courts?	Yes	Yes	Yes	Yes
Formality/informality of applicable administrative public hearing procedures	Formal	Formal proceeding before state's Environmental Hearing Board (an independent quasi-judicial agency)	Formal "public inquiry" where company seeks reverse of county permit denial before the Planning Inspectorate	Generally informal*

Opportunity for industry to appeal adverse decision to courts?	Yes	Yes	Yes	Yes, to a special national administrative court
Opportunities for neighborhood/ environmental group to appeal permit issuance to higher political authority	Yes	Yes	Yes, but on narrow legal grounds	No
Opportunity for neighborhood/ environmental group to appeal decision to courts	Yes	Yes	Yes, though with difficulty	Yes, to a special national administrative court

*As part of the process, anyone can request a hearing, and the authority must grant it. If not, the requesting party can appeal to the High Administrative Court. If the site is large and controversial, the process is more formal and is headed by a high-level provincial authority; if it is small, it is run by a lower provincial authority. In either case, lawyers need not be present. (Former Waste Corp. Dutch Environment Department director, telephone interview, March 18, 1998.)

landfill opponents with a large range of legal avenues to delay or prevent a landfill siting.

Landfills, by their very nature, impose concentrated costs upon the immediate locality but widely disperse benefits upon society as a whole. Thus a decentralized permit process places the landfill's fate primarily in the hands of local government agencies responsive to those bearing the majority of the landfill's concentrated costs. As a result, the use of a decentralized permitting process for landfills should benefit strong local opposition groups. Such groups are likely to influence permitting decisions by local decision makers whose political careers depend upon the community electoral process.

In contrast, landfill developers appear to be advantaged by the permitting system in Europe and even in a jurisdiction like Pennsylvania. The case-specific nature of the technical requirements provides the developer with opportunities to justify the adequacy of less elaborate environmental safeguards and deprives landfill opponents of a clear standard to use in litigation. Also to the advantage of the landfill developer are the issuance of the permits at the national level and the opportunity to appeal a locality's denial of a permit to a national authority.

Although harder to predict, it appears that a decentralized process demarcated by numerous permitting requirements leads to greater variation in the success of landfill developers to site new landfills or to expand existing ones. This is because the success of the siting or expansion effort would depend, to a greater extent than in a more centralized system, upon the existence, size, strength, and resources of local opposition groups, which can be expected to vary significantly among individual landfill projects, depending on a specific project's location, history, and media coverage, and on the groups' socioeconomic status and racial mix. On the other hand, the resources of the developer are not likely to vary much between projects. Hence the European model, which provides greater advantages for the developer, might be predicted to produce a higher siting or expansion success rate.

IV. CASE STUDIES

Waste Corp. currently operates approximately one hundred solid waste landfills in North America and over sixty landfill sites in twelve other nations. The majority of the sites are concentrated in the United States and Western Europe. The permitting histories of four sites, one each in California, Pennsylvania, the United Kingdom, and the Netherlands, are provided in the following to illustrate the actual operations and impact of each jurisdiction's distinctive legal and regulatory regime. Table 5.2 summarizes several key characteristics.

TABLE 5.2 Key Characteristics of the Four Sites and Their Permitting Processes

Characteristic	California Site	Pennsylvania Site	UK Site	Netherlands Site
Status of landfill	Expansion of existing landfill	New site, but area historically mined	New site, but site historically mined	Expansion of existing landfill
Type of waste disposed at site	Municipal and construction and demolition	Municipal and construction and demolition	Municipal and construction and demolition	Construction and demolition only
Total area land filled (acres)	215	154	99	32
Total weight capacity U.S. (tons)	17 million (with potential to expand to an ultimate capacity of 215 million tons)	16 million (but with potential for expansion)	4.8 million	300,000 tonnes (Dutch)
Expected life of landfill (years)	10	12	22	15
Approximate number of permits and compliance certifications and agreements necessary	National: 2 State: 4 Regional: 2 County: 3 City: 4 Total: 15	State: 4 Borough: 2 Total: 6	County: 1 National: 1 Total: 2	Province: 2 Total: 2
Time taken to prepare and process permits (years)	11 (1984–95)	5 (1987–91)	8 (1989–97)	5 (1991–96)

TABLE 5.2 (Continued)

Characteristic	California Site	Pennsylvania Site	UK Site	Netherlands Site
Permitting costs (includes only legal costs, costs of design and engineering studies, and any applicable permitting fees)	$45 million	$5.687 million	$440,000	Information not available (but all costs were internal, no outside lawyers or consultants)
Cost of preparing studies required by environmental impact regulations	$3.3 million	$45,000–65,000	$150,000	$8,500 for this small site, but average for landfills usually $40,00–50,000
Legal costs	$15 million	$250,000 (legal and engineering costs of 2 administrative appeals); $1.2 million (legal fees opposing land condemnation)	$136,714	$50,000 or less
Number of lawyers retained to work on permitting issues	9	3 part-time	2 part-time	none
Number of appeals during permitting	7	2	1	1
Number of court cases during permitting	3	0	0	0

NOTE: Figures in the table are approximations only.

A. *California*

In 1984, Waste Corp. initiated a permitting process for building a 215 million ton canyon landfill in California within a major metropolitan region. After eleven years devoted to fulfilling permitting requirements and five years pursuing and defending litigation, Waste Corp. is now constructing a 17 million ton expansion of an existing landfill.

The landfill expansion is in a semimountainous area with moderate development nearby. Waste Corp.'s holdings include roughly five hundred acres within the boundaries of a city and six hundred acres outside the city on county land. Two hundred acres of Waste Corp.'s holdings in the city are occupied by an inactive landfill currently in the process of post-closure reclamation.[54] A freeway separates the proposed landfill from an industrial area along one border, and a housing development (approximately three hundred houses) borders the property to the south.[55] Since the 1980s, city officials had been under public pressure to close the now inactive landfill because of dust, windblown litter, and other annoyances. Nevertheless, the county government was determined to expand the landfill to meet projected needs.

In order to build the landfill, Waste Corp. first had to obtain permits or agreements from eleven separate agencies: one federal agency, three state agencies, two regional agencies, three county entities, and two city agencies. These included five major permits: a land use permit; storm water and waste discharge permits; an air pollution permit (entailing six individual permits for construction and operation of gas flaring and collection stations and condensation systems); a Solid Waste Facilities Permit; and a Nationwide Permit from the Army Corps of Engineers for stream zone and wetlands alteration. The County Department of Regional Planning was the lead agency for the project, and the County Department of Health Services was the local enforcement agency. Each permit required extensive documentation and analysis of possible environmental impacts. Most of this information was combined into a voluminous EIR.

Waste Corp. originally proposed construction of a 1,016-acre, 215 million ton capacity landfill spanning county-owned and city-owned property. Upon meeting stiff opposition to its expansion plans from city officials, Waste Corp. proposed a 100-million-ton landfill.

In 1991, after demanding several amendments to the proposed project and the associated environmental analysis, the County Board of Supervisors approved a 17-million-ton landfill extension on county land only. The amendments included thirty-four conditions, including eliminating night-time landfill operations, granting the LEA authority to immediately shut down the landfill in the event of a threat to human health or safety, and additional monitoring (including citizen oversight) of mitigation measures designed to minimize truck traffic and other disturbances.[56]

Within six weeks of the county's approval, however, a coalition of neighbors and the city government filed separate lawsuits in the Superior Court of California against the county and Waste Corp., challenging the adequacy of the permit conditions granted by the county, the legal sufficiency of the EIR, and the county-approved conditional use permit. A few months after the lawsuits were filed, the city decided not to renew the permit for the existing landfill on city property, halting site disposal and commencing closure operations.[57] As a result, Waste Corp. limited its expansion plan to an area on county land. Angered by the city's unwillingness to allow expansion of the landfill, the county required Waste Corp. to apply for expansion on city land as a condition of its county use permit and restricted the city from using the landfill if it failed to approve a 20-million-ton or larger capacity landfill on city land.

In the consolidated trial of the two 1991 lawsuits, the trial court received into evidence twenty-one thousand pages of environmental and administrative records.[58] In April 1992 the trial court found, with a few exceptions, that the EIR was adequate and that the county had sufficiently supported its conclusions.[59] Nevertheless, the court found some defects in the EIR, which required Waste Corp. to modify it and seek recertification by the lead agency, the County Department of Regional Planning.

In June 1992 the city, the community coalition, and Waste Corp. each appealed portions of the trial court's judgment to a state appeals court. In the meantime, the trial court issued a second ruling vacating the county's approval of the modified EIR and requiring that the EIR be recirculated for review. Waste Corp. and the county appealed that second decision. The state appeals court ruled in favor of Waste Corp. with respect to the trial court's first ruling concerning the adequacy of the EIR. The community coalition unsuccessfully petitioned to the California Supreme Court for review of that appeals court decision. The appellate court then dismissed the county and the community group's appeal of the second set of trial court rulings. But the litigation was not over.

In the spring of 1994, the city and the community coalition returned to the trial court to complain that Waste Corp. had failed to comply with the trial court's first ruling. The community group also filed a second lawsuit against the company. City officials asserted that running heavy trucks on the only access road, which crossed city property (on company-owned land), required a zoning variance, since it was zoned only for agricultural uses. In settlement of that claim and the new lawsuit, the city agreed to process Waste Corp.'s zoning variance application in return for the county's agreement to allow the city use of the landfill on county land.

In January 1995 the city zoning administrator granted a variance, permitting Waste Corp. to use the access roadway. This decision was appealed to the city's Board of Zoning Appeals by the Community Coalition as well as by a Waste Corp. competitor.[60] In February 1995 the Board of Zoning Appeals reversed the zoning administrator's decision and denied the zoning variance. Waste Corp. unsuccessfully sought a city council override of the decision. Waste Corp. then filed a $400 million lawsuit against the city, alleging that the city's refusal to issue a zoning variance constituted an unconstitutional "taking" of the property.[61] A few months later that lawsuit was settled. In exchange for the city agreeing that no variance was necessary, Waste Corp. agreed to pay $3.2 million over fifteen years for a variety of community programs, including a direct payment of $500,000 to the city's general fund, support for recycling programs, and funds for environmental mitigation, including oak tree planting both on- and off-site.[62]

Meanwhile, the community coalition, battling Waste Corp. in another forum, appealed a permit for the landfill granted by the Regional Water Quality Control Board staff in the summer of 1994. The coalition asked the Regional Water Board to rule that the proposed landfill liner would not withstand potential seismic activity, but the board ultimately rejected this argument.

Thus, after three lawsuits, numerous appeals, and various claims and petitions, Waste Corp. obtained the permits necessary to extend the landfill. In total, the permitting process took eleven years. The appeals and litigation delayed the opening of the site for five years and cost the company a total of $15 million in legal fees.[63] While the city allegedly spent $750,000 in legal fees, we have not ascertained legal costs to the county or to other objectors.[64] Waste Corp. retained approximately nine lawyers for over five years to address these challenges. By the time appeals and lawsuits were over, the final EIR comprised an unruly 44,000 pages, approximately 25 percent of which pertained to legal actions.

What impact did this extended legal process have on the proposed landfill? As outlined in Table 5.3, the legal challenges did *not* yield changes in the environmental protections built into the project design—the liner, the leachate detection and collection system, and the groundwater monitoring system. Standards for these were determined primarily by federal and state laws and regulations. On the other hand, the expansion of the landfill, limited to undeveloped county land, is much smaller than initially proposed—approximately 17- as opposed to 70-million-ton capacity—with a life expectancy of ten years rather than thirty. However, because the tonnage limitation is expressed in terms of a maximum elevation for 215 acres, Waste Corp. may be able to increase the total waste capacity by 20 percent through advanced compaction technology. Although the county did not prohibit further expansion of the landfill on county land, it did require Waste Corp. to first attempt expansion of its inactive landfill on city land.

TABLE 5.3 California Case Study

	Waste Corp. Proposal	Permitted Landfill Operation
Date	1984 (date of initial permit application)	1996
Size/capacity of landfill	215-million-ton-capacity landfill encompassing 706 acres within both the county and city.	In 1996, Waste Corp. received the necessary permits for a 17-million-ton-capacity landfill on county land only. However, Waste Corp. is proceeding with its initial permit applications to expand the landfill to its originally proposed capacity.
Landfill liner design	Waste Corp. did not propose installation of a liner in its original 1984 proposal because liners were not then required of municipal waste landfills in California. When California required, in 1992, that municipal landfills be equipped with liners, Waste Corp. proposed installation of a composite liner consisting of at least a 30-mm flexible membrane upper component (60 mm if HDPE) and a low-permeability soil lower component that has a hydraulic conductivity of no more than 1×10^{-7} cm per/sec.	Same liner as proposed by Waste Corp. in 1992.

Leachate detection and collection system	Waste Corp. proposed construction of a granular drainage layer of 1-ft. thickness covering the floor of the landfill. The drainage layer was proposed to collect and direct the leachate toward leachate pumps, where it would be removed from beneath the waste. Leachate collection system was proposed to collect and remove twice the maximum anticipated daily volume of leachate from the landfill.	Same as proposed.
Groundwater monitoring	Waste Corp. proposed installation of 22 groundwater monitoring wells consisting of both shallow and deep wells.	Same as proposed.
Additional environmental safeguards		Additional dust and litter controls to reduce air-quality impacts. Assignment of county inspector to oversee Waste Corp.'s landfill operations full-time on-site. Inspector is authorized to enforce all county and state landfill regulations against Waste Corp. Waste Corp. must donate approximately 1,000 acres of adjacent undeveloped land to county for use as open space. $3.2 million in additional off-site environmental improvements in county at large.

Thus the county's deliberations resulted in its "preference" for the future use of already developed city land over undeveloped, natural county land on which there were ecologically valuable oak trees.

Other "benefits" to the county resulting from the permitting process include Waste Corp.'s agreement to (1) provide housing and pay the salary and expenses of a full-time county official stationed on-site during hours of operation and who has the authority to enforce all county and state regulations applicable to the facility; (2) provide vehicles for foresters and inspectors employed by the county; (3) donate approximately 1,000 acres of land for open space; (4) provide additional vegetation and dust and litter controls to reduce adverse impacts of the facility upon air quality; (5) give payments of $3.2 million for off-site environmental improvements, including hazardous waste cleanup within the county and forestry research.[65]

Overall, Waste Corp. estimated that these "side payments" cost the company over $10 million. Some of these exactions contribute specifically to site management, others provided benefits to the county at large and were not related to on-site management or mitigation, and still others, including the previously mentioned $3.2 million to the city, were for matters mostly unrelated to the site.

B. Pennsylvania

Beginning in the mid-1980s, Waste Corp. started constructing municipal solid waste landfill on land located in a semirural agricultural area in Pennsylvania. Waste Corp.'s parcel is adjacent to the site of a former iron-ore mining operation and to a river running through a wooded area fifty to two hundred meters from the landfill site. Two sides of the site are surrounded by woods and wetlands, and another by a highway. To the east, within one to two hundred meters, are two houses. Beyond the houses are an interstate highway and then a residential community of about forty houses, as close as five hundred meters to the border of the landfill.

Waste Corp. initially sought to construct two landfills at the site: a 154-acre facility on the southern portion of the site and a separate landfill on the northern portion that would fill in an abandoned "borrow pit" located near the adjacent abandoned mine. As required by the Pennsylvania DEP regulations, Waste Corp. proposed to include a double liner, leachate collection system, and groundwater monitoring.

Under Pennsylvania law, Waste Corp. was originally required to obtain just two environmental permits from the state: a water pollution discharge permit under Pennsylvania's Clean Water Act program, and a solid waste permit. Additionally, Waste Corp. was required to obtain numerous building permits and an earth disturbance permit from local ("borough") authorities. During the course of the permit process, and as a result of the enactment of the federal Clean Air Act Amendments of 1990, Waste Corp. was also required to obtain a state air quality permit for gas emissions from the landfill.

The company began the process of applying for a state solid waste permit in November 1987. As a result of local citizens' and the Pennsylvania DEP's concerns about possible subsidence at the borrow pit, the permitting process stalled while Waste Corp. reevaluated its plan and DEP evaluated the severity of the subsidence threats. The process was rejuvenated in 1991 when Waste Corp. abandoned the borrow pit, submitted an amended Part I application (concerning site characterization information), and submitted its Part II application (concerning the facility design). Waste Corp. received its solid waste permit from the State six months later, in June 1992.

Although the permit conditions generally reflected Waste Corp.'s proposal, several were new. DEP required Waste Corp. to monitor subsidence at the site and to install a pipe to increase the water flow out of the quarry into which the landfill's storm water runoff was discharged. Although Waste Corp. did not believe it was properly responsible for the cost of the pipeline,[66] it did not contest these conditions.[67] The corporation appealed three other conditions to the Pennsylvania Environmental Hearing Board, which (1) limited the type and geographic location of the waste to be disposed of at the facility; (2) specified performance criteria for the subcontractor which was to install the liner; and (3) barred future use of the borrow pit for landfill purposes. A settlement was reached before the board in the summer of 1993, resulting in compromises on points 1 and 2 and DEP's abandonment of point 3.

Waste Corp. also appealed several of the conditions in its water discharge permit concerning how to measure discharge flows and calculate effluent limits. This appeal was also settled by inserting clarifying language in the company's water discharge permit. In a separate appeal to the Hearing Board, the local citizens' group protested DEP's authorization of a landfill next to an abandoned iron-ore mine and close to an area that had experienced subsidence in the past. The group feared that subsidence at the mine site would result in destruction of the landfill liner and contamination of local groundwater supplies. In settlement of this appeal, Waste Corp. agreed to test the groundwater periodically and indefinitely, on all residential properties located within a half-mile radius of the landfill. The company also agreed once a year to provide the local environmental group with half of the groundwater sample obtained from its eighteen on-site monitoring wells so that the group could conduct independent contamination tests.[68] Furthermore, Waste Corp. agreed to donate $5,000 to a nearby school district and $1,000 to a community library.

Waste Corp. officials state that none of these appeals resulted in delay.

In each case, the company determined that its chances of winning were strong and hence moved forward with construction during the pendency of the appeals. Three lawyers worked part-time for Waste Corp. over a five-year period from 1991 to 1996. In Pennsylvania, Waste Corp. spent $45,000 to $65,000 on environmental studies required to comply with the state's environmental analysis requirements. The final environmental documentation included in the solid waste permit application comprised approximately ten thousand pages of text. As noted in Table 5.4, the ultimately permitted landfill site covers 154 acres, with a total capacity of 16 million tons over a life of twelve years. The entire permitting process consumed five years, at a cost to the company of $11.4 million.

C. The United Kingdom

The United Kingdom landfill is located in a semirural area on the southern periphery of a midsize village inhabited by approximately eight thousand people. Residential properties are located to the north, east, and west of the site, and a smaller village lies approximately one kilometer to the west. To the south and east are several hundred acres of heath land. The houses to the north are buffered from the landfill by a plateau with a dedicated lookout of the entire valley. The houses to the east are separated from the landfill by a small road, but about five residences are within 220 and 400 meters of the site.[69] The entire permitting process took eight years and involved only one appeal and no lawsuits.

The site has been mined for sand and clay by a local brickworks company for over fifty years. In the 1980s, the mining company and Waste Corp. formed a joint venture: the mining company would continue to make bricks, Waste Corp. would take over the extraction of sand and clay and backfill the void with domestic, bulky household waste, commercial and industrial waste, and inert materials. The entire operation comprises just under one hundred acres. Waste Corp.'s proposal projected the disposal of approximately 4.8 million tons of waste over twenty-two years. In terms of actual permitted capacity, it was the third-largest landfill in this study, with California as the largest and Pennsylvania a close second.

Although the mining operator conducted preliminary inquiries about in-filling the mining operation with refuse as early as 1983, Waste Corp. did not start its permitting process until 1989. As contrasted with the many permits required in California and Pennsylvania, two main permits are required in the United Kingdom: a planning permit from the local county planning authority[70] and a waste license from a regional office of the National Environment Agency. Waste Corp. initiated the permitting process through informal meetings and exchange of letters and draft proposals with the county planning officer, a process that took over three years. The

TABLE 5.4   Pennsylvania Case Study

	Waste Corp. Permit Application	Permitted Landfill Operation
Date	Part I (site characterization) of two-part permit application first submitted in Nov. 1987, revised and Part I and Part II (design of facility) permit application submitted Aug. 1991.	All permits issued in June 1992. Litigation over permits extended through summer 1993.
Size/capacity of landfill	Originally intended to construct two landfills on a single site: (1) borrow pit area landfill, and (2) 154-acre landfill with 16-ton capacity	Company dropped plans for landfill in borrow pit, although it succeeded in resisting the legal bar to such landfilling in the future. Company received permit for one 154-acre landfill with 16-million-ton capacity and a lifetime of 12 years.
Type of waste disposed	Municipal and construction and demolition waste	Municipal and construction and demolition waste
Landfill liner and leachate detection system design	Double liner consisting of primary liner of 60 mm. HDPE plastic underlain by 3 ft. clay and secondary liner consisting of 60 mm. HDPE plastic. Standard leachate collection system below secondary liner consisting of porous layer that can double as a leachate collection area in case of leak.	Same liner design as proposed. Same leachate collection system as proposed.

TABLE 5.4 (Continued)

	Waste Corp. Permit Application	Permitted Landfill Operation
Groundwater monitoring	At the site: series of monitoring wells at both the shallow and the deep aquifer at the site.	At the site: same system of groundwater monitoring as proposed by Waste Corp. In addition, however, Waste Corp. agreed to split samples taken from on-site groundwater monitoring wells with local citizen group for independent testing. Off-site: Waste Corp. agreed to monitor, on a quarterly basis, private wells of homes within half-mile radius of landfill.
Air pollution controls	No air pollution controls proposed for facility. At time of application, Pa. DEP did not require air-quality controls. Waste Corp. planned to install gas collection system at future time, if needed.	Due to enactment of federal Clean Air Act Amendments in 1990, Waste Corp. required to obtain air permit. Lawsuit by nearby waste incinerator against Pa. DEP over timing of Waste Corp. air permit forced state to change regulations to require facilities to obtain air permit at time of facility proposal.
Other environmental safeguards at the facility	None	Waste Corp. agreed to install monuments at site to monitor for land subsidence. Institution of regular meetings between Waste Corp. and local citizen group to discuss citizen concerns regarding landfill operation.

	Waste Corp. Permit Application	Permitted Landfill Operation
Local area environmental improvements	None	Waste Corp. stormwater runoff feeds into nearby quarry. Waste Corp. agreed to construct pipeline at quarry to increase flow and prevent possible overflow of quarry into nearby trout stream.
Local community improvements not environmentally related	None	$5,000 donation to local school district; $1,000 donation to a community library

public was not part of these meetings, nor did it have access to these preliminary documents. Nonetheless, public opposition to the site arose quickly. Even prior to the company's submission of its planning application, over 140 letters of objection were received by the County Planning Office.[71] The degree and type of public objection in this case seems comparable to that expressed at the California and Pennsylvania sites.

Prior to submitting the application to the County Planning Office in July 1993, Waste Corp. conducted informal discussions with planning officials and prepared an environmental statement, which took the company about a year to complete. The county council initially supported the proposal, but as public opposition grew, its support began to wane. Planning regulations stipulate that once the application is submitted, the county council has sixteen weeks to make a decision on the application. In this case, it took eighteen months. The planning officer recommended that the county council grant the permit, but seemingly as a result of public opposition, the county council refused permission in January 1995. One former council official characterized the decision as strictly political, noting that the council knew at the time that its decision would probably be overturned by the secretary of state for the environment because the landfill was needed and no viable alternative existed.[72]

In the United States, if a local government (such as the county in California or the borough council in Pennsylvania) declines a land use permit, the applicant has no legal recourse to federal officials to reverse such a decision, land use planning being strictly a state and local area of regulation. In the more hierarchically organized British government, however,

Waste Corp. was legally entitled to appeal the county council's decision to the secretary of state for the environment. Waste Corp. did so.

Upon receiving Waste Corp.'s petition, the secretary appointed an inspector from the Department of Environment[73] to conduct a public inquiry. Testimony and cross-examination during the inquiry lasted ten days—much longer than anticipated by the company. The inspector ruled in favor of Waste Corp. and approved the project. Once the inspector has made his decision, all parties have the right to challenge it to the High Court, but only on a point of law. The inspector's decision cannot be challenged simply because the aggrieved party does not like it. Thus, members of the local community as well as members of the county council were legally entitled to appeal the inspector's decision to the secretary of state, but they never did so. Company officials theorized that the narrow grounds for such an appeal as well as the British "loser pays" rule deterred an appeal of the inspector's decision.[74] Company officials estimate that their own appeal and the public inquiry delayed the project by a full year and incurred expenditures—including the part-time retention of two lawyers—costing approximately $130,000.[75]

After Waste Corp. received planning approval in 1996, it submitted its waste license application to the newly formed United Kingdom Environment Agency. Since the planning process had addressed so many of the controversial issues, the waste license review process was less contentious. However, Environment Agency authorities still requested additional studies, including a risk assessment regarding impacts to the heathland. The company received the waste license in January 1998.[76]

Documentation for the two permit proceedings totaled fifty-seven hundred pages. Waste Corp. officials estimate expenditures of approximately $155,000 preparing the information required for the permit applications. Most of the major and most costly exactions stemmed from the planning permit process and cost the company on the order of $1.8 million. As noted in Table 5.5, these included Waste Corp.'s commitment to create a special community trust fund, construct a special leachate detection system, provide additional road improvements and off-site tree planting, and conduct a more costly mining and reclamation process to mitigate concerns about the visual impacts of the mining process.[77] This does not include an estimated $4.8 million in opportunity costs incurred when the planning authorities insisted Waste Corp. remove the brickworks in about fifteen years, when the sand extraction is complete.[78]

D. The Netherlands

In 1991, Waste Corp. bought an existing landfill and commenced the permit application process for an expansion. The site is located in a fairly rural

TABLE 5.5 United Kingdom Case Study

	Waste Corp. Permit Application	*Permitted Landfill*
Date	Waste Corp. applied for a planning permit in 1989 and a waste license in 1996	Waste Corp. received its planning permit in 1996 and its waste license in January 1998
Size/capacity of landfill	Approx. 100 acres; 4.8-million-ton capacity; 22-year lifetime	Same as proposed
Landfill liner design	Proposed a composite liner consisting of 1 meter of clay and 2 mm HDPE	Agreed to increase the clay thickness to 2 meters.
Groundwater monitoring and leachate detection system	Proposed groundwater monitoring and leachate detection systems that are considered standard in the U.K.	Both the groundwater monitoring and leachate collection systems were more rigorous than originally proposed. The system ultimately agreed upon is more rigorous than usual because of the adjoining area designated as a Site of Special Scientific Interest (SSSI), but the required design standards do not exceed the maximum requirements in the government guidance.
		Required to sample wells more frequently and for more constituents than originally proposed.
		Waste Corp. was required by agency to install a special leachate detection system along the southern side of the site next to the SSSI. The details still have to be agreed upon, but it is equivalent to a composite liner with four lining systems.

TABLE 5.5   (Continued)

	Waste Corp. Permit Application	Permitted Landfill
Air pollution controls	Complied with standard dust control measures and the evolving national standards requiring the collection and flaring of landfill gases.	Same
Other environmental safeguards at the facility	None	Due to concerns over blowing litter and attracting birds, company agreed to conduct landfill operations under an enclosed net once the landfill reaches an agreed-upon height. Waste Corp. forfeited a previously obtained right to mine approximately 1/2 million tons of sand in a sensitive ecological area.
Local area environmental improvements	None	Off-site tree planting. Alterations in mining and reclamation process to reduce visual impacts of mining operation. As allowed under new landfill tax provisions (October 1966) Waste Corp. diverted up 20% of required landfill taxes into an approved trust fund to restore part of the site to public open space.*
Local community improvements not environmentally related	None	Waste Corp. agreed to make additional road improvements. Waste Corp. agreed to remove brickworks when sand extraction is complete in about 15 years.

*Introduction of the landfill tax provisions in October 1996 allows operations to divert up to 20 pecent of the tax payable (approximately $11.50/tonne) into an approved trust to spend on approved projects within a ten-mile radius of the landfill. The operator has to pay 10 percent of the 20 percent; the rest comes from customs and excise. (Senior Waste Corp. official, fax, March 24, 1998.)

agricultural area, but twenty-five houses are located within 250 to 300 meters of the site. Formerly, part of the site was mined for sand and used for disposal of industrial and demolition waste. Waste Corp.'s proposed expansion included two new operations: a recycling (sorting) facility and a new landfill for demolition and construction waste. In comparison with the other sites researched, the Dutch site is quite small: only thirty-two acres, three hundred thousand tons of total landfill capacity (twenty thousand tons/year), with an expected life of fifteen years. Although deemed by Waste Corp. to be fairly representative of the typical permitting process and to reflect typical design standards required in the Netherlands, the site is rather on the small side for Dutch landfills,[79] small enough that Waste Corp. was not required to prepare an EIR.[80]

Unfortunately, staff turnover and lack of documentation in English prevented us from completing as detailed an account of the permitting process at the Dutch site as those for the U.S. and U.K. sites. However, we obtained sufficient information to describe the permitting process's key steps and impacts. The permitting process took five years and involved administrative appeals both to the Provincial Council and to the high court of administrative law in The Hague.

In early 1991, Waste Corp. commenced dialogue with provincial authorities about the proposed landfill expansion. In September 1992 the company officially submitted what was then referred to as a "waste" license application to the Provincial Environment Authority and at the same time submitted the water permit application to the Provincial Water Purification Authority.[81] Both authorities published their concept permits in the spring of 1994. Generally after the concept permit is published, objections can be made by both the applicant and interested members of the public. On request by the authority concerned, the provincial council may hold a joint public hearing to air comments on both application proceedings.[82] No objections were made with respect to the wastewater discharge concept permit, but objections were expressed and a hearing held with respect to the waste license.[83] Nearby neighbors, mostly farmers, expressed strong concerns about possible health effects from proposed disposal of asbestos-bearing construction material.

Neighbors also expressed concern about noise and dust associated with the recycling facility. Another publicly owned waste management company, with a competing sorting facility nearby, expressed doubt about the need for another such facility. However, we were told that this company did not take a strong stand because waste companies commonly combine their various expertise to meet provincial disposal needs, and are thus reluctant to antagonize each other.[84]

After considering the advice and objections made about the draft permit, the Provincial Water Authority and the Provincial Environment Authority published the final decision for both the waste license and water permits in September 1994. The definitive water permit did not change and was again not objected to.[85] The definitive waste license now disallowed the disposal of the asbestos-bearing construction waste, which Waste Corp. begrudgingly accepted. However, Waste Corp. did appeal the waste license to the high court of administrative law in The Hague, contesting the landfill liner and cover conditions, which it argued were too vague and needed further definition. Initially, the provincial authorities wanted a traditional HDPE plus a fifty-centimeter sand/bentonite liner underlying the proposed expansion area. Waste Corp. insisted that a five-centimeter sand/bentonite liner was equally environmentally protective and would result in more landfill capacity at less cost. Rather than specifying the exact type of liner Waste Corp. must install, the final permit merely stated that the company must use "sophisticated technology."[86] Waste Corp. thus appealed the permit to the Netherlands administrative high court to obtain clarification of what type of technology satisfied this ambiguous standard.

While awaiting a hearing date before the high court judge, Waste Corp. and the province negotiated a compromise. Waste Corp. agreed to install a more protective composite liner, but only for the portion of the site that was as yet untouched by mining or landfill operations. The previously disposed waste would remain untouched and unlined. In July 1996 the high court judge ruled in favor of the negotiated agreement, which is common. The judge had also decided not to mandate a stop order while the case was pending, which enabled Waste Corp.—fairly confident that the judge would rule in its favor—to commence the landfill expansion while the court decision was pending.[87]

Waste Corp. did not rely on lawyers during the appeal process or at the hearings. Whereas this is usual for Waste Corp. in the Netherlands, it is fairly unusual for most parties to government proceedings concerning environmental permitting procedures. Although it is not mandatory for any appellant to use a lawyer during hearings before the high court, most parties do. We were told by Waste Corp. officials with cross-national experience, however, that the company itself rarely feels the need for legal expertise in the Netherlands, even when dealing with an appeal process. They stated that the company's environmental specialists rarely consult with lawyers or outside consultants. Waste Corp. officials estimate that they spent approximately $50,000 or less with respect to the site appeals. This is comparable to the U.K. site, but much less than the amount spent in California or Pennsylvania.

Although no EIR was required, Waste Corp. still prepared reports including typical EIR analyses (i.e., a groundwater quality report, a noise study, a traffic report). However, the company's EIR did not identify or explore possible project alternatives. Waste Corp. officials told us that typical EIRs for landfills in the Netherlands cost between $40,000 and $50,000. In this case, the cost was much less ($8,500) in part because no alternatives required environmental analysis and the studies were prepared mainly in-house rather than by consultants.

The entire process took 5 years, including the water permit amendment. Regulators claim a comparable landfill siting today would take on average only 2.5 to 3 years, now that the government structure to implement the EMA is in place (Table 5.6). However, Waste Corp. officials stated that although regulators may make this claim, in practice it takes longer. The law has been changed to reduce the time for provincial review of the definitive permit, but there is no sanction imposed on authorities if this period is exceeded. Hence, the only recourse for a project proponent is to appeal to the High Administrative Court on the basis of a rejected permit, it takes one to two years for a court ruling on such matters, and often the court simply orders the province to make a decision within a specified time. Occasionally, a company will use an appeal to put pressure on the authorities, but company officials claim that it generally does not save time and therefore does not merit the additional effort.[88]

E. Discussion

Total permitting costs differed radically across the jurisdictions. As shown in Table 5.2, total permitting costs were highest in California ($45 million) and Pennsylvania ($5.7 million), lower in the United Kingdom ($440,000), and least of all in the Netherlands (although Waste Corp. was unable to provide us with one overall figure for its permitting costs in that study). It is important to note that these permitting costs do not reflect the costs Waste Corp. incurred in order to construct and operate its facilities. In the United Kingdom, for instance, where government authorities required Waste Corp. to design and install a thicker liner and a more protective leachate collection system, the cost *redesign* is included in the permitting cost, but not the costs of construction or operation.

Legal costs constituted the largest single category of costs in both American jurisdictions ($15 million in California and between $250,000 and $1.2 million in Pennsylvania) and far exceeded those in either European jurisdiction ($137,000 in the United Kingdom and $50,000 in the Netherlands). Although these legal costs are undeniably part of the permitting process, it is difficult to determine whether, as some readers might conjecture, the higher legal costs in the United States may reflect a greater willingness on the part of *American* Waste Corp. officials to legally challenge or oppose decisions of the permitting authority. We were unable to ascertain whether the company officials in Europe accepted permit conditions or

TABLE 5.6 Netherlands Case Study

	Waste Corp. Proposal	Permitted Landfill
Date	Waste Corp. submitted its application for necessary licenses from provincial authorities in September 1992.	Administrative court approved negotiated agreement between Waste Corp. and province in 1996, resolving outstanding legal issues.
Size/capacity of landfill	32 acres; 300,000-ton capacity lifetime of 15 years	Same
Type of waste disposed	Waste Corp. proposed to dispose of asbestos-bearing construction wastes as well as other construction and demolition debris.	Waste Corp. was prohibited from landfilling asbestos-bearing construction waste. Waste Corp. was allowed to landfill all other types of construction and demolition debris it has proposed to landfill.
Landfill liner design	Underlie site excluding existing portion with an HDPE composite liner with only a 5-cm sand/bentonite layer rather than 50 cm. that the province initially wanted.	Same
Groundwater monitoring	Install 10 vertical monitoring wells throughout site, sampling each well twice a year. Existing site contained no leachate collection system, but the expansion proposal included a horizontal leachate collection system above the underliner.	Same
Other environmental safeguards at the facility	None	Same

	Waste Corp. Proposal	Permitted Landfill
Local area environmental improvements	None	None
Local community improvements not environmentally related	None	None*

*According to a former Waste Corp. Dutch Environment Department director (telephone interview, March 18, 1998), the public as well as the provincial authorities would be suspicious if the company proposed exactions. He said they would be concerned about what the company expected in return.

other requirements that their American counterparts would have contested.

We also observed significant differences between jurisdictions in changes to Waste Corp.'s landfill projects as a result of the permitting processes (administrative proceedings plus litigation). The project additions or changes observed can be divided into seven distinct categories, summarized in Table 5.7. Perhaps the most significant difference was that neither of the American cases show category 2 changes—technical design and operating standards intended to reduce the more severe risks of landfill operations. In both European case studies, regulatory processes did compel technical changes in the landfill's design. In the Netherlands case study, *all* the modifications were either category 2 technical changes or changes in the type of waste accepted (category 1).

Perhaps the most significant difference was that neither of the American cases resulted in category 2 changes, relating to technical design and operating safeguards aimed at severe environmental risks that commonly stem from landfill operations. The reason, it appears, is that the federal law and implementing regulations in the United States are detailed and prescriptive in that regard, as contrasted with the more flexible rules in the Netherlands and the United Kingdom. Because the United States has strict nationwide minimal standards, experienced companies such as Waste Corp. tend to incorporate them in their initial applications to local permitting authorities.

On the other hand, in both European cases regulatory processes, although based on flexible standards, did compel Waste Corp. to make technical changes in the initially proposed landfill design. The Dutch permitting process produced the fewest changes in the company's initial proposal, but it did result in the installation of a more protective liner (category 2)

TABLE 5.7 Categories of Changes between Proposed and Permitted Landfill in the Four Jurisdictions Studied

Type of Change Between Proposed and Permitted Facility	California	Pennsylvania	United Kingdom	Netherlands
Size/location of landfill; type of waste disposed of	X	X		X
Technical landfill design and operating safeguards			X	X
Monitoring and other technical assurances regarding the integrity and protectiveness of design safeguards		X		
Mechanism to assure government authorities that landfill operation is in compliance with regulatory requirements	X	X		
Mitigation of negative off-site externalities attributable to landfill operation (e.g., noise, dust, odors)	X	X	X	
Off-site environmental improvements to the local area	X	X	X	
Off-site nonenvironmental improvements to the local community	X	X	X	

and in restrictions on the type of waste accepted (category 1) (no asbestos-bearing construction wastes). In the United Kingdom the process resulted in category 2 improvements requiring a doubling of the thickness of the liner, better leachate detection, and intensified on-site groundwater monitoring, as well as some category 5 changes (reductions in blowing litter, road improvements) and category 6 changes (off-site tree planting and creation of a community fund for buying land for open space). In the Netherlands, Waste Corp. was not required or induced to provide off-site environmental improvements or contributions to the community. In the

United Kingdom, although we identified nonenvironmental off-site improvements, these were minor in comparison to those that resulted in the United States.

The regulatory process in the United States, and especially in California, resulted in larger changes, particularly with respect to reductions in the size of the landfill and pay for mechanisms to assure compliance with regulatory restrictions, mitigate off-site externalities, and fund off-site environmental and community improvements. In California, Waste Corp. had to reduce the landfill from a planned 215 million tons to 17 million tons, move it from undeveloped city land onto county land (category 1); reimburse the county for providing a full-time on-site inspector to monitor the corporation's compliance (category 4); install dust and litter controls (category 5); clean up abandoned off-site wastes caused by another party and donate one thousand acres to the county as open space (category 6); and $3.2 million in other county improvements, as well as in payments to the city (category 7).

Differences in the types of changes in Waste Corp.'s project that resulted from the permitting procedures of the four jurisdictions studied make it difficult to compare the overall social benefits of these processes. Furthermore, we do not have cost figures for all of Waste Corp.'s expenses at the various sites. Thus, it is impossible to do a reliable cost-benefit analysis of the different permit processes. Nevertheless, we can at least make some general comments about their efficacy.

From the case studies, it would appear that the American system, with its highly detailed federal law and regulations, reduces uncertainty concerning the technical design requirements for solid waste disposal facilities. Because of the highly prescriptive nature of the federal Subtitle D requirements, neither Waste Corp., the government, nor citizens' groups expended money pursuing either more or less stringent environmental design requirements.

It also appears that the U.S. landfill permitting system tends to guarantee more environmentally protective safeguards at landfills than do the more flexible British and Dutch permitting systems. Whether the inclusion of such safeguards resulted in a greater measure of actual protection of human health and the environment could not be determined from the factors examined in this study. Nevertheless, from a comparison of the designs of the landfills studied in the four jurisdictions, it appears that the liners (perhaps the most important environmental safeguard at a landfill) installed at the U.S. sites are more protective than the liners installed in either the United Kingdom or the Netherlands. In addition, the California and Pennsylvania landfills were outfitted with a sophisticated leachate detection system as a matter of course, which was not our understanding of the requirements at either the United Kingdom or the Netherlands site.

The American system also presents opportunities, mainly through litigation, for local government and citizens groups to obtain from a company a plethora of other non-landfill-related social welfare benefits that government and community groups in Europe did not attempt to obtain, or were less successful in obtaining. These opportunities allow the communities in the United States to command a higher effective "price" for the company's permission to operate a landfill than their counterparts in either the United Kingdom or the Netherlands. This "price" included benefits such as a greater measure of assurance that the design features permitted by the facility would, in fact, protect human health. In Pennsylvania, for instance, the local community negotiated for Waste Corp. to monitor their private drinking water wells for possible future contamination and to monitor the site for possible land subsidence. In California the county negotiated Waste Corp.'s agreement to reimburse the county for the costs of a full-time county compliance officer assigned to oversee Waste Corp.'s landfill operations. Finally, the American system afforded the local community the opportunity to obtain environmental and nonenvironmental off-site benefits, such as donations of open space, the company's agreement to clean up abandoned waste sites (both in California), and donations of funds to the local community ($3.2 million in California, $6,000 in Pennsylvania). Critics might say that these side-payment benefits demonstrate that the California process provides local interest groups with unwarranted extortive capacities. Social welfare economists, on the other hand, could argue that such side payments are fair compensation for the company's imposition of future environmental risks and other tangible negative externalities, such as reductions in nearby land values, dust, litter, odors, and noise.

Besides tangible economic and environmental benefits, the greater opportunities available in the United States for public involvement in landfill siting have yielded a greater measure of intangible benefits to neighboring landowners in terms of degree of knowledge concerning the health and environmental risks of a solid waste landfill and the comfort and satisfaction that attend involvement in a more transparent public process. (We say that the American process "may" have yielded such intangible benefits because we did not specifically interview neighbors and the interested public.) Although both the United Kingdom and the Netherlands had public comment periods on permits and publicly available environmental assessment reports, the sheer number of opportunities for public involvement and the total amount of information on the landfills that was made publicly available in the California and Pennsylvania permitting cases were greater. While, as demonstrated in our case studies, the greater transparency of the United States regulatory style can lead to many negative consequences in terms of delays and opportunities for vexatious and wasteful litigation, it also may generate more intangible benefits in terms of a more informed and involved public.

The primary factor driving costs, delays, and the size and number of additional environmental improvements required of the disposal company appears to be the degree of decentralization of authority within the jurisdiction's regulatory and permitting system. California, the jurisdiction with the largest associated permitting and legal costs, the longest permitting period, and perhaps the largest concessions in terms of company-funded environmental safeguards and community improvements, also had the most decentralized permitting process, with authority spread among local, regional, state, and national authorities. The Netherlands, whose system was the least complex, centralized its permitting process in two agencies, at the same level of government. Given the uniqueness of the Dutch site, the experience of Waste Corp. in other rather centralized jurisdictions such as Pennsylvania is instructive. In comparison to California, Pennsylvania's system is far more centralized. With the exception of land use permits, all environmental permits are controlled by state officials. Not surprisingly, the length of the permitting process and its costs were significantly lower in Pennsylvania than in California, despite the similar size of the landfill projects and despite strong opposition to the facility by local citizens groups in both jurisdictions.

The second factor that appears to account for the greater delays and costs associated with California's permitting system is the numerous avenues available to opposition groups to appeal administrative decisions to higher political authorities and to the courts. In California, not only are separate agencies at the city, county, region, state, and national levels responsible for separate permits at a single facility, but the decisions by lower-level decision makers in each are separately appealable to agency directors and, from there, to the courts. We found no requirement that appeals on one permit lodged by either the company or the public need be consolidated with the same or other party's appeals on any other permit; rather, appeals can be conducted concurrently and even simultaneously. Nor is the outcome in one proceeding binding upon the outcome in any other permit proceeding. The result is overlapping potentially duplicitous legal proceedings that allow groups opposing a landfill facility as well as the company proponents to drag out permit proceedings in endless rounds of appeals.

By contrast, the process of appealing administrative decisions in the other three jurisdictions is far more truncated. Although local construction and land use permits are subject to a local appeals process, the appeal of any environmental permit in Pennsylvania is made first to a single administrative hearing board with the power to consolidate appeals on different permits, and from there to the civil judicial system. Because of the extreme deference afforded Hearing Board decisions, appeals from the board to the courts are rare. In the Netherlands, all appeals from provincial authorities must be made to a single special administrative court with expertise in agency decision making. Because a single national environmental agency issues the environmental permits associated with a landfill in the United Kingdom, the range of appeals possible are similarly constricted. Appeals by marginally funded citizen groups in the United Kingdom are discouraged by the "loser pays" rule.

Yet a third factor explaining the varying results of the case studies concerns the jurisdiction's system for making land use decisions. Land use decision making can be an extremely important factor for landfill siting given that landfills provide broadly dispersed benefits to the region as a whole but impose negative externalities on the immediate surrounding area. By providing local governments with autonomy over land use planning, the United States converts the local problem into a legal stumbling block for landfill operators. Such operators must obtain permission for the site from the community most likely to resist the site. Thus, as demonstrated by the California case study, in the United States the power to veto land use planning permission augments the bargaining power of the local government. The significance of local land use permitting authority was not an issue in Pennsylvania in this particular case because of certain unique features of the local borough in which the Pennsylvania landfill site was located.[89]

In contrast, in both of the European jurisdictions studied, the legal structure is designed to reduce the power of localities over land use decisions. In the United Kingdom, local land use decisions may be appealed to the national government and overturned. In the Netherlands, disputes between provincial and national authorities over land use decisions are ironed out in the process of developing provincial land use management plans, which are drafted by the provincial authorities but must be approved by national authorities. The municipality where the landfill is located has far less leverage. To be permitted, a land use must be authorized by the provincial land use plan. These two characteristics of the United Kingdom and Dutch legal structure go far to reducing the influence of local government in posing obstacles to the siting of a solid waste landfill.

V. CONCLUSION

The case-study approach employed in the present investigation documented significant differences in the style of regulation among four jurisdictions in the United States and Europe: California, Pennsylvania, the United Kingdom, and the Netherlands. By comparing a landfill project proposed by the same multinational corporation with the project as permitted in each of the four jurisdictions studied, the case study also documented the effects of the different permitting processes in terms of the magnitude and the types of costs they require of private waste disposal operators and the magnitude and type of environmental benefits they can provide to government and community and environmental organizations.

The study documented that the most highly decentralized process, that of California, resulted in large costs as well as large social welfare benefits. The "costs" of California's highly decentralized system manifested themselves in delays, lengthy and duplicative permitting processes among different agencies at several levels of government, exhaustive environmental impact study requirements, and litigation costs associated with the company's, the public's, and the government entity's appeals of permit decisions both within administrative agencies and to civil courts. The "benefits" of the California system consisted primarily of additional assurances to the community of the environmental integrity of the site design, as well as a plethora of off-site environmental and nonenvironmental side payments unrelated to the particular environmental risks imposed by a landfill. The study documented that the permitting process of the Netherlands resulted in the smallest permitting costs and the smallest "additional" environmental benefits.

Overall, we found that it is wrong to assume that the style of regulation with respect to landfill permitting within a single country or even within a single continent will be similar, as differences between California and Pennsylvania, on the one hand, and the United Kingdom and the Netherlands, on the other, demonstrated. Nevertheless, we found that costs and benefits of particular styles of regulation were consistent across jurisdictions, with costs and benefits increasing with the jurisdiction's degree of decentralization and opportunities for uncoordinated legal challenges to permit decisions.

Whereas on the basis of four case studies, we were able to roughly characterize the size and nature of the monetary costs and environmental benefits associated with each permitting style, we were not able to make judgments concerning whether the benefits were "worth" the costs, or vice versa. Each style of regulation fostered its own type of costs and its own type of benefits. The advantage of this type of research is that it reveals categories of costs and benefits that may have been unintended by the regulatory authorities when they constructed the regulatory procedures being studied. For example, policy makers in California may not have intended that the donation of parkland constitute a "benefit" of the state's system for permitting solid waste landfills. Nevertheless, such a donation was a tangible public benefit resulting from the state's permitting process in the landfill we examined. If policy makers wish to prevent such donations from being required, they must change the dynamics that allow authorities to make such exactions.

The conclusions of the present study must be interpreted in light of limitations in the study's methodology. Most important, most of the information came from the multinational company itself. Furthermore, the study was limited to the permitting of a single landfill within each jurisdiction. The conclusions presented here would be strengthened by further research in which more sites are studied and a broader range of information sources are utilized.

NOTES

1. On siting opposition, see U.S. General Accounting Office, *How to Dispose of Hazardous Waste—A Serious Threat That Needs to Be Answered* (CED-79-13, December 1978); David Morell and Christopher Magorian, *Siting Hazardous Waste Facilities: Local Opposition and the Myth of Preemption* (Cambridge, Mass.: Ballinger Publishers, 1982); Daniel Mazmanian and David Morell, "The 'NIMBY' Syndrome: Facility Siting and the Failure of Democratic Discourse," in *Environmental Policy of the 1990s*, 2d ed., edited by Norman J. Vig and Michael Kraft (Washington, D.C.: CQ Press, 1994), 233–42; and Saraith Guerra, "NIMBY, NIMTOF, and Solid Waste Facility Siting," *Public Management* 73 (1991): 11. Many of the problems associated with the siting of solid waste facilities are addressed in the literature describing the siting of hazardous waste facilities. See Lawrence S. Bacow and James R. Milkey, "Overcoming Local Opposition to Hazardous Waste Facilities: The Massachusetts Approach," *Harvard Environmental Law Review* 6 (1982): 265–305; Michael Heiman, "From 'Not in My Backyard' to 'Not in Anybody's Backyard!': Grassroots Challenge to Hazardous Waste Facility Siting," *Journal of the American Planning Association* 56 (summer 1990): 359–62; Bernd Holznagel, "Negotiation and Mediation: The Newest Approach to Hazardous Waste Facility Siting," *Boston College Environmental Affairs Law Review* 13 (1986): 329–78; Michael O'Hare, Lawrence Bacow, and Debra Sanderson, *Facility Siting* (New York: Van Nostrand, 1983); Barry Rabe, *Beyond NIMBY: Hazardous Waste Siting in Canada and the United States* (Washington, D.C.: Brookings Institution, 1994); Louis Blumberg and Robert Gottlieb, *War on Waste: Can America Win Its Battle with Garbage?* (Washington, D.C.: Island Press, 1989); and Guerra, "NIMBY, NIMTOF, and Solid Waste Facility Siting," 11. Our research, together with that of others (e.g., Howard Kunreuther, Joanne Linnerooth-Bayer, and Kevin Fitzgerald, "Siting Hazardous Facilities: Lessons from Europe and America" [paper presented at the International Conference on Energy, Environment, and the Economy: Asian Perspectives, Taipei, Taiwan, August 22–25, 1995]; Don Munton, ed., *Hazardous Waste Siting and Democratic Choice* [Washington, D.C.: Georgetown University Press, 1996], confirms that strong opposition to siting large infrastructe facilities is common in other parts of the world, not just in the United States.

2. Although these landfills underwent permitting procedures that were typical at the time the facilities were permitted, many of these procedures, as well as the substantive environmental requirements, have changed since that time. Conse-

quently, the exact process today may be somewhat different than those we describe. Nevertheless, key informants concur that the overall trends have not changed.

3. It is impossible to find perfectly matched sites; too many factors vary among localities. For instance, some sites are new, others have a long history of expansion and repermitting. A landfill may be sited in an urban or rural community. The majority of the nearby population may be of high, medium, or low income. The site may or may not contain unique cultural resources, endangered or threatened flora and fauna, or be prone to earthquakes. The climate may be arid, moderate, or dry.

4. Section 4002 of the Resource Conservation and Recovery Act, 42 U.S.C. § 6942.

5. Section 4004 RCRA, 42 U.S.C. § 6944.

6. 42 U.S.C. § 6949a(c) (requiring EPA to revise and upgrade its earlier criteria for facilities that dispose of household wastes, including household hazardous wastes and hazardous wastes from small-quantity generators).

7. RCRA prohibits states from disposing of municipal solid waste in anything other than a "sanitary landfill" that meets the federal Subtitle D requirements. 42 U.S.C. 6944(b). The EPA's Subtitle D regulations require that landfill operators (1) install synthetic liners to curb leaks from the landfill that might contaminate groundwater; (2) install pipes and pumps to collect rainwater that percolates through the waste ("leachate") and accumulates in a layer on the top of the liner beneath the landfill; (3) treat the leachate to remove pollutants before releasing it from the landfill; (4) monitor the groundwater adjacent to the landfill to detect any contamination; (5) maintain and monitor the landfill for at least thirty years after it closes; and (6) provide financial assurances for closure, postclosure care, and for the cleanup of any contamination. See EPA Municipal Solid Waste Landfill Criteria, 40 C.F.R. § 258.1–258.74.

8. See 40 C.F.R. §§ 257–258. Municipal solid waste landfills must be outfitted with a "composite liner" consisting of another component of a "minimum 30-mil flexible membrane liner" and a lower component consisting of "at least a two-foot layer of compacted soil with a hydraulic conductivity of no more than 1×10^7 cm/ sec." 40 C.F.R. § 258.40(b).

9. Although many states have enacted solid waste landfill criteria that are more stringent than the federal Subtitle D criteria, both California and Pennsylvania being among them, the degree of variation from the federal criteria is not large.

10. Solid waste landfills with a design capacity of 2.5 million cubic meters and constructed after 1991 must comply with EPA emission guidelines promulgated under section 111(b) of the Clean Air Act, 42 U.S.C. § 7411(b), requiring that landfill gas be collected and controlled through a combustion device. 40 C.F.R. pts. 51, 52, and 60.

11. According to the federal Clean Water Act, all pollutant discharges to navigable waters must be permitted and must comply with effluent limitations. 33 U.S.C. §§ 1311, 1342. Discharge permits must be obtained from the federal EPA or, if the permitting program has been delegated to the state in which the facility is located, from a state agency.

12. 42 U.S.C. §§ 4321–4347.

13. Section 102 of NEPA requires that all federal agencies prepare a "detailed statement on the environmental impact" of any proposal for a "major federal

action." The requirement to obtain a federal permit renders a solid waste landfill a "federal action," and significant possible impacts upon the environment may render the landfill's construction and operation a "major" action. 42 U.S.C. § 4332.

14. The California Integrated Waste Management Board was created by the California legislature by the Integrated Waste Management Act of 1989 (Assembly Bill 939). CIWMB is part of the California Department of Environmental Protection (CAL/EPA) The CIWMB comprises six full-time board members.

15. For example, California requires a five-foot separation between the bottom of the landfill and the highest anticipated groundwater level. California regulations also contain more detailed geologic setting requirements. Telephone interview with California Integrated Waste Management Bureau (CIWMB) official, November 25, 1997.

16. In special cases, other approvals or permits may be required. For example, if the facility will require development of coastal land, the operator must obtain a Coastal Development Permit from either the California State Coastal Commission or a local agency authorized by the Coastal Commission. Similarly, if the project will require the filling of wetlands, the operator must obtain a dredge and fill permit from the United States Army Corps of Engineers (CIWMB, Permit Desk Manual, 1992, chap. 1, p. 1).

17. This consists of a finding of conformity with either the County-wide Integrated Waste Management Plan or a finding of consistency and conformance to the appropriate city or county general plan and the County Solid Waste Management Plan.

18. Typically, the landfill operator must obtain an air permit from the air pollution district (referred to as the Air Quality Management District or Air Pollution Control District, AQMD/APCD) that includes the facility.

19. Water discharge permits must be obtained from the applicable Regional Water Quality Control Board (RWQCB).

20. Cal. Public Resources Code § 21000 et seq.

21. Public Resources Code, § 21177.

22. Pennsylvania's solid waste management regulations are found at 25 Pa. Code Ch.271–285.

23. See 25 Pa. Code. § 273.251(b). The Pennsylvania DEP requires that a municipal landfill contain a primary synthetic liner and a secondary liner, which can be made of either a synthetic material or remolded clay. Federal EPA regulations require only that a landfill be equipped with a single composite liner, the upper component of which consists of a 30-mil flexible membrane liner and a lower component of at least two feet of compacted soil of a minimum conductivity. 40 C.F.R. § 258.40(b).

24. Telephone interview with Pennsylvania DEP official, December 8, 1997.

25. 25 Pa. Code § 271.127.

26. The entirety of Pennsylvania's environmental assessment requirements is spelled out in Form D, "Municipal Environmental Assessment Process for Municipal Waste Management Facilities," one of thirty-one forms that must be completed prior to the construction of a municipal landfill.

27. 35 P.S. § 7513.

28. European Council Directive 1999/31/EC of April 26, 1999.

29. Counties in the United Kingdom are a mid-tier level of government, above local district authorities but below national governing bodies.

30. In 1988, environmental assessment was introduced in the United Kingdom to implement an EC directive adopted in 1985. Preparation of an environmental analysis is mandatory for any municipal, industrial, or commercial landfill accepting more than 75,000 tons (U.K.) a year, whether being constructed and operated privately or by the government. However, if the site is in a designated sensitive location, then an EA may be required even if the proposed site will accept less than this amount of waste.

31. Telephone interview with Waste Corp. officials, March 7, 1997.

32. Telephone interview with Waste Corp. officials, March 7, 1997.

33. Although parties need not be represented by counsel, Waste Corp. officials told us that they routinely hire barristers to represent them in these public inquiries. Telephone interview with Waste Corp. officials, March 7, 1997.

34. A corps of some two hundred inspectors (professional planners, engineers, or architects) conducts the public inquiries. If the matter is regarded as having more than local significance, the secretary of state may conduct the public inquiry himself.

35. Telephone interview with Waste Corp. officials, March 7, 1997.

36. According to company officials, there is no clear dividing line between the issues raised in the land use planning procedures under the Town and County Planning Act and those raised in the pollution permit proceedings. Company officials expressed frustration at the degree of duplication between the county planning process and the pollution permit proceeding and stated that they thought it would be better to agree on the broad principles under planning first. Senior company official, telephone interview, March 24, 1998.

37. These three agencies consisted of the National Rivers Authority, the Waste Regulation Authority, and Her Majesty's Inspectorate of Pollution.

38. The U.K. government guidance documents provide key points to be considered (e.g., in selecting and specifying a liner), then identifies current useful reference documents. E-mail correspondence with U.K. environmental consultant, November 11, 1997.

39. See also David Vogel, *National Styles of Regulation* (Ithaca, N.Y.: Cornell University Press, 1986), 75–76 (describing the British government's approach to pollution control as particularly flexible, not only in comparison with the United States but also with most Western European nations). Nevertheless, in the past decade there has been a clear trend toward more stringent requirements for both waste generators and the waste disposal industry. This trend is likely to be accentuated once the European Union's environmental requirements are made final and apply to the United Kingdom.

40. See note 38.

41. Telephone interview with senior Waste Corp. U.K. official, March 24, 1998.

42. Dik Beker, "Sanitary Landfilling in the Netherlands," in *International Perspectives on Municipal Solid Wastes and Sanitary Landfilling,* edited by Joseph S. Carra and Raffaeloo Cossu (San Diego: Academic Press, 1990), 141–42.

43. Former Waste Corp. Dutch Environment Department director, telephone interview, March 18, 1998.

44. As mentioned earlier, the Environmental Management Act (EMA) of 1993

subsumed most environmental laws into one coherent act, including the Waste Management Act of 1979. This resulted in the change in license title from "waste license" to "EMA license." However, the Pollution of Surface Waters Act of 1970 is not superseded by the EMA, and it stipulates the requirement for waste water discharge permits. If site conditions are such that the Surface Water Purification Act requires that the site's wastewater is purified prior to discharge into the public sewage system, then the waste license must mandate the design features and technology necessary to achieve the required standards and a description of how any associated sludge will be disposed. Former Waste Corp. project manager, telephone interview, February 18, 1998.

45. A province can override a municipal zoning plan only during its preparation, not after its completion. Former Waste Corp. Dutch Environment Department director, telephone interview, March 18, 1998.

46. Thus, a solid waste landfill requires two permits: the EMA license (required by the EMA) and another for wastewater discharge (required by the PSWA). Potentially environmentally harmful activities can be controlled by a mixture of traditional regulation and cooperative agreements between government and business. VROM, Environmental Program, 1995 p. 4, http://www.rri.org/envatlas/europe/netherlands/nl-index.html=environmentalatlas. However, no such cooperative agreements have been made with respect to landfilling, but rather for activities such as recycling or car manufacturing. Former Waste Corporation Dutch Environment director, telephone interview, March 18, 1998.

47. Vogel, *National Styles of Regulation,* 143.

48. Environmental Protection Act 1993. For a detailed account of the EIR requirement in the Netherlands, see Huug H. Luigies, "Environmental Law of the Netherlands," in *Comparative Environmental Law and Regulation,* edited by Nicholas A. Robinson (Dobbs Ferry, N.Y.: Oceana Publications, 1996), 20–21.

49. Former Waste Corp. Dutch Environment Department director, telephone interview, March 18, 1998. See also Luiges, "Environmental Law of the Netherlands," 21.

50. Procedures followed in the existing administrative courts in the Netherlands are similar to the adjudicatory hearings held before U.S. administrative agencies. It is expected, however, that new administrative departments of the law courts will adopt the character and legal culture of their higher colleagues in the Administrative High Court in the Hague. E-mail from Waste Corp. official, the Netherlands, November 12, 1997.

51. General Administrative Law Act of the Netherlands, tit. 8 (The Hague 1994).

52. Sections 8:24 and 2:1 of the Dutch General Administrative Law Act.

53. Aalder's e-mail, August 31, 1998.

54. The closed landfill is just inside the city line and closed in 1991 after more than thirty years of operation when its permit expired and opposition blocked its reauthorization.

55. Supplemental EIR, 1997.

56. Company officials believe these requirements make this site the most conditioned of any of Waste Corp.'s landfills. Senior company official, telephone interview, June 22, 1998; Waste Corp. chronology.

57. Company official, personal interview, September 9, 1997.

58. Company chronology.

59. Waste Corp. file records; senior Waste Corp. manager, personal interview, September 9, 1997.

60. Waste Corp. officials allege that this competitor provided financial resources to a consulting firm hired by the community coalition to conduct seismic and groundwater analysis of the site presented to the California Regional Water Quality Control Board in 1994. See earlier discussion regarding the Community Coalition's appeal to the Regional Water Quality Control Board.

61. Newspaper article, April 25, 1995.

62. Newspaper article, August 26, 1994.

63. Telephone interview with Waste Corp. official, March 5, 1998.

64. Although we did not obtain estimates of public sector expenditure on legal fees, one company official (on September 9, 1997) stated that the city spent $700,000 just in its first lawsuit against the county.

65. In seeking approval of landfills, it is common for localities to demand special mitigation measures (sometimes labeled exactions, "amenities," or "side payments") over and above conditions required by regulation. These might include donated lands for parks and recreation, revegetation research, off-site tree planting, cleanup of hazardous waste facilities not created by the project proponent, inspection vehicle, salaries of county staff, purchase of water, and road access fees.

66. The department required the pipe to be installed to prevent water from the quarry area from possibly overflowing upstream and contaminating a nearby trout-fishing stream.

67. Waste Corp. determined that the anticipated results of the monitoring (that no subsidence is occurring) would bolster its future attempts to expand the landfill into the borrow pit area.

68. Personal interview, company official, September 25, 1997.

69. Environmental statement, June 1993.

70. Personal interview, Waste Corp. officials, June 17, 1997, and March 24, 1998.

71. Company files, November 15, 1994, memorandum.

72. Former council member, personal interview, June 19, 1997.

73. The Planning Inspectorate, at the time, was an executive agency in the Department of the Environment and the Welsh Office. The government recently renamed this the Department of Environment, Transport, and the Regions.

74. Company officials, conference call, March 7, 1997.

75. Company official, personal interview, June 18, 1997. Waste Corp. officials could have requested compensation for their appellate legal fees from the county but declined to do so because they would have had to prove to the inspectorate that the county had acted unreasonably, which would have been difficult. Furthermore, Waste Corp. knew that such a request would strap the county's already small budget, and the company recognized it would have to do business with the county for the foreseeable future. Company officials, personal interview, June 19, 1997.

76. Company official, telephone interview, October 26, 1999.

77. Concerns about visual impact required the company to alter their mining infill strategy. Rather than start mining at one end, which was more economical for

the company, they agreed to start at the opposite end so that the side most people overlooked would be reclaimed first.

78. Senior Waste Corp. official, telephone interview, March 24, 1998.

79. Dutch company official, personal interview, June 26, 1997.

80. In the Netherlands, only expansions greater than 500,000 cubic meters total capacity require an EIR. The public expressed concern that the company would simply apply for incremental expansions to the EIR requirement every few years, but this concern was not addressed directly by the Provincial Council. Former Waste Corp. staff, Dutch Environment Department director, telephone interview, February 18, 1998.

81. Personal interview, provincial EMA and water officials, June 26, 1997.

82. L. Verstappen, *Environmental Permits* (The Hague: Netherlands Foreign Investment Agency, 1993), 14.

83. The former Waste Corp. Dutch Environment Department director told us that it is typical to have objections on the waste license—the more political of the two permits—which spells out the majority of required standards and design features, whereas it is rare that the water permit is appealed. Telephone interview, February 18, 1998.

84. Former Waste Corp. Dutch Environment Department director, telephone interview, February 18 and March 18, 1998.

85. However, it was amended in 1997 to reflect the actual construction of the water discharge system and appropriate discharge standards. An amended concept and definitive permit were prepared with no appeals. Former Waste Corp. Dutch Environment Department director, telephone interview, February 18, 1998.

86. In 1992 or 1993, Waste Corp. internally raised the idea of mining the waste at the existing landfill to profit from usable materials and to increase the sites' disposal capacity. However, the old landfill waste contained large amounts of asbestos-bearing cement. The residue from this waste, after sorting and recycling, would have to be disposed of at another landfill, since disposal of asbestos had been banned at the new site. Ultimately, Waste Corp. dropped the idea without ever going public, due to the company's concerns regarding extra costs associated with additional health and safety mitigation needed for sorting and the cost of disposing asbestos residues at another landfill. Former Waste Corp. Dutch Environment Department director, telephone interview, March 18, 1998.

87. Former Waste Corp. Dutch Environment Department director, telephone interview, March 18, 1998.

88. Ibid.

89. Most important, the borough in which the site was located was separately incorporated largely as a result of the efforts of a land developer who originally owned the landfill site. This developer favored the landfill and was instrumental in appointing the elected heads of local government who also favored the landfill.

CHAPTER SIX

The Air Pollution Permit Process for U.S. and German Automobile Assembly Plants

John P. Dwyer, Richard W. Brooks, and Alan C. Marco

In this chapter, we use four case studies to compare the standards and procedures to obtain air pollution permits for automobile assembly plant "paint shops"—the part of the factory where new cars and trucks are painted—in the United States and Germany. The manufacturing facilities are owned by the same company, use nearly identical paint application technologies and paints, and use virtually the same air pollution control technologies. Moreover, both countries are federalist in structure, with the national government setting general standards, and the states issuing and enforcing individual permits. These similarities allow us to compare the permitting processes in the two countries, and to isolate the salient political and legal differences and economic consequences.

Despite these similarities, the two countries' *regulatory processes* are rather different. Air pollution control laws, regulations, and plant-level permits in the United States are somewhat more stringent, detailed, and prescriptive than in Germany. Moreover, U.S. law provides substantially greater opportunity for public participation in agency permitting decisions, and at one U.S. facility public participation significantly affected the regulatory outcome. For these and other reasons, the permitting processes in the U.S. plants were much slower and more conflictual than at the German plants, resulting in much longer delays in making production changes and installing new pollution controls.

I. INTRODUCTION

Ground-level ozone is harmful to humans, animals, and vegetation.[1] The primary constituent of smog, ozone is generated by the chemical interaction of volatile organic compounds (VOCs),[2] nitrogen oxides, and sunlight.

Consequently, a principal strategy to reduce urban smog in many industrialized countries is to regulate VOC emissions from industrial facilities and automobiles. For large industrial facilities, environmental agencies frequently implement and enforce VOC emission limits through individually negotiated air pollution permits.

In this study we compare the process to obtain VOC emission permits for automobile assembly plants in the United States and Germany. The project consists of four case studies in which we compare the costs of obtaining air pollution permits for assembly plant "paint shops"—the part of the factory where new cars and trucks are painted. The plants are owned by the same company (Ford Motor Co.), use nearly identical paint application technologies and paints, and use virtually the same air pollution control technologies. Moreover, both countries are federalist in structure, with the national government setting general standards, and the states issuing and enforcing individual permits. These similarities allowed us to compare the permitting processes in the United States and Germany, and to isolate the salient political and legal differences and economic consequences.

The next section describes the vehicle coating process and the technological means through which VOCs are emitted and controlled. Section III provides a brief summary of U.S. and German air pollution laws and regulations. Sections IV and V tell the permitting stories in the United States and Germany. Section VI concludes with a summary of our findings and a discussion of policy implications.

II. VEHICLE COATING PROCESSES AND VOC CONTROL TECHNOLOGIES

Painting the newly manufactured autobody is the most pollution-intensive aspect of automobile manufacturing, and consequently it is the principal focus of environmental regulation in the assembly plant. VOC emissions from the paint shop, which come predominantly from the paint solvents released in the paint application and curing processes, constitute an overwhelming fraction of the total VOC emissions from the assembly plant.[3]

After a vehicle body has been stamped, welded, and washed, it is dipped into an electrolytic deposition bath (e-coat), which provides the vehicle's primary corrosion protection coating. The coated body then is put into a "bake oven" to cure the coating, and thereafter sanded to prepare the surface for the next coat. VOCs are released by the curing process and while the vehicle body cools before sanding. After application of the e-coat, robots in a spray booth apply a "guidecoat," which is designed to prevent the topcoat from chipping and to provide a smooth surface for application of the topcoat. Again, the coating is cured in a bake oven; VOCs are released from the spray booth, the bake oven, and the cooling area. The body then goes to the topcoat line. Modern topcoats consist of a thin "base coat" (BC) containing the concentrated pigment and a thicker "clear coat" (CC) containing a gloss. After each application, the coating is cured in a bake oven, left to cool in a cooling area, and then sent to the assembly plant. VOCs are released from the spray booth, the bake oven, and the cooling area. The largest sources of VOC emissions in the assembly plant are the application of the topcoat, followed by the purging and cleaning of the spray guns, and then the application of the guidecoat.

Auto manufacturers use three strategies to reduce VOC emissions in the paint shop: reduce the VOC content of the coatings, modify the application technology to use less paint, and employ one or more emission control technologies. In response to Environmental Protection Agency (EPA) regulations, U.S. automakers have significantly reduced emissions by using coatings containing smaller amounts of VOC solvents[4] and by using more efficient application techniques. In the early 1980s, however, U.S. automakers faced competitive pressures from European and Japanese manufacturers using high-VOC BC/CC topcoats to produce high-quality, durable finishes. To meet increasingly strict air pollution standards, automakers and paint manufacturers began to develop low-VOC topcoats and more efficient transfer technologies.[5] U.S. manufacturers hoped that such technological advances would obviate the need for expensive emission control technologies. In some cases the new paint formulations and application technologies were not sufficient to meet the air pollution standards, and automakers had to install VOC emission control technologies.

Automakers rely on two emission control technologies to reduce VOC emissions: thermal oxidation and carbon adsorption. Thermal oxidizers burn VOCs in the exhaust stream before they are released through the plant's vents to the atmosphere. Manufacturers commonly use a thermal oxidizer (or "afterburner") to incinerate VOCs emitted from the bake ovens. Thermal oxidizers are much less efficient with dilute exhaust streams from the spray booths, where ventilation is required to protect worker health and safety and to prevent overspray from drifting to other vehicles. If not simply released to the atmosphere, such dilute exhaust streams first are passed through carbon filters, which adsorb the VOCs (the VOCs not adsorbed are released to the atmosphere). When the filters become saturated, the process is reversed and the desorbed (and now concentrated) VOCs are incinerated in a thermal oxidizer before the exhaust is vented to the atmosphere.[6]

III. REGULATORY BACKGROUND

A. *Air Pollution Regulation of Vehicle Manufacturers in the United States*

Under the federal Clean Air Act,[7] regulatory authority over nonhazardous air pollution from industrial and commercial facilities is divided between the federal EPA and state and local air pollution agencies.[8] The EPA's principal responsibilities are to set national ambient air quality standards (NAAQS) for common industrial and automotive pollutants,[9] and to adopt industry-specific emission standards for newly constructed or modified facilities, called new source performance standards (NSPS).[10] In 1977 Congress adopted two additional programs for new and modified facilities. The "nonattainment" program is designed for new and modified facilities in areas that have not yet achieved the NAAQS.[11] The "prevention of significant deterioration" (PSD) program is designed to restrict the degradation of air quality in areas where the air is cleaner than required by the primary NAAQS.[12] Together, the nonattainment and PSD programs constitute the so-called New Source Review program.

State and local environmental agencies implement and enforce the federal air quality and emission standards,[13] as well as any stricter state standards and state nuisance laws. Each state must adopt a state implementation plan (SIP) that specifies the emission limits for each source of pollution, that contains adequate provisions to monitor and enforce the emission limits,[14] and that has adequate procedures for public participation.[15] Significant sources of air pollution must obtain a five-year permit specifying emission limits, site-specific control technologies, and monitoring, record-keeping, and reporting requirements. The permits must meet the requirement that when emissions from all facilities are aggregated under local weather and geographic conditions, the resulting air pollution levels do not exceed the NAAQS.[16] The SIPs and individual air pollution permits are subject to EPA approval. In addition, the EPA oversees state enforcement and may file its own enforcement actions, even if the state agency already has sought enforcement.[17]

1. NEW SOURCE PERFORMANCE STANDARDS (NSPS)

The EPA's emission limits for categories of new and modified facilities[18] must be equivalent to limits achievable by the "best system of emission reduction" that has been "adequately demonstrated," taking into account control costs.[19] The 1980 standards for VOC emissions from automobile assembly plant paint shops consist of separate emission limits for the e-coat, guidecoat, and topcoat operations.[20] The regulations also require the manufacturer to conduct monthly performance tests to determine compliance with the emission limits,[21] monitor the temperature in thermal oxidizers,[22] and file quarterly reports on compliance and other issues.[23] The standards do not specify coating composition, application technologies, or control technologies. Manufacturers are free to use any methods, so long as they observe the specified emission limits.

The EPA may relax NSPS standards in certain circumstances: the agency may grant an "innovative technology waiver" for emission limits to "encourage the use of an innovative technological system" of emission reduction.[24] Before granting the waiver, the EPA must obtain the consent of the governor of the affected state and give public notice and an opportunity for a public hearing on the proposed waiver.[25] With the waiver, companies might avoid the need to install expensive control technologies soon rendered obsolete by new technological developments.[26]

2. NEW SOURCE REVIEW

In nonattainment areas, proposed new and modified major sources[27] of pollution must undergo New Source Review to obtain a permit.[28] The source must demonstrate that it has obtained sufficient "offsets"—reduced emissions from other facilities in the same nonattainment—so as to make "reasonable further progress" toward attaining the primary NAAQS.[29] For example, in a "severe" nonattainment area—which is the classification for Middlesex County, New Jersey, where Ford's Edison plant is located—a new or modified source must reduce VOC emissions by 130 tons for every 100 tons of additional VOC emissions.[30] Regardless of the offsets obtained, a new or modified facility also must install control technologies equivalent to the "lowest achievable emission rate" (LAER),[31] a standard that does not take into account the cost of controlling emissions. The facility owner must demonstrate that the owner's other major sources meet the SIP requirements and that the "benefits of the proposed source significantly outweigh the environmental and social costs" of the new facility.[32]

In attainment areas, proposed major new and modified sources of pollution must undergo New Source Review under the PSD program.[33] Before construction, the owner of a proposed "major emitting facility" must demonstrate that the emissions from the new facility will not cause air quality to degrade more than permitted by statute, that the facility will meet applicable NSPS, that the facility will meet an emission standard equivalent to the "best available control technology" (BACT), and that the agency has prepared an analysis of the projected air quality impacts arising from growth associated with the facility.[34]

There are important differences between the nonattainment and PSD programs. For example, LAER is more stringent than BACT, and only facilities in nonattainment areas must obtain offsets. But there are important similarities as well. Both programs focus on new and modified facilities, and both focus on "major" sources of pollution, although the definition of "major"—in terms of annual VOC emissions—is much smaller in heavily polluted nonattainment areas. Facilities in both areas are subject to technology-based emission standards that effectively require new or modified facilities to install certain types of control technologies to reduce emissions, with the details subject to negotiation between the facility and the state environmental agency. In addition, in both PSD and nonattainment areas the agency must prepare an analysis of the environmental impacts of the proposed new facility. Finally, regardless of the area's attainment status, the agency's findings and tentative decision to grant a permit are subject to public review and comment.

3. STATE NUISANCE LAW

Although VOC emissions are primarily governed by national air quality and emissions regulations, they also may be subject to state nuisance laws if they are odorous.[35] In the United States, state nuisance standards are quite general, and normally they are enforced through court litigation resulting in injunctive relief and damages.[36]

4. PUBLIC PARTICIPATION

Federal and state laws provide ample opportunity for public review and comment on proposed permit decisions. The U.S. regulatory system relies on public participation in permitting, monitoring, and enforcement to ensure that regulatory agencies adhere to statutory standards. For example, in deciding whether to grant an innovative technology waiver of the NSPS emission standards, the EPA must give public notice and an opportunity for a public hearing on the proposed waiver.[37] In addition, under federal law, the information submitted by the owner of a facility in a nonattainment area, as well as the agency's analysis of the data, are subject to a thirty-day public review and comment period.[38] Similarly, federal law provides that a state's tentative decision to issue a PSD permit is subject to a public hearing process.[39] State statutes (recall, it is states that issue the permits) typically require a public meeting to discuss the permit conditions, and many states also permit members of the public to petition the agency for a contested administrative hearing.[40]

Available data suggest that the federal air pollution control programs have significantly reduced both total VOC emissions and VOC emissions per vehicle from automobile assembly plant paint shops (Table 6.1).[41] Thus, in 1975, when most plants had not yet installed emission controls under the 1970 Clean Air Act, VOC emissions from automobile assembly plant surface coating operations were at an all-time high. Installation of new emission controls reduced emissions to 165,000 short tons in 1980 and 85,000 short tons in 1985, despite an increase in vehicle production,

TABLE 6.1   Automobile Production in the United States and VOCs
Emissions from Automobile Assembly Plant Paint Shops

Year	Passenger Vehicles (thousands)	Total VOC Emissions for Autos and Light Trucks (thousands of short tons)	VOC Emissions Per Passenger Vehicle (tons per vehicle)
1975	6,717	204	0.0304
1980	6,376	165	0.0259
1985	8,185	85	0.0104
1990	6,077	92	0.0151
1995	6,351	96	0.0151

thus reflecting the impact of NSPS standards (which became effective in 1980 for assembly plant paint shops) and the PSD and nonattainment programs (which began to take effect in the late 1970s). These standards and programs, of course, applied only to new and modified facilities. Thus, part of the decrease in VOC emissions was the result of moderate controls required for existing, unmodified facilities in nonattainment areas, such as the requirement for low-solvent paints. Emission increases in the 1990s (both total VOCs and emissions per vehicle) probably reflect the switch to the new high-gloss topcoats.

B. Air Pollution Regulation of Vehicle Manufacturers in Germany

The Basic Law (*Grundgesetz*) divides authority for air pollution control between the national government and the sixteen federal states (*Länder*).[42] Under this arrangement, the national government has adopted substantive standards and licensing procedures to control emissions from industrial facilities, and the *Länder* bear sole responsibility for implementation and enforcement, an arrangement that is strikingly similar to practices under the U.S. Clean Air Act. There are important differences, however. First, the *Grundgesetz* does not allow the federal government to oversee or take over the *Länder*'s functions.[43] Second, the federal government has no enforcement authority, and the Ministry for the Environment does not even have regional offices.[44] These two factors ensure that the *Länder* retain substantial discretion in the implementation of the federal statutes and regulations. Third, federal laws and regulations that the *Länder* must implement are subject to approval by the Bundesrat,[45] the upper house of Parliament whose members are ministers (commonly, they are environmental ministers) of the *Länder*. Thus, federal environmental regulations reflect broad consensus among the *Länder*.

Germany's main federal air quality legislation, the Federal Immissions

Control Act (*Bundes-Immissions-Schutzgesetzes*, or *BImSchG*), was enacted in 1974 and subsequently amended several times, most recently in 1995. The act provides general criteria to determine which industrial facilities must obtain a license—essentially facilities that would cause "considerable disadvantage" or "considerable nuisance."[46] Under the regulations of the federal Ministry for the Environment, Nature Conservation, and Nuclear Safety, automobile manufacturing plants must be licensed.

1. PERMITTING STANDARDS

The federal act provides two principal substantive requirements for licensed facilities. First, licensed facilities must not cause "harmful effects on the environment or other hazards, considerable disadvantages and considerable nuisance to the general public and the neighborhood."[47] This provision, which is subject to a general proportionality principle that balances costs and benefits,[48] is most closely analogous to nuisance laws in the United States. One important difference is that German regulations translate this statutory standard into specific emission limits.

Second, "precautions [must be] taken to prevent harmful effects on the environment, in particular by such emission control measures as are appropriate according to the state of the art,"[49] which is loosely analogous to the BACT criterion in the U.S. NSPS standards. Both the U.S. and German standards require some balancing of costs and benefits.[50]

A region with particularly polluted air must adopt a clean air plan (*Luftreinhalteplan*),[51] and the *Länder* are authorized to impose additional measures in areas that need special protection.[52] The *Luftreinhalteplan* are similar to the SIPs required under the U.S. Clean Air Act, especially in nonattainment and PSD areas, except that the criteria are vague, they have no force of law, and they are required only in certain areas.[53]

The general statutory requirements are implemented through the federal Technical Instructions on Air Quality Control (*Technische Anleitung zur Reinhaltung der Luft*, or *TA Luft*), which provide more detailed requirements to control and disperse emissions from licensed facilities. Although *TA Luft*'s provisions do not have the force of law, one court described them as "anticipatory expert testimony," which apparently means that they prima facie give operational definition to the statutory standards.[54]

TA Luft contains four types of substantive standards:[55] criteria to determine the height of exhaust stacks;[56] *immission* (air quality) values (analogous to the U.S. NAAQS);[57] general technological requirements and emission limits,[58] including emission limits for VOC emissions;[59] and emission limits and control technologies for specified categories of industrial facilities,[60] including automobile assembly plant paint shops (like the U.S. NSPS standards).[61] Generally speaking, facilities that do not cause *immissions* to exceed the established values satisfy the statutory requirement not to cause considerable disadvantage and substantial impairment.[62] Compliance with the height requirements for exhaust stacks, the general technological requirements and emission limits, and the requirements for specified industrial categories normally satisfy the statutory command to take "precautions."[63] German air pollution regulations have no provisions analogous to the U.S. nonattainment or PSD programs.[64] Moreover, given their emphasis on minimum stack heights, German regulatory standards are focused less on the relationship of emissions to air quality.

a. Stack Heights

TA Luft contains criteria to determine the minimum and maximum heights for exhaust stacks.[65] The evident purpose of these provisions is not to reduce emissions but to disperse emissions and thereby reduce local concentrations of pollutants. Control of VOC concentrations in the immediate neighborhood (which relates to both health protection and elimination of odors), not ozone control, is the primary object of these requirements.

b. Immission Values

The 1986 *TA Luft* established *immission* values to protect human health[66] and to protect against "considerable disadvantage and substantial impairment."[67] Using detailed criteria in *TA Luft*, the licensing agency must ascertain the actual, existing *immission* value for each pollutant ("initial load") and calculate the additional *immission* value that will result from the proposed facility, taking into account, for example, dispersion, weather conditions, nearby buildings, and terrain ("additional load").[68] As a general rule, the licensing agency must deny a license to a facility whose total load (initial load plus additional load) exceeds the *TA Luft immission* value.[69] The regulations make an exception if the additional load does not exceed the *TA Luft immission* value by more than 1 percent, and if the licensee obtains enough offsets from other facilities to "reduce the *immissions*."[70] The implication of this exception is that if *immissions* increase by less than 1 percent—which might be quite substantial in a polluted area— the agency must grant the license.

Because the 1986 *TA Luft* did not establish an *immission* value for ozone,[71] licensees whose facilities emit VOCs are subject to a slightly different procedure. In such cases the licensing agency must determine whether the proposed facility's VOC emissions should be considered "[health] hazards, considerable disadvantages, or substantial impairments for the general public or the neighborhood" based on "the state of science and general experience of life."[72] To determine whether the health hazards, disadvantages, or impairments are "substantial," the agency must consider whether the emissions create hazards to human health (which "are always substantial"); if not, the agency must consider the land uses specified in the zoning plans, other existing land use restrictions, the impact of pollutants, "the necessity of mutual consideration in neighbor relations," and control measures on the licensee's other facilities.[73] In other words, where there is no *immission* value, the agency may license a facility only where there are no health hazards and where it determines there are no other substantial adverse effects after weighing competing considerations. Because these considerations are quite general, the agency has considerable discretion over whether to grant the permit.

c. General Technological Requirements and VOC Emission Limits

TA Luft requires licensed facilities to have "emission control facilities corresponding to present state of [the art] technology."[74] In addition, special attention must be paid to "reducing the amount of waste gas," "optimizing processes," and "optimizing start-up and shut off processes."[75] The regulations also specify that VOC concentrations in the exhaust gas cannot exceed 20 mg/m^3.[76] In other words, the first provision is designed to reduce total emissions, and the second is designed to reduce VOC concentrations in the exhaust gas.

d. VOC Emission Limits and Control Requirements for Paint Shops

TA Luft, much like the U.S. NSPS, contains additional regulations for specific categories of industrial facilities,[77] including automobile assembly plant paint shops.[78] The regulations assert that the emission standards and control requirements can by met by state-of-the-art technology,[79] as required by the federal act. The 1986 VOC standards establish VOC emission limits of 60 g/m^2 of car body for nonmetallic paints and 120 g/m^2 for metallic paints.[80] That is, the emission limits depend on the type of paint used and are proportional to the size and number of vehicles produced. In 1991 the Ministry for the Environment revised both of these limits to 35 g/m^2, effective March 1, 1994.

The paint shop regulations also limit the VOC concentration in the exhaust gas from the dryers to 50 mg/m^3. In addition, the *Dynamisierungsklausel*—essentially a less stringent BACT requirement—requires further reductions if new control technologies become available.[81] These various requirements must be specified in the license "for each individual source."[82]

2. PERMITTING PROCEDURES

The *BImSchG* requires the licensing authority to give public notice of the project after it receives a permit application.[83] For new facilities, the agency must make public the permit application and any supporting documents submitted by the firm (except for documents that might reveal trade secrets).[84] For modified facilities, the agency need not make the permit application and documents available for public inspection if the modification does not increase emissions.[85]

Members of the public have one month to review the permit application and supporting documents and another two weeks to make written objections. There is no provision for a public hearing. The licensing authority must seek the opinion of other regulatory agencies, and it must "discuss the arguments against the project with the applicant and those having raised them."[86] Relative to the United States, the German licensing system is much less transparent to citizen groups, and much less subject to influence by interest groups, especially opposition groups.

The act does not specify a time limit in which the licensing agency must decide whether to issue a license for new facilities, although it provides that the agency must make a licensing decision for a modified facility within six months. That period can be extended for successive three-month periods "if the difficult nature of verification so requires."[87]

C. Summary and Comparison

Although it is difficult to make precise comparisons (because the two countries use different types of standards), it appears that the U.S. standards are stricter, more detailed, and more intrusive, especially in nonattainment areas, and it is evident that U.S. procedures provide much greater opportunity for public participation in agency permitting decisions.

1. DIVISION OF REGULATORY AUTHORITY

Under both U.S. and German law, the federal government is responsible for setting air quality standards, and the states are responsible for permitting and enforcement. The U.S. regulatory system, however, involves greater federal oversight; the EPA must approve the SIP—which contains each facility's emission limits—and air pollution permits are subject to EPA approval. In addition, the EPA has concurrent enforcement authority, and may even take over permitting and enforcement functions if it deems state efforts systematically inadequate. In Germany, there is no federal oversight of the permitting or enforcement process.

2. AMBIENT STANDARDS AND AIR QUALITY PLANS

Both countries establish air quality standards and have provisions for air quality plans, although the U.S. requirements are more demanding. First, the NAAQS are set at a level designed to protect public health without regard to control costs. The German *immission* values are subject to the proportionality principle, which requires a balance of costs and benefits.

More importantly for this study, Germany has not adopted a numerical *immission* value for ozone; regulators must decide on a case-by-case basis whether VOC emissions, which eventually cause ozone, may endanger human health or the environment. Whereas every state in the United States must have an SIP—or face serious economic sanctions—only certain areas in Germany need to develop such plans, which in any event do not have the force of law.

3. EMISSION LIMITS FOR CERTAIN INDUSTRIAL CATEGORIES

Both the U.S. and German laws establish emission limits for categories of industrial polluters. In both countries, the air pollution statute instructs the federal environmental agency to set such limits for categories of industrial facilities that might endanger public health or the environment. In addition, the U.S. and German agencies must establish emission limits that reflect the best control technology, taking into account costs.

The established emission limits are somewhat different, however. The U.S. EPA has set separate emission limits for the three different coating processes in the automobile assembly plant, proportional to the volume of applied solids. The German Ministry for the Environment, on the other hand, has set a single overall emission limit (proportional to the area of the painted surface).[88] The single emission standard gives German manufacturers greater flexibility during the production process and potentially reduced monitoring and reporting requirements.

4. EMISSION LIMITS DESIGNED TO ACHIEVE OR MAINTAIN AIR QUALITY

Although both countries establish air quality standards, they have adopted rather different means to achieve those standards. In U.S. nonattainment areas, the facility must obtain offsets, must install control measures reflecting the "lowest achievable emission rate" regardless of offsets obtained, and must show that the benefits of the new facility outweigh its environmental and social costs.[89] In other words, the facility must both reduce pollution *and* install state-of-the-art control technologies. In U.S. attainment areas (PSD), the facility need not obtain offsets, but it must adopt controls equivalent to the BACT.

The German approach is potentially simpler and probably less demanding. Where the agency has established an *immission* value, the sum of the initial load and the additional load may not exceed the *immission* value by more than 1 percent.[90] If the agency has not established an *immission* value for a particular pollutant, the agency must assure itself that the new pollution load will not threaten human health or the environment. In short, the German regulations are focused exclusively on not significantly increasing the exceedence of the *immission* value, whereas the U.S. system emphasizes both reducing the exceedence and employing the best technological controls.

5. ODORS

The U.S. Clean Air Act does not address odors, which generally are left to state pollution regulations and nuisance law. However, because state pollution agencies normally issue air pollution permits, they may include provisions designed to control odors from industrial operations. State environmental agencies are more likely to require control of odors in relatively clean areas located near residential areas, where new industrial odors would be noticeable or more easily traced to a particular source.

By contrast, the *BImSchG* and *TA Luft* deal explicitly and extensively with odors. The act specifically defines air pollution as including "odorous substances,"[91] and *TA Luft* contains detailed provisions to ensure the dispersion of air pollution that is vented to the atmosphere.[92] As in the United States, the agency is likely to be more attentive to odorous emissions (e.g., require taller emission stacks for better dispersion) in areas that are not already heavily polluted.

6. PUBLIC PARTICIPATION

Both U.S. and German regulatory procedures allow some opportunity for public participation in the agency's permit decision, although the opportunities are more extensive in the United States. For example, under U.S. law, members of the public are permitted to review and comment on all air pollution permit applications, and in many states they may petition the agency to initiate a formal contested administrative hearing, replete with counsel, cross-examination, and an administrative law judge to decide whether to issue or deny the permit.

Under German law, the licensing authority must give public notice of each project, but it must permit public review and comment only if the facility is new or if the modified facility is expected to cause additional or new types of air pollution. Proposed modifications that would not result in a net increase in emissions are not subject to public review and comment. There are no provisions requiring public meetings or administrative hearings in advance of the agency's decision to grant or deny the permit.

IV. THE U.S. PERMITTING PROCESS

A. *The Permitting Process in an Ozone Attainment Area*

Turning the corner of a curving road in the Highland Park area of St. Paul, Minnesota, the last thing one expects to see is a truck assembly plant. The lawns are trimmed, the hedges are sculpted, and the roads are tree-lined and recently paved. Many of the homes are single-family houses, with a scattering of small apartment houses and a few larger apartment buildings. Located a few miles from downtown St. Paul, the neighborhood has a middle-class, suburban look. Many of the residents are professionals, including lawyers, doctors, government officials, and business owners.

Yet the residential neighbors sit in uneasy juxtaposition with Ford's Twin Cities Assembly Plant. Located immediately east of the Mississippi River, the facility is just west of a shopping center and is surrounded by the Highland Park residential neighborhood. The proximity of the assembly plant to the neighborhood has been a source of conflicts, some arising from odors and potential health effects of air pollutants emitted by the plant's paint shop.

The EPA has designated the St. Paul area (indeed, the entire state) as an attainment area for ozone. One reason for the good air quality in the state is the relative dearth of large VOC emitters. None of the largest twenty-five VOC emitters is located in Minnesota,[93] and the EPA lists only five industrial facilities with VOC emissions greater than 1,000 short tons per year, and only one hundred facilities with more than 100 short tons per year.[94] At the time of this study, the Ford assembly and painting operations emitted about 1,000 tons of VOCs annually, making it one of the largest VOC emitters in the state.[95]

Over 13,000 people live within a mile of Ford's assembly plant, and approximately 150,000 live within three miles, for a population density of 6,200 people per square mile. Within a mile of the plant 5 percent of the population is minority, and 12 percent is below the poverty line; within a three-mile radius, the percentages are 8 and 15, respectively. These percentages are significantly smaller than the corresponding numbers for the county, and well below the national figures.[96] The median household and per capita income for the county are slightly greater than the national medians, and in 1994 the unemployment rate for the county was 3 percent. The area near the Ford facility is wealthier than the rest of the county.

Ford Motor Company opened its Twin Cities truck assembly plant in 1925. In recent years the facility has employed approximately 2,000 workers, who annually produce more than 100,000 trucks.[97] Most of the VOCs come from the coating lines—the e-coat, the guidecoat, and the topcoat. Because the Ford facility is a "major" facility under the Clean Air Act, any significant modification to the facility would subject Ford to federal NSPS emission limits and potentially to the federal PSD New Source Review process.

1. THE PERMIT PROCESS: DELAYS FROM PUBLIC CONCERNS ABOUT ODORS AND HEALTH EFFECTS

a. The Plan for a New Paint Shop

In the early 1980s, Ford decided to make substantial changes at the Twin Cities facility—it wanted to produce a new model, a light-duty pickup truck called the Ford Ranger, to increase the line speed, and to build a new paint shop. The new paint shop would include a new e-coat line, a new urethane anti-chip coating line, and a new BC/CC topcoat line. Ford planned to incinerate the VOCs from the drying ovens before releasing the treated exhaust to the atmosphere. The company believed that these modifications would increase the efficiency of its operations, improve the quality of its product, and, in vain as it turned out, reduce odors in the nearby community.

Ford announced its plans in October 1983.[98] Within a month, the St. Paul Department of Planning and Economic Development gave its approval after concluding that the plans would impose no new burdens on traffic and would satisfy zoning and land use planning requirements. In early January 1984, the Minnesota Pollution Control Agency (MPCA), which had responsibility to implement state and federal air pollution laws, granted Ford an installation permit.[99] To avoid disrupting production, Ford continued to use the existing paint shop while it constructed the new facility. The company completed the new facility in August 1985, at a cost of $236 million.

b. The Innovative Technology Waiver from NSPS Emission Standards

In February 1984, shortly after it had begun construction, Ford applied to the EPA for an "innovative technology waiver" from the NSPS standards for its new BC/CC topcoat line.[100] Along with other U.S. manufacturers, Ford wanted the new line to compete successfully with foreign manufacturers in Europe and Japan, which also were using a BC/CC topcoat for automobiles and light-duty trucks.[101] According to U.S. automakers, the BC/CC topcoat was more appealing to customers and was more durable than the single-coating topcoat.

The BC/CC topcoats applied by foreign manufacturers used high-VOC-content coatings, which in the United States would require additional, expensive control equipment to meet federal NSPS standards. To meet the competition and achieve federal emission standards at a reasonable cost, automakers and paint manufacturers had embarked on a research program to develop low-VOC-content coatings and more efficient application technologies. To gain time while developing the new coatings, and not waste money on expensive end-of-the-pipe controls, Ford sought a waiver for its new BC/CC topcoat line.

In September 1984, the EPA gave public notice of its intent to grant the requested waiver and invited public comment.[102] Leslie Davis, president of Earth Protector, a local environmental group, and organizer of grassroots opposition efforts, objected.[103] Davis also gave Governor Rudy Perpich a petition with 250 signatures, urging him to withhold his consent for the waiver.[104] Perpich gave his consent.[105]

Roughly a year later, the EPA granted the waiver until December 31, 1986.[106] The EPA explained that for Ford to achieve the NSPS standards on the topcoat line it must limit production of vehicles using the BC/CC coating or install new emissions control equipment. The EPA deemed both options unreasonable, the first because it amounted to an "economic penalty," and the second because the $15 to 20 million price tag for controls was too high. The EPA expressed confidence that Ford and its paint suppliers would be able to comply by the end of 1986 and that the waiver created only a slight risk to public health.[107] Davis sought judicial review of the waiver, but the court of appeals upheld the EPA's decision.[108] As the EPA had predicted, Ford was able to meet the NSPS standards by the end of 1986 with the reformulated paints.[109]

c. Neighbors' Complaints about Odors and MPCA's Denial of Ford's Operating Permit

Although the political and legal battle over the waiver did not slow Ford's efforts to bring the new paint shop on line, it signaled a broader grassroots opposition to the Ford plant that grew out of long-standing complaints about odors from the paint shop and evolved to include health concerns. These concerns did not abate with the opening of the new paint shop in August 1985 (which included a new incinerator) or with Ford's use of low-VOC solvent-based coatings in 1986.

Neighbors' complaints about odors from the paint shop dated back at least to 1979.[110] In 1984, the last year of operation of the old paint shop, the MPCA received over 300 complaints from residents, and Ford received 140 complaints directly. The complaints continued after Ford closed the old paint shop and began operating the new shop.[111] Citizens complained not only about the disagreeable odors but also about minor health effects and potentially more serious health risks.[112]

Leslie Davis led the initial grassroots effort, which evolved into the Ford Oversight Community Task Force.[113] Davis sought political support from a number of sources. In addition to a 250-signature petition opposing the NSPS waiver, Davis contacted United Automobile Workers (UAW) officials about worker exposure to chemicals, which caused union officials to ask the MPCA about the best controls for solvent vapors.[114] He wrote letters to local newspapers,[115] succeeded in generating news stories on odors from the facility,[116] and contacted *60 Minutes* in an unsuccessful effort to get the investigative television show to report on the facility.[117] He took his case to the St. Paul City Council,[118] which eventually adopted a resolution requesting health studies of the VOC emissions from the facility.[119]

Davis's political activity began to pay off. In December 1986, the MPCA asked Ford to undertake an odor abatement study and delayed Ford's "total operating facility" permit application, which it had submitted in March 1986, thus giving activists, such as Davis, an opportunity to seek redress for their concerns.

In March 1987, the MPCA scheduled a public meeting to consider a staff recommendation to approve the permit.[120] An MPCA official contacted Davis about finding neighborhood representatives to work with the agency on the draft permit. In the meantime, however, another citizen group, the Highland Area Citizens Task Force on Ford Emissions, formed to demand changes to the proposed permit. The new group, which was less confrontational than Earth Protector, thought the permit should include requirements for emissions testing and a health-risk assessment by an independent consultant.[121]

In late May 1987, the MPCA rescheduled the public meeting on the proposed permit and reopened the comment period. In correspondence with the new neighborhood group, MPCA staff indicated that they did not think that Ford was required to install additional emissions controls to meet federal standards. However, MPCA staff proposed to recommend a facility emissions cap of 1,095 tons of VOCs to address the odor concerns.[122]

d. The Ford Air Quality Task Force and the Negotiated Operating Permit

The controversy had become heated, and there was danger that the disputants' positions would irremediably harden. Both Earth Protector and the Highland Area Citizens Task Force requested a formal administrative hearing.[123] However, MPCA officials feared that a hearing would delay issuance of a final permit by several months, and private citizens feared that it would be expensive and perhaps futile.

The solution was a new task force that included representatives from all points of view—the Ford Air Quality Task Force. This group, formed in June 1987, included elected officials, members of the University of Minnesota School of Public Health, and representatives from the Minnesota Department of Health, the St. Paul Division of Public Health, MPCA, Ford, and the community, including Leslie Davis and Judith Krasnow from the Highland Area Citizens Task Force.[124] After appointing the task force, the politically appointed MPCA Board[125] authorized Ford to continue production under the 1984 construction permit while a new facility permit was being prepared, so long as Ford limited its production to forty-five vehicles per hour and limited total annual VOC emissions to 1,095 tons.[126] Contemporaneous accounts indicate that the task force quickly reduced the adversarial atmosphere, which was replaced by a spirit of cooperation.[127]

On the task force's recommendation Ford retained two environmental consulting groups—TRC Environmental Consultants to test for odors and other air emissions and Clement Associates to perform a health-risk assessment of emissions from the paint shop.[128] The consultants' studies and the task force report were not completed until early 1990, two and one-half years after MPCA staff formed the task force.

TRC Environmental Consultants confirmed that Ford's facility was causing disagreeable odors in the residential community, and it identified the central spray booth stack as the main culprit.[129] TRC also concluded that the final repair spray booth, the final repair oven, and the e-coat cooling tunnel might be contributing to the odor problem.

In May 1989, before the task force could make a formal recommendation, Ford obtained permission from the group and a permit from the MPCA to raise the stack from 139 feet to 189 feet and to change the shape of the stack opening.[130] The higher, reshaped stack would not reduce VOC emissions, but it would disperse them better. In October 1989, Ford formally proposed two additional improvements that tracked the consultant's report: to improve the emissions collection system and replace the afterburner on the e-coat bake oven, and to combine the eight, relatively short stacks for the final repair operations into a single hundred-foot stack.[131] Together, these changes, which cost Ford $4.4 million and took more than a year to complete, totally eliminated odor complaints from Ford's facility.

Meanwhile, in November 1988, Clement Associates presented its results estimating both short-term and long-term (e.g., cancer) health risks. After the MPCA submitted its own methodology to calculate health risks, the Ford Air Quality Task Force spent several months discussing the consultant's report and the MPCA's comments. Based on this study, the task force concluded that "developmental effects" and "adverse health effects due to long-term exposure to substances emitted from the plant are highly unlikely,"[132] although it also acknowledged the potential for short-term minor effects.

The task force prepared a draft report by August 1989 and issued its final report in late February 1990. The group recommended that Ford reduce VOC emissions by 10 percent "to compensate for these uncertainties in the [health] assessment," and that Ford periodically evaluate the need for a new health-risk assessment. Ford agreed to the 10 percent reduction in emissions to assure members of the public that they faced no health risks from the VOC emissions.[133]

Meanwhile, Ford continued to seek authorization to make additional improvements to its paint shop. In October 1989 the company sought authorization to update the anti-chip coating operation.[134] In addition, Ford wanted to increase the number of Rangers receiving a BC/CC from 20.6 to 32.2 per hour.[135] Although the Ford Air Quality Task Force had not yet issued its report, Ford knew it would recommend a 10 percent reduction in emissions. Consequently, Ford proposed to install a new VOC emission control system for the topcoat line, namely, to replace the afterburner on the spray booth with a carbon adsorption system to concentrate the VOCs and an incinerator to burn the desorbed VOCs.

In April 1991, after a year of negotiations, MPCA staff and Ford reached agreement on a draft operating permit. Aside from the technical permit conditions, the principal effect of the permit was that it imposed an annual VOC emissions limit of 934 tons, roughly a 14 percent decrease from VOC emissions of 1,088 tons in 1987–88, when the task force commissioned the health-risk assessment. However, the proposed cap was a net increase of 39.2 tons of VOCs when measured under federal criteria (i.e., average emissions over the previous four years).[136] Because this increase was still less than the "significant" threshold level under the PSD regulations,[137] the permit was not subject to the burdensome requirements of New Source Review; nonetheless, the emission controls met the stringent LAER standards normally required in nonattainment areas.[138] Plainly these stringent requirements were not necessary to meet the federal PSD standards; the MPCA required them to address the odor and health concerns of the neighbors.

Neither the task force nor the EPA had any significant comments or suggestions that threatened to derail MPCA approval of the permit.[139] On May 28, 1991, the MPCA held a public meeting to discuss the proposed permit. Only fourteen people attended. At its June 25, 1991, meeting, the MPCA Citizens Board approved the permit. Ford installed the new pollution control equipment over the next eighteen months at a cost of $24 million.

2. PERMIT CONDITIONS

The thirty-four-page permit imposed several categories of "special conditions," including VOC emission limits, operating requirements, compliance demonstration requirements, construction schedule requirements, and requirements to undertake periodic health-risk assessments.[140] Many of the permit provisions were required by the federal Clean Air Act, but some, especially those concerning odors, were solely the product of state law.

a. Emission Limits

The permit required the coating lines to meet the mandatory federal NSPS emission standards for the various coating lines,[141] and it imposed an annual VOC emissions cap of 934 tons from all painting operations, including repair and touch-up operations in the assembly plant,[142] as well as monthly emission limits.[143]

The permit included special provisions for odors. In addition to requiring the spray booth stack to be 189 feet above grade, the permit imposed "odor emission limits" as required by state regulations. In particular, it specified that the emission limit for the assembly plant touch-up operations and paint shop paint mixing operations was 25 "odor concentration units,"[144] for the spray booth stack the emission limit was 1 million odor concentration units, and for all other stacks the emission was 150 odor concentration units. In addition, there could be no detectable odors outside the facility's borders.[145]

b. Operating Requirements

The permit established numerous operating requirements.[146] For example, it required Ford to notify the MPCA of the cause and duration of breakdowns of control and continuous monitoring equipment;[147] to maintain and monitor a minimum temperature in the incinerators;[148] to keep daily operating records and calculate monthly emissions to demonstrate compliance with emission limits;[149] and to ensure that the emissions control equipment meets minimum efficiencies.[150] Most important, from Ford's point of view, the permit imposed two sets of production limits—53 vehicles per hour in the paint shop, and 44.5 vehicles per hour in the assembly plant, an increase from 40 vehicles per hour specified in the temporary operating permit.[151] Thus, as a result of the five-year delay in obtaining a final operating permit, Ford's truck production potentially was reduced by more than 100,000 trucks.[152]

c. Compliance Demonstration

The permit required Ford to undertake a variety of testing procedures to ensure that control technologies are functioning properly. For example, the company must determine the efficiencies of the carbon adsorption system and the incinerators[153] and must file monthly reports demonstrating compliance with federal emission limits and the total annual emissions cap of 934 tons.[154] Every three years, or whenever Ford makes a change that "substantively bears on the health risk of the emissions," Ford must undertake a new health-risk assessment.[155]

B. The Permitting Process in an Ozone Nonattainment Area

The area immediately surrounding Ford's assembly plant in Edison Township, New Jersey, is a mixed-use area, with light and heavy industry, commercial strips, and blue-collar residential neighborhoods. According to the local chamber of commerce, Edison has "crowded industrial parks," including the largest industrial park in New Jersey. The Ford plant borders U.S. Highway 1, along with car dealerships and strip malls.

The EPA has designated Middlesex County as a "severe" nonattainment area for ozone. Some of the ozone is the product of VOC and nitrogen oxides emissions from the substantial vehicular traffic in the area, which is crisscrossed by four major highways.[156] Local industrial operations also contribute to the VOC load, as do more distant sources. New Jersey itself is relatively industrialized. Two of the largest twenty-five VOC emitters in the nation are located in or border New Jersey, and twenty-one industrial facilities in New Jersey (eight of which are in Middlesex County or adjacent counties) emit more than 1,000 short tons of VOCs annually, compared with only five facilities in all of Minnesota. The total annual industrial VOC emissions for the state are approximately 89,000 short tons, compared with 31,000 short tons in Minnesota.[157] Moreover, because New Jersey is downwind from the heavy industrial region of the Ohio Valley, it receives that region's ozone.

The demographic profile of the residential area near the Edison plant is similar in some respects to that near Ford's St. Paul facility, as illustrated by Table 6.2. Although the per capita income of Edison Township is slightly higher than the New Jersey average and nearly 50 percent greater than the U.S. average,[158] the residential neighborhoods closest to Edison's Ford facility are blue-collar, whereas the corresponding neighborhoods near the St. Paul facility are middle-class and largely professional. Thus, although the overall county demographics are similar, the demographics of the immediate neighborhoods are different.

The Edison assembly plant, which opened in 1948, produced Pintos in the 1970s and Escorts during the 1980s. In the late 1980s, when demand for the Escort fell, Ford decided to consolidate Escort production from two plants. In part because of the significant additional capital investment that would be required for pollution controls to meet the stringent nonattainment requirements, Ford seriously considered closing the Edison facility.

An area's air quality attainment status may be a significant factor in a company's decision whether to retool or relocate.[159] One reason may be that federal law requires more stringent pollution controls in nonattainment areas so that the state can demonstrate "reasonable further progress" toward attaining the national ambient air quality standards. Not only do stricter emission standards in nonattainment areas usually require more expensive pollution control technologies; they also may engender regulatory delay and conflict as state agencies seek to ensure compliance with federal law, and manufacturers seek to maintain or improve their competitive position. A state agency in nonattainment areas may insist on particularly stringent controls in order to avoid even more stringent federal regulations that would become mandatory if the state missed its attainment deadline. Such requirements, including greater offset ratios, would

TABLE 6.2   Demographics Near Ford Facilities in Edison, New Jersey, and St. Paul Minnesota

	New Jersey	Minnesota
Population density within 3 miles of the facility (people/square mile)	4,879	6,212
Population density within 1 mile of the facility (people/square mile)	4,852	4,731
% Minority population within 3 miles of the facility	12%	8%
% Households below the poverty line within 3 miles of the facility	8%	15%
% Unemployment in county	6%	3%
% Jobs in manufacturing in the county	20%	20%

increase the cost of modifying or constructing new industrial facilities and thus negatively affect the state economy.

Despite the potential advantages of building a new facility in an attainment area, Ford decided to retool the Edison plant to produce Ford Ranger and Mazda B-series trucks.[160] Ford also decided to upgrade the paint shop to install a BC/CC topcoat line for better vehicle finishes.

1. THE PERMIT PROCESS: DELAYS CAUSED BY AGENCY CONCERNS

In August 1987, Ford filed an application for a construction and operating permit with the New Jersey Department of Environmental Protection (NJDEP). In the application, Ford proposed to upgrade the paint shop to allow the use of new coatings such as the BC/CC topcoat. After a year of negotiations over Ford's data and emissions calculations and the adequacy of the control technologies, the NJDEP denied the application, specifically refusing to permit the BC/CC system.

In September 1989, Ford submitted a revised application for the guide-coat and topcoat lines. This application sought only a single-coating line, not a BC/CC line. Ford was desperate to open the new Ranger truck line, even if it meant using an old and less competitive paint technology. Ford's calculations showed that the bulk of the VOCs (87 percent) came from the spray booth, and a much smaller proportion (13 percent) came from the bake oven. Nonetheless, the permit application proposed no controls on the spray booth; an afterburner would do little to reduce VOCs in the relatively dilute exhaust stream from the spray booth, and Ford did not want to install a relatively expensive carbon adsorption/afterburner system for what would be a temporary paint line. The application proposed an afterburner for the relatively concentrated VOC exhaust from the bake oven, which would eliminate nearly 95 percent of the bake oven VOCs. Ford estimated the topcoat line, based on a reduced rate of forty Ranger trucks per hour and two work shifts, would emit approximately 500 short tons of VOCs annually.[161] In mid-December 1989, the NJDEP approved the permits, relying on reduced solvent concentrations and the afterburner to ensure that the modification would not result in an increase in emissions.

In March 1990, Ford resubmitted its permit application for the BC/CC topcoat line. The application proposed not only an afterburner on the bake oven but also separate carbon adsorption systems for each portion of the topcoat line and an afterburner for the desorbed VOCs. Despite these controls, the VOC emissions would increase to 740 tons annually. A month later, Ford submitted a "state-of-the-art analysis" to demonstrate that a proposed carbon adsorption system would adequately control emissions from the proposed BC/CC topcoat line.

Ford and the NJDEP continued to meet and negotiate over the terms of the permit. According to Ford officials, the relationship was strained: they describe the NJDEP as antagonistic, bureaucratic, and uncooperative, and the delays caused Ford to reconsider its decision to retool the Edison plant. The NJDEP thought the delay resulted from Ford's repeated failure to provide critical information necessary to evaluate the permit application and ensure that the air quality region would make "reasonable further progress" toward achieving attainment. The NJDEP did not approve the final permit until November 1994. The modifications to the control technologies cost Ford $31.7 million.

2. PERMIT CONDITIONS

The 1994 construction permit imposed several sets of conditions, including emission limits, operating requirements, monitoring requirements, testing requirements, and record-keeping and reporting requirements. These requirements were more demanding, more intrusive, and ultimately more burdensome than the requirements in the St. Paul permit. A principal factor was that the Edison plant was in a nonattainment area, and thus had to meet stricter federal and state standards, but the differences also may have reflected NJDEP's more aggressive approach.

a. Emission Limits

The NJDEP established hourly, daily, and annual VOC emission limits for both the prime coat line and the topcoat lines, including separate hourly emission limits for different parts of the spray booth and the bake oven. The St. Paul permit, by contrast, imposed only monthly and annual limits for each coating line, with no separate limits for the spray booths or ovens.

Such detailed emission limits, which were more than EPA regulations required, significantly constrained Ford's flexibility during production and effectively increased the monitoring and reporting requirements.

b. Composition of the Paint

In addition to emission limits, the NJDEP imposed restrictions on the amount of volatile organic solvent (VOS) in the different coatings, including both a maximum amount of VOS for each coating category and a weighted average for all paints of that category.

c. Operating Requirements

The permit imposed numerous conditions on the type of fuel and rate of fuel usage for the afterburners,[162] and it specified detailed operating conditions for the emission controls, including the minimum destruction efficiency, operating temperature, and residence time for the afterburners,[163] and the minimum removal efficiency for the carbon adsorbers.[164] In addition, the permit limited the plant operating time to 4,700 hours per year, or roughly two shifts, and it imposed hourly, daily, and annual production limits.[165]

The permit required Ford to install a continuous VOC monitor and recorder after each carbon adsorber.[166] Ninety days before installing the monitors, Ford must submit for NJDEP approval detailed information on the monitors and recorders.[167] After reviewing the stack tests, the NJDEP may require installation of continuous emission monitors in the afterburner stacks.[168]

d. Testing Requirements

Within 180 days of beginning operations, Ford must verify compliance with emission limits. The required tests include (1) stack tests to measure the concentration of VOCs in the gas vented from the thermal oxidizers and carbon adsorbers at the maximum production of 50 Rangers per hour;[169] (2) determination of the efficiency of various technological controls;[170] and (3) determination of the solvent content of the prime, BC, and CC coats.[171] Ford must test the solvent content of the paint monthly, and must undertake a stack test every five years.[172] The permit specified the test methods[173] and required Ford to obtain prior approval for its testing protocols and test date.[174]

e. Record-Keeping and Reporting Requirements

The permit established substantial record-keeping and reporting requirements. It required Ford to maintain all records—daily production rates, colors, paint and solvent usage, VOS content of the paint, natural gas consumption (for the thermal oxidizers), and monitoring data—on-site for at least five years, to be made available to regulatory officials on demand.[175]

Ford must report any violations of the emission limits or operating conditions within two days of their discovery, along with a description of the cause of the violation and the measures taken to correct it "as expeditiously as practicable."[176] If emissions, including odors, pose "a potential threat to public health, welfare or the environment, or . . . might reasonably result in citizen complaints," Ford must notify the NJDEP immediately.[177]

Ford must submit a quarterly report to the NJDEP and the Middlesex County Health Department. The report must include (1) tables showing the daily use of coatings and solvents in the spray prime, the topcoat, and the "purge and wipe"; (2) tables demonstrating compliance with requirements establishing emission limits from paint and solvent content of paint; (3) all excess emission reports from the continuous emission monitors; and (4) a summary of all exceedences and corrective actions.[178]

C. Comparing the Permit Process at St. Paul and Edison

Although Ford experienced substantial delays in obtaining its air pollution permit at both the St. Paul and the Edison facilities, the permit processes were quite different. Ford officials bemoan the antagonistic relationship with NJDEP officials but describe their relationship with MPCA officials in positive, constructive terms. Moreover, Ford officials do not have a negative view of public participation at the St. Paul facility. On the contrary, they view it—especially when it took the form of the Ford Air Quality Task Force, which brought all interested parties together—as an opportunity for Ford to understand the public's concerns and to take reasonable steps to address them, and as an opportunity for the company to explain the actions it took to mitigate environmental harms.

This variability is not necessarily related to the fact that St. Paul is in an attainment area and Edison is in a severe nonattainment area. First, Ford officials did not press the MCPA to complete the permit process quickly. Indeed, they acknowledged that the interim St. Paul permit, which permitted Ford to use the BC/CC line in the new paint shop while the task force completed its studies and then while Ford and the MPCA negotiated a permit, imposed few burdensome or inflexible controls on the company's operation. Ford was confident that so long as the MPCA and the public viewed it as working in good faith to address the health and odor concerns raised by the neighbors, the MPCA eventually would issue a reasonable permit. However, had Ford needed to obtain the permit more quickly, it might have viewed the extensive, slow process of public participation with alarm. Second, Ford was able find a relatively inexpensive, quickly implemented solution to the long-standing concerns about odors from the plant. If Ford had been unable to find a satisfactory solution to the odor problem,

the permit process probably would have been more rather than less contentious.

V. THE PERMITTING PROCESS IN GERMANY

A. Cologne

Located on the Rhine River in the *Land* of Nordrhein-Westfalen in western
Germany, Cologne is a cultural and industrial center of approximately one
million people. The federal government has designated the region as an
area of serious air pollution. This designation requires the *Land* government to monitor air quality and draft an air quality plan.[179]

Ford's body and assembly plant in Cologne, which produces Fiestas,
Scorpios, and Pumas, employs more than five thousand workers. Much of
the paint shop was designed, built, and permitted in the late 1970s and
early 1980s.

1. THE PERMIT PROCESS: EXTENDED NEGOTIATIONS WITH A MODERATE AMOUNT OF PUBLIC PARTICIPATION

In February 1986, the federal Ministry for the Environment promulgated
TA Luft, imposing a new regime of air pollution controls on industrial
facilities, including emission standards for paint shops in automobile assembly plants. About the same time, Ford decided to modernize and re-
organize its paint shop at the Cologne plant, including the construction of
two new topcoat lines that could handle one-color, two-color, and metallic
painting. Because of the large scale of the construction project, Ford
wanted to complete it in three stages over a period of two and one-half
years. Because the project involved fundamental changes (*wessentlichen Än-
derung*) to the facility, Ford needed a new permit that would comply with
TA Luft requirements.

In March 1987, Ford applied to the Cologne factory inspectorate (*Staatliches Gewerbeaufsichtsamt Köln*) for a permit to modify its paint shop. The
agency sent the permit application to local agencies for comment (e.g., fire
service, water quality). Over the next eight months Ford and the inspectorate negotiated the details of the permit. Both Ford and agency officials
felt somewhat handicapped because it was their first experience with the
new *TA Luft* requirements.

In early November 1987, the *Staatliches Gewerbeaufsichtsamt Köln* announced the project in local newspapers and the official gazette for Cologne, informing the public that the proposed permit and supporting documents were available for review until mid-January 1988. During the review
period, several neighbors in the Merkenich and Flittard areas of Cologne
filed written objections to the project on the ground that the existing fa-

cility emitted noxious odors and that the new facility would continue to do so. In early February 1988, after the agency agreed to study and address the problem in the new permit, the neighbors withdrew their objections.

In response to these concerns, Ford retained a consulting firm to determine whether extending some of the emission stacks would adequately disperse the odors. The consulting firm used a dispersion model to estimate whether odors would be perceptible after construction of the new facility. According to the model, the Flittard residents would encounter perceptible odors less than 5 percent of the time, and some residential blocks in the Merkenich area would experience odors a bit more frequently.[180]

The agency concluded that this level of odors was acceptable, since the land development plans for both areas allowed a mixture of residential and industrial uses, and the permit would reduce VOC emissions from the plant and improve the area's air quality.[181] The agency concluded that there would be no harmful environmental effects related to the odors, as long as Ford extended the two stacks to ninety-nine and fifty-eight meters. These measures, the agency concluded, would meet the statutory requirement of "state-of-the-art" (*Stand der Technik*) controls. Ford readily agreed to raise the stacks.

The consulting firm also used the dispersion model to determine whether there would be any health effects from Class II or Class III organic chemicals, and concluded there would be none. Nonetheless, the inspectorate prohibited use of carcinogens and Class I organic chemicals.[182]

In late August 1988, seventeen months after Ford filed its application, the *Staatliches Gewerbeaufsichtsamt Köln* issued the permit. Although the agency approved most of the permit application, it rejected two important elements. The first issue arose in connection with the use of metallic paint. In the past, metallic paints had been a large source of VOC emissions, and a switch to water-based metallic paints would significantly reduce VOC emissions. Ford, however, wanted the flexibility to be able to switch back to VOC solvent-based metallic paints if the water-based paints gave poor-quality results. Ford argued that the air purification system described in the proposed permit would ensure that VOC emission levels were no greater than with water-based paints. The agency, however, rejected Ford's request, citing insufficient data about the air purification system.

The second issue concerned the VOC control technologies for the electrostatic application zone (*ESTA Zone*) of the prime coating line. The proposed permit contained plans to construct a specific carbon adsorption/afterburner system and a more generally described air purification system. The agency found the description of the latter too vague to meet *TA Luft* requirements for this part of the paint shop, and it required Ford to install the specifically described control system.[183]

The permitting process, although not lengthy by U.S. standards, was exacerbated by three factors. First, the agency's review was more comprehensive because the application was for a new paint shop rather than the modification of an existing one. Second, this was Ford's and the agency's first attempt to negotiate a permit under new *TA Luft* requirements. Because *TA Luft* is not specific about the type or extent of monitoring, for example, it took the parties additional time to work out the details. Ford officials claimed that their experience with the Cologne permit helped expedite the process of obtaining subsequent permits, such as the Saarlouis permit, which took less than five months. Third, the neighbors' objections to odors delayed the permit process somewhat—perhaps as much as three months, according to Ford officials.

2. PERMIT CONDITIONS

The forty-five-page permit specified the construction schedule, stack heights, VOC emission limits, and monitoring and record-keeping requirements. Relative to the U.S. permits, the Cologne permit was less detailed (except regarding stack heights) and allowed the facility greater flexibility to achieve compliance.

a. Construction Schedule

The permit provided a detailed construction schedule (negotiated with Ford) for the new paint shop. The permit was set to expire by March 1991 if the new facilities were not operational by that date.

b. Stack Heights

The permit specified in great detail the heights and diameters of the various stacks at the facility, including the ninety-nine-meter and fifty-eight-meter stacks to control odors.[184]

c. VOC Emissions

The permit listed the VOC emission concentration limits (*Massenkonzentrationsbegrenzungen*) for various parts of the paint shop, including technical requirements for measuring the concentrations.[185] In general, the maximum concentrations were smaller than the *TA Luft*, although the permit followed *TA Luft* for carcinogens and Class I organic materials.[186] Because this set of standards was focused on concentrations, it probably was related to odor control and health effects from VOCs.

The permit also listed the VOC emission rates (*Massenstrombegrenzungen*) for different parts of the paint shop, as well as technical standards for measuring the emissions.[187] In contrast to emission concentrations, this set of limits restricted total VOC atmospheric loading, and thus probably was more related to ozone formation. Total annual VOC emissions could not exceed 1,275 metric tons.[188]

d. Monitoring and Record Keeping

The permit required continuous monitoring of certain parameters, including VOC emission concentrations and emission rates of the gas escaping from the afterburners and the carbon adsorption systems.[189] The permit also required Ford to undertake a performance test of VOC emission concentrations and emission rates within three to twelve months of beginning operations in the paint shop and to report the results, including measurement techniques and operating conditions, to the factory inspectorate.[190] Thereafter, it must undertake performance testing every three years.[191]

In addition, the permit required Ford to keep careful records of its solvent use in different parts of the facility and the number of vehicles painted.[192] The permit required the company to use this information, as well as the data from the continuous VOC monitors, to demonstrate that it did not exceed the annual VOC emission limit of 1,275 metric tons or the *TA Luft* emission limit of 60 g/m² (for most paint) and 120 g/m² (for metallic paint).[193]

Finally, Ford must keep records of all disturbances, including the type, cause, time, duration, and measures taken to rectify the problems.[194]

B. Saarlouis

Saarlouis is located in Saarland, a small, heavily industrialized *Land* in southwestern Germany, on the French border. Saarlouis is a small town of thirty-eight thousand, and the Ford assembly plant, with six thousand workers, is the largest employer in the town.

Ford's Saarlouis assembly plant, which began production in 1970, today produces more than 250,000 Ford Escort sedans and wagons annually. The facility is located next to a steel factory. The federal government has designated parts of Saarland, but not specifically Saarlouis, as a site of serious air pollution.

1. THE PERMIT PROCESS: SPEEDY ISSUANCE AND NO PUBLIC PARTICIPATION

In the early 1990s, Ford decided to modernize the topcoat line at the Saarlouis facility to permit both single-color painting and metallic paints, and to increase its production by 40 percent. Ford also needed to install new air pollution control technologies to meet stricter emission limits in *TA Luft,* which would take effect in early 1994. Because the modifications to the topcoat line and the increase in production were fundamental changes (*wesentliche Änderungen*), Ford needed to obtain a new permit.[195]

A few months before submitting its permit application, members of Ford's environmental and production staffs met with regulators from the Saarland Ministry of the Environment (*Ministerium für Umwelt*) in an effort to avoid any undue delays during the permitting process. At these meetings, company and agency officials discussed the agency's data requirements for the permit application. When the agency gave Ford a lengthy list of data requirements, company officials and regulators spent one month negotiating the level of detail required for the application.

On February 3, 1993, Ford submitted its permit application to the *Ministerium für Umwelt*. The Ministerium distributed various parts of the application to local regulatory authorities (i.e., water and construction agencies, each of which had participated in the earlier negotiation regarding the required data). The local agencies had four weeks to submit any objections to the *Ministerium für Umwelt*, during which time they met regularly with Ford representatives and visited the plant. As it turned out, these agencies had no objections to the draft permit negotiated by Ford and the Ministerium für Umwelt.

There was no public participation during the permit process. In fact, Ford deliberately avoided public participation by invoking a statutory provision that relieved the agency and Ford of any sort of public notice or hearing process.[196] That provision states that as long as the modification would not be expected to result in an increase in emissions, the agency need not give public notice of the modification nor make publicly available the permit application, the draft permit, or any other associated documents.[197]

The *Ministerium für Umwelt* issued the permit on June 28, 1993. In marked contrast to the permit process in Minnesota and New Jersey, the German permit process for the Saarland facility took less than five months. The capital cost of the emission controls for the modified facility was approximately $24 million.

2. PERMIT CONDITIONS

The Saarlouis permit is somewhat simpler than the Cologne permit. Although it specifies production and emission limits, control technologies, and monitoring requirements, the permit does not micromanage emissions in different parts of the facility. Rather, it imposes an annual emissions limit and an emissions limit based on the area of painted surfaces.

a. Production and Emissions Limits

Under its old permit, Ford's assembly plant produced approximately 1,400 vehicles daily. For vehicles receiving a regular paint coating, VOC emissions for each vehicle averaged 55 g/m^2, and for those receiving metallic paint, VOC emissions for each vehicle averaged 104 g/m^2. The plant emitted an average of 1,776 metric tons of VOCs annually.

Under the new permit, Ford was allowed to increase production to 1,950 vehicles per day, roughly a 40 percent increase (as a practical matter, this meant that Ford would add a third work shift). The permit required the VOC emissions per vehicle to be reduced to 35 g/m^2, regardless of the type of paint used, as required by the new *TA Luft* regulations that would become effective March 1994. The total VOC emissions for the facility would be 1,613 metric tons per year, a 9 percent decrease despite the 40 percent increase in production.[198]

b. Control Technologies

Much like the U.S. NSPS standards, *TA Luft* does not specify the particular controls a manufacturer must use to meet the numerical emission limits. Rather, it suggests using water-based or powder paints, carbon adsorption technologies, or some combination of the aforementioned. Ford's Saarlouis permit, however, was quite specific and left Ford no options. It required the company to install on the two topcoat lines three carbon adsorption wheels with a flow-through capacity of 200,000 m^3/hour, and to keep on reserve an additional carbon wheel in the event of a breakdown.[199] The purified air, which would be vented through a nineteen-meter stack, must contain no more than 100 mg VOCs/m^3.

The permit also required Ford to install two afterburners to incinerate the desorbed VOCs after the carbon wheels become saturated. The purified air, which also is vented up through a nineteen-meter stack, must contain no more than 20 mg VOCs/m^3. The agency specifically found that these controls met the statutory standards.[200] Together, the carbon adsorption systems and afterburners would ensure that the VOC emissions did not exceed 35 mg VOCs/m^3.[201]

c. Monitoring, Reporting, and Record Keeping

Ford must report the actual emission rate from the carbon adsorption wheels three months after beginning operations, and thereafter every six months. If the measurements are stable, and below the permit limits, Ford need only measure and report the emission rate every three years.[202] To ensure compliance with the emission rates from the afterburners, the company must continuously monitor and record the incineration temperature.[203]

Although the permit is not clear on the matter, Ford officials report that the air vented from the carbon wheels and the afterburners is continuously monitored. In addition, Ford must keep records of solvent usage (it relies on paint manufacturers for data on the solvent content of the paint), the amount of solvent disposed, the amount of solvent incinerated in the afterburners, and the number of car bodies painted.[204] From these data, Ford must estimate emissions and report the results annually.

Ford also must report any breakdown in the air purification system for the topcoat line, which must be armed with a visual and audio alarm system, within twenty-four hours, and it must promptly take measures to limit emissions as much as possible.[205] Ford must keep records on all disturbances on the topcoat line that might cause an increase in emissions—including the time, duration, type, cause, and corrective measures—for two years.

VI. ANALYSIS AND CONCLUSIONS

There are important similarities in the U.S. and German air pollution permit processes in this study. The permits required the facilities to use similar pollution control technologies, and the capital costs for the control technologies were comparable—in the range of $20 to $30 million. The emissions monitoring requirements also were similar. Although reporting requirements in the U.S. permits were somewhat more burdensome, the additional costs were not significant compared with the capital costs of the controls.

The principal difference—the time between the application and issuance of the permit—is striking. The German agencies approved the permits in five and seventeen months, whereas the U.S. agencies took over several years. At the St. Paul, Minnesota, facility, Ford was allowed to use its new paint technology but had to reduce production by as much as 100,000 trucks during the period of delay. At the Edison, New Jersey, facility, Ford had to reduce the rate of production *and* was barred for a few years from introducing the popular new topcoats. The opportunity costs potentially were substantial.[206] Several important factors—especially the degree of public participation, the stringency and detail of legal requirements and permits, and the extent of federal oversight—probably account for this substantial difference.

A. Public Participation

Public participation, and thus politicization of the permitting process, potentially plays a more prominent role in air pollution permitting processes in the United States than in Germany.[207] The U.S. legal structure strengthens the role of politics. In the United States, federal and state law requires every permit decision to be preceded by public notification, an opportunity for public comment, and a meeting where members of the public can voice their concerns and demand answers from regulators (and often company officials). Typically, state implementation plans provide an opportunity for contested administrative hearings (as well as judicial review) to resolve factual disputes underlying the permit decision. Entrepreneurial activists can use these procedures to generate publicity, create and energize a political constituency, and force the agency to address their concerns.

Under German law, by contrast, the opportunities for public participation are restricted. Most important, the *Land* environmental agency has no legal obligation to give public access to the proposed permit and supporting documents when the permit is for a facility modification, so long as the modification does not increase pollutant emissions. This limitation on public participation is not trivial. The Saarlouis permit expressly states that Ford requested the agency not to notify the public of the facility modification. A Ford memorandum confirms that the company wanted to install control technologies that would reduce total facility VOC emissions in part to avoid public notification of and comment on the draft permit.

Even when a German environmental agency must make the draft permit and supporting documents available to the public, the opportunity for public participation is more restricted than in the United States. German agencies accept written comments and objections from members of the public, but they are not required to hold a public meeting or initiate a contested administrative hearing. As a result, the opportunities for activists to generate political action are much more limited. Absent an extremely controversial issue—such as shipping nuclear waste, which literally brings protesters into the streets—political expression about permit decisions is suppressed.

The politicization of the U.S. permitting process—and the resulting delay and relative stringency of the permit—often is magnified by the political complexion of some agencies. In Minnesota, for example, the MPCA governing board is appointed by the governor and evidently is prepared to ignore the recommendations of its expert staff in controversial cases. In Germany, by contrast, the agency is viewed as neutrally implementing public policy expressed in *BImSchG*.

This is not to say that U.S. environmental agencies pander to activists' demands; indeed, such agencies may be more attentive to the needs of economically powerful interests. But they also may be more likely than the German air pollution agencies to take political pressures seriously and to look for political solutions. Bombarded with a steady stream of newspaper articles detailing the neighbor's concerns, and threatened with requests for a potentially divisive contested case hearing, the MPCA forged a political solution—it brought the entire range of disputants together in the Ford Air Quality Task Force, which systematically addressed public concerns about odors and health. Whether the MPCA was seeking a rational, nonadversarial and politically legitimate solution to a difficult problem, or whether it was seeking cover from political criticism and legal challenge, its approach led to a solution that Ford officials and most members of the public found acceptable.

As it turned out, odors from the paint shop at the St. Paul facility were a real and substantial problem whose solution came out of the process of public participation. Ford and the MPCA had had years to address the neighborhood's complaints about odors, but they failed to make significant progress on the issue until activists forced the issue in the context of a permit renewal.

The controversy over the odors eventually spawned a separate concern about public health. To a substantial degree, the very existence of this issue was Ford's fault for letting the odor controversy fester for so long. The controversy over health effects was also the predictable result of a style of political activism that seeks to create and energize a political constituency through predictions of dire consequences.[208] It bears noting, however, that the Ford Air Quality Task Force carefully addressed the issue by bringing in experts to evaluate the problem. The task force's conclusion and recommendation—that VOC emissions probably presented no significant threat to health but that total VOC emission should be reduced by 10 percent to provide a margin of safety—were hardly irrational or extreme.

As with the St. Paul facility, the modification of the Cologne facility was an occasion to raise community concerns about odors from the paint shop. The public announcement of the permit application gave neighbors an opportunity to file objections and caused the agency and Ford to investigate ways to reduce odors. There were important differences from the St. Paul process, however. First, in Cologne, the neighbors' only option was to file written objections. There were no opportunities for public meetings or administrative hearings to air disputes. The neighbors' only remedy was to file suit asserting that the permit violated their rights; such suits are costly and, given the usual deference to agency judgments, not likely to be successful. Second, the Cologne neighbors were not allowed to participate in choosing the consulting firm or in reviewing the consulting firms' methodology, assumptions, or conclusions. There was no agency-endorsed task force to oversee the technical process of analyzing odors and health effects. Third, the agency made no effort to eliminate all odors. Whereas the St. Paul permit expressly prohibits any perceptible odors beyond the plant boundaries, the Cologne permit recognizes that two neighborhoods would experience odors 5 to 6 percent of the time, but that such odors were acceptable in light of the overall reduction in VOC emissions and improvements in air quality. In short, the Cologne permit was less demanding than the St. Paul permit.

Without doubt, extensive public participation and the resulting politicization bring delay. Delay may be costly if it needlessly restricts production or delays introduction of new products. But delay also can be useful if it allows the agency to gather more information and find solutions to demonstrated problems. It is not clear how much Ford suffered from the delay in issuing the permit for the St. Paul facility. The EPA allowed Ford to have an "innovative technology waiver" from the NSPS standards for seventeen months, thereby allowing Ford additional time to attempt to meet the air pollution standards and eliminate noxious odors through new paint formulations and application technologies. When the odors (and complaints) persisted, the MPCA allowed Ford to use the new BC/CC line while the permit process proceeded. Under an agreement with the MPCA, Ford restricted its production rate and the total annual VOC emissions but otherwise operated under few restrictions. Ford officials commented that this arrangement was satisfactory to them, and although they surely wanted the permit controversy resolved, they never expressed great dismay with the slowness of the permitting process. In other words, although the delay was substantial, the legal system permitted agency officials enough discretion to accommodate the company's needs during the permit process.

B. Stringency and Detail

It is evident that U.S. statutory and regulatory requirements, and the resulting permit conditions, often are more detailed and stringent than the corresponding German requirements, especially in polluted areas. The Clean Air Act's NSPS program requires each coating line to meet separate emission limits. The nonattainment program requires the facility to achieve an overall reduction in emissions through offsets at other facilities, and separately to meet the LAER standards, which do not take control costs into account. The U.S. permits also are remarkably detailed. Some requirements, such as the extensive testing, monitoring, and reporting requirements, probably are irksome but not especially burdensome to a large company such as Ford (more detailed reporting requirements, however, may lead to greater compliance costs, since permit violations are easier to detect). Other requirements, however, such as the separate emission limits for numerous points in the paint shop and the specifications for paint formulations, severely limit Ford's flexibility to address sudden changes in the production line without providing corresponding environmental benefits. When the company regards such requirements as burdensome, conflict between the company and the agency is more likely to be exacerbated, resulting in delay.

A potential aspect of stringent and detailed standards, especially when coupled with large control costs, is the tendency to view permit disputes as legal matters rather than as technical matters. Conceivably, lawyers and the legal process may play a larger role in resolving disputes. In the two U.S. case studies, however, lawyers and litigation had virtually no direct role in the permit decisions. One reason may be that standards of judicial review are deferential to agency judgments; within boundaries defined by "substantial evidence" or "arbitrary, capricious, or an abuse of discretion," courts will uphold agency permit decisions. Another reason may be that because the firm and the agency have an ongoing relationship, the parties turn to litigation only as a last resort.

In Germany, by contrast, the number of standards and the monitoring requirements are less detailed, thereby affording the facility greater flexibility to deal with changes on the production line. The statutory "state-of-the-art" requirement, contrary to the U.S. LAER requirement in nonattainment areas, is based on the proportionality principle under which benefits and costs are balanced. Because the German permits involve fewer, less stringent, and inherently more flexible requirements, there is less for the agency and the company to fight about.

C. Federal Oversight

There is considerable federal oversight built into U.S. air pollution regulation—including the EPA's authority to approve SIPs and individual permits, to strip state agencies of the permitting and enforcement authority, and to impose economic sanctions on states that do not meet attainment deadlines. The oversight helps to motivate state agencies to apply federal standards vigorously and to demand greater proof that the facilities will meet the legal requirements, even in the absence of discernible public concern. Quite possibly, the existence of the federal nonattainment program, which together with EPA oversight can limit economic development in nonattainment areas unless new and modified sources make "reasonable further progress" to attainment, motivates state agencies to deal more aggressively with facilities seeking a new permit. Obtaining reductions in VOC emissions leaves room for other new or modified facilities.

In Germany there are no provisions for federal oversight; there is no federal approval of the *Länder* decisions, no federal authority to assume permitting and enforcement responsibilities, and no concurrent federal enforcement authority. These differences, which flow from fundamental structural differences in the *Grundgesetz* and the U.S. Constitution, relieve the *Länder* of political pressure that environmental activists might be able to exert through the federal government.

APPENDIX

For this study, we interviewed officials from Ford Motor Company, as well as representatives of other American, Japanese, and European automakers, the American Automobile Manufacturers Association, the Environmental Protection Agency, the New Jersey Department of Environmental Protection, the Minnesota Pollution Control Agency, and BASF (a paint manufacturer). We also reviewed agency documents, including permits, and emissions data.

PERSONS INTERVIEWED

Danielle R. Bigari, Environmental Quality Office, Ford Motor Co. (Dearborn, Mich.)

Kevin Butt, Manager of Environmental Affairs, Toyota Motor Corporate Services (Lexington, Ky.)

Hugo Clysters, Environmental Quality Office, Ford Motor Co. (Cologne, Germany)

Leslie Davis, Earth Protector (Minneapolis, Minn.)

Paul Harris, Environmental and Safety Engineering, Europe, Ford Motor Co. (Essex, England)

Robert Hitt, Manager of Community Affairs, BMW Manufacturing Corp. (Greer, S.C.)

Steve Hitte, Operating Permits Group, EPA (Research Triangle Park, N.C.)

Andy Hobbes, Ford Motor Co. (Essex, England)

Robert Johnson, Managing Engineer, Ford Motor Co. (St. Paul, Minn.)

John Kallush, Environmental Engineer (St. Paul, Minn.)

Neil Ledbetter, New United Motor Manufacturing, Inc. (Fremont, Calif.)

Joseph F. Lennon, Regional Manager Environmental Programs, Ford Motor Co. (Dearborn, Mich.)

Karin Lis, General Motors Corp. (Detroit, Mich.)

Roger Martin, Environmental Engineer, Ford Motor Co. (St. Paul, Minn.)

Pat McCarroll, General Motors Corp. (Detroit, Mich.)

Dean McGrath, American Automobile Manufacturers Association (Washington, D.C.)

Robert Niemi, Environmental Engineer (Dearborn, Mich.)

Frank Partee, Manager of Air Quality, Ford Motor Co. (Dearborn, Mich.)

Gene Praschan, American Automobile Manufacturers Association (Raleigh, N.C.)

Geoffrey T. Stevens, Environmental Planning and Control Section, Ford Motor Co. (Dearborn, Mich.)

Naomi Suss, PPG Industries (Troy Mich.)

NOTES

We would like to thank the members of the Comparative Legal Systems Project at U.C. Berkeley for their contributions to this work, and Heather Elliott for her assistance in translating the German permits. Also, this effort would not have been possible without the many industry and agency representatives who kindly and candidly shared with us the facts, figures, opinions and insights.

1. Office of Technology Assessment, *Catching Our Breath: Next Steps for Reducing Urban Ozone* (1989), 40–91; U.S. EPA, *Review of National Ambient Air Quality Standards for Ozone: Assessment of Scientific and Technical Information,* QAQPS Staff Paper (1996).

2. Because not all VOCs contribute to ozone formation, VOC regulations focus on so-called reactive VOCs. Some VOCs also are toxic or carcinogenic, and are subject to additional regulations.

3. According to the U.S. Environmental Protection Agency, U.S. auto assembly plants are the sixth-largest source of industrial VOC emissions when analyzed by SIC category, constituting 2.9 percent of all industrial VOC emissions. U.S. EPA Office of Air Quality Planning and Standards, *AIRSWeb, United States VOC Air Pollution Sources* (May 27, 1998).

Because of the importance of nonindustrial pollution sources (e.g., automobiles on the road and architectural coatings), however, auto assembly plants represent a significantly smaller fraction of the total VOC pollutant load nationwide. In 1996, VOC emissions in the United States totaled 19.086 million short tons. Of that total, 2.881 million short tons of VOCs (15 percent) came from solvents used in surface coatings, including architectural coatings, and 123,000 short tons of VOCs (0.64 percent of total VOC emissions) came from automobile and light truck painting. Only one auto assembly plant (not one considered in this study) is in the list of the top fifty VOC emitters. By comparison, 5.202 million short tons (27 percent of total VOCs) came from the exhaust of on-road vehicles. EPA, *National Air Pollutant Emission Trends, 1900–1996,* Appendix A (EPA-454/R-97–011, December 1997).

4. In the early 1970s, automobile paint shops used high-solvent-based lacquer or enamel topcoats. These coatings were easy to apply and repair. Even after the topcoat dried, scratches and other imperfections could be repaired by heating the surface locally to smooth out the imperfections. Air pollution standards introduced in the 1980s forced manufacturers to reduce the amount of solvents in the topcoat paints.

When foreign manufacturers introduced high-quality finishes, U.S. automakers began to introduce BC/CC topcoat lines to stay competitive. Because the BC/CC coatings had VOC solvents (although much lower VOC content than the 1970s lacquer and enamel paints), manufacturers had to rely more heavily on control technologies to meet the EPA's increasingly strict emission standards.

5. 49 Fed. Reg. 37548 (1984). In 1984, Congress enacted the Cooperative Research Act, 15 U.S.C. §§ 4301–4306, which permitted the U.S. automakers to cooperate on research without violating the antitrust laws. The manufacturers began collaborating on research for low-VOC paints in 1987, eventually forming the United States Council for Automotive Research (USCAR).

6. The exhaust from the bake oven is not sent to the carbon adsorption system because it is too hot for efficient adsorption. Fortunately, the exhaust is sufficiently concentrated to incinerate the VOCs directly without first concentrating them.

7. 42 U.S.C. §§ 7401–7671q.

8. Congress has broad authority under the Commerce and the Spending Clauses

to regulate virtually any aspect of the environment. Although the states also possess broad authority under their traditional police powers to regulate the environment, the Supremacy Clause generally preempts inconsistent state laws and regulations, unless Congress allows the inconsistency. Under many federal environmental statutes, the federal government sets national policies and standards, which state agencies implement, monitor, and enforce. State governments generally want to help implement federal environmental policies, and federal threats to withhold federal funding for important public works projects effectively coerce recalcitrant states to do so. Often, the federal government retains authority to approve state permitting decisions, and it usually retains independent enforcement authority. See, generally, John P. Dwyer, "The Role of State Law in an Era of Federal *Preemption:* Lessons from Environmental Regulation," *Law and Contemporary Problems* 60 (1998): 203; Dwyer, "The Practice of Federalism under the Clean Air Act," *Maryland Law Review* 54 (1995): 1183.

9. Section 109(a)-(b), 42 U.S.C. § 7409(a)-(b). To date, the EPA has set standards for sulfur dioxide, particulates, nitrogen oxides, carbon monoxide, ozone, and lead. See 40 C.F.R. pt. 50 (specifying primary and secondary national ambient air quality standards). The EPA must set these standards without regard to the magnitude of control costs. *Lead Industries Ass'n v. EPA,* 647 F.2d 1130, 1149 (D.C. Cir.), *cert. denied,* 449 U.S. 1042 (1980).

10. Section 111(a)(1), (b), 42 U.S.C. § 7411(a)(1), (b) (specifying general criteria for NSPS standards). See also 40 C.F.R. pt. 60 (specifying NSPS standards for more than seventy-five industrial categories).

11. The 1970 version of the Clean Air Act required states to meet the primary NAAQS by the mid-1970s. The act contained no provisions to address the possibility that the air quality in some areas would not meet the national standards by the statutory deadline. In 1977, when scores of urban areas failed to meet the primary NAAQS for ozone, Congress added a new "nonattainment" program to the Clean Air Act. See Sections 171–179b, 42 U.S.C. §§ 7501–7509a. In 1990 Congress adopted a more elaborate program with longer deadlines and more stringent control measures in areas with more serious air pollution problems. See Sections 181–192, 42 U.S.C. §§ 7511–7514a.

12. Sections 160–169B, 42 U.S.C. §§ 7470–7492.

13. Section 111(c), 42 U.S.C. § 7411(c) (legal authority to delegate NSPS program to state air pollution agencies); 40 C.F.R. § 60.23 (procedures to prepare and submit for EPA approval a state plan to implement the NSPS program).

14. Section 110(a)(2), 42 U.S.C. § 7410(a)(2). States that fail to submit acceptable SIPs are subject to sanctions, such as increases in "offsets" required for new or modified sources and a cutoff of federal funds for highway construction projects. Section 179, 42 U.S.C. § 7509. In addition, the EPA may assume primary responsibility by issuing a federal implementation plan. Section 110(c)(1), 42 U.S.C. § 7410(c)(1).

15. Section 110(a)(2), 42 U.S.C. § 7410(a)(2).

16. Section 110(a)(1), 42 U.S.C. § 7410(a)(1).

17. Section 113(a), 42 U.S.C. § 7413(a).

18. Section 111, 42 U.S.C. § 7411. The EPA's regulations exempt (1) routine maintenance, repair, and replacement; (2) an increase in production rate if it does

not require additional capital expenditure; and (3) an increase in the hours of operation. 40 C.F.R. § 60.14(e)(1)-(3).

19. Section 111(a)(1), 42 U.S.C. § 7411(a)(1). The EPA has established NSPS emission standards for dozens of industrial categories, including surface coating operations in auto assembly plants. 40 C.F.R. pt. 60, subpt. MM.

20. Id. § 60.392.

21. Id. § 60.393. The EPA specifies the reference methods and procedures to conduct these tests. Id. §60.396.

22. Id. § 60.394

23. Id. § 60.395.

24. Sect. 111(j)(1)(A), 42 U.S.C. § 7411(j)(1)(A). To grant a waiver, the EPA must determine (1) that the proposed control system has not been adequately demonstrated; (2) that there is a "substantial likelihood" the proposed control system will achieve greater emission reductions than otherwise required by NSPS; (3) that the proposed control system would not contribute to "an unreasonable risk to public health, welfare, or safety"; and (4) that the emissions will not prevent attainment or maintenance of air quality standards. Section 111(j)(1)(A), (B)(i), 42 U.S.C. § 7411(j)(1)(A), (B)(i). The waiver cannot extend longer than seven years after it is granted or more than four years after the beginning of operations. Section 111(j)(1)(E), 42 U.S.C. § 7411(j)(1)(E).

25. Section 111(j)(1)(A), 42 U.S.C. § 7411(j)(1)(A).

26. In the early 1980s, EPA granted several automobile manufacturers waivers for their topcoat lines. See 40 C.F.R. § 60.398 (describing waivers for several plants).

27. A "major source" is a facility that has the potential to emit more than a specified number of tons of VOCs annually. In a "severe" nonattainment area, such as Edison, New Jersey, where Ford's Edison assembly plant is located, a "major" source is one with the potential to emit 25 tons of VOCs annually. Section 182(d), 42 U.S.C § 7511a(d). Automobile assembly plants typically emit between 500 and 2,000 tons of VOCs annually.

28. Section 172(c)(5), 42 U.S.C. § 7502(c)(5); 40 C.F.R. §51.165 (regulations for new source review in nonattainment areas). Regardless of the amount of current emissions, if the proposed modification would result in no net increase in emissions (e.g., because emissions in other parts of the facility were reduced), the modification would not be subject to the nonattainment provisions. See 40 C.F.R. § 51.165(a)(1)(v).

29. Section 173(a)(1)(A), 42 U.S.C. § 7503(a)(1)(A).

30. Section 182(d)(2), 42 U.S.C. § 7511a(d)(2).

31. Section 173(a)(2), 42 U.S.C. § 7503(a)(2). The act defines the "lowest achievable emission rate" as the rate of emissions that reflects the following:

> (A) the most stringent emission limitation which is contained in the implementation plan of any State for such class or category of source, unless the owner or operator of the proposed source demonstrates that such limitations are not achievable, or
> (B) the most stringent emission limitation which is achieved in practice by such class or category of source, whichever is more stringent.

Section 171(3), 42 U.S.C. § 7501(3). In any event, the LAER is as least as stringent as the NSPS standards. Id.

32. Section 173(a)(3), (5), 42 U.S.C. § 7503(a)(3), (5).

33. Sections 165, 42 U.S.C. § 7475; 40 C.F.R. § 51.166 (regulations for new source review in PSD areas). In most cases (including automobile assembly plants), a "major source" is a facility with the potential to emit more than 250 tons of VOCs annually, and a major modified source is a major source whose modification results in a net increase in emissions. 40 C.F.R. § 51.166(b)(1)(i)(*b*), (b)(2). Thus, as with facilities in nonattainment areas, if the proposed modification would result in no net increase in emissions, it would not be subject to the PSD permitting process. Because the modifications to the Minnesota facility resulted in a net decrease in VOC emissions, it was not subject to PSD review.

34. Section 165(a), 42 U.S.C. § 7475(a).

35. There are no nationally formulated standards covering odors.

36. *Restatement (Second) of Torts* §§ 821A-840E. For a study of local enforcement of nuisance standards as applied to odors, see Noga Morag-Levine, "*Chasing the Wind: Reactive Law, Environmental Equity and Localized Air Pollution Regulation*"(Ph.D. diss., University of California, Berkeley, 1995).

In Minnesota, for example, state law specifically requires a person causing "obnoxious odors constituting a public nuisance" immediately to take "reasonable steps to minimize" the emissions. Minn. Stat. § 116.061.1(b). However, the Minnesota statute also provides an exception if the state air pollution agency has granted the polluter a permit that authorizes the odorous emissions. Id. § 116.061.3(4).

37. Sect. 111(j)(1)(A), 42 U.S.C. § 7411(j)(1)(A).

38. 40 C.F.R. § 51.161. See also 40 C.F.R. § 60.9 (information the agency has collected regarding compliance with NSPS requirements must be made available to the public, subject to trade secret claims); 40 C.F.R. § 60.23(c), (d) (public notice and hearing procedures on state adoption of a plan to implement NSPS requirements).

39. Section 165(a)(2), 42 U.S.C. § 7475(a)(2); 40 C.F.R. § 51.166(a)(5), (q).

40. In all states, hearings are open to the public, and all state studies, reports, orders, and other final documents are open to public inspection. See, e.g., Minn. Stat. § 116.075.1. See also Minn. Rules § 7000.1800 (any person may petition the Minnesota Pollution Control Agency for a contested hearing to challenge the decision to grant an air pollution permit). The procedures contemplate a formal proceeding in which the parties are represented by counsel, witnesses are subject to cross-examination, and the issue is decided by an administrative law judge. Minn. Stat. §§ 14.57–14.69; Minn. Rules §§ 1400.5100–1400.8401. The statute also provides for recovery of attorney fees. Minn. Stat. § 15.472.

41. EPA, *National Air Pollutant Emission Trends, 1900–1996,* Appendix A (EPA-454/R-97–011, December 1997); American Automobile Manufacturers Ass'n, *U.S. Motor Vehicle Production,* http:www.aama.com/data/table1.html (6/29/98).

42. *Grundgesetz,* art. 74(24).

43. Id. art. 83–85.

44. Hans D. Jarass and Joseph DiMento, "Through Comparative Lawyers' Goggles: A Primer *on* German Environmental Law," *Georgetown International Environmental Law Review* 6 (1993): 47, 55; Susan Rose-Ackerman, *Controlling Environmental Policy: The Limits of Public Law in Germany and the United States* (New Haven, Conn.: Yale University Press, 1995), 8.

45. *Grundgesetz,* art. 84.

46. *BImSchG,* art. 4, ¶ 1. Modification of such facilities also requires a license. Id. art. 15, ¶ 1. In the United States, by contrast, the criterion for whether a facility is subject to NSPS, PSD, or nonattainment requirements is numerical, e.g., the potential to emit more than 100 tons of VOCs annually.

47. *BImSchG* art. 5, ¶ 1.

48. David P. Currie, "Air Pollution Control in West Germany," *University of Chicago Law Review* 49 (1982): 359–60.

49. *BImSchG* art. 5, ¶ 2.

50. Currie, "Air Pollution Control in West Germany," 370.

51. *BImSchG* art. 47.

52. Id. art. 49.

53. Currie, "Air Pollution Control in West Germany," 374–80.

54. Ibid., 361–62.

55. The regulations also contain detailed provisions to monitor emissions, including requirements specifying the location of measurement sites, the frequency of measurements, and the selection of measurement procedures. *TA Luft* § 3.2.

56. Id. § 2.4.

57. Id. § 2.5.

58. Id. § 3.1.

59. Id. § 3.1.7.

60. Id. § 3.3.

61. Id. § 3.3.5.1.1.

62. *TA Luft* §§ 2.2.1.2, 2.2.1.3.

63. Id. § 2.2.1.4.

64. *TA Luft* contains special measures, including low-emission fuel and operating restrictions, which are required in areas that are subject to stationary weather conditions that cause a considerable increase in immissions. Id. § 2.2.1.4. These provisions, however, are far less burdensome and cover far fewer areas than the U.S. nonattainment provisions.

65. Id. § 2.4

66. Id. § 2.5.1.

67. Id. § 2.5.2.

68. Id. § 2.6.

69. Id. §§ 2.2.1.1, 2.2.1.2.

70. Id. § 2.2.1.1(b).

71. Although there are no *immission* values for ozone, a 1995 amendment to the *BImSchG* provides that if the hourly average ozone concentration exceeds exceed 240μg/m³ the government may impose driving restrictions. *BImSchG* art. 40a. The *BImSchG* value is roughly equal to the U.S. NAAQS value of 0.12 ppm. See 40 C.F.R. § 50.9. There is an important difference, however. The German standard is not an air quality limit that the *Länder* must meet or face sanctions. Rather, it is a threshold that is the basis for government-imposed restrictions on driving. The U.S. standard, which can be violated only one day annually, is a mandatory standard that states must meet by statutory deadlines or face federal sanctions.

72. *TA Luft* § 2.2.1.3(b).

73. Id. § 2.2.1.3.

74. Id. § 3.1.2.

75. Id.

76. Id. § 3.1.7.

77. See *TA Luft* § 3.3 (the 1986 version of *TA Luft* has air pollution regulations for ten categories of industrial facilities).

78. Id. § 3.3.5.1.1.

79. Id. § 3.1.

80. Id. § 3.3.5.1.1.

81. Id. § 3.3.5.1.1.

82. Id. § 3.1.

83. *BImSchG,* art. 10, ¶ 3.

84. Id.

85. Id. art. 15, ¶ 2.

86. Id. art. 10, ¶¶ 5–6.

87. Id. art. 15, ¶ 1.

88. *TA Luft* § 3.3.5.1.1.

89. Section 173(a), 42 U.S.C. § 7503(a).

90. Even if the additional load causes the initial load to increase by more than 1 percent, the agency will still grant a license if the proposed source can obtain enough offsets to reduce *immissions. TA Luft* § 2.2.1.1.

91. *BImSchG* art. 3, ¶ 4.

92. *TA Luft* § 2.4.

93. EPA, *AIRS Graphics, Largest VOC Emission Sources in the United States* (May 1, 1998).

94. EPA Office of Air Quality Planning and Standards, AIRSWeb, *Minnesota VOC Air Pollution Sources* (May 27, 1998).

95. For plant emissions in recent years, see EPA, *U.S. Automobile Assembly Plants and Their Communities: Environmental, Economic, and Demographic Profile,* No. 34 (Ford Motor Co., St. Paul, Minn.) (December 1997).

96. Nationally, approximately 20 percent of the population is minority, and 20 percent is below the poverty line. EPA, *U.S. Automobile Assembly Plants and Their Communities.* The population data are for 1990.

97. From 1991 through 1994, annual production ranged from 119,712 to 208,325 trucks. EPA, *U.S. Automobile Assembly Plants and Their Communities.*

98. "St. Paul Ford Plant May Build Ranger," *St. Paul Pioneer Press & Dispatch,* October 3, 1983.

99. MPCA, Installation Permit for an Emission Facility and Air Pollution Control Equipment (Permit No. 249–84-I-2).

100. 49 Fed. Reg. 37,548 (1984).

101. Id. at 37,548–49.

102. Id. at 37,548.

103. Davis argued that EPA did not have adequate information to assess public health risks from the excess emissions, that the waiver might permit Ford to violate other regulatory standards, and that granting Ford a waiver to meet foreign competition was not a legal basis for a waiver.

104. "Area Residents Oppose Waiving Air Quality Rules for Ford Plant," *Minneapolis Star & Tribune,* January 31, 1985. Under federal law, the EPA could not approve the waiver without the governor's consent.

105. "Perpich Backs Ford Request for Waiver on Air Standards," *Minneapolis Star & Tribune*, February 8, 1985.

106. 50 Fed. Reg. 36,830 (1985). The EPA also granted a waiver for two other Ford plants and a Chrysler plant, each of which, unlike the St. Paul facility, were in nonattainment areas. Id. at 36,830.

107. Id. at 36,832.

108. *Davis v. EPA*, 804 F.2d 1324 (1986). Davis did not file his suit until March 1986, and the court did not rule until late November 1986, about five weeks before the waiver terminated of its own accord. Because there was no injunction pending the outcome of the litigation, the suit had no impact on Ford's operations or the ongoing processes to draft an acceptable permit.

109. MPCA, Ford Motor Company St. Paul Assembly Plant Permitting Fact Sheet (Mar. 30, 1987).

110. Letter from Helen Marr to MPCA, October 1979.

111. In fiscal 1987, MPCA received 135 complaints about odors from the Ford plant, and in 1988 it received 65 complaints. "Ford Plant's Smokestack Extended to Disperse Odors from Paint Shop," *Minneapolis Star Tribune*, July 7, 1989.

112. Ford officials confirmed that there was a problem with odors. "How could we deny that [an odor problem] existed with over 300 complaints," the official admitted. "When it was damp and humid it just hung in the air."

113. "Earth Protector's Davis Sparks Controversy over Ford Paint Shop," *Highland Villager*, July 11, 1984.

114. Letter from Leslie Davis to Tom Laney, President, Local 879 UAW (August 2, 1984); Letter from Tom Laney, President, Local 879 UAW, to Leslie Davis (August 13, 1984); Letter from Tom Laney, President, Local 879 UAW, to MPCA (October 9, 1984); Letter from V. H. Sussman, Director, Stationary Source Environmental Control, Ford, to Tom Laney, President, Local 879, UAW (January 17, 1985).

115. "Ford, Drop 'Wet Look' Paint," *St. Paul Pioneer Press & Dispatch*, April 19, 1985; "Ford Motor Story Failed to Clear the Air on Waiver Issue," *Highlander Villager*, March 12, 1986; "Fighting Ford," *Highland Villager*, June 25, 1986; "Residents Urged to Take Action," *Highland Villager*, July 16, 1986.

116. "Environmental Group Says Ford Expansion May Create Toxic Emissions," *Minneapolis Star & Tribune*, November 28, 1984; Editorial, "Fumes, Fear Creep in Window," *St. Paul Pioneer Press & Dispatch*, January 10, 1985; "Environmentalists, Ford Co. Discuss Plant," *Minneapolis Star & Tribune*, January 17, 1985.

117. Letter from Leslie Davis to 60 Minutes (December 24, 1984); Letter from Marjorie Holyoak, Director, Audience Services, 60 Minutes, to Leslie Davis (January 23, 1985).

118. "Highland Park Neighbors Protest Odors Coming from Ford Plant," *Minneapolis Star & Tribune*, September 11, 1986.

119. Letter from John Drew, Councilman, St. Paul City Council, to Lisa Thorvig, Chief, Regulatory Compliance Section, MPCA (April 30, 1987).

120. MPCA, Public Notice on Proposed Air Emission Facility Permit (March 20, 1987).

121. "Neighborhood Task Force Seeking Changes in Ford Operating Permit," *Highland Villager*, June 17, 1987.

122. Letter from Lisa Thorvig, Chief, Regulatory Compliance Section, MPCA, to Judith Krasnow, Liaison, Citizen's Task Force (May 27, 1987); Memo from Michael Valentine, Director, Division of Air Quality, MPCA, to Air Quality Committee, MPCA Board (June 17, 1987).

123. "Neighborhood Task Force Seeking Changes in Ford Operating Permit."

124. Task Force Meeting Minutes (July 1, 1987).

125. Minn. Stat. § 116.02(1) (commissioner and eight board members are appointed by the governor, subject to senatorial confirmation); § 116.02(3) (no member, other than the commissioner, may be an officer or employee of the state).

126. The emissions cap was the same as that in the proposed but never issued 1986 operating permit. The MPCA also imposed a limit on the VOC content of the paint. MPCA, *Summary of Comments and Responses: Public Meeting re Draft Air Emission Permit, #249–91-OT-1* (May 28, 1991).

Because two thousand jobs hung in the balance, it was politically infeasible for the MPCA to close the plant until it issued the operating permit. Ford officials felt there was little danger that the MPCA would deny an extension so long as Ford continued to make a good faith effort to reach a solution. Although the construction permit imposed some restrictions, Ford was not unhappy with the permit. Because the permit established performance standards (e.g., 1,095 tons per year), rather than specific environmental controls (except for the required afterburners), Ford had substantial flexibility to meet the permit requirements. Moreover, the construction permit did not impose onerous monitoring, record-keeping, and reporting requirements.

127. "Cooperative Spirit Smooths Way for Ford Plant Monitoring," *Highland Villager,* October 21, 1987.

128. These evaluations costs Ford $750,000. Ford also incurred personnel costs during the extended permitting process. Ford officials estimate that two members of its environmental staff worked an average of four hours daily over the course of five years, for an estimated total cost of about $182,500.

129. See Ford Air Quality Task Force, *Task Force Report on Air Emissions Studies, Ford Motor Company—Twin Cities Assembly Plant* (February 28, 1990).

130. "Ford Plans Plant Changes to Cut Odor," *Minneapolis Star Tribune,* June 7, 1989; "Ford Plant Smokestack Extended to Disperse Odors from Paint Shop," *Minneapolis Star Tribune,* July 7, 1989. Because the exhaust stack is in the flight path of the Minneapolis–St. Paul International Airport, Ford also needed to obtain approval from the Federal Aviation Administration.

131. See MPCA, *Fact Sheet: Ford Motor Company Twin Cities Assembly Plant* (May 1991); Letter from Frank Partee, Ford Motor Co., to J. Michael Valentine, Director, Division of Air Quality, MPCA (October 31, 1989).

132. Ford Air Quality Task Force, *Task Force Report on Air Emissions Studies, Ford Motor Company—Twin Cities Assembly Plant* (February 28, 1990).

133. Ford Task Force Minutes (November 2, 1989).

134. Letter from Frank Partee, Ford Motor Co., to J. Michael Valentine, Director, Division of Air Quality, MPCA (October 31, 1989).

135. With this change, all Rangers would receive the BC/CC coating. Letter from Frank Partee, Ford Motor Co., to J. Michael Valentine, Director, Division of Air Quality, MPCA (October 31, 1989).

136. See MPCA, *Public Notice on Proposed Air Emission Facility Permit* (May 9, 1991).

137. EPA regulations provide that the threshold for a significant net increase is VOC emissions is 40 tons per year. 40 C.F.R. § 51.166(b)(23)(i).

138. MPCA, *Issue Statement,* June 25, 1991, p. 2.

139. After reviewing the draft permit, the task force recommended that Ford be required to participate in any task force formed to study emissions. The MPCA incorporated that recommendation into the permit. See also Letter from William MacDowell, Chief, Regulation Development Section, Air Enforcement Branch, EPA, Region 5, to Ahto Niemioja, Supervisor, Permit Unit, Regulatory Compliance Section, Division of Air Quality, MPCA (June 10, 1991) (informing MPCA about the need for minimum efficiencies in the VOC control equipment, which MPCA subsequently implemented as §III.I of the permit).

140. Air Emission Permit No. 249–91-OT-1, § II.C. The EPA regulations are found at 40 C.F.R. § 60.392.

141. Air Emission Permit No. 249–91-OT-1, § III.E.1.

142. Id., § III.E.2.

143. The permit defines an "odor concentration unit" as "The number of standard cubic feet of odor-free air needed to dilute each cubic foot of contaminated air so that at least 50% of the odor concentration test panel does not detect any odor in the diluted mixture." Air Emission Permit No. 249–91-OT-1, § III.

144. Id., § II.E. See Minn. Rules 7005.0920.

145. To ensure that Ford would not delay installation of the control equipment, the permit provided that the company may not begin operation of the modified PVC/guidecoat/anti-chip system until the new carbon wheel adsorption/incineration system was in operation on the main topcoat line. Air Emission Permit No. 249–91-OT-1, § III.H.

146. Air Emission Permit No. 249–91-OT-1, § III.A. Ford and MPCA staff were unable to agree on monitoring equipment for the carbon adsorption system. The permit requires Ford to submit a report on alternative monitoring systems, after which the MPCA director will select a particular system. Air Emission Permit No. 249–91-OT-1, § III.B.5.

147. Air Emission Permit No. 249–91-OT-1, § III.B. There are analogous requirements for the cleaning ovens in the assembly plant. Id.

148. Air Emission Permit No. 249–91-OT-1, § III.F.

149. The minimum efficiencies for the control equipment are 90 percent destruction efficiency for each incinerator, 85 percent capture efficiency for the carbon wheel adsorption unit on the main enamel line, and overall control efficiencies of 18 percent for the PVC/guidecoat/anti-chip line, and 50 percent for the main topcoat line. Air Emission Permit No. 249–91-OT-1, § III.I.

150. Air Emission Permit No. 249–91-OT-1, § III.G.

151. Ford lost the capacity of 4.5 trucks per hour, for about 4,700 hours per year (twenty-hour days for 234 days), for five years, totaling 105,750 trucks. Ford officials claim that they would have used the full capacity.

152. Air Emission Permit No. 249–91-OT-1, § IV.B, C, F.

153. Air Emission Permit No. 249–91-OT-1, § IV.E. These calculations are prescribed by 40 C.F.R. § 60.393.

154. Air Emission Permit No. 249–91-OT-1, § VI.

155. U.S. 1, Interstate 287, and the New Jersey Turnpike pass within a mile of Ford's plant. The Garden State Parkway is less than four miles away.

156. EPA Office of Air Quality Planning and Standards, AIRSWeb, *New Jersey VOC Air Pollution Sources* (May 27, 1998).

157. EPA, *U.S. Automobile Assembly Plants and Their Communities.*

158. Middlesex County, Office of Economic Development, *Demographics, Mean Income* (1990). This is also true for Middlesex County as a whole. EPA, *U.S. Automobile Assembly Plants and Their Communities.*

159. Randy Becker and Vernon Henderson, *Effects of Air Quality Regulation on Decisions of Firms in Polluting Industries* 29–39 (National Bureau of Economic Research Working Paper No. 6160, 1997).

160. At the time, Ford owned 30 percent of Mazda.

161. Application for Permit to Construct, Install or Alter Control Apparatus or Equipment and Certificate to Operate Control Apparatus or Equipment (September 26, 1989). Before Ford adopted low-VOC paints in 1986, the topcoat line emitted almost 1,000 tons of VOCs annually. Most of the difference was due to the low-VOC paints, not the afterburner on the bake oven.

162. § II.F.

163. §§ II.G.1, II.G.2. Deviations from the specified temperature do not constitute a permit violation if the annual duration of the deviations is less than 1.5 percent of the total operating hours, although all deviations must be reported. § II.H.

164. § II.I.2. Deviations less than three hours are not a violation of the permit, although Ford must still meet the daily emission limits. Ford must submit a report on the deviation that describes the cause, duration, remedial steps taken, and measures taken to prevent recurrence. § II.I.4–5.

165. §§ II.A–II.E.

Average hourly production	40 Ranger trucks
Maximum jobs/hour	50 Ranger trucks
Maximum jobs/day	800 Ranger trucks
Maximum jobs/year	188,000 Ranger trucks

166. § III.A. The monitors must meet EPA's specification in 40 C.F.R. pt. 60, App. B.

167. § III.C.

168. § III.B.

169. § IV.A.1. The stack tests must measure both the rate of total VOC emissions (lb./hour) and concentrations (parts per million) in the exhaust stream.

170. § IV.A.2.

171. § IV.A.3.

172. §§ IV.A.3, IV.F.

173. § IV.B.

174. §§ IV.A.3, IV.C, IV.D.

175. § V.A.

176. § V.B.1

177. § V.B.2.

178. § V.C.

179. *BImSchG* arts. 44–47.
180. Permit at 14.
181. Permit at 14–15.
182. Permit at 16.
183. Permit at 2, 13–14.
184. Permit at 20–24.
185. Permit §§ 3–4.
186. Permit §§ 3, 8.1
187. Permit §§ 5–6.
188. Permit § 9.1.
189. Permit §§ 7.2–7.3.
190. Permit §§ 7.1.1–7.1.2.
191. Permit § 7.1.3.
192. Permit §§ 9.1.1–9.9.6.
193. Permit § 9.1.3. *See TA Luft* § 3.3.5.1.1.
194. Permit § 8.4.
195. *BImSchG* art. 15, ¶ 1.
196. See Permit at 4 (stating the Ford requested the *Ministerium* to refrain from making a public announcement about the permit process and making the permit application and supporting documents available for public inspection); Ford Brief Comments on the Project Appropriation Request—Waste Air Purification, Saarlouis (undated) ("Prerequisite for licensing *without making* Ford's *application public* is that the specific and annual emission levels are not higher than the emissions of the two existing shift operations"; emphasis in original).
197. See *BImSchG* art. 15, ¶ 2.
198. At present, the facility operates only two shifts and emits approximately 900 to 1,000 metric tons of VOCs annually.
199. Permit at 5–6.
200. The agency found that the afterburners were state of the art (*Stand der Technik*). The agency also found that the technological controls would satisfy the statutory requirements that the modifications would not cause harmful environmental effects (*schädliche Umwelteinwirkungen*) or other dangers (*Gefahren*), considerable disadvantages (*erhebliche Nachteile*), or considerable nuisance (*erhebliche Belästigungen*) for the neighborhood or the general public (*Allgemeinheit*). *BImSchG* art. 5.
201. Permit ¶ 28.
202. Permit ¶ 34.
203. Permit ¶ 40. Ford must also report the incineration temperature three months after beginning operations, and thereafter every six months. If the measurements are stable, Ford need submit reports only every three years. Id. The permit also specifies the type and amount of fuel that may be used in the *TNV*. Permit ¶¶ 41–42. See also Permit ¶¶ 47–51 (specifying other requirements for record keeping and reporting of continuous measurements).
204. Permit ¶ 45.
205. Permit ¶¶ 35–36.
206. There were other costs—including personnel costs and the costs of health studies—but these paled in comparison with the capital and delay costs. It is not

possible to calculate the delay costs precisely. For example, while Ford's production at the St. Paul facility was forty rather than fifty trucks per hour, it is not possible to know whether Ford would have used the additional production capacity if given the opportunity, or whether Ford was able to make up for the shortfall at another facility.

It is also difficult to calculate the relative benefits from the environmental controls. Even if, as appears to be the case, the U.S. controls are more stringent, it is not clear how much environmental and health benefits result from that additional stringency.

207. As the New Jersey case study makes clear, not every permitting controversy involves public participation. Indeed, not all permitting processes are controversial.

208. Mary Douglas and Aaron Wildavsky, *Risk and Culture: An Essay on the Selection of Technical and Environmental Dangers* (Berkeley: University of California Press, 1982).

PART II

Legal Rights and Litigation

CHAPTER SEVEN

Employee Termination Practices in the United States and Canada

Laura Beth Nielsen

I. INTRODUCTION AND OVERVIEW

In all economically developed democracies, the trend this century has been to temper the traditional liberal theory of employment-at-will. The employment-at-will doctrine holds that absent a written contract or collective bargaining agreement, an employer may terminate an employee at any time for any legal reason or for no reason, just as an employee may choose to quit.[1] Employment-at-will eroded as countries began to provide legal protections against arbitrary dismissal and discriminatory firing, and, in some cases, imposed requirements of due process, reasonable notice, and severance pay. Significant cross-cultural legal differences persist, however. Whereas most European states and Canada emphasize guarantees of continued employment, the United States emphasizes the employer's interest in efficiency—while providing strong legal protections against termination based on race, gender, age, or disability. Moreover, national legal systems vary in whether employee rights are protected by courts or administrative bodies.

Some large domestic corporations offer stronger guarantees against arbitrary dismissal than are required by law, and some multinational companies pride themselves on implementing similar personnel practices regardless of the law of the host countries. This is the corporate philosophy of PCO, a pharmaceutical company with operations in more than twenty countries. This case study examines whether and how differences in national legal regimes affect actual corporate personnel practices, by comparing PCO's U.S. and Canadian operations.

PCO Canada employs 525 people, and PCO U.S. employs approximately

9,500 people. In both countries the workforce of PCO consists mainly of white-collar workers whose major tasks include sales, marketing, manufacturing, research, and development. PCO has no unionized employees in either country; it contracts out jobs performed by people in occupations traditionally dominated by strong labor unions. In both countries, women slightly outnumber their male counterparts and are well represented even in top management positions. In Canada, 12.3 percent of PCO employees are "visible minorities," as opposed to about 18 percent racial minorities in PCO U.S.

In the course of the research, we conducted thirty-two interviews with PCO's human resources staff in both the United States and Canada as well as the corporate officials involved with termination, including the affirmative action officers, the legal departments, and human resources managers in most of the regional offices. In Canada we were able to read the personnel files of all the employees who left PCO over a two-year period. In PCO U.S. we did not have access to such files, but we were provided summary figures and quantitative estimates that correspond to the results generated by the analysis of the Canadian employment files.

Some scholars have argued that the liberal theory of employment-at-will has been slowly eroded by common law and statutory developments, but the United States retains the employment-at-will presumption for private sector, nonunionized employees working without a contract.[2] Canada, in the European tradition that emphasizes continuity of employment, provides greater common law protection to employees in that country, requiring that an employee receive reasonable notice prior to termination unless "just cause" for immediate dismissal is shown.[3] There are various exceptions to the common law standards in both countries. For example, in *Toussaint v. Blue Cross & Blue Shield* (1980), the Supreme Court declared that provisions in employee manuals and oral statements made by employers can be considered contractually binding exceptions to the common law presumption of employment-at-will.

Additionally, in both countries, statutes protect employees from dismissal as a result of discrimination on the basis of race, gender, age, and disability.[4] A number of Canadian provinces, including Ontario, provide statutory protection from discrimination on grounds of sexual orientation as well.[5]

When forced to separate or terminated from PCO, an employee can leave without contesting the termination, can contest the termination in some way other than filing a lawsuit, or can file a lawsuit. PCO corporate data show much *less* posttermination disputing, including lawsuits, in Canada. As Figure 7.1 shows, of employees who were terminated in Canada in the 1995 fiscal year, 71 percent raised no dispute. In the United States, only 39 percent of those terminated left without dispute. On the other end

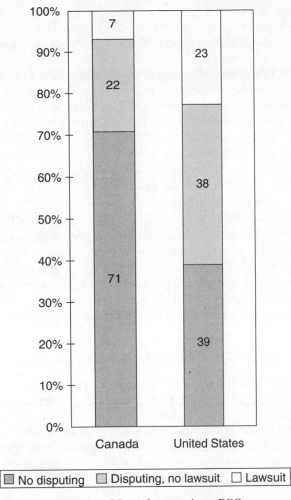

Figure 7.1. Results of forced separations, PCO, 1995
(PCO company data).

of the spectrum, of terminated employees, 7 percent of Canadians eventually filed a lawsuit against PCO, whereas 23 percent in the United States filed a lawsuit.[6] "Midlevel" disputing ranges from simply writing a letter contesting a severance package or the termination itself to hiring an attorney to do the same. In PCO Canada, 22 percent of those who were fired engaged in midlevel posttermination disputing, whereas in the United States, 38 percent did so.[7]

In one respect, PCO's posttermination litigation experience was the same in both the United States and Canada. In the years studied, not a single terminated employee won a lawsuit against PCO in either country. Even more striking, PCO has never lost a posttermination lawsuit in either country.

Despite PCO's uniform corporate personnel policy, PCO U.S. and PCO Canada termination procedures vary noticeably, both in terms of the organization of the Human Resources Department and in terms of day-to-day decision making. PCO U.S. has more deeply entrenched bureaucratic structures to process legal claims. These differences reflect the fact that PCO U.S. employees have access to both a greater variety of legal claims and more potent legal remedies. Thus PCO U.S. officials face greater legal uncertainty than their Canadian counterparts regarding the source and effects of a posttermination legal claim.

Although it is difficult to estimate precisely how much PCO spends on the termination process in each country, it seems clear that U.S. prelitigation and litigation processes are generally more expensive. Not only does PCO U.S. spend more money on the termination process, but the money spent is channeled largely to legal and quasi-legal professionals, whereas the expenditures made by PCO Canada go toward providing severance packages and services to the terminated Canadian employee.

II. NATIONAL DIFFERENCES IN LAW

Cross-national legal differences relating to employee termination law may be roughly divided into three categories. First, there are differences in substantive law of all sorts—common law, statutory law, and regulatory requirements. Second are differences relating to the institutional and procedural features of the different national legal systems. Third, there are economic differences associated with lawsuits, including attorneys' fees and typical awards for successful wrongful termination cases.

A. Substantive Law

The most striking difference in substantive law between the two countries is that unqualified employment-at-will has never been the law in Canada. At the most general level, Canada follows the European model of providing a somewhat higher threshold of protection from termination for all workers. In Canada the employment-at-will doctrine does not prevail; the common law presumption in that country is "reasonable notice" prior to termination, unless the employer has "just cause" to terminate an employee.[8] This suggests that Canadian employers might be more vulnerable to unjust dismissal lawsuits than their American counterparts—at least in legal theory.

Because of the increase in statutory and regulatory rules regarding termination, the common law difference between the United States and Canada hardly reflects the entire law. However, the basic common law difference reflects the countries' variant traditions regarding employment. In Canada the just cause presumption was and is designed to protect all employees, reflecting a commitment to protecting continued employment.[9] In the United States the employment-at-will tradition demonstrates a commitment to the fluidity of markets and employer flexibility.

In Canada, employees terminated without just cause are entitled to receive "reasonable notice," which can take the form of either actual notice or monetary compensation in lieu thereof.[10] Reasonable notice is a secure legal principle, now embodied in statute, and is applied to quasi-employees, part-time employees, temporary workers, and even nonemployee workers.[11] The reasonable notice requirement can be overridden for a number of reasons such as a valid contractual term of employment, or if the employee's performance or conduct constitutes "just cause" for dismissal. Exactly how much notice is "reasonable" remains somewhat vague despite explicit statutory guidelines, because of an evolving common law doctrine that typically provides protections above the statutory minimum.[12] Nevertheless, as a practical matter, legal publications provide guidelines for notice, based on factors such as type of job, years of service, and future employability of the terminated worker. In addition to the common law protections, as mentioned earlier, Canadian provinces have a comprehensive statutory regime that protects workers from arbitrary treatment.

In contrast, in the United States the trend has been to allow companies to define workers out of employee status by labeling them "independent contractors," thus circumventing legal requirements for employment relationships. U.S. law, then, is less comprehensive and less protective of workers, and more protective of employer autonomy. On the other hand, piecemeal statutory, common law, and regulatory protections have increased protection for many American employees. Some legal scholars argue that the employment-at-will standard no longer exists in the United States,[13] since it has been eroded both by common law developments and by statutory employee protections. Common law courts in many states have found employers liable for discharging an employee for reasons that violate public policy;[14] for violating the implied covenant of good faith and fair dealing;[15] and for violating an implied contract.[16] Moreover, statutory protections against discrimination against particular groups have eroded the employment-at-will presumption. These include the Civil Rights Act of 1964, the Americans with Disabilities Act, and the Pregnancy Discrimination Act. Over 70 percent of the total U.S. workforce—including minorities, women, and older and disabled workers—is now "protected" as defined by the Equal Employment Opportunity Commission (EEOC).[17]

Additionally, government workers protected by civil service legislation are entitled to continued employment absent just cause for dismissal. Collective bargaining agreements provide the same for many unionized employees in the private sector. Finally, many large corporations, like PCO, include guarantees of due process in their employee manuals, which provide employees certain protections associated with the contract exception to employment-at-will.

B. Legal Institutions and Mobilization of Law

Numerous factors affect a disgruntled employee's decision to pursue a legal claim regarding a termination. The employee's age, education, and prior encounters with legal disputes may influence her decision to invoke or "mobilize the law."[18] The availability of broader social insurance benefits may help explain lower levels of legal mobilization in Canada.[19] Thomas argues that widely available health insurance and disability compensation in Canada dampens litigation (compared with the United States) concerning product liability. Similarly, in Canada a secure social safety net provides stability for terminated employees, thus making litigation more a choice than an economic necessity.

In addition to these factors, institutional arrangements make it easier for U.S. employees to take legal action to vindicate their claims under the law, and encourage them to take legal action even if it is unclear whether their rights have been violated. American rules concerning lawyer compensation arrangements, rules concerning the role of government agencies, and damage awards all provide greater incentives for terminated PCO employees to pursue legal action in the United States.

1. COUNSEL FEES

In the United States, lawyers can and do take cases on a contingency fee basis whereby an attorney charges a client nothing at the outset but agrees to take a percentage of an award if, and only if, one is granted or a settlement negotiated. A typical U.S. attorney's contingency fee is 33 to 40 percent, large enough to encourage many U.S. attorneys to take chances on weak cases with potentially high damages. Although most Canadian provinces allow some form of the contingency fee system, Ontario does not.[20] The majority of PCO Canada employees work and live in Ontario, and PCO Canada's corporate headquarters are located there. Thus, terminated PCO U.S. employees can pursue legal action with no "up-front" costs in a way that is not available to most PCO Canada employees.

Canada's "loser pays" system of assigning trial costs and attorney's fees makes it less likely that Canadians will pursue legal claims to trial and encourages them to make earlier, more realistic assessments of their likelihood of success. In Canada, unlike most cases in the United States, at the end of the trial the loser is required to pay some of the winner's legal costs, generally about 60 percent of her actual legal expenses.[21] In the United States the costs of *successfully* defending a wrongful termination lawsuit usually must be absorbed by the defendant; conversely, if the employer loses, it need not defray the successful plaintiff's legal costs. But when a terminated PCO Canada employee thinks of filing a lawsuit, besides having to pay her lawyer at least some money at the outset, she must consider the risk of losing and having to pay not only all her legal costs—which may amount to thousands of dollars[22]—but also PCO's legal costs. Similarly situated PCO U.S. employees know that even if they lose, they need not pay PCO U.S.'s legal bills—which might reach tens of thousands of dollars.[23] Hence PCO U.S. employees have weaker disincentives to sue.

2. ADMINISTRATIVE AGENCIES

In the United States, lawsuits claiming discrimination based on race, sex, age, and disability must initially be channeled through the federal EEOC or one of its state-level equivalents. Once an employee with an antidiscrimination claim (in this case, regarding termination) files a complaint with the EEOC, the agency then has a statutorily prescribed time of 180 days to investigate the claim. If the agency investigates and determines that the claim is meritorious, it issues the employee a "right-to-sue" letter (which allows her to file a lawsuit in federal court) or else the EEOC itself may sue the employer.[24] If the agency is unable to investigate and dismiss or affirm a complaint within 180 days, the EEOC is required to issue a "default" right-to-sue letter, which gives the employee/claimant the right to file a suit in federal court.

Unfortunately for all parties involved, the EEOC currently faces a backlog of over 100,000 charges. One study of 782,000 discrimination complaints filed with the EEOC and various state equivalents found that the average complaint languishes more than one year before any action is taken. The average time for a *meritless* complaint to be dismissed is thirteen months. Of complaints filed, about 66 percent are ultimately dismissed as meritless. Although terminated employees whose complaints are not being acted on can pursue the action in court, this option is realistic only for employees who can find the attorneys willing to take the case on contingency.

PCO officials report that very few EEOC complaints against it are resolved through the time-consuming agency process. The wait alone provides some incentive for disgruntled employees to attempt a compromise with PCO. Typically the employee moves on to another job and simply waits out the administrative process, hoping that her complaint is eventually ruled meritorious.

Nevertheless, the availability of the EEOC process, which is free to complainants, makes it easier and cheaper for terminated PCO U.S. employees than PCO Canada employees to take legal action.[25] Additionally, the fruits of the EEOC investigation and PCO's documents regarding that investigation are "discoverable"; the terminated employee has the right to gain access to these documents as her case progresses. Thus, by filing an EEOC claim, an employee who has only suspicions of discrimination in her termination may have a significant investigation conducted for her at no cost.

When a violation of the Human Rights Code is lodged in Canada, the commission established by the statue typically provides an investigating officer. As is the case in the United States, an investigation is conducted, a report is filed, and a tribunal may be established if evidence of a violation is shown. The difference is that the employee is locked into this process and cannot take her case outside the commission. Thus, despite similar remedies and similar difficulties obtaining a remedy, the PCO U.S. employee has greater legal leverage in discrimination claims because she can use the EEOC to gather evidence and then opt out of the administrative process to pursue the claim for damages in federal court.

3. THE LURE AND RISK OF HIGHER DAMAGES

In both countries the terminated employee's calculus about whether to enter the complicated, often-costly legal system includes a prediction about the likelihood of prevailing coupled with the size of the damage award that might be granted. In Canada, civil litigants are not constitutionally guaranteed the right to a jury trial.[26] Ontario alone, by statute, gives a party the prima facie right to request a jury.[27] But Ontario also has instituted a policy whereby eight of ten civil cases filed are diverted to a mediator.[28] In the United States, jury trials are widely available, and American law gives juries considerable discretion in determining damages, including (in appropriate cases) punitive damages. A study of wrongful discharge lawsuits in California that went to trial, 1980–86, found that the median jury award was $177,000, the average award $650,000, and the largest award $8 million.[29] We do not have a comparable study of Canadian damage awards, but it appears from studies in other legal contexts, such as medical malpractice suits, that Canadian civil damage awards tend to be much smaller than their American counterparts.[30]

C. Perceived Legal Risks to the Employer

The differences in law and legal institutions discussed earlier make the U.S. legal system a more threatening environment for employers, creating greater legal uncertainty, higher risks of incurring high defense costs, and a greater potential for large damage awards (with the accompanying adverse publicity). Lauren Edelman and others have found that American employers overestimate the actual incidence of wrongful dismissal lawsuits in the United States.[31] Nor are the aggregate costs of wrongful termination civil suits as high as employers may think.[32] Moreover, PCO U.S., its attorneys say, rarely faces causes of action based on common law claims. Over 65 percent of PCO U.S.'s posttermination legal actions entail statutory antidiscrimination claims first filed with the EEOC.[33] What does trouble PCO U.S. is the high level of legal uncertainty and the unpredictable possibility of the occasional very large civil damage award.

Because the implied contract theory of wrongful discharge is a common law creation—developed by the courts rather than by legislatures—the law varies from state to state, and the substance of the law can also be fairly ambiguous. The ambiguity is multiplied because crucial decisions often are made by a diverse array of juries, whose decisions are not explained and are largely unreviewable. This leaves employers unclear about the best way to protect themselves from liability. Certainly, many employers guess incorrectly. The study of 120 California jury verdicts between 1980 and 1986 found that 68 percent of plaintiffs won their wrongful discharge lawsuits, and that awards averaged $650,000.[34]

It is the highly publicized large losses that command employers' attention. In a study of nine professional personnel journals, Edelman, Abraham, and Erlanger found inflated reporting of both the rate at which employees win their wrongful discharge cases and the commensurate jury awards.[35] In our interviews, PCO U.S. officials often discussed very large wrongful termination awards,[36] as well as the damages *claimed* in lawsuits filed against PCO itself. PCO therefore tailors its termination policy to prevent any (even a small) chance of losing a lawsuit with a large award.

The majority of the cases that PCO faces, as noted earlier, originate in EEOC claims.[37] Here, too, the threat lies in those antidiscrimination claims that eventuate in lawsuits for damages. Statistically, the rate of large damage awards in these cases is small. In a study of Title VII race-based lawsuits, Shea and Gardner, a large Washington, D.C., law firm, found that plaintiffs were awarded compensatory and punitive damages in only 68 of 576 reported cases between 1980 and 1989.[38] Of those 68 cases, in only 3 did compensatory and punitive damages combined amount to more than $200,000.[39] Nevertheless, as with the common law claims, PCO U.S. officials focus on the highly publicized large antidiscrimination awards. It makes economic sense in their minds for the company to allocate greater resources to prevent the worst possible outcome—no matter how remote the chances of that outcome—because the American legal system makes that outcome hard to predict.

III. CORPORATE CULTURE

Notwithstanding cross-national differences in law and legal institutions, PCO has a strong commitment to uniform corporation-wide practices and policies. The PCO "Guidelines of Company Policy" declare that "[a]dherence to a uniform worldwide standard of conduct to guide our behavior is essential and must be maintained in each country where we do business."[40] Every PCO executive we spoke to claimed that there are no official differences in the termination process between the United States and Canada.[41] PCO sponsors annual training, which all human resources representatives from both the United States and Canada are required to attend. Because the corporate philosophy is claimed to derive from principles of equity for employees rather than from legal requirements, PCO asserts that the company does not tailor the termination process to the legal requirements of the particular countries in which it operates.

Uniform cross-national policies, regardless of differences in law, allow PCO to train U.S. and Canadian human resources personnel together.[42] After the training, PCO can transfer human resources personnel from country to country without retraining those employees in local law. Additionally, PCO officials claim that the practice of implementing a generous and consistent human resources policy makes it easier to attract and retain quality employees.[43]

Except in unusual circumstances, PCO is confident that its standard practices in termination go above and beyond the legal requirements of the United States and Canada. The company's executives do believe, however, that following the PCO policy insulates termination decisions from serious legal challenge.[44] This emphasis on consistency and the very real attempt made by PCO officials to meet the corporate goal of uniformity allows us to rule out cross-national differences in corporate culture as an explanation for the cross-national differences in termination practices.[45]

A. PCO's Rapid Termination Procedure

In both the United States and Canada, PCO has a two-tiered termination policy. A "rapid termination" occurs when an employee commits one of PCO's "five deadly sins"—absence of three days without notice, dishonesty, insubordination, possession of firearms or violation of the substance abuse policy, and misconduct.[46] In those cases, the termination process is not drawn out over many months but occurs virtually "on the spot." The Human Resources Department is consulted to provide verification that the incident was sufficient to merit termination and to ensure that PCO has the evidence to prove the violation, but beyond that the department's involvement is minimal. PCO greatly values ensuring rapid, decisive resolution in these cases. Rapid termination not only eliminates the presence of the problem employee but also provides an example to other employees that certain behavior will simply not be tolerated. In a typical year, PCO Canada and PCO U.S. terminate about the same percentage of employees using rapid termination—less than 1 percent of the workforce, by executives' estimate.[47] In rapid termination cases, there is little cross-national difference in the corporation's procedures, and the law in both countries allows rapid termination for the offenses PCO designates the five deadly sins.

B. PCO's Incremental Discipline Process

When an employee's performance declines, PCO policy calls for implementation of the "Incremental Discipline Process, designed to provide the problem employee with notice about specific inadequacies in her performance, to ensure that the company's expectations are clear and realizable, and to provide a fair chance for the employee to rehabilitate her performance. PCO officials, both in law and in human resources, insist that the rationale for the required procedures and documentation is not a legal defense but fair treatment as an aid to rehabilitation of the employee. The process, however, does generate a thorough paper trail about the employee's poor performance, which provides both legal justification for any eventual termination and better evidence supporting PCO's decision. In addition, the Incremental Discipline Process is designed to prevent two costly outcomes. First, it seeks to prevent termination of an employee who, all things considered, *should not* be fired; thus the process is designed to deter or expose a manager who has an unjustified desire to terminate an acceptable employee. Terminating an employee for a bad reason could expose PCO to legal liability,[48] but it is also bad business: PCO would bear the costs of training the employee's replacement and retaining an arbitrary or biased supervisor. Second, PCO policy strives to reduce the risk of retaining an employee who *should* be terminated. The Incremental Discipline Process provides the vehicle by which a manager who regrets terminating a "friend" can invoke an impartial, routinized assessment of the employee's performance. On the other hand, the Incremental Discipline Process—with its carefully scheduled phases of documentation, probation, and termination, is costly in itself, in terms of delay and personal time.

1. DOCUMENTATION

As an employee's performance begins to wane, the line manager—the employee's direct supervisor—is expected to step up consultations with the problem employee to clarify which expectations are not being met. When the line manager determines it is appropriate, she begins to document these meetings, sending copies to the employee and to the employee's file. The length of the documentation phase varies according to factors such as the sensitivity of the position, the attitude of the line manager, and the line manager's perception of how long the employee has been performing inadequately.

2. PROBATION

If the employee fails to improve, the next step is probation. All employees who have been with PCO for one year or longer are entitled to a six-month probation before termination.[49] Prior to placing the problem employee on probation, the line manager must consult with the Human Resources Department concerning the nature of the problem, the amount of discussion and documentation that has already occurred, and other pertinent factors. If it is agreed that the employee should be placed on probation, a probation letter is drafted by the line manager and the human resources manager. An attorney typically reviews both the letter and the case history, including documentation about the performance problems. Lawyers in the United States, it was told, undertake a more thorough review than their Canadian counterparts, but in both countries the attorney is expected to make sure that the employee's behavior provides the basis for a legally justifiable termination and that there is adequate "proof" in the form of documentation to back up PCO's side of the story.

The next step is a "probation meeting" among the employee, the line manager, and the human resources manager[50] to discuss the company's expectations. The problem employee is asked whether the expectations are unrealistic.

Sometimes the probation period or the probation meeting is used to suggest that there is simply a "bad fit" between PCO and the employee and that it is in the employee's interest to leave the company. One human resources manager told us, "I ask myself, 'Is this a will problem or a skill problem?' "[51] If it is a "skill problem," the probation meeting is used to explore what PCO can do to bring the employee's skills up to the required level. Typically, however, a "skill problem" will not reach the probation phase but will have been identified and rectified earlier. Sometimes the skill problem is simply too large. Then, "we try to convince the employee that the opportunities at PCO are not going to meet their expectations. We try to help them get on with other life opportunities."[52]

Most probation meetings, however, address "will problems," encouraging the employee to recognize that she is not putting all she can into the job and that she has to make her own turnaround. Probation for "will problems" often is short, PCO officials say, because an employee either shapes up or does not.

Throughout the probation, typically a period of six months, the line manager is expected to continue meeting regularly with the problem employee and to make clear whether performance is improving satisfactorily. The extended probation process is expensive for PCO. The costs include (1) productivity losses that stem from retaining a poor employee for up to six months, (2) lost manager time, because managers have to spend more time supervising problem employees, and (3) consultation with attorneys and other specialists (such as affirmative action officers).[53]

3. TERMINATION

At the end of the six-month probation period, assuming the employee has not left, a decision to retain or terminate the employee is made. PCO officials in both the United States and Canada indicate that by the time a problem gets to this stage, the decision is not difficult. The actual decision is made jointly by the line manager, the human resources manger, and, in some cases, the attorney and/or the affirmative action officer.

The "hard part" of termination is setting the terms, especially the amount of the severance pay. In both countries the officials say that PCO tries to make the first severance offer a fair one, in the belief that fairness prevents time-consuming negotiations, inconsistent results, and escalating posttermination disputes. PCO usually does not budge much from the initial offering in either country.

In both the United States and Canada, human resources executives described particular terminations that eliminated or accelerated steps of the Incremental Discipline Process when weak performance by the employee in question was deemed particularly harmful to PCO.[54] PCO's willingness to deviate from the stated policy under particular circumstances not only reflects the company's conviction that the Incremental Discipline Process goes beyond the legal requirements in both countries but also shows that when business risks are obvious and severe, even a legally risk-averse company like PCO is willing to move closer to legal liability to prevent other costs to PCO that would result from retaining the employee. A number of PCO officials who described deviations from the stated policy indicated that in their view the deviation made it no more likely that the termination would lead to legal wrangling.

IV. LEGAL, ORGANIZATIONAL, AND PROCEDURAL OUTCOMES

Despite PCO's emphasis on uniform corporate policy, and its belief that its termination policy clearly meets legal standards in both countries, in the United States, PCO's terminated employees challenge their termination decisions more than their Canadian counterparts. Moreover, in the United States there are many causes of action with which PCO must be concerned, while in Canada there is only one cause of action that poses an actual litigation threat to PCO; this means legal uncertainty for the company is greater in the United States. To deal with legal risks, PCO U.S.'s Human Resources Department has established two offices that do not exist in PCO Canada. Finally, there are procedural differences: PCO Canada is more inclined to use probation, and PCO U.S. uses attorney services more.

A. Dispute Pattern Differences

In 1995, as Table 7.1 shows, PCO Canada had a higher overall termination rate than PCO U.S., but much of the disparity may reflect idiosyncratic reasons, due to particular business-related changes in the Canadian operation.[55] For the purposes of this study of regulatory and legal system differences, the crucial finding is that at each phase of the termination process, PCO Canada and PCO U.S. incur different levels of disputing. According to PCO's detailed records, and our analysis of personnel files, as a percentage of all employees, there was a higher rate of "separations" (termination, resignation, or retirement) in PCO Canada than in PCO U.S. in the years studied. But the ratio of "forced separations" (meaning the employee was fired) to all separations was similar in the two countries. As Table 7.1 shows, in the fiscal year studied, 24 percent of total separations in Canada were forced; in United States, 23 percent of total separations were forced.

In Canada, 36 percent of those who were fired were first placed on formal probation. In the United States, on the other hand, only 9 percent of those who were fired were first placed on probation, suggesting a higher incidence of managerial recourse to "rapid termination" or to special case deviations from the formal termination process.

As noted at the outset of this chapter, former PCO U.S. employees were twice as likely to engage in posttermination disputes with PCO; 60 percent of them did so, compared with 29 percent of former PCO Canada employees. And former PCO U.S. employees were three times as likely to file a lawsuit—23 percent (more than one in five), as compared with 7 percent in Canada.

B. Organizational Differences

Although the termination philosophy of PCO does not vary cross-nationally, the organization of the Human Resources Department does vary. PCO U.S. employs in-house attorneys; PCO Canada does not. PCO U.S. uses its attorneys differently than PCO Canada. PCO U.S. has an Affirmative Action Office (AAO) that is active in the termination process; PCO Canada has no counterpart. These structural differences represent costs to PCO U.S. that are not incurred by PCO Canada. More in-house offices and officials to handle legal and quasi-legal questions reflect the higher rate and risk of serious legal disputing in the United States.

TABLE 7.1   PCO Termination and Disputing Rates in 1995

	United States	*Canada*
Total employees	9,603	525
Total separations	282 3% total employee	58 11% total employee
Forced separations	66 23% total separations	14 24% total separations
Formal probations	6 9% forced separations	5 36% forced separations

Forced separations
  without postseparation
  disputing
	26
	39% forced separations
		10
		71% forced separations

Forced separations
  with
  postseparation
  disputing
  but no lawsuit
	25
	38% forced separations
		4
		22% forced separations

Lawsuits filed	15 23% forced separations	1 7% forced separations

SOURCE: PCO company data.

1. LAWYERS

In Canada, when either the human resources representative or the line manager believes that legal advice is required, termination issues are brought to an outside attorney. This occurs routinely at the probation and termination phases of the Incremental Discipline Process but infrequently at other times.[56] More typically, however, attorney contact in Canada is brief and is done by telephone.[57] One senior official in the Canadian human resources office told us that she had never been to PCO Canada's attorney's office.

In the United States, in contrast, attorney contact is more frequent, more substantive, and occurs earlier in the termination process. In the United States, PCO been willing to pay to have in-house corporate counsel present every day in the corporate headquarters to deal with personnel matters.

2. THE AFFIRMATIVE ACTION OFFICE

Unlike PCO Canada, PCO U.S. has a specialized AAO that employs 2.5 full-time executives who perform regulatory tasks required by the EEOC and the Office of Federal Contract Compliance Program (OFCCP). PCO's AAO personnel split their time between termination issues and regulatory requirements (which include quarterly reports about the demographics of the workforce, training on special topics such as sexual harassment, and producing PCO's annual affirmative action plan). When termination of a "protected" employee (such as a racial minority, a woman, or an employee over forty years of age) is being considered, the line manager or the human resources manager contacts the AAO. The AAO can also become involved when a terminated or disciplined employee threatens to or actually files a complaint with the EEOC.

Although PCO officials insist that employees who fall into protected categories receive no different treatment in the termination process, a "protected" employee is *always* routed through the AAO prior to termination. According to the director of the AAO, this practice ensures that similar employee malfeasance is treated similarly and that all legal requirements are met. However, this practice also appears to reflect the greater perceived legal risk under civil rights laws. For example, the affirmative action officer and corporate human resources personnel all expressed concern about compliance with the Americans with Disabilities Act (ADA). Because some disabilities may be hidden, there is a concern that an employee may be misidentified as *not* belonging to a protected class when he does, in fact, merit special legal protection. Furthermore, the ADA is troubling to PCO U.S. officials because its legal requirements are ambiguous. PCO Canada, on the other hand, does not feel compelled to undertake special administrative reviews to deal with the risk of posttermination lawsuits by employees who allege that PCO failed to accommodate their disability.

In addition to consultation during the Incremental Discipline Process, the AAO is PCO U.S.'s interface with the EEOC and state equivalents. If an EEOC complaint is filed by an employee who believes that she has been terminated because of race, gender, or age, then PCO has thirty days to file a response.[58] At this point PCO must be very careful, say the AAO officials, because the complaint signals that the termination might result in a lawsuit. For reputational reasons, too, PCO wants to end the dispute quickly. Any complaint to the EEOC, therefore, is investigated by the AAO. The director of the office claims that responding to each complaint requires approximately two full workweeks for one person—at least eighty hours.

Although PCO Canada employees enjoy legal rights against discrimination, there is no separate corporate bureaucracy in PCO Canada to field these legal claims. The AAO in PCO U.S. presumably reflects the cross-national differences discussed earlier concerning the methods, incentives, and likelihood of legal mobilization. The PCO U.S. Affirmative Action Office is costly, and the EEOC response function is one of the most costly tasks that the AAO has to perform.

C. Procedural Differences

In the United States, PCO's termination process involves more work, more time, and higher costs. The reason, it appears, is that in the United States there is a more complex and detailed body of legal rules surrounding termination, more legal uncertainty, and a more threatening and more frequently activated litigation system. In Canada, PCO seeks waivers from dismissed employees without concern for increasing the risk of future litigation. PCO U.S. takes the opposite position. In termination cases in the United States, formal consultations with legal or quasi-legal professionals are more frequent, involve more people, are more open-ended and deliberative.

1. USE OF WAIVERS AND SEVERANCE PACKAGES

There is cross-national variation in the frequency with which PCO asks a terminated employee to sign a waiver indicating acceptance of the terms of the severance and agreeing to forgo legal action. For PCO Canada, disputes over the severance package (or "reasonable notice" payment) is the source of virtually all litigation. Thus, when a severance package is agreed upon, officials ask the employee to sign a waiver confirming her agreement.

In PCO U.S. the terminated employee only rarely is asked to sign a waiver, and the negotiation process is more constrained by law. For PCO U.S. the terms of the severance package are determined in accordance with the Employment Retirement Income Security Act (ERISA), which requires employers to adhere strictly to the terms of the formal employee benefit plans.[59] There is little room for negotiation; PCO does not have the discretion to "sweeten the deal" by supplementing one person's benefits. Thus, in PCO U.S., the termination meeting is simply a notification rather than a dialogue. The severance package in the United States, therefore, is more limited. It includes the payment of any pension or investment plan to which the employee has contributed through his tenure. In contrast to the Canadian practice, lump sums equivalent to an employee's salary for a particular period of time are not made at the time of termination.

Since liability for PCO U.S. centers not on the severance package but rather on the termination itself, an employee waiver, although rarely obtained, is intended to shield PCO from various forms of legal liability. But U.S. managers are reluctant to request a waiver for fear that if the idea of legal liability is mentioned, the employee is more likely to retain an attorney or pursue legal action.[60] In Canada, on the other hand, requests for waivers are standard practice. At the termination meeting, the waiver (preapproved by PCO's attorney) is presented to the Canadian employee, who usually signs it—either on the spot or after consulting an attorney (often at PCO's encouragement) to ensure the fairness of the offer.

In Canada, when an employee is terminated without just cause, she is entitled, pursuant to statutory law, to reasonable notice or compensation in lieu thereof. Just cause exists when the employee engages in serious misconduct, insubordination, theft, dishonesty, incompetence, competing with the employer, conflict of interest, absenteeism, or chronic illness. Adverse economic conditions, redundancy, and reorganization of the company do not constitute just cause for termination. Some commentators suggest, and PCO Canada's experience confirms, that employers face a difficult challenge if they attempt to prove in court that a termination meets the just cause requirement. Thus PCO Canada routinely offers "reasonable notice compensation" in lieu of actual notice. The amount of compensation provided is not specifically dictated by the law; court decisions refer to a variety of factors, including length of service, salary, job status, labor market conditions, and the year of the decision.[61] Studies indicate that severance awards in Canada as a whole average almost nine months of pay, and more for larger employers.[62]

Given the legal ambiguity concerning what must be paid in lieu of actual notice, PCO Canada tends to err on the side of safety and fairness, offering the employee outplacement assistance, severance pay, and short-term (usually six weeks) extension of medical benefits. Unlike in the United States, PCO Canada officials and employees have some room to negotiate. This negotiation occurs informally in many of the termination meetings or semiformally after the termination meeting, by way of letter or phone call from an attorney-friend of the terminated employee. PCO Canada invests heavily in pretermination resolution and thus sees fewer posttermination disputes and lower costs.

Severance packages in the United States are much lower, and rarely is time spent negotiating a waiver of legal liability. It is possible, too, that PCO Canada, with its greater use of probation, spends more management time on pretermination dispute resolution. But PCO Canada spends less than PCO U.S. in posttermination disputes and lawsuits and on definitively expensive, pretermination consultations with legal and quasi-legal personnel. It is difficult to compare the larger PCO Canada expenditures on severance pay and pre-termination negotiations with the higher legal and administrative costs in the United States. But overall, the more complex, detailed, and potentially punitive legal rules faced by PCO U.S. officials seem to lead to higher expenditures on both pre-termination and posttermination mechanisms.

2. USE OF ATTORNEYS

Not only do PCO U.S. officials consult attorneys more often, but they also use them somewhat differently. In the United States, according to officials, they typically present to the corporation's attorney a more open-ended question, along the lines of "What should we do in this situation?" In Canada, according to PCO Canada's outside counsel and officials, the usual question typically asked is narrower, along the lines of "Is the following step we are about to take legally defensible?" In both countries the attorneys also function as troubleshooters. But unlike the Canadian attorney, PCO U.S.'s in-house lawyers provide ongoing training to department personnel. The PCO U.S. in-house attorney tries to speak with every human resources worker and as many line managers as possible at the outset of their employment, encouraging them to consult her too early and too often rather than too late.

In PCO Canada, there are more rules about when the attorney should be consulted. Generally, the attorney is consulted later in the process as a routine "last check." The attorney reviews the probation letter and analyzes or discusses the file to determine whether PCO Canada has solid justification for placing an employee on probation. In the United States, in contrast, a line manager or human resources representative often consults an attorney not to seek approval for a decision but to participate in formulating a plan. The attorney consultation is intended not only to ensure that PCO is on sound legal footing for posttermination disputing that may eventually arise but also to help apply PCO's policy of attempting to rehabilitate problem employees.

The U.S. attorney, then, is more of a "partner" in the decision-making process, and indeed often seeks a larger role. PCO's Canadian attorney had nothing but praise for PCO Canada's Human Resources Department. The PCO U.S. attorney, on the other hand, asserted she often wishes that the representative or the line manager would consult her earlier in the process.[63] The American lawyers sometimes want additional steps to be taken regarding a problem employee, even if doing so will lengthen the documentation phase and extend the tenure of an unwanted employee.

The PCO U.S. attorney also seems to work much harder at ensuring consistency—ensuring that employees who have committed similar blunders are treated alike. This may partly reflect differences in scale and organizational structure. In Canada the department is smaller, and all human resources representatives are in the same location, which allows consultation to ensure consistency. In the larger, more decentralized PCO U.S. operation, both the attorney and the AAO take affirmative responsibility for ensuring consistent treatment. Differences in law, however, also stimulate the U.S. attorney's extra efforts. Since PCO Canada need only be concerned with one cause of action—reasonable notice—it is easier for nonlegal actors to perform many of the quasi-legal tasks reserved for the attorney at PCO U.S., whose former employees may resort to a complex and legally confusing array of statutory causes of action, in more legal forums.

3. USE OF PROBATION

Probation is one of the most important and potentially costly elements of the Incremental Discipline Process. Although PCO officials claim otherwise, the probation process almost surely helps insulate the company from legal liability. Probation demonstrates the employer's attempt to rectify a problem fairly and provides a written record of employee nonperformance, which could be used at trial to bolster PCO's legal argument that the termination was the result of employee nonperformance rather than some other, illegal reason. As Table 7.1 shows, probation is used much more frequently by PCO Canada (36 percent of employees) than by PCO U.S. (9 percent).

Probation, however, is drawn-out, costly, and usually unsuccessful. One executive estimated that only one or two out of five employees who begin the Incremental Discipline Process reachieve good standing with PCO.[64] The higher probation rate in Canada thus seems to contradict the theory that PCO U.S. is more risk-averse and incurs more costs in the termination process. After all, wouldn't the division of the company that is more risk-averse employ this defensive strategy more frequently? Secondly, does PCO U.S.'s less frequent use of probation help *explain* its higher rate of posttermination legal disputing and litigation? The answer to both questions is no. In fact, PCO U.S.'s less frequent use of probation is misleading and actually *reflects* its greater sensitivity to legal risk.

Probation procedures in PCO U.S. historically have been more complex and expensive than in PCO Canada. Until very recently, PCO U.S. offered a step prior to formal probation known as a "performance plan." This plan was essentially a probation period that did not start the six-month probation clock and could be entered into informally, without consulting the attorney or the AAO. Like probation, during a performance plan a problem employee was under close supervision and received a clear statement of performance expectations.

The performance plan was required neither by the law nor by PCO corporate policy. It was instituted, PCO U.S. officials say, to guard against legal liability. It gave problem employees *additional* opportunities to reform and gave the line manager *more* evidence to justify further discipline, if necessary. Moreover, the performance plan allowed line managers to attempt the same rehabilitative process attempted by probation without all the formal requirements.

More recently, PCO U.S. officials have been moving away from the performance plan because it simply delays the point at which inefficient employees can be terminated.[65] PCO U.S. officials currently are reanalyzing each of the complex termination procedures to evaluate their legal necessity.[66] Although the increased use of probation might suggest that PCO Canada is more risk-averse, this actually demonstrates PCO Canada's willingness to move forward with the termination process and PCO U.S.'s aversion to doing so.

V. PERCEPTIONS OF LEGAL RISK

Despite PCO's desire for a uniform corporation-wide personnel policy, a detailed analysis of its termination processes, as we have seen, highlights significant cross-national differences in structure, procedures, dispute patterns, and process costs. The Canadian law on the books, with its broader protections against arbitrary dismissal, might lead one to expect that PCO Canada would be more legally risk-averse and would incur greater costs in the termination process. In fact, we have seen that PCO U.S. is more risk-averse, as evidenced by its establishment of more elaborate defensive structures and procedures, and by its employment of more legal and quasi-legal personnel. These measure entail substantial costs not incurred by PCO Canada.

PCO Canada, too, makes expenditures to avoid legal risk. It pays terminated employees larger severance packages that tend to be more generous than the law requires and more generous than those paid by PCO U.S. It uses the formal probation process more often, and it perhaps retains nonproductive employees longer—although that is not clear because of PCO U.S.'s use, until recently, of an informal preprobation performance plan for questionable employees.

PCO U.S. officials perceive their legal environment as more threatening than do their counterparts in Canada. The threat arises from the higher level of legal uncertainty generated by the American legal system and the risk of extremely costly and embarrassing jury awards in statutory antidiscrimination or wrongful discharge lawsuits. This threat leads PCO U.S. to employ a strategy of minimizing exposure of the worst-case scenario of maximum liability.

The greater legal uncertainty in the United States arises in part, as mentioned earlier, from the fact that PCO U.S. faces the possibility of claims arising from a multitude of statutory and common law theories, whereas PCO Canada faces a threat from only one cause of action. PCO Canada's legal risk focuses almost solely on the "reasonable notice" requirement.[67] In the two years of employment records we examined, there were only two posttermination lawsuits, both based on that claim. Also, all of PCO

Canada's postseparation legal disputes that fell short of a lawsuit revolved around the same issue. The law on the subject is somewhat blurred by the case-by-case nature of judicial elaboration of the doctrine. Nevertheless, as noted earlier, its requirements are summarized in books that provide Canadian employers detailed advice about the required amount of compensation in lieu of reasonable notice.[68] Thus PCO Canada's human resources managers express reasonable confidence about knowing how to avoid litigation, and about what their maximum exposure will be if a case is brought and goes to trial. This higher level of legal certainty is manifested in the ability of PCO Canada's human resources managers to function with relatively little input from lawyers.

In contrast, according to its attorney, 25 percent of lawsuits against PCO U.S. in 1995 (the year studied) claimed race discrimination under Title VII of the U.S. Civil Rights Act, 17 percent claimed gender discrimination, 33 percent age discrimination (pursuant to the Age Discrimination in Employment Act [ADEA]), 8 percent were based on the Americans with Disabilities Act, and 17 percent "other," primarily ERISA, the law governing employee benefit programs. This distribution is displayed in Figure 7.2. It is notable that none involved common law wrongful discharge claims, and PCO attorneys say they worry less about that kind of suit.[69] Under all the relevant statutes, as well as the common law area, the large number of lawsuits in the United States as a whole constantly generates new law and ambiguous, difficult-to-summarize requirements.

Even more important to PCO U.S.'s sense of unpredictable legal risk is the greater propensity of Americans to bring lawsuits; the higher incidence of trial by jury; and the potential, under the expansive American law of damages, for very large damage awards and the adverse publicity they generate. As noted earlier, American rules on counsel fees (availability of contingency fee arrangements; absence of a "loser pays" rule) make it easier and less risky for former PCO U.S. employees to retain an attorney and bring a lawsuit. Not surprisingly, research in other areas of law suggests that when confronted with similar problems, Americans are considerably more likely than Canadians to assert legal claims for compensation.[70] PCO U.S. officials also view jury decisions on liability and damages as difficult to predict and are deeply concerned about the risk, however small the statistical odds, of a very large verdict against the company. In addition to the direct costs, PCO executives repeatedly said they feared that a highly publicized large award in a civil rights case would have an adverse effect on employee morale, as workers "take sides" in discussing the case. To cope with such unpredictable maximum legal risks, PCO U.S. attempts to reduce uncertainty by employing more legal and quasi-legal professionals than does PCO Canada, by involving them earlier and more intensively in personnel management, and by routinely involving a special Affirmative Action Office in

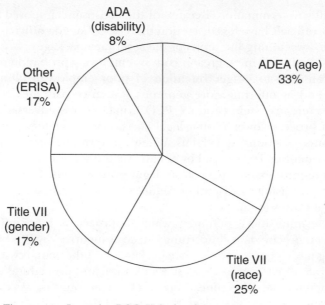

Figure 7.2. Lawsuits, PCO U.S., by claim, 1995
(PCO company data).

consultation and decision-making processes involving various categories of employees.

VI. CONCLUSION

In Canada, substantive legal protections against arbitrary discharge arguably are broader than in the United States, for they require just cause or reasonable notice for all employees, regardless of race, gender, or other characteristics. Nevertheless, the discharge process in PCO Canada engenders less legal disputing and less corporate bureaucracy, both formal and informal, than in PCO U.S. This can be linked to the larger variety of legal causes of action available to the American employees, the higher money damages awarded by American courts, and the greater ease of legal mobilization in the United States. These factors generate more perceived legal uncertainty and legal risk for the company than does Canadian law, leading it to expend more on lawyers and regulatory affairs personnel. These factors also lead to a higher incidence of posttermination lawsuits in PCO U.S.

Confronted with a more adversarial legal environment, PCO U.S. employs a more adversarial model of employment relations when considering termination. PCO U.S. is less likely to pursue probation and less likely to move swiftly to termination. Because of the constraints imposed by ERISA, PCO U.S. officials have less discretion than PCO Canada officials to defuse conflict by sweetening the terms of the severance package.

PCO Canada may incur greater costs by employing probation more often (which can lead to longer retention of poor employees ultimately dismissed), and by offering more generous severance packages. These policies, however, may help produce PCO Canada's less adversarial posttermination process, lower *ex ante* legal costs, and lower legal costs arising from posttermination legal claims. When posttermination disputes do occur, they can often be resolved by enhancing the severance package, which does not require extensive aid from legal professionals. In PCO U.S., the threat of postdismissal disputing requires more investment in legal and quasi-legal professionals.

To determine more definitely which approach is more efficient, we would need precise data concerning the costs incurred by PCO Canada in providing more generous severance packages and the actual costs incurred by PCO U.S. in making its expensive structural and procedural alterations to the Incremental Discipline Process. PCO's accounting systems do not readily generate that data. Given the nature of the organizational and procedural "extras" observed at PCO U.S., it seems safe to say that PCO U.S. probably spends more money per terminated employee. Regardless of which division of PCO spends more on termination, it is clear that in Canada, the "extra" money is largely going to "paying workers" in the form of more generous severance packages and the increased use of probation, whereas in PCO U.S., the money is going to "paying lawyers" because it is largely channeled to legal and quasi-legal professionals.

NOTES

1. *Adair v. United States,* 208 U.S. 161 (1908).

2. Some U.S. state courts have held that employer-issued employee manuals (or other oral or written statements by the employer) may be considered implied contracts, and that those terms may limit the employment-at-will doctrine and create liability for termination without just cause.

3. H. W. Arthurs, D. D. Carter, J. Fudge, H. J. Glasbeek, and G. Trudeau, "Canada," in *International Encyclopaedia For Labour Law and Industrial Relations,* edited by R. Blanplain (Kluwer Law and Taxation Publishers, 1993); Ellen E. Mole, *The Wrongful Dismissal Handbook* (Toronto: Butterworths, 1990). *Toussaint v. Blue Cross & Blue Shield,* 292 N.W.2d 880 (Mich. 1980)

4. In the United States, protection from race and gender discrimination is found in Title VII of the Civil Rights Act of 1964, 42 U.S.C. §§ 2000e et seq., and enforcement is delegated to the Equal Employment Opportunity Commission (EEOC) and the federal courts. In addition, each state in which PCO operates has similar laws that prohibit employment discrimination.

In Canada, race and gender discrimination are prohibited at both the federal and the provincial level. For federal employees (not most PCO employees), private sector labor relations are governed by the Canada Labour Code, R.S.C. 1990, c.E-14, but race, sex, national origin, and ethnic origin discrimination are prohibited by the Canadian Human Rights Act, R.S.C. 1985, c.H-6.

Almost all of PCO's Canadian employees work in Ontario and are protected by the Ontario Employment Standards Act, R.S.O. 1990, c.E-14. Like the federal law, protection against discrimination in Ontario is embodied in a human rights code: the Ontario Human Rights Code, R.S.O. 1990, c.H-19. It should be noted, however, that each province in Canada has its own statute that may vary somewhat.

In the United States, protection from age discrimination is found in the Age Discrimination in Employment Act (ADEA). 29 U.S.C. §§ 621–34 (1988). In Ontario, age discrimination is prohibited by the Employment Standards Act, R.S.O. c.E-14.

In the United States, the law governing employment abuses on the basis of disability is the Americans with Disabilities Act, 29 U.S.C. §§ 621–34 (1988). Discrimination based on disability is prohibited in Ontario by the Ontario Human Rights Code, R.S.O. 1990, c.H-19.

5. Protection from discrimination on the grounds of sexual orientation is also found in the Ontario Human Rights Code, R.S.O. 1990, c.H.

6. Although it is difficult to find data of this nature specific to certain corporations, some empirical studies about the rate of disputing in the corporate United States indicate that PCO may have a higher level of disputing than other companies do. In fact, many authors of empirical studies about dispute patterns conclude that a large percentage of aggrieved employees do not pursue their claims of employer mistreatment. Moreover, when the source of the claim is discrimination, as is frequently the case in PCO U.S. (see Figure 7.2), scholars suggest that the number of people who will pursue a claim falls even further. See, e.g., Kristen Bumiller, *The Civil Rights Society: The Social Construction of Victims* (Baltimore: Johns Hopkins University Press, 1989).

There are any number of reasons that the experience of PCO may be different than the ones mentioned here. First, PCO is a very large corporation, which may lead to higher disputing rates because of a lack of community. Second, the employees at PCO are largely upper-middle-class, well-educated employees. This population is more likely to know their legal rights, have access to the legal system, and either have an attorney or know how to go about getting one. Thus, many of the barriers to the legal system that may be present for the subjects of the other studies are not faced by PCO employees. Of course, since this case study focuses only on the experience of PCO, there is no way of knowing exactly why these numbers are higher; these are simply some hypotheses.

7. In both countries, the data are from the calendar year 1995. In Canada, we also collected comparable data for the calendar year 1994—there were no significant differences between the 1994 and 1995 data.

8. For more on how the just cause presumption is translated to PCO procedures, see section IV.

9. For more on the common law principle regarding employment, see Mole, *The Wrongful Dismissal Handbook.*

10. Employment Standards Act, R.S.O. 1990, c.E-14, pt. 57.

11. Id. at 5.

12. Arthurs et al., "Canada."

13. See, e.g., Mary Ann Glendon and Edward R. Lev, "Changes in the Bonding of the Employment Relationship: An Essay on the New Property," *Boston College Law Review* 20 (1979): 457.

14. *Petermann v. International Brotherhood of Teamsters,* 174 Cal.App. 2d 184, 344 P.2d 25 (1959) (holding that an employer cannot terminate an employee for failing to commit perjury at his employer's direction).

15. *Monge v. Beebe Rubber Co.,* 114 N.H. 130, 316 A.2d 549 (1974) (holding that an employer may not discharge an employee for failing to go on a date with her employer).

16. *Toussaint v. Blue Cross & Blue Shield,* 292 N.W.2d 880 (Mich. 1980) (holding that an employee can sue an employer for wrongful termination where a contract requiring good cause for termination can be inferred from oral or written statements made by the employer).

17. John J. Donohue III and Peter Siegelman, "The Changing Nature of Employment Discrimination Litigation," *Stanford Law Review* 43 (1991): 992 n. 18

18. Bumiller, *The Civil Rights Society.*

19. Bruce A. Thomas, "The Canadian Experience with Alternative Dispute Resolution in Products Liability Cases," *Canada–United States Law Journal* 17 (1991): 363.

20. Ont.Rev.Stat. ch. 478 (1980).

21. See Thomas, "The Canadian Experience with Alternative Dispute Resolution," 368 (discussing civil trials more generally).

22. A study conducted by the *Civil Justice Review* found that the typical cost to a plaintiff to pursue a civil claim in Canada is $38,000 Canadian. Reported by Charles Harnick in a speech to the Annual Institute on Continuing Legal Education, Canadian Bar Association of Ontario, Toronto, January 26, 1996 [available Westlaw, Database BCA].

23. In a study of 120 wrongful dismissal jury trials in California, the average legal cost to a company defending a dismissal case that goes to trial was over $80,000 U.S. James Dertouzos, Elaine Holland, and Patricia Ebmer, "The Legal and Economic Consequences of Wrongful Termination, RAND: The Institute for Civil Justice" (Santa Monica, Calif.: RAND, 1988).

24. Testimony of Gilbert F. Casellas, Chairman, U.S. Equal Employment Opportunity Commission before the House Committee on Economic and Educational Opportunities, July 25, 1995,

25. The costs to the employer are, however, great and occur whether or not the EEOC investigates. Simply filing the complaint triggers expensive responsive action on the part of PCO, so that even claims later dropped or deemed meritless are expensive for the company.

26. *Crupi v. Royal Ottawa,* 12 C.P.C.2d 207 (Ont.Dist.Ct.1986).

27. Courts of Justice Act, Ont.Stat. ch. 11, § 121 (1984).

28. "Ottawa's Lawyers Told to Settle Out of Court More Often," *Financial Post Daily,* September 26, 1995, 133.

29. Dertouzos, Holland, and Ebmer, *The Legal and Economic Consequences of Wrongful Termination.*

30. Peggy Berkowitz, "In Canada, Different Legal and Popular Views Prevail," *Wall Street Journal,* April 4, 1986, 21. Medical malpractice fees paid by Canadian physicians are approximately one-twelfth the average U.S. premium. Patricia Danzon, "The 'Crisis' in Medical Malpractice: A Comparison of the Trend in the United States, Canada, the United Kingdom and Australia," *Law, Medicine and Health Care* 18 (spring–summer 1990): 50–51; Donald N. Dewees, Michael J. Treblicock, and Peter C. Coyte, "The Medical Malpractice Crisis: A Comparative Empirical Perspective," *Law and Contemporary Problems* 54 (1991): 217.

31. Lauren B. Edelman, Steven E. Abraham, and Howard S. Erlanger, "Professional Construction of Law: The Inflated Threat of Wrongful Discharge," *Law and Society Review* 26 (1992): 47.

32. Dertouzos, Holland, and Ebmer, *The Legal and Economic Consequences of Wrongful Termination.*

33. Interview, Susan Tuern, PCO U.S. attorney, March 6, 1996.

34. Dertouzos, Holland, and Ebmer, *The Legal and Economic Consequences of Wrongful Termination.*

35. Id. at 65

36. The awareness about very large wrongful termination awards was discussed in interviews of all PCO human resources managers throughout the United States. Interviews with Bill Richmond (a pseudonym), PCO U.S. Human Resources Manager of Marketing and Sales, January 30, 1996; Robert Burns (a pseudonym), PCO U.S. Human Resources Manager of Marketing and Sales, January 23, 1996; and Ryan Jackson (a pseudonym), PCO U.S. Human Resources Manager of Marketing and Sales, January 15, 1996.

37. Interviews, Hank Brown, PCO U.S. Affirmative Action Officer, March 6, 1996; Interview, Susan Turner, PCO U.S. attorney, March 6, 1996.

38. Reported in 136 Cong. Rec. E 2478.

39. Id.

40. PCO Guidelines of Corporate Policy, p. 5.

41. Interviews, Bill Richmond (a pseudonym), PCO U.S. Human Resources Manager of Marketing and Sales, January 30, 1996. Similar statements were also made by Robert Burns (a pseudonym), PCO U.S. Human Resources Manager of Marketing and Sales, January 23, 1996, and Ryan Jackson (a pseudonym), PCO U.S. Human Resources Manager of Marketing and Sales, January 15, 1996.

42. Interviews, Norma Lanning (a pseudonym), PCO Canada Human Resources Representative, October 18, 1995; Eric Samson (a pseudonym), PCO Canada Human Resources Representative, October 18, 1995.

43. Interviews, Bill Richmond (a pseudonym), PCO U.S. Human Resources Manager of Marketing and Sales, January 30, 1996, Norma Lanning (a pseudonym), PCO Canada Human Resources Representative, October 18, 1995; Eric Samson (a pseudonym), PCO Canada Human Resources Representative, October 18, 1995.

44. There is more confidence in this philosophy in Canada than in the United States. Interviews, Norma Lanning (a pseudonym), PCO Canada Human Resources Representative, October 18, 1995; Eric Samson (a pseudonym), PCO Canada

Human Resources Representative, October 18, 1995; Erica James, PCO Canada Senior Human Resources Representative, October 18 and 19, 1996.

45. Of course, there is a distinction between formal and informal differences in corporate culture. While the corporate standard emphasizes cross-national continuity, the corporate philosophy cannot eliminate all cultural differences.

46. Obviously, "misconduct" is a broad category designed to give PCO officials some flexibility. Some of the executives with whom we spoke even laughed about the ambiguity of the category. Erica James, PCO Canada Senior Human Resources Representative, October 18 and 19, 1996. However, consistent with PCO general philosophy to err on the side of caution, misconduct would have to be quite severe to circumvent the implementation of the progressive discipline process.

47. PCO officials terminate about five each year with rapid termination in Canada and about one hundred in the United States, according to corporate officials.

48. For more on the actual liability, see sections II.A.2.c. and II.A.3.

49. PCO Human Resources Policy Manual, p. 12.

50. There is a strong commitment to conducting the probation meeting in person regardless of how far the human resources personnel and the line manager may have to travel to attend the meeting. In fact, the vice president for human resources in Canada told us that one of her "worst" terminations—meaning that the posttermination disputing was quite protracted—was one in which she did not attend the probation meeting. She attributes at least some of the problems in that case to her absence.

51. Interview, Bill Richmond (a pseudonym), PCO U.S. Human Resources Manager of Marketing and Sales, March 7, 1996.

52. Interview, Bill Richmond (a pseudonym), PCO U.S. Human Resources Manager of Marketing and Sales, March 7, 1996.

53. For more on the role of the Affirmative Action Officer, see section III.B.2.

54. For example, "Steve Smith" was brought in at a fairly high level as the product manager of one of PCO's largest-selling drugs in Canada. At the time Smith's performance began to decline, the drug was only months away from being made available by competitors under a generic label—a period during which PCO had a large business interest in ensuring brand loyalty and market share. When Smith missed deadlines, failed to create and implement development plans, and failed to manage the budget properly, his direct supervisor implemented a "development plan" to help Smith rehabilitate his performance. Smith was quickly terminated before the designated probation period, however, when it became obvious that he had no intention of implementing the development plan. In Smith's case, none of the formal steps of the Incremental Discipline Process had been taken. The development plan was not a formal probation, and yet Smith was terminated without fear of legal ramifications.

55. A group of six PCO Canada employees were dismissed, according to company officials, because their jobs became obsolete and they were either unreceptive to or unsuccessful in retraining efforts. In addition, an entire sales office was closed due to nonprofitability. Also in the year in question, PCO Canada had a higher rate of retirements.

56. For example, a PCO Canada human resources representative was approached by a PCO Canada line manager who claimed to be having trouble with a

female employee. The human resources representative later learned that the conflict arose because the employee was not responsive to the manager's sexual advances. The human resources representative, who had been working with the line manager, immediately sought legal advice.

57. For more on the substance of the interaction, see section II.C.2.

58. At the time of our interview, the EEOC had been recently giving PCO sixty days to file the response. PCO's AAO did not know why this change in policy had taken place and, grateful for the extra time, had not sought out an explanation from the regulatory agency.

59. 29 U.S.C. §§ 1001–1461.

60. None of the U.S. regional human resources managers interviewed had used the waiver more than five times, although all of them were thinking about using it more and wanted to use it more.

61. Steven L. McShane and David C. McPhillips, "Predicting Reasonable Notice in Canadian Wrongful Dismissal Cases," *Industrial and Labor Relations Review* 41 (1997): 108.

62. Steven L. McShane, "Reasonable Notice Criteria in Common Law Wrongful Dismissal Cases," *Relations Industrielles* 38 (1983): 618; cited in Terry H. Wagar and Kathy A. Jourdain, "The Determination of Reasonable Notice in Canadian Wrongful Dismissal Cases," *Labor Law Journal* 43 (1992): 58.

63. There is an interesting parallel between this suggestion by the PCO U.S. attorney and the human resources personnel in PCO Canada. Although the PCO Canada attorney had no complaints once a termination reached his desk, the human resources personnel expressed some dissatisfaction with the speed at which problems were brought to *their* attention by line managers—it was too late. This supports the argument that the human resources personnel in PCO Canada are performing some of the quasi-legal tasks.

64. Interview, Bill Richmond (a pseudonym), PCO U.S. Human Resources Manager of Marketing and Sales, March 7, 1996.

65. Interviews, Bill Richmond (a pseudonym), PCO U.S. Human Resources Manager of Marketing and Sales, January 30, 1996. Similar statements were also made by Robert Burns (a pseudonym), PCO U.S. Human Resources Manager of Marketing and Sales, January 23, 1996, and Ryan Jackson (a pseudonym), PCO U.S. Human Resources Manager of Marketing and Sales, January 15, 1996.

66. Because the Incremental Discipline Process and specifically probation are expensive and time-consuming, PCO U.S. executives are currently making efforts to reduce the costs PCO incurs from problem employees, including limiting the time of poor performance that precedes probation, reducing the number of probations by helping employees understand that PCO is not the right place for them, and reducing the need for legal and affirmative action consultations by training the line managers and the human resources managers to handle these situations properly.

67. Obviously, employers in general and PCO Canada in particular could be vulnerable to lawsuits based on any number of causes of action under Canadian law. However, PCO Canada has never been the subject of a lawsuit on any grounds other than reasonable notice. PCO Canada officials were, of course, aware of the various causes of action but reported little concern about them because of what they

regarded as the high level of integrity in the organization and based on PCO Canada's past history.

68. See, e.g., Mole, *The Wrongful Dismissal Handbook*. This book has pages and pages of charts describing type of employment, years of service, and so on, and it prescribes the amount of reasonable notice compensation sufficient to avoid possible litigation.

69. Interview, Susan Tuern, PCO U.S. attorney, March 6, 1996.

70. Herbert Kritzer, W. A. Bogart, and Neil Vidmar, "The Aftermath of Injury: Cultural Factors in Compensation Seeking in Canada and the United States," *Law and Society Review* 25 (1991): 515. Another survey found that American employees are substantially more likely than Canadians to assert claims regarding workplace discrimination. Herbert Kritzer, W. A. Bogart, and Neil Vidmar, "To Confront or Not to Confront: Measuring Claiming Rates in Discrimination Grievances," *Law and Society Review* 25 (1991): 882.

CHAPTER EIGHT

Credit Card Debt Collection and the Law

Germany and the United States

Charles Ruhlin

If the extension of credit is the lifeblood of a dynamic commercial society, the forcible collection of unpaid debts is its backbone. Debt cases account for a substantial part of the business of virtually every country's court system.[1] At the same time, democratic governments face political pressures to protect debtors from unfair debt collection practices and sometimes, in the case of hardship, from having to pay their debts on time. Just as the political balance of forces between creditors and debtors varies from country to country, and from era to era, so do the laws and institutional arrangements that constrain the collection process. This chapter represents an exploratory effort to assess the extent and consequences of cross-national differences in debt collection laws and practices. It does so by examining the experience of a multinational bank that conducts consumer credit card operations in the United States and Germany. It finds, in brief, that the high cost and uncertainty of the U.S. legal system, in which debtors also have greater access to bankruptcy protection, encourage U.S. operations of multinational banks to delay formal legal collection action longer than in Germany. In Germany, the weakness of formal legal protections for debtors, coupled with the presence of uniform and simple court procedures facilitating debt collection, make it relatively easy for banks to press their claims at an early date without the risk of pushing debtors to file for bankruptcy.

I. INTRODUCTION

Multinational banks, increasingly challenged by global competition and the loss of corporate borrowers to bond markets, have sought to recover profits from consumer banking. In the United States, credit card returns far surpassing those in other areas of banking have enticed creditors to issue cards at record levels. Banks have increased credit card loans 20 percent in each of the last two years, and these loans now represent approximately 11 percent of banks' total loan portfolios.[2] Credit card debt per household nearly doubled between 1992 and 1996, yet innovative practices (like BancOne's introduction of retirement-savings-account-linked cards) are extending credit even further.[3] In countries such as Germany, the credit card market is less highly developed, yet it has grown rapidly in recent years and piggybacks on a longer tradition there of cheque cards (combination ATM and bank credit cards),[4] variants of which are now being introduced in the United States.

Notwithstanding excellent revenue potential and generally unproblematic repayments of credit card obligations, banks still must contend with serious delinquencies in repayment—whether as a result of illness, marital problems, unemployment, or overextension. In the United States, one study indicated, credit card debts in 1997 accounted for 53 percent of bank loan losses, although they represented less than 11 percent of all debt held by banks.[5] In 1996 the Bank of New York, reflecting generally growing losses in the credit card business, set aside $360 million to cover bad debts.[6] According to one news article, in 1997 Visa and Master Card International were losing more than $8.5 billion in unpaid credit card debts.[7]

To a large extent, banks have routinized their handling of credit card delinquencies in their operations at home and abroad. Hence any cross-national distinctions in governance mechanisms are likely to reflect differences in the institutional environment, which includes (1) formal legal rules delineating the rights and responsibilities of creditors and debtors; (2) legal institutions and practices governing the enforcement of these rights and responsibilities; and (3) national or regional norms and attitudes surrounding indebtedness, bankruptcy, and litigation.

The extent to which national legal rules and institutions influence the relationship between consumers and banks can be examined by comparing similar bank operations in different national systems. Two major economic powers—the United States and Germany—have strikingly different institutional environments with which multinational banks must contend in debt collection. These environments generate different levels of uncertainty in the debtor-creditor relationship, and these in turn prompt different organizational responses to breakdowns in the relationship.

A complete analysis of consumer debt collection in the United States and Germany would consider the degree to which institutions constituting respective national social safety nets help alleviate the problems that cause personal delinquencies and default in the first place. Differences in the comprehensiveness of health insurance, unemployment insurance, and other forms of social insurance coverage may influence the extent to which consumers incur debt and, indirectly, how legal rules and institutions buffering individuals from debt burdens have evolved. Such analysis is beyond the scope of this paper, but the relevance of social safety nets should at least be noted. Moreover, to focus on how German and American laws and regulations concerning debt collection affect actual collection practices, as in this case study, cannot provide a full-blown evaluation of the two nations' debt collection or consumer credit policy. A complete welfare analysis would examine from a societal perspective the trade-offs between the costs that flow from the U.S. system's greater propensity to expand (and write off) credit to risky customers and the benefits that flow from a more generous credit system.

II. METHODS

This research began with interviews of in-house counsel and collections managers in several U.S.-based multinational banks with operations in the United States and Germany. Additional interviews with representatives of government agencies, law firms, industry associations, academic institutions, and independent research institutes helped build descriptions of the institutional frameworks in these two countries. In Germany, I interviewed several research scholars and attorneys who have participated in the process of creating a new consumer bankruptcy law there, and representatives from consumer debt-counseling agencies. In the United States. I interviewed twelve in-house counsel and collections managers from five multinational banks, an official at the Federal Trade Commission (FTC), which is formally charged with enforcing the federal Fair Debt Collection Practices Act, and three academic researchers. I conducted some of these interviews by telephone and others in person. These initial interviews were largely information-gathering exercises, intended to open discussion of the legal frameworks in both countries.

Based on these initial discussions, we reached agreement with one bank, called Credit Co. here, to conduct more in-depth interviews of its staff and gain access to internal documents. I interviewed in-house counsel and collections managers from Credit Co.'s national and regional offices in the United States, and their counterparts in the bank's German headquarters. I used a common questionnaire with both open-ended questions, to elicit qualitative information on their bank's experiences with the two legal cultures, and specific questions pertaining to quantitative data regarding their collections experience. The percentages shown in Tables 8.1 and 8.2 were calculated from Credit Co.'s 1995–96 collections records. They indicate percentages of total accounts in each of Credit Co.'s two operations.

TABLE 8.1   U.S. Accounts

A. As Percentage Share of Account Status

	Days Overdue			Post-Write-Off %	Percentage of Total
	5–64 %	65–134 %	135–185 %		
Original contract	86.23	9.29	4.47	0.00	52.03
Partial payment arrangement	10.42	12.50	16.67	60.42	0.67
Bankruptcy	23.08	23.08	19.23	34.62	0.36
Collection agency	0.21	0.33	1.02	98.43	46.55
Creditor-initiated litigation	0.00	0.00	0.00	100.00	0.38

B. As Percentage Share of Each Stage of Delinquency

Treatment Level	Days Overdue			Post-Write-Off
	5–64 %	65–134 %	135–185 %	
Original contract	99.44	93.75	77.93	0.00
Partial payment arrangement	0.16	1.63	3.76	0.87
Bankruptcy	0.19	1.63	2.35	0.27
Collection agency	0.22	2.99	15.96	98.05
Creditor-initiated litigation	0.00	0.00	0.00	0.81
Percentage of total	45.12	5.16	2.99	46.73

Statistics referred to represent averages or approximations compiled from Credit Co.'s records during this time period, and so try to depict its parallel practices in the two countries.

III. UNITED STATES

A. Institutional Framework

The formal legal portion of the U.S. debt collection system consists of both collection and bankruptcy law. The former is primarily state-based law codifying early English common law doctrine. This body of law permits individual creditor collection action on a first-come, first-served basis, subject only to state and federal statutes that (1) restrict the character and intrusiveness of collection efforts; (2) exempt certain assets from seizure; (3) limit wage garnishment; and (4) provide debtors with defenses based on the Truth-in-Lending Act, and so on. The federal Bankruptcy Code enables debtors to obtain an automatic stay that halts state-remedy procedures and prevents creditors from individually liquidating the debtor's assets. Instead,

TABLE 8.2   German Accounts

A. *As Percentage Share of Account Status*

| | Days Past Due | | | Post-Write-Off % | Percent of Total |
	1–59 %	60–119 %	120–179 %		
Original contract	98.34	1.66	0.00	0.00	43.79
Partial payment arrangement	30.46	45.30	23.44	1.12	6.16
Mahnverfahren	0.00	0.00	100.00	??	39.63
Collection agency	10.84	10.84	47.88	30.44	10.42

B. *As Percentage Share of Each Stage of Delinquency*

| | Days Past Due | | | |
	1–59 %	60–119 %	120–179 %	Post-Write-Off
Original contract	93.48	15.64	0.00	0.00
Partial payment arrangement	4.07	60.04	3.12	2.12
Mahnverfahren	0.00	0.00	85.75	???
Collection agency	2.45	24.31	10.79	97.88
Percentage of total	45.99	4.64	46.14	3.23

the bankruptcy court coordinates liquidation proceedings under Chapter 7 of the code or a type of reorganization proceedings for wage earners under Chapter 13.

This legal framework seeks, on one hand, to prevent debtors from reneging on their obligations by granting creditors the right to collect debts by reasonable extrajudicial methods and, if these fail, to obtain from courts remedies such as attachment, garnishment, and execution liens against debtors' assets. On the other hand, collecting consumer debts via formal legal channels is costly and yields uncertain benefits. To varying degrees across states, creditors are constrained both substantively and procedurally in their collection efforts. Due process rules entitle debtors to adequate notice and an opportunity for an adversary proceeding. In some states, prejudgment wage garnishment is prohibited and other prejudgment remedies are restricted. Title III of the Consumer Credit Protection Act provides federal protection against garnishment as well; it exempts a minimum of 75 percent of debtors' wages and preempts those state laws that are less protective of debtors.

Other legal rules aim to protect debtors and scrupulous creditors alike from unethical actions by debt collectors. The federal Fair Debt Collection

Practices Act (FDCPA) of 1978 regulates the activities of third-party debt collectors, excluding parties (such as large banks) that collect their own debts. Many state laws, however, apply similar restrictions to all debt collectors, including creditors (such as banks) collecting their own debts. State laws also forbid debt collectors from invading debtors' privacy, harassing or abusing them, making false or deceptive representations, or engaging in a variety of other unfair collection methods. Contacts with debtors' families, friends, employers, and other third parties with access to debtors are strictly limited under these laws. Once debtors are contacted, they may insist that collectors deal exclusively with their attorneys, or even completely stop all collection contacts. Under most of these laws, in all communications made to collect a debt, the collector must disclose that it is attempting to do just that and that any information obtained will be used only for that purpose.

Fair debt collection laws rely to a great extent on private enforcement (i.e., debtors must raise claims or defenses based on these laws in court), although the FTC is formally charged with enforcing the FDCPA. Debtors who are successful in their claims against debt collectors under the FDCPA, as well as under many state statutes, are entitled to actual damages, statutory damages, the costs of litigation, and reasonable attorney's fees. Many courts have ruled that even where there are no actual damages, but only technical violations of the law (such as failure to provide all relevant notice provisions in every communication), successful debtor-plaintiffs can recover statutory damages, costs, and attorney's fees. These rulings have emboldened consumer attorneys to bring cases based on technical violations committed by creditors, to make settlement demands unrelated to any damages, and to earn more in attorney's fees than clients are entitled to collect. Creditors typically settle these cases before the complaint is even answered for around $7,500.[8]

Large banks claim that they are careful to follow the strict letter of the law in their collection activities, and even to go beyond what is required because they are eager to avoid legal action. This task is difficult and costly, however, because the laws are very detailed and, in the case of state laws, vary across jurisdictions. It is becoming more common with respect to consumer credit practices that banks are signing negotiated assurances with state attorneys general, committing themselves to the discontinuation of certain collection practices such as number of communications per week with debtors and permitted communications with persons other than a debtor or persons residing in the household of a debtor. If they fail to live up to these agreements, they can be (and increasingly are) sued.

Even where written law is uniform, as is the case with the FDCPA, federal courts vary in interpreting legal provisions. For example, in theory, debt collectors who are charged with violations of the FDCPA may rely in good faith on FTC formal advisory opinions to shield themselves from liability. In practice however, the FTC has issued only informal advisory opinions. Although these informal decisions declare strict compliance with notice provisions to be unnecessary, they also are not binding on courts. Courts have split on the question of strict compliance, and the resulting uncertainty, according to attorneys, has forced creditors to settle most debt collection cases out of court to avoid the risk of paying attorney's fees and litigation costs.[9]

Creditors' collection efforts in the United States are also constrained by the threat that a debtor will file for bankruptcy. Personal bankruptcies have risen to record levels in recent years as consumers' debt burdens have increased. Since 1981, filing rates have tripled, reaching a projected one million cases projected in 1996.[10] Filing for bankruptcy triggers an automatic stay that cuts off all debt collection efforts. This blunts the instruments that creditors use to put pressure on debtors—informal methods such as telephone calls, letters, and visits; or formal lawsuits, with their threat of property seizure or garnishment. Only for a very small subset of consumers is credit card debt the main cause of bankruptcy, but it still represents on average about one-sixth of debt in bankruptcy filings.[11] Just as the debtors' bar has facilitated fair debt collection actions by debtors even where there are no actual damages, so, too, a bankruptcy bar has emerged that advertises its services aggressively and encourages and enables debtors to pay rather nominal fees to discharge tens of thousands of dollars in debt.

Consumers who file bankruptcy petitions come from all sections of society. They have the choice of filing either a Chapter 7 bankruptcy, which discharges their preexisting debts but liquidates their nonexempt assets, or a Chapter 13 bankruptcy, which permits them to keep all their assets but requires repayment of some portion of their debts over three to five years, as specified by a court-supervised plan. In addition, state laws exempt a variety of debtors' assets—sometimes rather substantial assets—from liquidation under Chapter 7.[12] To various degrees, state laws also constrain promised plan repayments under Chapter 13 (or under a Chapter 7 reaffirmation agreement).[13] Lenders are subject to legal liability for violating state laws protecting debtors from creditors who press for reaffirmation agreements. In 1997, Sears, Roebuck & Co. took a $475 million write-off in connection with a settlement with tens of thousands of consumer-debtors who had filed for bankruptcy, following revelations that Sears had used threatening wording in seeking reaffirmation agreements and had failed to comply with a Massachusetts law requiring the creditor to file such agreements with the bankruptcy court judge for review.[14] Further legal uncertainty in bankruptcy procedures stems from the great diversity of legal cultures across districts, in which repeat players—judges, attorneys, bankruptcy trustees, and others—exert enormous influence over debtors' decision making.[15] Hence, creditors with far-flung operations, such as large bank credit card issuers, must check the intensity of their collection efforts not only to avoid litigation under fair debt collection practices laws but also to avoid pushing debtors into bankruptcy, thereby enmeshing the creditors in automatic stays and the vagaries of local legal cultures.

B. Bank Collection Operations

Banks generally receive full repayment of credit card debt, subject to normal trends in the business cycle. It is not clear how important collection efforts are in maintaining this record, but banks feel that it is necessary to establish extensive operations to deal with delinquent credit card accounts, and they regularly rely on third parties to assist them in their collection efforts. A guiding principle in these operations, according to bank collection officials, is to avoid the great uncertainty and high costs inherent in the U.S. legal system by taking measures that will prevent any formal legal action, or, if that is not possible, to delay litigation for as long as possible. Preventive measures involve reliance on the negotiating skills of in-house collection personnel and third-party collectors. Constrained both by fair debt collection laws and by the availability of bankruptcy, collection personnel must be skillful enough to negotiate with debtors sufficiently to extract payments, while guarding against either pushing debtors into taking formal legal action (because collection methods are too extreme) or filing for bankruptcy (because debt burdens are too onerous).

Credit Co. typically categorizes accounts according to the period they are overdue. Accounts that are 5 to 64 days overdue are placed in "buckets" 1 or 2. They are shifted to buckets 3 through 6 for every subsequent 30 to 35 days that they remain unpaid. When an account is 180 days overdue, it leaves bucket 6 and enters the post-write-off stage. The actual governance of these accounts as they "pass" through these stages depends largely on the legal and institutional framework in place in a given state or nation.

At a single point in time, Credit Co. may manage up to 25 to 30 million credit card accounts. Table 8.1 and Figure 8.1 show that 52 percent of delinquent accounts represent original contracts and do not involve either bank partial payment arrangements or third- party action (i.e., collection agency, bankruptcy court).

The vast majority of delinquent accounts in any one of the pre-write-off stages have not been renegotiated or sent to third parties. However, once accounts are written off, the bank becomes much more aggressive in negotiating partial payment arrangements or sending them to collection agencies: 60 percent of all partial payment arrangements are negotiated

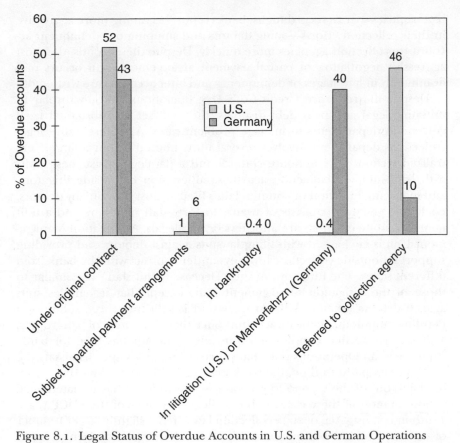

Figure 8.1. Legal Status of Overdue Accounts in U.S. and German Operations of "Credit CO"

after write-off, whereas 98 percent of all accounts sent to collection agencies occur at this stage. Nearly all of the accounts written off are sent to collection agencies.

Because legal action is so costly and outcomes so uncertain, the bank sues delinquent debtors in less than 1 percent of these cases. Practically all of this litigation occurs only after accounts are written off and sent to collection agencies. Pre-write-off litigation occurred in only 15, 10, and 25 cases, respectively, in three recent months at Credit Co's U.S. operations— making these numbers virtually negligible when compared with the total number of accounts. According to bank officials, this delay is due mainly to the perceived costliness and uncertainty of legal action. Any threat of bankruptcy—real or perceived—doesn't necessarily force banks to postpone sending accounts to collection agencies. In fact, even as consumer bankruptcies soar to record highs, banks report becoming more aggressive in their collection efforts—suing debtors and shipping out delinquent accounts to collection agencies more quickly. Despite these trends, the most aggressive negotiation of partial payment arrangements still occurs predominantly in late stages of delinquency and after accounts are written off.

Despite the reticence Credit Co.'s U.S. operations typically display in initiating legal action in debt disputes, they still set up substantial legal collections departments to manage problem cases. A representative legal collections department involves several units housed within a large, centralized section. One in-house counsel and a paralegal assist these units with bank-initiated collection activities, supervision of outside litigators, and managing litigation or counterclaims filed against the bank by debtors. Each unit generally consists of twenty to forty staff members and a unit manager, none of whom are attorneys or paralegals. A Litigation Management Unit is encharged with filing lawsuits against debtors and providing support for outside collection attorneys under contract with the bank from different states. The functions of the "Deceased Unit staff" are similar to those of the Litigation Management staff, except that it handles suits against debtors' estates. A Bankruptcy staff is split into three subunits, a Pending subunit that handles accounts once there is a threat of bankruptcy; a Recovery staff that handles accounts after a debtor has filed for bankruptcy; and an Operations staff that processes petitions and dismissals.

At a given point in time, the bank may deal with fewer than sixty counterclaims out of the 25,000 to 30,000 cases in which it has initiated legal action. In most of these cases, debtors allege violations of the FDCPA, the Truth-in-Lending Act, or state collection laws. In the slightly larger number of cases in which debtors initiate litigation (about 70 at a given point in time), just more than one-half allege violation of these laws. Two factors seem to hold down the rate of legal claims by debtors. First, large banks apparently do take extra precautions to comply with debt collection laws to avoid exposing themselves to any legal action by debtors. Second, debtors in trouble tend to seek out relatively convenient and efficient forms of protection offered by bankruptcy, rather than filing claims against creditors in regular court procedures. Debt collection by banks in the United States typically begins when their collection personnel contact delinquent debtors via telephone calls and dunning letters (letters requesting payment). In contrast to its minimal legal collections staff, a large bank with national credit card operations employs approximately 2,500 full-time equivalent collection personnel (management and support staff) working in regional centers.

Entry-level collectors deal almost exclusively with accounts that are in the first two months of delinquency. They simply remind customers of their payment obligations. Traditionally, collectors employed by Credit Co. have dealt with accounts in five to fifteen states, meaning they must be familiar with the laws and regulations from those particular states (in addition to federal collection laws). More recently, in an attempt to identify effective collection practices, the bank now randomizes collectors' account portfolios so that all will work with accounts from every state. Collections personnel thus need to become familiar with laws and regulations from all fifty states rather than just five to fifteen. To some extent this adds to the work of the legal counsel for collections, who is responsible for providing training for collectors and for drafting written legal prompts for them to refer to when contacting customers.

Once accounts are between two to four months overdue, more experienced collectors take over, informing debtors that their delinquencies have become more severe and that a decision is being made whether to keep their accounts open. If an agent does not negotiate a satisfactory arrangement by the fourth month of delinquency, the account is automatically closed. During the fifth and sixth months of delinquency, before accounts are written off, the bank makes intensive efforts to close out balances owed it. The most experienced collections agents with the sharpest negotiating skills attempt in repeated contacts with debtors to extract payments. If, after these communications, a debtor cannot make even current payments, the bank attempts to enter into a partial payment arrangement, negotiating an immediate payment based on ability to pay, and subsequent payments to make the account current. These efforts extend through the sixth month of delinquency into the post-write-off stage, where, as Table 8.1 indicates, most partial payment arrangements are finalized (though they are also worked out as early as the second or third months of delinquency).

If it becomes clear at any point in the delinquency that a debtor will never make any payment large enough to roll an account back toward current status, the bank will attempt right then to negotiate a partial payment arrangement. Recently, partial payment arrangements have been conducted somewhat more frequently during each of the two-month periods leading up that stage (see Table 8.1). If, even after these renegotiations, serious delinquencies continue and the debtor shows a lack of discipline in paying, the bank offers to close out the account for good, settling for a specified amount; 60 percent of these settlements occur in the post-write-off stage, but if early on it is clear that the risk of bankruptcy is high, the bank will settle then. Banks estimate that up to half of their write-offs are the result of bankruptcy or bankruptcy risk. Typically, this risk is determined by collection agents listening for signs that the customer blames his delinquency on persistent unemployment, on levels of debt greater than income, or on pressure from other creditors. Under such circumstances, Credit Co. officials assume, debtors face strong temptations to pay $300 to file a bankruptcy petition that will discharge, say, $25,000 worth of debt.

If in-house efforts are unsuccessful and the debt is still deemed collectible, Credit Co. typically contracts out its collection work to outside counsel or collection agencies. Collection agencies are often employed if the debtor appears to be judgment-proof. The amount of the debt may be small or large. The bank pays the collection agency a commission rate that ranges from 20 to 50 percent of the amount collected, depending on their prior handling of accounts and on the number of months that an account has been in the post-write-off stage.

Just as the bank is striving to spot trouble cases early and renegotiate or settle more quickly to avoid legal action, so, too, is it beginning to ship out a small percentage of cases to collection agencies in pre-write-off stages. However, as mentioned previously, the vast majority of accounts contracted out occur at the post-write-off stage. This enables banks to deploy their own large collection staffs in the most effective manner—gradually turning up the heat over several months with increasingly skilled negotiators.

IV. GERMANY

A. Institutional Framework

Compared with those in the United States, German laws and institutional arrangements place more emphasis on the integrity and binding quality of the original debt obligations. German debtors can count on far less legal and institutional support than do their American counterparts. There are no fair debt collection laws shielding borrowers from creditors' collection efforts. Even if debts become too onerous, German debtors cannot seek refuge in consumer bankruptcy procedures.

The importance of the original debt obligation—whether due to the long-held norm of contract-as-promise in civil law or to the notion of creditor-debtor equality—is evident in the Mahnverfahren procedure found in Chapter 7 of the Civil Procedure Code. Mahnverfahren is a summary procedure that greatly expedites the collection of debts.[16] The creditor files an allegation in court without presenting evidence other than a contract and a statement that payment is overdue. Paralegals and other law office assistants rather than attorneys handle the filing of these claims. Court clerks, working under formal supervision of a judge, screen the forms for correctness and issue an injunction. If the debtor, who may consult a debt-counseling agency or a private attorney, wishes to contest the claim, he or she may file a petition; this must be done within four weeks of the creditors' filing. Typically, a debtor's petition argues that the creditor failed to meet good faith requirements under contract law or that the contract is void because the creditor failed to meet disclosure and interest rate requirements under the Consumer Credit Act (Verbraucherkreditgesetz). At this point, formal litigation procedures may begin.

Between 1982 and 1984, 9,118 cases for every 100,000 in total population went to Mahnverfahren procedures, but only 17 percent of these cases were challenged by debtors and ended up in litigation.[17] But, as noted in the following, the rate at which debtors challenge Mahnverfahren actions for credit card debt appears to be much lower. By 1991 these numbers had changed very little: only 10 to 15 percent of debtors contested creditors' claims in Mahnverfahren. When a debtor does not contest a creditor's claim in Mahnverfahren, the court simply enters a judgment in the creditor's favor. Enforcement of this judgment resembles the U.S. procedure. A civil servant (Gerichtsvollzieher) is sent to the debtor to collect, much like a sheriff in the American context. In Germany, too, creditors face difficulty in collecting on judgments or in obtaining assignment of the debtor's assets to cover repayment; as in the United States, the consumer debtor typically has few, if any, assignable assets. Compounding the difficulty in Germany is the fact that wage garnishment is prohibited. This is perhaps the only significant way in which German law and institutions are more debtor-friendly, although in 1999 some garnishment remedies will be authorized by law.

A major difference is that in Germany, the right to execute on a judgment lasts for thirty years, compared with the ten-year statutory limits in most U.S. jurisdictions. This makes it more feasible for German creditors to wait until the debtor has regained control over his personal finances, and then seek to collect on the judgment. On the other hand, bank credit card operations sometimes offer a prompt final settlement for 50 percent of the amount owed, or even less in some cases. Overall, Mahnverfahren has proved so successful in Germany (especially from the creditors' perspective) that harmonization of civil procedure codes throughout the European Union is forcing the introduction of similar procedures throughout member states.[18]

Beginning in 1999, Chapter 13–like protection will become available for German consumers. Germany's generous social safety net has shielded debtors somewhat from this necessity, but as economic globalization and East-West reunification, among other factors, have forced cutbacks in social spending, bankruptcy and other forms of legal protection for debtors are likely to become more important.

Consumer organizations in Germany, which played important roles in drafting the new consumer bankruptcy law (Insolvenzordnung), claim that the law will encourage debtors and creditors to reach out-of-court settlements through the mediation of debt-counseling agencies. Historically, German creditors, vested with strong legal rights, have had no need to resolve consumer debt disputes outside of courts. It is uncertain whether their incentives will shift sufficiently under the new bankruptcy law so that they will need to rely on debt-counseling agencies' assistance. Staffed predominantly by social workers rather than attorneys, these agencies primarily help debtors gain control over their personal finances and renegotiate their debts with creditors. Under the new bankruptcy law, if the parties (with or without mediators' assistance) do not settle out of court, then debtors may go to court, where they must present a debt rescheduling plan to the judge. Using this plan, the judge will attempt to forge an agreement between the parties, with the approval of a majority of creditors (measured by amount of debt) required. Only if the judge's efforts fail will a trustee be appointed to manage the case. The trustee will then oversee the development of a seven-year rescheduling plan much like a Chapter 13 plan in the United States. Thus, in German bankruptcy cases, informal compromise will be sought at two levels before formal legal action comes into force.

One formal legal protection currently available to consumers is called "oath of disclosure" *(Eidesstattliche Versicherung)*. This procedure resembles bankruptcy in that debtors, under oath, disclose that they are unable to repay their debts and petition the courts for relief from collectors' actions. But the relief is limited; if granted, it lasts for three years, during which time the debtor is cut off from all normal forms of credit and may not open a business. And, unlike bankruptcy, after three years, the debtor must reassume the original obligation.

B. Bank Collection Operations

Credit Co.'s operations in Germany enjoy the procedural and institutional advantages all creditors enjoy there—that is, the convenient, low-cost Mahnverfahren system, the relative absence of bankruptcy, and the minimal legal protections for consumer debtors against aggressive creditor collection efforts. Instead of avoiding formal legal action as in the United States, managers in the bank's German operations move more quickly to file claims in Mahnverfahren. As shown in Figure 8.1, whereas Credit Co. resorts to litigation in less than 1 percent of delinquent accounts in the United States, its German operations employ the Mahnverfahren legal collection method in 40 percent of delinquent accounts. Banks in Germany do not have to worry about debtors filing for bankruptcy as in the United States, while their own legal action against debtors is encouraged by the convenience and inexpensiveness of procedures such as Mahnverfahren.

This dynamic is reflected in the account statistics compiled by Credit Co.'s German operations. This operation employs a system categorizing accounts much like its U.S. counterpart. Accounts that are 1 to 59 days overdue are placed in "buckets" 1 or 2, moving to buckets 3 through 6 for every subsequent 30 days that they remain unpaid. Accounts that are 180 days overdue are written off, as in the United States. The scale of the German subsidiary's operations is far smaller than in the United States, averaging from 200,000 to 300,000 credit card accounts. About 98 percent of all accounts not yet subject to partial payment arrangements or third-party actions are current (compared with 87 percent in the United States), while the remainder are two to four months overdue (compared with 9 percent in the United States).

Typically, as shown in Figure 8.2, a far lower percentage of delinquent accounts enter the post-write-off stage in Germany (3 percent) than in the United States (46 percent). Only 1 percent of partial payment arrangements, 5 percent of Mahnverfahren actions, and 30 percent of collection agency action occur in the post-write-off stage. In the United States, as described earlier and presented in Table 8.1, 60 percent of partial payment arrangements, just less than 100 percent of creditor-initiated litigation, and 98 percent of collection agency action occur in the post-write-off stage.

Thus, despite recent increases in consumers' debt burdens in Germany, an even higher percentage of credit card debtors keep their accounts current than in the United States, and the bank is compelled to write off a much lower percentage. Moreover, these patterns prevail despite the high German rates of long-term indebtedness (rather than higher credit turnover) that seemingly lie behind the rise in debt burdens. This is all the more noteworthy because German bankers say they have less access to consumers' credit records than do their American counterparts, and thus are less able to prescreen customers for credit risk, which in theory would diminish the credit quality of German relative to U.S. card portfolios. On the other hand, American operations may be more aggressive in selling credit card services to lower-income and other higher-risk consumers.

Regardless of why German accounts are kept current, bank operations there spend much less effort than their U.S. counterparts in managing trouble accounts. About 10 percent of all credit card accounts are closed at a given point in time, but almost three-fourths of these are closed by customers. In the cases where Credit Co. itself closes accounts, it frequently does so automatically because the accounts are 60 days past due. Once accounts are closed, they are sent to in-house collections for an additional 60 days, where collections staff attempt to collect in full or negotiate partial payment arrangements. German operations staff the equivalent of thirty full-time agents to handle approximately ten thousand delinquent accounts. Since all law governing credit transactions is federal, there are no differences between legal rules across *Länder*, and hence no need for regional centers and extra training for collection agents. Before initiating Mahnverfahren, creditors must remind debtors of their obligations at least three times. German operations do not send dunning letters; reminders sufficient for Mahnverfahren purposes are attached to account statements regularly sent to each customer. Between days 60 and 119 of delinquency, agents telephone customers to remind them of their obligations. At day

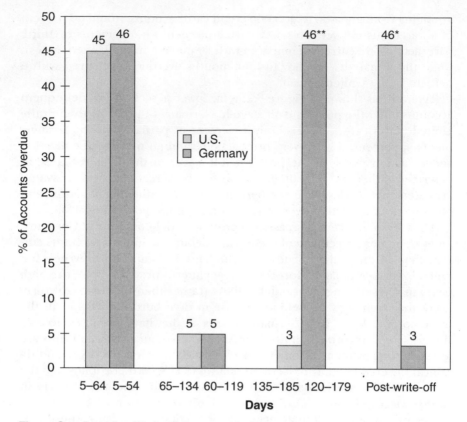

Figure 8.2. Length of Debt Delinquency in U.S. and German Operations of "Credit CO"

** Mostly in Manverfahren.
* Mostly referred to collection agency.

120, the bank proceeds directly to Mahnverfahren, as contrasted with the stepped-up negotiating efforts that U.S. operations begin around that time. Of the approximately five thousand accounts (on average) closed by the bank in Germany at a given point in time, about 75 percent have been sent to Mahnverfahren and are working their way through the legal system. The bank sends the remaining 25 percent of accounts to collection agencies, where they are worked for up to ten weeks. Collection agencies manage most of the bank's card accounts that are 150 or more days delinquent (including those that the bank has written off). Payment arrangements are similar to those used in the United States, where the collection agency's commission depends on the account's vintage.

Like the banks themselves, collection agencies in Germany waste little time in trying to extract payments from debtors through letters or telephone contacts. The incentives to use Mahnverfahren quickly are just as strong as for banks, and collection agencies acting for creditors will file the necessary court petitions. Thus, as shown in Figure 8.2, whereas 46 percent of Credit Co.'s delinquent accounts in the United States are classified as "referred to collection agency," that status applies to only 10 percent of the company's delinquent accounts in Germany.

Once a suit is filed in Mahnverfahren, banks expect to receive a summary judgment in their favor, in large part because the consumer debtor rarely files a defense or counterclaim. According to bank officials in Germany, operations on the scale examined here typically might face only five to fifteen such counterclaims to the approximately four thousand claims they file in court. This rate is far lower than the 10 to 15 percent rate for overall consumer credit filings in Germany, though higher than the U.S. rate. Debtors file oath of disclosure petitions at a very low rate as well.

As in the United States, the legal staff involved in legal collections activity in Credit Co.'s German credit card unit is minimal, with one counsel for collections and three paralegals responsible for all litigation initiated by the bank. The paralegals' main task is to file Mahnverfahren claims. No separate in-house counsel is responsible for managing claims filed against the bank by debtors, as is the case in U.S. operations. This suggests that although the ratio of debtors' claims to total cases may be similar in the two countries, the legal complexity of these claims might be sufficiently greater in the United States to warrant the presence of a separate legal division. The possibility of class action damages in the United States, unlike in Germany, may be part of this explanation.

Like their U.S. counterparts, German operations are learning to spot potential problem cases early and act even before accounts are 60 days overdue. Examining Tables 8.1 and 8.2 shows that the bank in Germany is more aggressive in pursuing partial payment arrangements or contracting out to collection agencies than it is in the United States. Overall, the bank has little incentive to negotiate partial payment arrangements with German debtors, doing so in less than 0.5 percent of all cases (although this rate is higher than in the United States). But in Germany, only one-quarter of these renegotiations occur after accounts are more than 120 days overdue, and only 1 percent occur in the post-write-off stage, whereas in the United States the majority of renegotiations occur in the post-write-off stage. The bank in Germany contracts out a lower percentage of delinquent accounts to collection agencies, and employs this method at an earlier stage of delinquency, than in the United States; the largest number of such cases fall between four and six months of delinquency (as opposed to the post-write-off stage in the United States).

V. CONCLUSION

The behavior of multinational banks and their credit card operations is influenced, of course, by a variety of cultural factors and market incentives in addition to legal and institutional frameworks. Nevertheless, it appears that the high cost and uncertainty of the U.S. legal system, with its high bankruptcy risk and the presence of many local legal cultures, encourages American operations to delay formal legal action much longer than in Germany, where uniform and simple legal procedures make it relatively easy for banks to press their claims at an early date without the risk of pushing debtors to file for bankruptcy. Second, the legal costs and bankruptcy risk posed by the U.S. legal system seem to encourage American bankers to engage in much more extended and aggressive informal collection efforts, which in turn has prompted the enactment of detailed regulation of collection efforts. Third, U.S. banks write off a larger proportion of debts and must cope with delinquencies in a much larger proportion of cases, although it is not clear how much these differences stem from the varied influences of the two legal systems.

There is some evidence from general sources (rather than from the banks we studied) that because of the more complex set of debtors' rights and litigation methods that prevail in the United States, both debtors and creditors face greater incentives to engage in opportunistic behavior. Visa USA has estimated that over 25 percent of its credit card losses arise from situations in which the debtor could pay, but does not, due to use of bankruptcy, other legal claims, or fraud.[19] At the same time, frustrated by debtors' expansive use of bankruptcy rights, creditors are tempted to use unethical methods to convince debtors who file for bankruptcy to reaffirm their debts, or aggressively oppose bankruptcy filings in courts, thereby pressing debtors who can ill afford the resulting legal fees to enter into reaffirmation agreements.[20] In Germany, where the law is more straightforward and court procedures are less expensive, such temptations to opportunism presumably are far lower.

A more complete analysis would examine whether greater consumer protections in the United States actually promote credit use. If so, the welfare (and policy) implications of greater adversarial legalism in the United States are unclear. If the risk creditors face, and the costs of the system as a whole, are greater in the United States than in Germany, those risks and costs still must be weighed against the benefits to consumers and the economy as a whole of greater access to credit. Although this study indicated that the American debt collection system is more legally uncertain, costly, and inefficient, it cannot tell us which system produces a more efficient consumer credit market.

NOTES

1. Robert A. Kagan, "The Routinization of Debt Collection," *Law and Society Review* 18 (1984): 323.

2. "The Cutting Edge," *The Economist,* July 27, 1996, 63–64.

3. "Cracking Open the Nest Egg," *The Economist,* July 27, 1996, 64.

4. The German market has only recently taken off, with three million cards in circulation in 1994. Still, German consumers have had extensive experience with bank credit since at least the 1960s, the fastest-growing form involving the use of EC cheque cards. As of 1994, there were about twenty-one million cheque cards in circulation, which consumers can use to overdraw their personal bank accounts by up to three times their monthly income. They are charged overdraft interest by their bank on any withdrawal and are penalized with higher interest rates if they fail to comply with payment agreements negotiated ex ante with their bank. Udo Reifner, "Consumer Credit Regulation in Germany," mimeo, School of Economics and Politics, Hamburg University, September 1994.

5. "Consumer Loans: Good Debts," *The Economist,* July 15, 1997, 72–73.

6. Ibid.

7. Albert Crenshaw, "Creditors Go for Broke to Collect," *San Francisco Chronicle,* February 17, 1997, B3.

8. Mark Hansen, "When Rubin Sues, Defendants Settle; Unscrupulous Debt Collectors Pay the Bills for New Mexico Consumer Lawyer," *American Bar Association Journal* 79 (1993): 29; Anthony P. Pecora, "The Unyielding Miranda Requirement of the Fair Debt Collection Practices Act: Strict Textualism or Statutory Myopia," *Commercial Law Journal* 99 (1994): 231.

9. Pecora, "The Unyielding Miranda Requirement," 249.

10. Fred R. Bleakley, "Personal Bankruptcy Filings Are Soaring," *Wall Street Journal,* May 8, 1996, A2; see also "Consumer Loans: Good Debts," *The Economist,* July 15, 1997, 72–73 (more than 121,000 personal bankruptcies filed in one month, May 1997).

11. Bankruptcy Petition Study, May 1997, Visa U.S.A.

12. Often, for example, the debtor's home is exempt from liquidation, enabling unscrupulous debtors to shield assets by making large investments in home improvements before filing for bankruptcy. Although such behavior surely is not the norm, it has been estimated that close to 90 percent of debtors who file for Chapter 7 do not liquidate any assets to pay debts. Dian Culp Bork, "Why Personal Bankruptcies Are Surging," *Wall Street Journal,* January 29, 1997, A11.

13. A reaffirmation agreement is a formal, legally enforceable agreement signed with a creditor to repay a debt notwithstanding a bankruptcy discharge.

14. Barnaby Feder, "The Harder Side of Sears," *New York Times,* July 20, 1997, sec. 3, p. 1.

15. Teresa Sullivan, Elizabeth Warren, and Jay Lawrence Westbrook, *As We Forgive Our Debtors: Bankruptcy and Consumer Credit in America* (New York: Oxford University Press, 1984).

16. Erhard Blankenburg, "The Infrastructure for Avoiding Civil Litigation: Comparing Cultures of Legal Behavior in the Netherlands and West Germany," *Law and Society Review* 28 (1994): 789.

17. Id. at 797.

18. Id. at 800.

19. Crenshaw, "Creditors Go for Broke to Collect," B3.

20. Ibid. See also Feder, "The Harder Side of Sears."

CHAPTER NINE

Obtaining and Protecting Patents in the United States, Europe, and Japan

Deepak Somaya

In the 1970s, ACME, a highly innovative U.S. chemical firm, pioneered a technology involving an inert polymeric substance that subsequently found wide application in products around the world. ACME sought to obtain patent protection for this pioneering innovation, as well as for related follow-on innovations, in the United States and elsewhere, sometimes with very different results. This chapter describes ACME's experiences obtaining and enforcing patents in the United States, Europe, and Japan, analyzes the cross-national differences in legal regimes for granting and protecting intellectual property rights, and provides some insight into the resulting economic consequences.

I. INTRODUCTION

In an era of increasing global trade and information flows, innovative companies are increasingly sensitive to cross-national differences in patent protection. This is because an invention, once disclosed, ostensibly becomes freely available to everyone, including firms in a country that does not protect the invention adequately. A CEO of a U.S. company that invents and manufactures products for the semiconductor industry wrote: "To be valid, a patent must describe how to make the invention, complete with recipes. A U.S. patent is therefore a free 'how to' book for every potential offshore competitor. For a modern software or manufacturing enterprise, a U.S.-only patent can be worse than no patent."[1] Multinational companies, therefore, are acutely sensitive to the differences in international patent systems that determine the extent of protection accorded to their innovations in each market.

This chapter has three primary objectives. First, it documents significant differences between the patent systems in the United States, Japan, and Europe. Second, by recounting ACME's experience, it addresses the implications of these differences for a company trying to obtain and enforce patents internationally. I focus on the costs, delays, and inconveniences imposed on the company by different patent regimes, their impact on company revenues, and the strategic responses and tactics the company employed to overcome hurdles imposed by the different systems. Finally, the findings are related to the ongoing process of harmonizing patent laws and regimes.

The research shows that in Europe and Japan, as well as in the United States, ACME encountered adversarial legal opposition to its patent claims, resulting in costly delays and uncertainties. In both Europe and Japan, legal conflict occurred primarily in administrative forums and was related to the initial governmental decision to grant a patent. In the United States, the most serious legal challenges occurred later, through litigation in the federal courts. Overall, the U.S. system granted ACME broader protection for its innovation. The lesser (or less consistent) patent protection in Europe and Japan set back ACME's marketing efforts to some extent; nevertheless, its innovative products eventually achieved considerable commercial success in all its markets.

As a consequence of lobbying by multinational companies, cross-national differences in patent regimes have been subject to strong pressures toward convergence, particularly through international forums such as the General Agreement on Tariffs and Trade (GATT) and the World Intellectual Property Organization (WIPO). Bilateral trade negotiations, especially those between the United States and its trade partners, have been another important force for convergence. In Japan and the United States, and to a lesser extent in Europe, important changes are being implemented in the patent systems as a result of the GATT Trade Related Intellectual Property Rights (TRIPS) agreement, and Intellectual Property Rights (IPR) agreements under the U.S.-Japan Framework talks. It will be some time before the full impact of these changes can be objectively assessed. However, this case study (together with other research) suggests that nonstatutory cross-jurisdictional differences persist at the national patent office level and, more important, that patent enforcement processes, which are vested with the courts, are likely to remain an enduring source of differences between national patent regimes for some time.

II. RESEARCH METHOD

After collecting detailed information about the differences among national patent regimes from secondary sources, I sought a more nuanced understanding of them through interviews with experts and patent law professors in the United States and at the Max Planck Institut (in Munich), and with examiners from the Japanese Patent Office (JPO) and the European Patent Office (EPO). Our primary respondents in ACME were the general counsel (who had substantial cross-national patent experience) and the chief patent counsel, with whom we conducted one round of lengthy in-person interviews and several follow-up discussions by telephone. The interviews and discussions delved into broad questions about differences in patent systems as well as more specific ones dealing with a set of five patents that we identified as both important to and representative of the company's experience. Where possible, company records, court documents, and other public sources were used to corroborate the accounts of ACME lawyers. Finally, our findings were reviewed by eight practicing international patent attorneys, three of whom provided very detailed feedback. Because of confidentiality concerns, it was not possible to interview the patent examiners or judges involved with the specific ACME patents we studied. However, interviews with other patent examiners and attorneys corroborated this chapter's general findings.

III. GENERAL DIFFERENCES AMONG PATENT REGIMES

The patent law regimes of the United States, Japan, and Europe all reflect a basic consensus concerning the importance of intellectual property rights in developed economies. Patent grants have two purposes. On the one hand, patents provide economic incentives for the creation of valuable innovations by conferring upon the inventor a limited monopoly in the new technology. On the other hand, the patent system facilitates the diffusion of these inventions in industry by mandating public disclosure of innovations. In interpreting and applying patent law, national patent offices and judges who hear patent cases strike a somewhat different balance between the competing goals of providing incentives and diffusing technology.

Among practitioners, the United States is generally regarded as being particularly supportive of patentees and their exclusive property rights over inventions. The Japanese patent system, in contrast, emphasizes the rapid dissemination of innovations in industry and encourages the sharing of technology, rather than providing broad exclusive rights to patentees.[2] In the words of one scholar, "[T]he Japanese view inventions more as a public, and less as a private, good," and they thus view patents "more as a means to reward inventions and less a right to exclude others from use than in the United States."[3]

European national systems are often described as somewhere between the United States and Japan, with the United Kingdom leaning more toward the U.S. pole and Germany somewhat more toward the Japanese. The

EPO, which was established in 1976 to provide a "common window" facility for a basket of national patents, is still far from being an issuer of a homogeneous European patent. Outcomes within the EPO, according to ACME's attorneys, may vary with the nationality of the examiners and panels involved. Further, the enforcement of patents in Europe remains within the jurisdiction of national courts, which differ substantially in their procedures, interpretation of patents, and provision of enforcement mechanisms.[4]

Apart from core ideological differences, there are institutional and procedural differences between the jurisdictions as well, often reflecting the historical development of their national patent systems and the character of their political and legal institutions. Unlike the United States, patent offices in Japan and Europe provide administrative "opposition" systems for adversarial contestation of a patent at the time it is issued. In Japan, prospective foreign patent holders, and U.S. firms in particular, have long complained that they are disadvantaged by the costs and delays of the patent system (including the "pre-grant" opposition process), which favor the strategic patenting practices of their rival Japanese firms. In the United States, courts are less deferential to administrative authority than Japanese or European courts, and they often second-guess the patent office's assessment of the validity of patents. At the same time, U.S. courts provide the most powerful legal weapons against infringers, including preliminary injunctions, far-reaching pretrial discovery, and large pecuniary damages. But these adversarial measures are very costly for litigants and, combined with the high level of uncertainty in the U.S. courts, can be used strategically to hold competitors at bay. In Europe a different type of uncertainty and variation results from the autonomy retained by national patent systems and courts, despite efforts to provide a "common European patent" through the EPO.

The following description lays out some of the main differences between patent regimes as they existed in 1993, before the latest burst of harmonization.[5] For the purposes of understanding ACME's experiences in patenting, this 1993 "snapshot in time" is probably more relevant than the current, evolving scenario, which I shall discuss in a later section in this chapter.

A. Differences in Patent Prosecution

In all economically developed countries, obtaining a patent, or patent "prosecution," as it is called, begins with filing an application at a national patent office or, for Europe-wide coverage, in the EPO.[6] In the patent office, a patent examiner, who is an expert in the relevant technology, evaluates the claimed innovation using such criteria as "novelty," "nonobviousness," and "usefulness." In doing so, she conducts searches for prior art (existing public domain knowledge, including prior patents) and arrives at an interim decision on whether to grant the patent, which she then communicates to the applicant through an "office action." Typically, such a decision may find that the invention that is being "claimed" in the patent is too broad when compared with the technological advance made by the patentee, or that the patentee has not disclosed adequate information about the innovation, and so forth. Applicants are given an opportunity to respond to objections raised in the office action(s) and to alter their application to the examiner's satisfaction. Third parties may be allowed to intervene in this process by contesting the patent, but the ways in which they may do so vary across patent offices.[7] The following subsections describe important cross-national differences in the regulations and procedures for obtaining a patent.

1. PRIORITY

The United States is the only country except the Philippines to grant patents on a first-to-invent, rather than first-to-file, basis. Consequently, the U.S. Patent and Trademark Office (USPTO) provides for an adversarial proceeding, called an "interference," to resolve disputes over inventive priority. The first-to-invent provision presumably benefits small inventors, who may have more difficulty in writing up the invention, comparing it with prior art, and rushing the application to the patent office. However, interference proceedings are costly.[8] Only about two hundred interferences are filed each year (out of roughly two hundred thousand applications), and only a fraction of these have resulted in a patent award to the second (or later) firm to file.[9] The costs involved, some observers contend, raise "doubts as to whether independent or small inventors . . . really fare better under the first-to-invent system."[10] Irrespective of its actual impact on the ground, the logic of a first-to-invent system pervades the USPTO and is a unique feature that sets it apart from its foreign counterparts.

2. LANGUAGE

The USPTO allows patent applications to be written in any language. English translations are required within two months, but the original language remains the source document in the event of future litigation. In contrast, the JPO permits filing only in Japanese and, much to the distress of U.S. firms surveyed in an earlier study, does not permit corrections if they would change the gist of the claims (even for errors in translation).[11] In the EPO, applications can be filed in any member-state language, followed by a translation in English, French, or German, the official languages of the proceedings. Subsequent translations are required when registering the patent in any of the member states. Although language alone might not be a major issue, when added to other difficulties of obtaining patents abroad, it can be a significant irritant for patentees. Competent skills in drafting patents in foreign languages are hard to find, and firms have to be extremely careful lest they discover too late that the essence of their patent has been lost in the translation.

3. PATENT TERM, PUBLICATION, AND EXAMINATION

In the United States, patents are awarded for seventeen years from the date of grant. Patent applications are not published unless and until the patent is granted, enabling applicants to continue to use the invention as a trade secret if they are not successful in obtaining a patent. Patent applications, once filed, are automatically examined in the USPTO. However, some applicants find ways to delay examination of their patents through manipulative tactics, giving rise to "submarine patents." These patents, still unpublished, lurk in the system while unsuspecting firms "reinvent" the same technologies and build substantial market stakes in them. When the submarine patent eventually issues, the patentee can sue and collect large royalties from the surprised "second" inventors. Since the patent term is from the date of grant, patentees could still enjoy the entire seventeen-year life of the patent, no matter how long the application is delayed in the system.

In Japan and the EPO, applications are published eighteen months after filing. Submarine patents are nearly impossible in systems that require timebound publication, irrespective of the patent term, because the publication puts potential infringers "on notice" and enables them to avoid making sunk investments in a technology that will be covered by another's patents in the future. Mandatory publication also means that every patent application is freely available to one's competitors within a fixed time from the application date. This not only leaves the applicant without recourse if the patent is refused but also facilitates strategic practices on the part of competitors such as "patent flooding." In the EPO, patents are granted for twenty years from the date of application, but patent applicants can choose to delay examination for up to six months after the eighteen-month publication. In Japan, patents were awarded for fifteen years from the date of provisional grant (i.e., before opposition) or twenty years from application, whichever is less. Applicants are required to request examination within seven years of their application date, or their application lapses. Thus, both the EPO and the JPO allow the applicant to defer examination of the patent application for some length of time. Besides lowering the overall workload of the patent office, deferral is also useful for applicants because it enables them to delay legal costs while assessing the commercial value of their innovation.

4. ADVERSARIAL PROCEEDINGS

In the past, the USPTO permitted competing inventors or firms to challenge a patent and request a "reexamination" by submission of "prior art which raises a substantial new question of patentability," a standard that was considered too demanding.[12] The EPO and the JPO, on the other hand, invite intervention from third parties more directly by early publication of the application and by providing formal "opposition" procedures. This sometimes leads to contentious and lengthy skirmishes between prospective patentees and their competitors. But opposition proceedings probably also discourage later litigation, resolving in a quasi-administrative forum certain issues that would otherwise be raised by nonpatentees in postgrant lawsuits. In jurisdictions such as Japan and Germany, courts do not delve into issues of "validity" in patent suits (i.e., whether the patent should have been granted) but instead defer to the Patent Office. By contrast, in the United States, with its initial secrecy, limited ability to challenge a patent at the Patent Office level, and substantial court powers, challenges to validity are more likely to arise later and be decided by the courts.

In Japan, opposition proceedings are notorious for lasting very long—from three to five years. Unlike the EPO, the JPO's opposition is a pregrant process, with the applicant enjoying only a provisional, legally unenforceable patent grant during the opposition. Further, each opposing party's claim is contested in a separate proceeding. Thus, the opposition process can impose significant costs and delays on the applicant, thereby encouraging technology-sharing settlements with its competitors.

5. PATENT STANDARDS AND SCOPE

Patent practitioners generally agree that the USPTO, in judging the patentability and scope of inventions, is inclined to favor inventors. At the other extreme, the JPO has interpreted similar principles rather strictly, against the applicant.[13] For example, the JPO requires that claims be narrowly specified and supported by working examples. Further, its examination policies also narrow the breadth of a patent by lenient interpretation of the novelty criterion as applied to subsequent improvement innovations made by other firms.[14] ACME's patent attorneys felt that, in the past, Japanese patent policy has been geared more toward incremental "engineering" innovations and technology sharing than toward encouraging and protecting sweeping "pioneer" inventions. The literature supports this view.[15] ACME lawyers said that in Japan, it is "assumed that patents are to be shared and cross-licensed," but they also acknowledged that the Japanese "do not have a pirating mentality."

Despite some harmonization through the EPO, the standards applied to patent applications in Europe are quite varied. At the national level, some countries (e.g., France, Italy) grant patents readily, based on a registration process alone. This leaves substantial issues regarding validity and scope for the courts to resolve. The United Kingdom is regarded as having relatively easy standards of patentability,[16] whereas the Netherlands, Austria, and especially Germany are considered to have very demanding standards. The EPO, in conducting its examination, has generally pursued a median path between these different national approaches. But ACME's experience suggests that some variation has found its way even into the EPO, depending on the nationality of examiners and panels.

6. STRATEGIC PATENTING PRACTICES

Japan's patent procedures and standards, it is argued, are particularly conducive to strategic use of the system by Japanese firms, particularly against foreign patent applicants. One common strategy is known as "patent flooding."[17] When a company files an application for a significant patent, its potential competitors file numerous related patent applications claiming "improvement" patents for new uses or slight variants of the technology. These patents, if granted, "surround" the original patent, thus preventing the patentee from using the technology freely in the market and forcing the patentee to license its technology. In addition, Japanese firms have often vigorously contested important patents in the JPO, keeping applications tied up in lengthy opposition proceedings.[18] Foreign firms, less capable of dealing with these tactics in Japan, have frequently succumbed to the pressure to license their technology.

In one infamous case, a start-up U.S. firm (Fusion Systems) that manufactured (and patented) innovative ultraviolet lamps encountered difficulties when Mitsubishi Electric apparently reverse-engineered the product, flooded the JPO with improvement patents, and used them to badger Fusion Systems into licensing its patents at near-giveaway rates. Eventually, the intervention of the United States trade representative relieved the pressure on Fusion Systems.[19] Allegations of unfairness toward foreign applicants in Japan have gained credibility because the JPO is under the direct administrative control of the Ministry of International Trade and Industry (MITI), Japan's chief trade policy agency, and the JPO's director general is appointed by MITI and returns to it after his two-year tenure.[20] MITI has a reputation, particularly in the United States, for orchestrating Japanese trade policy in a strategic and nationalistic manner.

Other patent regimes are also subject to strategic patenting practices, as illustrated by the use of "submarine patents" in the United States. A great deal of strategic gaming also occurs in U.S. patent litigation, which is generally considered very costly and uncertain. European jurisdictions appear to be comparatively less amenable to strategic gaming because of their less adversarial civil law tradition.[21]

7. DELAYS AND COSTS

The JPO is notorious for delays in the patent examination process. These delays (and the accompanying costs) greatly exacerbate the problems faced by foreign firms in protecting their innovations in Japan. In part, these delays are engendered by the large numbers of patent applications filed in the JPO. In the late 1980s and early 1990s, the JPO averaged more than five hundred thousand patent and utility model applications per year, compared with roughly two hundred thousand in the United States. Even though only about two-thirds of Japanese patent applications are actually examined,[22] the number is still about 1.5 times that in the United States. Among the causes commonly cited for this flood of applications are the patenting practices of Japanese firms,[23] the focused single-claim nature of Japanese patent applications,[24] and the large number of utility model applications (over two hundred thousand applications per year in the early 1990s).[25] Yet, in 1991 the JPO had only 955 examiners, as compared with 1,890 in the USPTO. In the late 1980s and early 1990s, the JPO's average time for processing examination requests was around thirty months from the date of request for examination, compared with eighteen to nineteen months[26] in the USPTO (from the date of application) and twenty-four months in the EPO (from the date of application).[27]

Obtaining a patent in Japan is not only time-consuming but also quite expensive (approximately $30,000 in 1993 for a typical twenty-page, ten-claim, two-drawing application), primarily because of high JPO examination fees and costly patent agent services.[28] But comparable costs for Europe-wide patent coverage are even higher (approximately $120,000 for registration and maintenance in 8.3 countries)[29] because in addition to the costs incurred in the EPO, additional fees and translation costs are incurred for each member state in which the patent is registered.[30] In the United States, a foreign filer would have had to spend only about $13,000 for a similar patent.[31]

B. Differences in Enforcing Patent Rights

The worth of a patent, once granted, depends in significant measure on the powers, attitudes, and efficiency with which national court systems enforce patent rights against these alleged infringers. The three major aspects of court-based enforcement are reassessment of validity, determination of infringement, and the strength of legal enforcement. The strength of legal enforcement depends primarily on the powers to collect evidence, the availability of injunctions against alleged infringers, and the availability of punitive damages. According to the chief patent counsel of a large U.S.-based multinational chemical company whom we interviewed, "Enforcement in the United States and the United Kingdom is forceful but very expensive. In continental Europe, enforcement is not costly, but also much less effective. And in Japan, enforcement is both expensive and less effective." These descriptions are also supported by ACME's patent attorneys and by the general literature.

1. THE UNITED STATES (AND THE UNITED KINGDOM)

Litigation costs are very high in the United States and the United Kingdom, with their lawyer-dominated (rather than judge-dominated) modes of litigation, but the courts also offer the strongest enforcement mechanisms. Both jurisdictions allow parties to demand pretrial discovery; although, as one lawyer has put it, the U.K. version is a "gentle domesticated animal" compared with the "ravenous beast of the jungle" that one sees in the aggressively adversarial U.S. litigation system.[32] In addition, injunctions (including preliminary injunctions pending trial) are widely used in both the United States and the United Kingdom. In cases of willful malfeasance, treble damages may be awarded in the United States, and in recent years the use of this punitive remedy has sharply accelerated. Treble damages are not available in Japan or in Europe, although broader damages (beyond lost profits or reasonable royalties) are available in the United Kingdom.

In patent cases, as elsewhere, U.S.-style litigation is extremely expensive. Each party typically hires its own expert witnesses.[33] Discovery is time-consuming and costly. The American Intellectual Property Law Association (AIPLA) estimated that, in 1995, the median litigation cost through pre-trial discovery alone ranged from $190,000 (in cases in which the amount at risk was under $1 million) to $1,983,000 (in cases greater than $100 million), and from $301,000 to $2,975,000 through trial.[34]

In addition to costs, U.S. patent litigation is also subject to a disturbing level of legal uncertainty, at least at the district court level. Probably because patents cannot be adequately challenged by competitors during prosecution, infringement suits often become a forum for contesting validity issues as well. Unlike in Europe and Japan, the courts determine both infringement and the patent's validity in the United States and the United Kingdom. To the dismay of Japanese and European patentees who are used to having specialized benches hear patent cases, in the United States, such cases are decided not by experts but by lay jurors or technically untrained district court judges, who may be influenced by the adversarial manipulations of competing lawyers and partisan expert witnesses.[35] To address the problem of legal uncertainty, the United States in 1982 established the Court of Appeals of the Federal Circuit (CAFC), which handles all patent appeals nationwide, and this has increased uniformity in the lower courts.[36]

In most respects, enforcement in the United Kingdom is a paler image of the American system. There, too, courts wield substantial powers. The

United Kingdom does not use juries in civil cases, however, and the outcomes are somewhat more predictable than in the United States.[37] The costs of using the British courts are high, in part because of the expense of hiring specialized barristers, and in part because unlike in the United States, the losing party must pay the legal fees of the winning party.[38] Nonetheless, as in the United States, the measures available to patentees are quite potent for seeking redress in the event of clear infringement. The effectiveness of these measures, combined with the uncertainty inherent in the system, can be a two-edged sword, however. U.S. and U.K. pretrial discovery and litigation in general can be used strategically by a firm with a broad patent to compel its competitors to abandon commercial and technological development in related areas.[39]

2. JAPAN

In patent enforcement, as in many other areas of civil litigation,[40] courts in Japan are expensive, understaffed, and slow, which is often interpreted as part of a deliberate policy of discouraging litigation and encouraging compromise.[41] When a patentee sues an alleged infringer in a Japanese district court, judicial proceedings—an experienced patent lawyer writes—are intermittent, slow, and costly.[42] The small, guildlike patent bar charges high counsel fees,[43] which the winning party cannot recoup from the loser. Defendants may impose additional delays on a patentee in an infringement case by requesting a redetermination of the patent's validity by the Trial Board of the JPO. Pending redetermination of validity by the Trial Board, the court suspends its hearings on infringement, further delaying any relief to the patentee. Japanese courts rarely issue preliminary injunctions pending determination of infringement charges.[44] Nor do the courts offer pretrial discovery, which makes it very difficult to prove violations of process patents. They also interpret patent claims narrowly and literally, and eschew such principles of equity as the doctrine of equivalents,[45] construing even minor improvements on the technology by the defendant to be grounds for noninfringement. Thus, the predominant effect of the Japanese court system in patent enforcement, as in other areas of commercial dispute, appears to be to mediate a settlement between the parties rather than to determine the just allocation of property rights.[46]

3. CONTINENTAL EUROPE

In Europe, litigation costs in patent enforcement are lower than in the United States, the United Kingdom, and Japan. Fact-finding and legal argumentation are controlled by judges rather than by the parties' lawyers. In France and Italy, proceedings are based almost entirely on written documentation and testimony. In Germany there are two oral hearings, but they are far shorter and less elaborate than U.S. (or even British) trials,

TABLE 9.1 Comparison of the Patent Systems of the United States, Japan, and Europe (circa 1993; subsequent and impending changes marked with *)

Prosecution Features	United States	Japan	Europe (EPO)
Basis of deciding patent priority	First to Invent*	First to File	First to File
Native language filing permitted?	Any language (English translation for record)	Japanese (but can file in English, with translation to follow)*	Any EPC member language, with English, French or German translation; translations required for each country designated
Patent term	17 years from grant*	Lesser of 15 years from grant and 20 years from filing*	20 years from filing
Publication of patent	No*	Yes, 18 months from filing	Yes, 18 months from filing
Examination deferral	No	Yes, 7 years from filing	Yes, 6 months from publication
Third-party contestation of patent	Limited reexamination* and interferences*	Pre-grant oppositions*	Post-grant oppositions
Patentability standards	Least unfavorable to applicants (1 year grace period for prior publication)	Strict standards—claims need working examples, very limited grace period*	Moderate standards; some variation by nationality, limited grace period
Breadth of claims awarded	Very broad	Narrow	Broad

	United States and United Kingdom	Japan	Continental Europe
Time taken	18–24 months	~36 months + oppositions (3–5 years)*	~30 months + opposition (expeditious)
Overall comparable costs	$13,000	$30,000	$120,000
Enforcement Features			
Jurisdiction over validity of patent	With Courts, and often exercised	With Patent Office Appeals Board	Varies by national court system
Strength of Enforcement:	Very strong	Weak	Medium (varies)
Discovery and depositions	Widely used ("rampant" in U.S.)	Not available	No, but alternatives exist in some countries
Preliminary injunctions	Yes	Not available in practice	Yes, but sometimes difficult (e.g. Germany)
Interpretation of claims	Literal interpretation, propatentee court systems, equivalents applied	Narrow interpretation linking back to specifications, equivalents not applied	Interpreted less literally; equivalents applied, but under different principles
Prior user rights available?	No	Yes	Yes
Judicial style	Adversarial court trials, jury trials often seen	Brief intermittent hearings with judge, written testimony is widely used	Largely by written testimony, some oral hearings, court experts used
Uncertainty in outcomes	High, due to lay judges (in District Courts) and juries. Not in U.K.	High, especially due to delays, and pressure to settle out of court	Relatively low in all jurisdictions

and in the words of one ACME attorney, they tend to offer "rough and ready justice." European courts are much less open to hired expert testimony; the judges consult their own experts or technical publications when necessary. In Germany (as in Japan, but unlike the United States), invalidity proceedings must be brought separately in the patent court, but unlike Japan, infringement actions usually will not be stayed while a validity suit is pending. For all these reasons, European court proceedings, in a cross-national perspective, are expeditious and not costly for the parties. One author describes European patent litigation costs as less than those in the United States even if enforcement actions are pursued in several nations simultaneously.[47] In Europe, however, aggrieved patent holders do not have access to the potent and extremely effective legal weapons afforded by U.S. and U.K. law. Party-directed pretrial discovery is limited, although French and Italian courts provide some investigative assistance.[48] In terms of remedies, treble damages are not assessed. Injunctions are available, but preliminary injunctions are employed infrequently, and not at all in Germany.[49]

In most spheres of law, European courts, with their judge-dominated procedures, emphasis on legal uniformity, and highly professional bureaucratically supervised judiciaries, are regarded as more predictable than U.S. courts. But for a company seeking cross-national protection of patent rights, European courts entail a different kind of uncertainty, stemming from the different interpretive standards applied by different national judiciaries to the centrally granted EPO patent.[50] In the absence of a common European Appeals Court, firms have no recourse against the ruling of a national court on a patent obtained even through the EPO. Nonetheless, many lawyers we spoke to were positively disposed toward European enforcement because it afforded effective justice at reasonable costs and risks.

The overall differences between the patent systems of the United States, Japan, and Europe, circa 1993, are summarized in Table 9.1. Laws or practices that have changed, or are in the process of being changed, are marked with asterisks.[51]

IV. ACME'S PATENT EXPERIENCES

Although ACME has ultimately been very successful in commercializing its innovative polymeric products, it has not had an easy time with patent regimes in the United States, Europe, or Japan. Everywhere, its efforts to obtain and protect patents have encountered some delays, legal uncertainty, and inconsistency. In general, Japan and Germany were somewhat less favorable to ACME than the United States. This section provides a narrative of ACME's experience in each regime, first for its basic invention, and then for several follow-on innovations.

A. ACME's Basic Invention

In the late 1960s, ACME's scientists discovered a process to modify a polymeric substance, making it tremendously useful in an array of new areas. In 1970, ACME applied to the USPTO for a patent on this innovation, with claims that covered both the process and the product(s) made by it. One year later, it filed similar applications in Japan (only for the process)[52] and in several Western European countries.

1. UNITED STATES

The USPTO examiner issued office actions challenging ACME's application and rejecting some of the claims therein. ACME's counsel felt that the examiner had misunderstood the character of the innovation, noting that compared with the best patent offices abroad, the USPTO is characterized by a high level of personnel turnover, and hence significant variation in the quality of examiners.[53] ACME responded to the office action, making additional arguments and recharacterizing its claims, but again met with objections and eventual rejection. ACME appealed to the USPTO's Board of Appeals but then learned of a patent on a similar process held by ZCO, a Japanese company. Although ZCO's patent had not played a role in the USPTO's rejections of ACME's application, ACME was compelled by U.S. law to disclose such prior art. ACME therefore amended its application in mid-1973 and refiled,[54] carefully distinguishing its process from ZCO's patent. A new examiner, however, apparently failed to see the difference between the two patents. The examiner also asked ACME to elect to prosecute either its process or its product claims first.[55] ACME decided to begin with the process claims. But as ACME was waiting for an interview it had requested with the examiner, it discovered another patent on a similar process from the USSR, and refiled once again. On this third application, the assigned USPTO examiner recognized the distinctiveness of ACME's process, and in 1976, six years after the initial application, the patent was granted. ACME reactivated its application for the product patent in 1977. At first it was rejected by the examiner in an office action, but eventually it was allowed in mid-1979.

ACME also had to resort to the U.S. courts to enforce its rights under the patent, and its experience in that arena conforms to the general description of U.S. litigation as cumbersome, costly, and unpredictable. In 1979, after the product patent was allowed, ACME sued a large U.S. corporation for infringement of both its product and process patents. After a costly pretrial litigation phase, a five-week trial ensued. The bitterly contested case involved more than two years of pretrial discovery, the testimony of thirty-five witnesses, and over three hundred exhibits.[56] The defendant challenged the validity of ACME's patents as a defense against the infringement suit, and the U.S. District Court agreed. The judge, in his opinion, cited a combination of processes that were in the prior art (and were known to the USPTO examiner who approved the patent), and the existence of other forms of public knowledge about the process. ACME appealed to the recently established CAFC, and in 1983 obtained a reversal of almost all the important invalidation decisions of the District Court.

In 1984 ACME filed suit in a U.S. District Court in another state against a different company that was allegedly infringing its patents. Again, true to U.S.-style litigation, the ten-week trial in 1986 involved fifty-four witnesses, the evidence from twenty-five depositions, and nearly four hundred exhibits. The trial judge held that ACME had failed to prove infringement and, despite the earlier CAFC ruling, that a number of claims in the patents were invalid. ACME appealed, but it experienced long delays at the CAFC, and with less than two years to go on the seventeen-year patent term (in 1991), ACME decided to settle the case with the defendant.

In sum, in the U.S., legal uncertainty plagued ACME from the very start. Yet, the potent legal remedies, high litigation costs, and large monetary penalties associated with U.S. patent litigation also may have worked in the company's favor by deterring potential infringers. ACME successfully served notice to two firms to stop infringing its patent.[57] So while ACME's U.S. patent faced difficulties in prosecution and uncertainties in enforcement, ACME appears to have used it to effectively protect its technological turf from infringers.

2. JAPAN

Even before making its basic pioneering invention, ACME had formed a joint venture with a Japanese company to manufacture a different range of products. Recognizing its partner's complementary technological skills in process engineering, the company decided to form another joint venture with it for the new technology in 1974. ACME licensed its basic process to the venture royalty-free in return for future licenses to technological improvements that its Japanese partner might develop.

ACME's Japanese partnership did not, however, smooth the way for JPO approval of its basic patent. After filing in May 1971, ACME requested immediate examination from the JPO. Following several office actions requesting clarifications, the application was rejected. One of ACME's lawyers complained about dealing with JPO examiners because it was "difficult to understand what their concerns really are." ACME appealed this original rejection to the JPO appeals board, which in late 1975 agreed with ACME's position. The patent was published for opposition, and challenges were subsequently filed by the aforementioned ZCO, a member of a major Japanese *kieretsu* (interlocked business group), and three other Japanese companies. The JPO upheld the opposition and invalidated ACME's patent.

ACME appealed to the JPO Appeals Board and, in 1980, won the patent. ACME's problems did not end there, however. ZCO appealed the board's decision to the Tokyo High Court, which in 1982 overturned the board and invalidated ACME's patent. According to ACME's lawyers, such a reversal of the Appeals Board by the High Court is a very rare occurrence. ACME appealed the High Court decision to the Japanese Supreme Court in 1986, but the appeal was unsuccessful.

Predictably, the Japanese courts were slow and costly; ACME's legal fees amounted to several hundred thousand dollars. Meanwhile, after ACME's patent application was published, ZCO filed for and obtained some related patents, which enabled it to get a toehold in the technology. As soon as ACME obtained the favorable decision from the JPO Appeals Board, it brought an infringement action against ZCO, but the court suspended proceedings until the validity of the patent had been determined in ZCO's appeal to the Tokyo High Court.

Throughout the prosecution phase, ACME and its Japanese partner used the technology to make and market products that had considerable commercial success in Japan. As soon as there was uncertainty about the status of ACME's patent, however, competitors moved vigorously into the market the joint venture had developed. Just as the joint venture was beginning to reap the rewards of its market development efforts, it suffered huge losses of revenue, and its market share declined to about a tenth of its original level.

ACME's frustrating experience with the Japanese patent system is not unique, especially for pioneer inventions. Texas Instruments' patent on the integrated circuit (the "Kilby" patent) was holed up in the Japanese system from 1960 to 1989.[58] Corning Inc.'s pioneering optical fiber innovations, which were promptly awarded patent protection in the United States, were stuck in the JPO for ten years, and when issued were practically worthless.[59] Allied-Signal officials suspect that the JPO colluded with its Japanese rivals in delaying the patent for Allied's breakthrough amorphous metal technology "Metglas."[60]

3. EUROPE

When ACME sought to protect its basic innovation in Western Europe, the EPO had not yet been established, and ACME applied for patents in various national patent offices. In France, Belgium, and Italy, the patents issued automatically upon registration, without administrative examination. In the United Kingdom, the examiner initially objected to the application but, upon clarification and resubmission, approved it in 1973.[61] In West Germany, a jurisdiction regarded as applying stringent standards for patentability, the examiner strongly objected to ACME's application, citing lack of novelty. ACME's attorneys generally respect the expertise of German patent examiners, but they were frustrated by what seemed to be an ideological bias against granting the patent. Twice, in response to office actions, they were unsuccessful in convincing the examiner. After a third submission the patent was granted in 1976.

As in Japan, the German system encourages opposition at the administrative stage, rather than leaving validity issues for the courts to decide in later enforcement actions. Oppositions to ACME's German patent were filed by ZCO, a second Japanese firm, and a Dutch company.[62] The requisite hearing before the German Patent Court was not held until 1981. After a daylong hearing, ACME's German patent was invalidated by the court, which, with characteristic European emphasis on documentary evidence, allowed ACME only a truncated physical demonstration of why its process was not obvious. ACME's appeal to a higher court, which employs a limited standard of review, was unsuccessful. In the Netherlands, oppositions were filed by the same parties making the same arguments, but there the tribunal upheld ACME's patent claims.

B. ACME's Subsequent Patents

ACME continued to develop new products and processes related to its basic polymeric patent. In the different jurisdictions, ACME's subsequent patent applications have often met with disparate treatment, as described below.

1. MEDICAL DEVICES

Using the basic polymeric form that it invented, ACME developed a new type of material that proved to be extremely useful in a number of medical devices. In late 1982 it filed for a patent in the USPTO. An office action initially rejected a number of claims in the application, but following ACME's response the U.S. patent was granted in 1984. ACME filed in Japan in 1983 but deferred examination for the full seven years, until 1990. The JPO examiner then granted the patent (provisionally). An opposition was filed by ZCO, which had a commercial interest in the market for these products, too, but ACME's patent was upheld in 1992.

In 1983, ACME filed for a patent from the EPO. There, too, after the examiner granted the patent, ZCO filed an opposition. The EPO Opposition Board held against ACME in 1990, in what ACME's attorneys felt was a "bizarre" decision. The opposition panel, relying only on the court's own experts, rejected affidavits from ACME's engineers as "not trustworthy," although such evidence would have been usually permitted in the United States. ACME persisted, however, in appealing the patent rejection, and four years later the EPO Appeals Board reversed the decision and upheld ACME's patent.

2. COATING POLYMER

This innovation had particular promise as a weatherproof coating for ACME's polymer-fabric products, but it had other applications as well. ACME's primary innovation involved a completely solid monomer from which to manufacture the coating, which reduced the pollution hazard associated with the coating process considerably. ACME filed its patent application in the USPTO in 1984. The examiner's office action stated that the innovation failed the nonobviousness criterion. The examiner accepted ACME's request for an interview to argue its case, and was persuaded about the merit of the patent. The patent issued in 1985, twelve months after filing.

The EPO process, initiated in 1985, was more difficult. The examiner, a German and a former employee of a major chemical firm, was very knowledgeable about prior art but was also skeptical about whether the product truly had an "inventive step" (the European version of nonobviousness). His office action, issued in 1987, criticized the vagueness of language in the application and cited the existence of similar prior art. When three written responses (in 1988, 1989, and 1990) failed to convince the examiner, ACME arranged an interview between the inventor and the examiner. After the interview, the examiner again criticized the application, this time on new grounds. After yet another negative office action and an ACME response, a second interview was arranged in October 1992, this time between the examiner and ACME's attorney. In 1993 the EPO patent finally issued. ACME lawyers said they would have appealed a rejection. This time, competitors did not file oppositions.

In Japan, ACME filed in 1984 but deferred examination until 1991. The examination went smoothly, and a provisional patent was granted within fifteen months. A Japanese firm filed an opposition, citing seven Japanese articles as proof that the innovation was not novel. ACME officials estimated that the patent, once issued, would be good for only ten more years, three or four of which would be spent fighting the opposition. This battle would entail considerable legal costs and would take up the time of ACME's lawyers and the inventor. Moreover, ACME's experience in other countries suggested that imitation of this invention was not a great threat commercially. Hence, ACME abandoned its Japanese patent application. In this case the deferral process appears to have delivered the desired result— ACME was able to avoid some of the costs associated with obtaining the patent because it was able to evaluate its commercial position better during the time afforded by deferral.

3. LAMINATION TECHNOLOGY

This ACME innovation helped produce a more uniform laminate (primarily on fabrics) using a polymeric support. ACME sought to patent both the process and the resultant products. In the United States, the company applied for the patent in 1987 but soon after discovered relevant prior art in the search report compiled by the EPO. Thus it refiled in the United States in 1989, disclosing the prior art. In 1990 the U.S. examiner issued an office action citing vagueness of language and obviousness of the innovation. ACME filed a detailed and ultimately persuasive thirteen-page response. The U.S. patent issued shortly thereafter, in 1991.

ACME filed in the EPO in 1988. The examiner's office action raised objections similar to those of the USPTO, and ACME responded with the same arguments that had prevailed in the United States. The EPO responded quickly and favorably, awarding the patent in mid-1992. The process had taken a mere six months from the time the first office action was issued, which was unusually fast, according to ACME's lawyers. A major European chemical company then filed an opposition. In March 1995 an EPO panel upheld ACME's patent, after a hearing that was unusually informal, and allowed ACME's inventor considerable opportunity to present his case orally. The European objector decided not to appeal, partly on the basis of ACME's reassurances that the patent would not threaten certain processes already in use by that company's customers.

In Japan, ACME filed in 1988, requested examination in 1991, and was granted the patent in 1993. Office actions were dealt with quickly, and no opposition was filed. The final patent issued in 1994, with less trouble than in either the United States or Europe.

4. LAMINATED INDUSTRIAL FILTER

ACME has been active in the industrial filter business since the 1970s. The laminated filter was a new, more resilient product, constituting another application of ACME's basic technology. The U.S. application, filed in 1989, was granted in twenty-one months after one office action. In the EPO, virtually the same scenario occurred; the European patent, filed in 1990, was issued in two and a half years, and no opposition was filed.

In Japan, however, ACME requested examination in September 1993 and received a very negative office action eighteen months later. The examiner cited three earlier patents, which ACME's lawyers did not initially recognize as being technologically similar to its submission. Unsure about how to proceed, ACME asked its Japanese affiliate to discuss the case with its Japanese attorneys. On learning that the objections might have some merit, ACME narrowed its claims, and the patent issued in 1996.

C. Conclusions from ACME's Patent Experience

As noted earlier, patent systems in the United States, Europe, and Japan are marked by significant ideological differences concerning the relative importance of incentives for innovation versus diffusion of technology. The United States is more pro-incentive, whereas Japan is more pro-diffusion, with the various European jurisdictions lying somewhere in between. Partly because of these ideological differences, and partly because of the history and influence of various domestic institutions, the patent systems in these countries exhibit many specific differences in rules, laws, and practices. In Europe and Japan, adversarial contestation between parties occurs early, through opposition proceedings in the administrative forum of the Patent Office. In the United States, adversarial contestation is typically deferred until a suit is brought in the courts. These differences were clear in ACME's experience in the three jurisdictions.

In every jurisdiction ACME encountered frustrating delays, costs, and uncertainties, albeit in different stages of the process, and stemming from different sources. In Japan, ACME experienced extremely costly delays, and eventually its patent was struck down in the Japanese Supreme Court. In the United States, the company managed to obtain patents for its pioneering invention after a six-year-long process. Subsequently, when ACME sought to enforce its patent against infringers, two different U.S. District Courts sought to nullify the patent, only to be reversed by the CAFC in one instance. In Europe, ACME met with inconsistent treatment among nations, and among panels in the EPO. ACME's pioneering patent, approved in other countries in Europe, faced opposition and eventual invalidation in the German Patent Office.

ACME's recent patenting experience with its four follow-on innovations suggests that such variation persists. ACME's follow-on patents were obtained relatively quickly in the United States. But in the EPO and Japan, the same patents on some occasions encountered delays and opposition proceedings. In the EPO, two patents faced major delays, as the result of a "surprising" opposition verdict in one case and a long-drawn-out process of convincing the examiner in the other. But the opposition proceeding for another patent was dealt with very expeditiously by the EPO panel. In one instance, ACME abandoned its patent application in Japan, rather than pursue costly opposition proceedings and get a patent that was soon to expire. Yet, in another case, the JPO granted ACME's application more smoothly than either the USPTO or the EPO.

Table 9.2 attempts to summarize ACME's legal experience in the United States, Japan, and Europe. For each patent application in each jurisdiction, the table includes a somewhat subjective score for ACME's "degree of procedural difficulty," based on the number and expense of the procedural hurdles encountered. Although the pattern may reflect the different types of inventions being patented (pioneering versus follow-on), and the number of cases is very small, the procedural difficulty score has tended to be lower and more similar across jurisdictions in the later patent applications,

TABLE 9.2   ACME's Experience in Obtaining Patents
(Degree of Difficulty in Parentheses)

	U.S.	Japan	Europe
Basic process	Granted in 1976 (6-year delay); district court(s) invalidate patent during enforcement	Denied after opposition and all levels of appeal	Granted in some countries; denied in Germany after opposition and appeal; Limited enforcement obtained in the U.K.
	(5)	(6)	(2) to (6)
Medical devices	Granted in 1984	Deferred examination; granted after opposition in 1992	Granted 1987; "surprising" reversal in opposition; granted on appeal: 1994 (11-year delay)
	(0)	(1)	(3)
Coating product	Granted in 1985	Deferred examination; abandoned when opposed	Granted after many office actions in 1993
	(1)	(1)	(2)
Lamination product	Granted in 1991	Granted in 1994; very quick	Granted in 1992; upheld after opposition in 1995
	(1)	(0)	(1)
Industrial filter	Granted in 1991	Granted in 1993	Granted in 1993 after a strong office action
	(0)	(0)	(1)

Coding scheme for degree of procedural difficulty (maximum possible score = 8; but realistic range = 0 to 6). *The sum of* Office actions (one or less = 0 to 1; two or more leq 1 to 2); opposition/reexamination procedure encountered = 1 to 2; patent revoked in opposition, and appealed = 1 to 2; uncertainty in court outcomes = 1 to 3.

suggesting perhaps that pressures for harmonization may be having some effect. But this may also reflect the fact that these later patents were for less important follow-on inventions and did not require enforcement actions anywhere.

ACME's officials have difficulty estimating the financial impact on the firm of the different procedural obstacles and delays in each jurisdiction. But it is clear, at least in some cases, that they are quite significant. For example, after its basic patent was struck down in Japan, ACME's market share fell by a factor of ten, after it had spent several years developing a market for its product. However, in other cases the impact has been marginal at best. In Germany, even though its patent was overturned in opposition, ACME faced no competition from imitation products in the market. Moreover, it appears that the patent on the company's pioneering innovation offered broad protection for subsequent related innovations, most notably in the United States and the United Kingdom. In the United States, the pro-patentee bias of the system and the power of the courts have enabled ACME to obtain satisfactory protection of its technological turf. In Japan and in some parts of Europe, ACME appears to stand on weaker legal ground but has nevertheless been economically successful, apparently as a result of its innovative products and the strength of its brand name.

D. Evaluating the Different Patent Regimes

Do ACME's experiences suggest any normative conclusions for patent policy? Clearly, the costs and hassles of obtaining and enforcing patents vary substantially across jurisdictions. The different patent jurisdictions, because of their ideological biases, also elicit different strategic responses from firms trying to get inventions patented. In the United States, overall, ACME received strong protection for its innovations and was eventually successful in preventing competitors from copying it. This strong exclusive protection, it can be argued, encourages important pioneering innovations in the United States. ACME, as we have seen, was responsible for making and commercializing important innovations relating to fabrics, medical products, and industrial filters, which were of considerable social value and generated revenues for the company. In Japan, however, as a result of weak patent protection for its basic innovation, ACME's competitors were able to benefit from knowledge spillovers, arising (presumably) from ACME's innovations, without paying royalties. As a consequence, ACME's ability to appropriate returns for its innovation in Japan was severely hampered.

However, ACME's experiences reflect the trials and tribulations of an innovator trying to obtain patent protection in various patent systems, not the experience of innovative firms that are compelled to defend themselves against patent claims. A system that arguably "overprotects" patentees may squelch socially useful follow-on innovations or diffusion of technologies to other companies. The difficulty of obtaining adequate patent protection in Japan reflects that country's bias toward greater diffusion of innovations, even at the cost of discouraging pioneering inventions to some extent. Some follow-on innovations to ACME's basic invention were indeed made by Japanese firms, as evidenced by ZCO's patents. In no other country did ACME's competitors learn from ACME's technology successfully and build on it in any substantial way.[63] It may be argued, therefore, that the Japanese system encourages competition in the creation of useful follow-on innovations and in finding new applications for technology, at the expense of incentives for pioneering innovations, which the U.S. system provides. Europe appears to straddle the middle ground in this trade-off.

Furthermore, the U.S. system encourages strategic gaming between patent adversaries mainly in the courts, rather than in the administrative forum of the Patent Office. This "late stage" adversarial contestation is very costly and involves high stakes. This feature is also present to a lesser degree in the United Kingdom, the other common law country in this study. By contrast, the civil law traditions of Japan and continental Europe provide incentives for earlier interfirm competition in the less expensive administrative forum of the Patent Office. This makes patent prosecution more cumbersome but reduces post-grant uncertainty and risk. In the civil law systems, courts generally defer to the Patent Office for determination of validity, and thus play a more limited role. Despite the lengthy prosecution for its basic patent, ACME's real challenge in the United States was enforcement through the courts, a process so costly and cumbersome that the company's lawyers could only pursue one such action at a time. In contrast, almost all of ACME's expenditures of time and resources in Japan, Germany, and the EPO stemmed from opposition proceedings in the respective patent offices, where competitors vigorously contested its patents.

Despite the cost and delays of litigation in the United States, American courts also make a very strong enforcement apparatus available to patentees. Admittedly, this apparatus is extremely costly and unpredictable, but for a firm such as ACME, seeking to commercialize an important innovation, it can provide an important means of survival and growth. Yet this powerful and uncertain apparatus can also stymie innovation. One patent lawyer I spoke to offered examples of software start-ups threatened with lawsuits by large, resource-rich, patent-wielding firms—threats made possible by the very broad claims allowed for recent software patents in the USPTO. Another lawyer, practicing in the biotech field, voiced similar concerns about biotech patent decisions by the U.S. Patent Office. Without the resources to survive protracted legal battles, small but innovative firms often give in, at the social cost of reduced competition in the creation of valuable new innovations. Practitioners often hail Europe, on the other hand, for its nations' typically efficacious, low-cost adjudication.

What does all this tell us about which type of patent system is better, or offers superior overall social benefits? Answering this question is problematic. If one believes that broad pioneering innovations (as compared with follow-on innovations) are made "available" by the progress of the general "science," innovative firms require fewer legal protections. If, however, one believes that these innovations will be produced and successfully commercialized only if the inventors are well rewarded, then those legal incentives are critically important. Which belief is more "true" is a difficult conundrum, inextricably related to the stage and pattern of development of a country; to the structure of its economy, markets, and industries; to its institutions of scientific pursuit and education; and to the extent it benefits from external worldwide advances in technology. Moreover, multinational firms increasingly plan their research efforts with a global market in mind and may not be as sensitive to the individual national levels of protection they receive as compared with the cumulative global level (as appears to be the case with ACME). In sum, ACME's experiences enable us to frame and address important questions about the social welfare consequences of the differences in patent systems, but our answers to these questions must remain somewhat inconclusive.

V. HARMONIZATION

ACME's struggles, as recounted earlier, took place over nearly two decades ending in the early 1990s. But the world's patent regimes are changing. Waves of harmonization have been sweeping international patent regulation in recent years, changing opportunities for firms trying to obtain patents in major developed countries. A country's patent system can be used to advantage domestic industry by providing weaker protection to the kinds of innovations that foreign firms are good at, thus compelling them to license their technologies to local firms under favorable conditions. It is no surprise, therefore, that international firms have demanded greater cross-national uniformity in patent regimes, and regimes of protection for all intellectual property rights. At a global level, harmonization has been pursued in two forums—the Uruguay round of GATT negotiations (resulting in the TRIPS agreement) and the less successful initiatives (primarily the Patent Harmonization Treaty—PHT) being undertaken by the WIPO.[64] Within Europe, multilateral efforts are under way through the EPO and the European Commission. Changes in the Japanese and U.S. systems have been engendered through bilateral trade negotiations, especially the Structural Impediments Initiative (SII).[65] Many of the differences analyzed in the 1993 GAO study and recounted earlier in this chapter either have disappeared or are ostensibly in the process of being removed.

All the jurisdictions discussed in this chapter, including the United States, now have a uniform twenty-year patent term from the date of application.[66] Further, under the TRIPS agreement, signatory nations have accepted common "minimum" guidelines on such broad issues as the types of innovation that can be patented, uniformity of treatment irrespective of nationality,[67] and the granting of compulsory licenses. In the recent past, only minor changes have been made in the European patent system. The establishment of a "community patent" still appears a distant goal.[68] Through its bilateral and TRIPS commitments, the United States has undertaken to provide for mandatory eighteen-month publication, removal of compulsory licensing provisions, and a fixed patent term of twenty years from grant. The scope of reexamination in the USPTO has also been broadened to allow for more third-party participation—although how it will be applied in practice remains to be seen. Further, in a recent ruling, the U.S. Supreme Court empowered lower federal court judges to play an important role in determining the construction of patent claims, thus decreasing the role of juries in jury trials.[69]

The biggest changes have occurred in Japan. Responding to the strong international criticism about delays, the JPO has taken several steps to remedy its application process. These include phasing out the examination of utility models, hiring additional staff, computerization, issuing "administrative guidance" to major Japanese firms to control their patent applications in the JPO, and instituting special fast-track examination procedures for key patents. The JPO has also issued guidelines to its examiners to permit much broader claims,[70] apply stricter novelty criteria for improvement patents, be more clear in their office actions, and be more generous in awarding interviews. In its bilateral agreements with the United States, Japan has undertaken to end its pre-grant opposition system, further accelerate examination, permit initial filing in English, allow for the correction of translation errors, and restrict the power to grant compulsory licenses. The Japanese courts appear to have been undergoing changes as well, with some recent verdicts awarding fairly large damages to foreign litigants against Japanese firms.[71]

The main shifts (completed and prospective) toward patent harmonization among these jurisdictions are listed in Table 9.3. Many features of the patent systems of the major developed countries appear to be converging. Some differences made obvious by their impact on ACME appear to be disappearing. However, this may be deceptive. The forces of convergence operate predominantly at the level of the laws and standards embodied in the patent statutes. Even at this level, certain national features, such as the American "first-to-invent" system, live on. Convergence in

TABLE 9.3   Major Shifts Towards Patent Harmonization

Major Shift in (Country)	Nature of Change	Source of Change	Remarks
COMPLETED CHANGES:			
United States	Patent term changed to 20 years from the date of filing	TRIPS (minimum 20 years) and U.S.-Japan Agreement (abolition of the 17-years-from-issue option)	Lobbying efforts are under way to restore the 17-year (from issue) option
United States	Ability to introduce inventive acts in foreign countries as evidence for claiming patent priority under first-to-invent	National treatment provision under TRIPS	The U.S. is not fully in compliance with the national treatment provisions in TRIPS
United States	Broader reexamination provision	USPTO reform	Impact of the provision is still unclear
United States	Judges given more power (versus juries) in patent cases	Supreme Court decision	Court opinion states that judges are better suited to interpret some technical patent issues
Japan	Changed patent term to 20 years from date of filing	TRIPS accord	
Japan	Filing in English, and permit corrections in translation	U.S.-Japan Agreement	

TABLE 9.3 (Continued)

Major Shift in (Country)	Nature of Change	Source of Change	Remarks
Japan	Move to postgrant opposition system	U.S.-Japan Agreement	
Japan	Restrict powers to grant compulsory licenses	U.S.-Japan Agreement	
Japan	Patent Office procedures to grant broader claims	U.S.-Japan Agreement	A U.S. patent counsel felt that these had yet to have an effect
Japan	Accelerated examination procedures	U.S.-Japan Agreement	It remains to be seen how effective the JPO is in achieving faster rates of examination
PROSPECTIVE CHANGES:			
United States	18-month publication	U.S.-Japan Agreement	Bill stalled in Congress
United States	Restriction of compulsory licensing provisions	U.S.-Japan Agreement	Bill stalled in Congress
Japan/EPO	Grace period	WIPO-PHT	Still being negotiated
United States	Prior user rights	WIPO-PHT	Still being negotiated

patent prosecution, which is amenable to change through changes in laws, appears to be proceeding at a reasonable pace. However, here, too, substantial national differences persist in the attitudes and values of each nation's patent examiners and in office-level procedural biases.[72]

The process of enforcing patents through the courts, which are subject to unique national legal traditions, appears much more resistant to the forces of convergence. The adversarial, expensive, and powerful nature of the U.S. litigation system, the diversity of European national judicial systems, and the slow, consensus-driven approach of the Japanese trial system will be persisting features of these nations' patent regimes. As one expert remarked, "[I]n ten years, there will be no arguments about standards; the arguments will be exclusively over enforcement, because that is such a nebulous process."[73] Forcing countries to adopt similarly worded patent laws is one thing; obtaining similarly enforceable patent rights is quite another.

That said, there is pressure to harmonize enforcement systems as well. The GATT TRIPS accord contains sections that appear to address several areas in "enforcement."[74] However, the language of these provisions is loose, and developed countries may not need to make any changes to conform to them. In Japan the Osaka High Court has recently made a decision that appears to apply the doctrine of equivalents,[75] suggesting that political pressure applied by Japan's major trading partners may affect the courts, too. Overall, however, full-scale cross-national convergence is likely to remain elusive in the medium term—partly because of differences in applying similarly worded standards, but primarily because of the entrenched legal traditions of court-based patent enforcement systems.

VI. CONCLUSION

ACME's experiences of divergent treatment in the United States, Japan, and Europe are generally consistent with the literature on cross-national differences in patent regimes. Of course, ACME's experiences may be distinctive in some respects. They are concentrated in a specific area of technology (polymer chemistry), in which ACME has had particular success innovating and marketing new products. While we did speak to legal practitioners about different areas of technology, and relied on their input in interpreting our findings, other research suggests that in many areas of technology patents are not very important in appropriating returns to innovations.[76]

ACME's experience does highlight the particular strengths and weaknesses of the U.S. system of patent protection. Although the USPTO does not always appear to provide the highest level of technical proficiency compared with some foreign offices, it continues to be comparatively friendly to inventors. And because the U.S. system does not encourage adversarial contestation at the administrative level, it defers contestation on validity issues to the court-driven enforcement stage, which may extend the period of uncertainty. On the other hand, because U.S. courts offer more powerful legal weapons against infringers than do the courts of continental Europe and Japan, patent holders in the United States are under less compulsion to compromise their claims to exclusive rights (e.g., by agreeing to disadvantageous licensing arrangements).

At the same time, U.S. courts, with their reliance on juries, unspecialized trial court judges, sweeping powers to reassess validity, and very high costs, appear to be a more risky proposition than their civil law–based counterparts in Japan and continental Europe. The combination of high litigation costs, high penalties, and legal uncertainty means that the parties' relative financial capacity to endure the expense, delay, and risk of litigation, rather than the technical merits, may often have a significant effect on outcomes. ACME appears to have both suffered and gained from these characteristics of U.S. adversarial legalism.

These conclusions do not resolve the debate about which methods of patent protection best serve the public good or best balance the goals of stimulating and diffusing innovation. But they do indicate that the impact of different patent regimes cannot be deduced merely from the law on the books, which has been the focus of most recent attempts at patent harmonization, but only by reference to the character of national legal regimes and to informal differences in interpretation and procedures. Further, they temper our expectations about the impact of patent harmonization in the short term.

NOTES

The author gratefully acknowledges help, advice, and feedback from Rosemarie Ham, Robert Merges, David Mowery, Pamela Samuelson, David Teece, and participants in a seminar at Berkeley, as well as the invaluable counsel and support of the editors of this volume. Thanks are also due to ACME's lawyers and many attorneys and patent professionals, too numerous to list here, but without whose help this chapter would not have been possible. Responsibility for all errors however, are strictly the author's.

1. Bill Budinger, "Modernizing Patent Law," *Inventor's Digest*, September/October 1995, 35.

2. Samson Helfgott characterizes the U.S. system as one whose emphasis is "to protect the patentee," whereas the Japanese system seeks "to teach industry new innovations." Samson Helfgott, "Cultural Differences between the U.S. and Japanese Patent Systems," *Journal of the Patent and Trademark Office Society* 72 (1990): 231–38.

3. Arthur Wineberg, "The Japanese Patent System: A Non-tariff Barrier to Foreign Businesses?" *Journal of World Trade* 22 (1988): 12.

4. This also means that there is no unified body of case law that feeds back into the prosecution of patents at the EPO.

5. See, in particular, the "U.S. General Accounting Office Study on Intellectual Property Rights: U.S. Companies' Patent Experiences in Japan" (Washington, D.C.: GAO, 1993) (henceforth GAO Study); and Michael Helfand, "How Valid Are U.S. Criticisms of the Japanese Patent System?" Stanford Law School (unpublished ms., on file with author, 1991).

6. Except in some European countries, which have a simple registration system.

7. For example, in the United States, an administrative reexamination process is available, whereas in other jurisdictions adversarial "opposition" proceedings can be initiated.

8. In 1990 it was estimated that the average interference lasted a year at a cost of about $7,000 per month for each side in attorneys' fees. Further, they often spilled over into lawsuits on appeal, which sharply raised the costs. Andrew H. Thorson and John A. Fortkort, "An Analysis of Patent Protection in Japan and the U.S.," *Journal of the Patent and Trademark Office Society* 77 (1995): 310–12.

9. Some observers aver that this is mainly because the firms usually agree on a settlement involving a royalty-free license to the second firm. To the extent that this is true, it alleviates some of the problems associated with the absence of prior user rights in the United States.

10. Thorson and Fortkort, "An Analysis of Patent Protection in Japan and the U.S.," 311.

11. GAO Study, 54. Language, according to the report, was one of the biggest hurdles faced by U.S. industry in effectively using the Japanese patent system, which (according to many Japanese lawyers) was often compounded by hasty translation of the application under time pressures.

12. N. Thane Bauz, "Reanimating U.S. Patent Reexamination: Recommendations for Change Based upon a Comparative Study of German Law," *Creighton Law Review* 27 (1994): 951.

13. For example, in Japan, prior publication of an innovation anywhere in the world leads to rejection of an application's claim to novelty, whereas in the United States applicants have a grace period of one year after publication within which to file an application.

14. For example, a version of a patented component with slightly improved features may be deemed patentable in the JPO but not in the USPTO. Further, broad "means plus function" type claims, which may be used in the United States, are rarely allowed in Japan. See Helfand, "How Valid Are U.S. Criticisms of the Japanese Patent System?" 9.

15. Helfgott, "Cultural Differences between the U.S. and Japanese Patent Systems," 234.

16. Simply put, a standard of "patentability" implies a bar that the innovation must clear to be actually considered one by the patent office (e.g., it should be sufficiently novel, or sufficiently nonobvious to persons who are skilled in the relevant art).

17. Jinzo Fujino, "Understanding the Flood of Japanese Patent Applications," *Patent World,* July–August 1990, 30–31.

18. The GAO Study indicates that, in 1991, 6.5 percent of all applications were opposed, and each opposed application had an average of 1.8 opponents.

19. Donald M. Spero, "Patent Protection or Piracy—A CEO Views Japan," *Harvard Business Review* 68, no. 5 (September–October 1990): 60–67.

20. Robert Girouard, "The Japanese Patent System: Trade and Industrial Policy Implications" (master's thesis, University of California at Berkeley, 1995).

21. Nonetheless, one lawyer we spoke to cautioned us that in biotech patents, some stalling practices are used in Europe, especially by appealing to "Green" political interests.

22. As we have seen, JPO procedures require an applicant to specifically request examination (in seven years), and some applicants choose not to do so based on their commercial assessment of the patent.

23. Employee incentives within Japanese firms, and organization-level incentives to obtain cross-licenses encourage rampant patenting in Japan.

24. Despite changes in the rules of the JPO in 1988 permitting inclusion of multiple claims in a single application, Japanese firms predominantly continue to use their earlier practice of including only a single claim per application. What this means is that to cover the same innovations or set of innovations, more patents are filed in Japan as compared with the United States.

25. Utility models are lesser patents awarded by the patent office; they are subject to a lower standard of patentability and have a shorter duration. Procedurally, however, the utility models were subject to the same type of examination. Recently, the JPO has discontinued examination of utility models and supplanted it with a registration process, with examination being invoked in the event of litigation over infringement.

26. This figure excludes the time taken on parent applications that were "continued" in the successful application. A patent lawyer we spoke to believed that this mismeasurement could be fairly significant in some areas, such as biotechnology.

27. GAO Study. The figure for the JPO was estimated by dividing the number of patents that were pending to be examined in 1991 by the number of patents that were examined in that year. The time taken was less when no oppositions were filed twenty-one to twenty-four months), but commercially important innovations are usually opposed.

28. Samson Helfgott, "Why Must Filing in Europe Be So Costly?" *Journal of the Patent and Trademark Office Society* 76 (October 1994): 787–92. Helfgott cites results of a recent study conducted by the FICPI (International Federation of Intellectual Property Attorneys) at 788. A large fraction of the costs in Japan can be delayed by deferring examination, since the costs of merely filing an application are quite low.

29. Ibid., 789; 8.3 countries represents the approximate equivalent U.S. market size in Europe.

30. A survey of European patenting costs by the American Intellectual Property Law Association in 1995 ("Position Paper on the Costs of European Patent Prosecution," October) found that costs in Europe split roughly evenly between official fees, translation costs, and attorney fees.

31. Helfgott, "Why Must Filing in Europe Be So Costly?" 789. Such estimates provided by other authors vary somewhat but are in roughly the same range. For example, see Budinger, "Modernizing Patent Law," 35: "[I]t costs about $10K to

$15K to patent one innovation in the United States. In Europe, the cost is about $100K (for a market comparable in size to the United States) and in Asia [presumably including many countries besides Japan] it is somewhere over $200,000 per invention!"

32. Michael J. Pantuliano, "The U.S. View of European Patent Litigation," *European Intellectual Property Review*, no. 9 (1993): 307. For a more detailed analysis of the same topic by the author, see "A U.S. House Counsel's Comparative View of European and Japanese Patent Litigation," *International Patent Litigation* (1994 supplement), edited by Michael N. Meller (Washington D.C.: BNA Books, 1994), 1–21.

33. James Maxeiner, "The Expert in U.S. and German Patent Litigation," *IIC: International Review of Industrial Property and Copyright Laws* 22 (1991): 595–605.

34. Report of Economic Survey 1995, by the American Intellectual Property Law Association, Fretzer-Kraus Inc.: Washington D.C. (henceforth AIPLA Report), 69–70. One patent attorney warned patent owners that U.S. litigation could take from six months to ten years (with two to five years being common), and out-of-pocket costs could range from $100,000 to $1 million (with an average of about $350,000). John D. Vandenburg, "The Truth about Patent Litigation for Patent Owners Contemplating Suit," *Journal of Patent and Trademark Office Society* 73 (1991): 301–8.

35. For example, the Tokyo and Osaka courts in Japan, and the Düsseldorf court in Germany, all have specialized patent divisions and judges with considerable experience in patent cases. In the United Kingdom, the Patents Court (which is the court of the first instance) has had specialized judges for a long time. But only recently was a former patent barrister appointed to the High Court. In the United States, only the Court of Appeals of the Federal Circuit is specialized in patent cases.

36. The CAFC, it is widely believed, has also engendered a stronger pro-patent bias in the U.S. legal system. A 1986 *Fortune* magazine article declared, "Thanks mostly to a new appeals court, patent holders are winning many more suits against infringers. Damage awards have driven some defendants close to bankruptcy"; quoted in Ronald D. Hantman, "Patent Infringement," *Journal of the Patent and Trademark Office Society* 72 (1990): 454–518.

37. In part, legal uncertainty in the United Kingdom is lower because the Patents Court in the Chancellery Division, which is the court of first instance, has traditionally had specialist judges who deal with patent cases.

38. A patent lawyer we spoke to felt that this "English Rule" curbed the incidence of rogue lawsuits filed by lawyers working for clients on a contingency fee basis. However, another lawyer felt that the rule also undermined the fairness of the system by raising the stakes in litigation, and thus making it more risky in marginal cases, especially for small, resource-strapped firms. For a discussion, see Curtis E. A. Karnow, *Daily Journal*, July 27, 1997, 4.

39. For example, Joshua Lerner, "Patenting in the Shadow of Competitors," *Journal of Law and Economics* 38 (1995): 463–95; Edmund Kitch ("The Nature and Function of the Patent System," *Journal of Law and Economics* 20 [1977]: 265–90), however, has argued that such protection of technological "prospects" may be the main explanation of how the patent system operates.

40. John Haley, "The Myth of the Reluctant Litigant," *Journal of Japanese Studies* 9 (1978): 359; Takao Tanase, "The Management of Disputes: Automobile Accident

Compensation in Japan," *Law and Society Review* 24 (1990): 651; Frank Upham, *Law and Social Change in Postwar Japan* (Cambridge, Mass.: Harvard University Press, 1987).

41. Wineberg, "The Japanese Patent System," 18.

42. Mark F. Wachter, "Patent Enforcement in Japan—An American Perspective for Success," *AIPLA Quarterly Journal* 19, no. 24 (1991): 59–85.

43. In particular, fees are high because Japanese patent lawyers charge a fraction of the amount at stake in the case, which they keep even if the case is settled favorably very early.

44. Helfand, "How Valid Are U.S. Criticisms of the Japanese Patent System?" 39. See also Osamu Takura, "Practical Aspects of Patent Litigation in Japan" (mimeo, on file with author, 1993), 478. However, in 1992 the Tokyo District Court granted a petition for preliminary injunction against seven Japanese manufacturers of the drug Tagamet.

45. Thorson and Fortkort, "An Analysis of Patent Protection in Japan and the U.S.," 306–9. In patent law, courts apply the doctrine of equivalents to enlarge the scope of the claims if the allegedly infringing device works on essentially the same principles. In the past, Japanese district courts have applied the doctrine, but were struck down by the appeals courts.

46. Wineberg, "The Japanese Patent System," 18. *Asamura Guidelines: Patent and Utility Models in Japan* (Tokyo: Asamura Patent Office, 1991), 22–23. One lawyer we interviewed told us that around 80 percent of patent suits in the United States did not go to trial either, reflecting the high costs of U.S. litigation. However, it is very likely that these suits are settled on much more favorable terms to patent holders than in Japan.

47. Pantuliano, "The U.S. View of European Patent Litigation," 308.

48. Pantuliano, "A U.S. House Counsel's Comparative View of European and Japanese Patent Litigation," 11–12.

49. Ibid., 9.

50. Stephen M. Bodenheimer Jr. and John Beton, "Infringement by Equivalents in the United States and Europe: A Comparative Analysis," *European Intellectual Property Review*, no. 3 (1993): 83–90. See also Pantuliano, "A U.S. House Counsel's Comparative View of European and Japanese Patent Litigation," 13.

51. See Table 9.3 and the associated section on patent harmonization for an explication of these changes. Nor are these the only differences between the patent regimes in these countries. Numerous other differences of varying importance abound, but we have covered adequate ground to understand and appreciate ACME's experiences.

52. At the time, product patents (which protect the product from imitation, irrespective of small differences in the method used to manufacture it) were not available in Japan, but this changed in the late 1970s.

53. It is not unusual, however, to receive an office action on an application. One ACME attorney believed that if an application was accepted without any office actions, the "quality" of the application was probably poor, because it did not stretch the limits of the claims that could have been allowed.

54. Since the refiling was done as a "continuation," ACME did not lose its priority on the invention.

55. This apparently is a normal action when process and product patents covering the same invention are filed simultaneously.

56. Court opinion. (Full citation withheld to protect confidentiality of the company.)

57. Court opinion.

58. "Dimmer of Great Ideas," *Business Tokyo,* May 1990, 30–35.

59. Statement of Dr. David A. Duke, Corning Incorporated, before the Senate Subcommittee on Trade of the Committee on Finance, July 1993 (copy available from the Director of Public Policy, Corning Inc., Washington, D.C.). Corning's pioneering innovations in the area of optical fiber received prompt patent protection in the United States in 1971 and 1972. In Japan, however, the patent took five years to issue and five more years to address all the oppositions. In the meantime, a number of licenses were also being negotiated, and exclusion of nonlicensees was a pressing problem. By the time the oppositions were completed, a number of firms had invented around the Corning process, and since only the process patent had been granted, the company had no recourse against them.

60. GAO Study, 30–31. The composition patent issued after seven years of examination and opposition, whereas the process patent took almost ten years.

61. ACME's British patent, enforceable in the effective British courts, proved somewhat useful, for in 1981 the company brought a suit against a British importer of infringing products. Even though some of the claims in the patent were held invalid on a technicality (and had to be modified), ACME negotiated a reasonable settlement with the U.K. firm.

62. Interestingly, ACME faced no direct competition for its products in Germany through "infringement" of its rejected patent. In light of the strong opposition from its competitors, this is an unsolved puzzle for ACME's attorneys.

63. A particularly surprising case was Germany, where ACME had no patent protection for its basic innovation.

64. The Patent Harmonization Treaty (PHT) is focused on the more limited set of countries in the developed world and is more ambitious than TRIPS. But these negotiations have been plagued with problems and were set back severely in January 1994, when the United States announced that it would not seek to resume WIPO negotiations.

65. Two agreements were concluded relating to intellectual property, on January 20 and August 16, 1994.

66. However, there are concerted efforts being made in the United States to reinstate the option of the old "seventeen years from grant" patent term, which would constitute a reversal of U.S. commitments under the U.S.-Japan Framework Agreement(s).

67. This has substantially affected the USPTO, forcing it to accept evidence of inventive acts outside the United States in order to establish priority in its first-to-invent system. Some scholars, however, have argued that the changes in the United States have not gone far enough to honor its "national treatment" treaty commitments under the TRIPS accord. Harold C. Wegner, "TRIPS Boomerang—Obligations for Domestic Reform," *Vanderbilt Journal of Transnational Law* 29 (1996): 535–58.

68. As one commentator put it, "[T]he EC's explicit policy objective of achiev-

ing harmonization has been thwarted by politics, industrial opposition, the question of whether harmonization will truly maximize the collective economic interests of the EC, and the sovereignty concerns of the EC's member countries." Mitchel B. Wallerstein, Mary Ellen Mogee, and Roberta A. Schoen, eds., *Global Dimensions of Intellectual Property Rights in Science and Technology* (Washington, D.C.: National Academy Press, 1993), 152. The fate of European harmonization appears to be inextricably linked to the success of European integration efforts in general, and the growth in influence of the European Court of Justice.

69. *Markman v. Westview Instruments, Inc.*, 116 S.Ct. 1384 38 USPQ2d 1461 1463 (1996), stating that "judges, not juries, are the better suited to find the acquired meaning of patent terms" (at 1470).

70. Specifically, they have been instructed to allow claims unless they are circumscribed by the prior art.

71. Relentless trade pressure—primarily from the United States—appears to be affecting court decisions. And the issuance of some important patents to foreign firms has put pressure on Japanese firms to protect themselves from lawsuits by agreeing to substantial settlements. "When Copying Gets Costly," *The Economist*, May 9, 1992, 91.

72. These relate to how examiners approach patent applications and what ideological and procedural biases they continue to hold. Often, supporting institutions and the government machinery are also reluctant to change. One U.S. patent counsel, with recent experience in Japan, was unhappy with the compliance by patent examiners there with the new guidelines and laws.

73. Michael Kirk, former deputy director of the USPTO and former U.S. trade negotiator, at a seminar on "Globalization and the Political Economy," at the University of California at Berkeley, in spring 1996. Firms are also recognizing this, leading some authors to comment that "meaningful enforcement, in contrast with statutory protection, is emerging as a major issue for the rest of this decade." Herbert F. Schwartz and Vincent N. Paladino, "Key Shifts in Patent Protection," *Managing Intellectual Property, Patent and Design Yearbook* (1994), at 8.

74. For example in "discovery" (Article 43), injunctions (Article 44), and damages (Article 45).

75. Shusaku Yamamoto and John Tessensohn, "Doctrine of Equivalents Breakthrough in Japan," *Managing Intellectual Property*, July/August 1996, 12–15. The decision (*Genentech Inc. v. Sumitomo Pharmaceutical Co. Ltd.*, H-6 [ne] No. 3292), was dated March 29, 1996, and overturns a first instance ruling in Sumitomo's favor. This is the first time a Japanese appeals court has handed down a decision applying the doctrine of equivalents, although courts of first instance have occasionally done it in the past.

76. In particular the "Yale Study," which found that patents were important only in the ethical drug industry, and (to a lesser extent in) the chemical industry. See Richard Levin, Alvin Klevorick, Richard Nelson, and Sidney Winker, "Appropriating the Returns from Industrial Research and Development," *Brookings Papers on Economic Activity*, no. 3 (1987): 783–831.

PART III

Regulating Product Safety

CHAPTER TEN

Licensing Biologics in Europe and the United States

Martine Kraus

We got approval in the U.S. and we thought: If we can get it approved in the U.S., we can get it approved everywhere; the U.S. has the highest standard. That was a great mistake.

REGULATORY AFFAIRS OFFICER, MULTINATIONAL
PHARMACEUTICAL COMPANY

I. INTRODUCTION

The conventional wisdom, based on a number of cross-national comparative studies, is that American regulatory processes are much more legalistic, adversarial, and costly than those of European nations, where more informal, negotiated policy making and implementation prevail and recourse to courts is rare.[1] In the 1970s, for example, the U.S. Food and Drug Administration (FDA) was criticized for its legalistic conservatism, which, in comparison with other countries, led to higher costs and longer delays in the introduction of beneficial new drugs.[2] FDA enforcement of Good Manufacturing Practices (GMP) regulations was described as legalistic and inflexible.[3] Cross-national comparative studies also typically indicated that American regulatory processes were much more complex and organizationally fragmented than their European counterparts.

During the 1980s and 1990s, however, political and bureaucratic pressures arose for regulatory reform and for cross-national *harmonization* of regulatory controls. The European Union (EU) adopted a multistate approval process for pharmaceuticals. The FDA announced its intent to harmonize new drug testing standards used in the United States with those in other countries,[4] and to carry out joint reviews of important new therapies with the Canadian Health Protection Branch. Regulatory and company officials from the EU, Japan, and the United States founded the International Conference on Harmonization (ICH) to discuss the harmonization of pharmaceutical regulation and the mutual recognition of data among the three trading blocks.[5] In the United States, the FDA has been subjected to powerful political pressures to accelerate its regulatory procedures. In 1992 the U.S. Congress enacted a user fee system tied to performance goals for the

FDA.[6] An FDA advisory committee urged quick approval of a new class of promising AIDS drugs,[7] and the Center for Biologics Evaluation and Research (CBER) hired three hundred new reviewers and introduced reviewer deadlines to hasten the approval process.[8] Conversely, regulation at the *transnational* level in Europe has been criticized for becoming more legalistic than regulation at the national level. In the 1990s, as companies specializing in genetically engineered health products grew much more rapidly in the United States than in Europe, the disparity was widely attributed to the more favorable regulatory system in America.

In consequence, it is not entirely clear whether the national differences in regulatory style identified ten or fifteen years ago still persist in this policy area. To provide some perspective on this issue, this study investigates the regulation of biotechnology-derived "biological" products. Biologics are products made from or with the aid of living organisms, as opposed to pharmaceuticals produced through chemical synthesis. Biologics include human blood products or blood-derived products, vaccines, peptides, and carbohydrate products produced by cell culture. In all economically advanced democracies, the manufacture of biologics is closely regulated to guard against the risk of deadly viral and bacteriological contamination. Regulatory authorities in both the United States and the EU require manufacturers to obtain licenses both for their manufacturing facilities and for each new product, based on detailed descriptions and analyses of their facilities and quality control measures. This chapter compares the efforts of Company Y, a multinational manufacturer, to win regulatory approval from agencies in the EU and the United States for the manufacture of a medically valuable genetically engineered biological product.

II. RESEARCH METHOD

The research was based primarily on numerous, lengthy, in-person interviews with Company Y's director and vice president of regulatory affairs. These officials are responsible for obtaining regulatory approval of Company Y's products and manufacturing facilities in the United States and Europe. We discussed in detail the regulatory approval process for one of Company Y's genetically engineered blood products, because it was said to illustrate the characteristics of both regulatory systems. I asked the officials to describe the similarities and differences Company Y experienced with regard to the substantive requirements for regulatory approval, the amount of time it took to obtain approval, changes that had to be made to satisfy EU and U.S. regulators, and the cost to the company of the compliance and approval process. Company Y officials allowed me to review the voluminous documents submitted as part of the approval process and the responses they received from the regulating agencies, after which I was able to ask follow-up questions, clarify any confusion, and confirm details discussed in interviews.

I also asked the Company Y officials for examples of either legalistic or cooperative interactions with both sets of regulators and reviewed FDA and European regulatory officials' responses to Company Y's submissions. Finally, I asked Company Y officials about their impressions of whether either system demanded a higher margin of safety or entailed higher "accountability costs" or "opportunity costs." Company Y officials, who have had ongoing interactions with both sets of regulators, did not appear to have an "ax to grind" with either system; they are generally supportive of this form of product safety regulation, since the stakes for making a faulty product are extremely high. Thus I found their responses knowledgeable and credible.

To test the generalizability of Company Y's experiences, I conducted a series of telephone interviews with similarly situated officials in other multinational pharmaceutical companies.[9] I presented these officials with a summary of the findings with respect to Company Y and asked them to comment, based on their own company's experiences. The results of this process, as well as my own subsequent experience working in the pharmaceutical industry and informal interactions at conferences and other gatherings of professionals in this field, give me confidence that the findings from Company Y's experience are accurate and typical.[10]

III. SUMMARY OF FINDINGS

Based on Company Y's experience, in the 1990s the U.S. and European approaches to the regulation of biological products continued to diverge in several areas:

1. Despite increasing progress toward centralization, the European system, viewed as comprising both member states and EU agencies, was more institutionally complex and fragmented than the American system.

2. In certain respects, the European regime was as legalistic and *more* stringent than the American one. Although FDA regulatory interactions with companies had grown somewhat more flexible, both regulatory systems remained highly prescriptive and prone to regulatory unreasonableness. Both regulatory regimes insisted on certain regulatory requirements that Company Y's quality control officials regarded as unnecessary under the particular circumstances and costly to comply with. The European regulatory review process, however, was more analytically searching and less mechanical than the American one.

3. There remained some differences in substantive requirements concerning manufacturing safety and reliability: the FDA focuses more on manufacturing *facilities,* the European authorities on process control analysis. Clinical study requirements still differ between Europe and the United States, as well as among member countries of the EU.

4. Both regulatory review systems imposed substantial delays in marketing new biologic products. A six-month wait for regulatory approval, once the product was ready for manufacture and marketing, was estimated to cost the company $48 million in revenues, while delaying benefits to patients eager for the product. In the case at hand, the application approval time by the EU Committee for Proprietary Medicinal Products (CPMP) (approximately twenty months) was substantially shorter than by the FDA (approximately thirty-one months). However, if we add delays stemming from individual country approval in Europe (an additional five months), overall differences in review times are less striking. Once manufacturing has begun, moreover, regulatory reviews of proposed process changes are much slower in Europe than in the United States.

5. Although both regulatory systems entail costly and burdensome transaction and opportunity costs, neither was clearly more cost-effective. The faster process change review in the United States was offset to an unpredictable degree by a higher rate of turnover and inexperience among regulatory reviewers at the FDA. In the case at hand, nonetheless, the cost of compliance was slightly higher in Europe than in the United States, because more tests were required and authorities insisted on tighter tolerances in manufacturing processes.

Generalizations from the particular case study must be qualified, however. The case studied reflected Company Y's first submission of a genetically modified product to the newly created EU authorities. Today, Company Y officials say, company and government officials alike would be more experienced, and the process might be significantly faster and less troublesome. Second, since the approval of the described product, the EU "concertation" procedure has been superseded by a *more* centralized procedure, which promises to streamline the process.[11] More generally, the 1990s have been characterized by increased convergence of the two regulatory regimes. Product application review times between Europe and the United States are clearly converging and by 1999 had been reduced to less than 12 months, as agencies in both places strive to be more efficient.[12] A recent EU directive promises convergence of the review times for process changes as well. For specified biotechnology and synthetic biological products, the FDA is moving away from an exclusive focus on the manufacturing facilities and toward a more European-style process control analysis.[13] Conversely,

European authorities have increased inspections of U.S. manufacturing facilities. Finally, EU guidelines on clinical trials and the International Conference on Harmonization's focus on preclinical and clinical trial requirements have led to rapid convergence in the area of clinical studies.[14]

IV. THE PRODUCT AND ITS CONTROL

All industrial democracies have established regulatory regimes to control the testing, manufacture, and marketing of pharmaceutical, biological, and medical device products. The harmful side effects of products such as thalidomide demonstrated that consumers and health care professionals cannot fully evaluate the safety of products that they use on a daily basis, and that liability law may not always provide sufficient additional incentives for manufacturers to test for and maintain the highest standards of quality control.[15] Government regulation attempts to fill that gap for therapeutics by requiring extensive premarket research and testing concerning the safety, quality, and efficacy of new pharmaceutical and biological products, as well as controls on sanitary conditions and quality assurance during manufacture.

Governments impose special regulations on the manufacture and approval of biologics because, compared with pharmaceuticals, they are chemically less stable, more heat- and shear-sensitive, difficult to assay, and more subject to contamination. Contaminated intravenous medicines can rapidly spread disease and even cause death. In the early 1980s, many French patients became infected with the AIDS virus from contaminated blood banks. As recently as 1995, 350 people worldwide contracted hepatitis from a biological drug treatment for immune deficiency.[16] Thus, in the United States, the regulation of biologics manufacture is more stringent than for pharmaceuticals; special attention is paid to the cleanliness of the production area, the operation of the equipment, and the control of the manufacturing process.

Genetically engineered blood products, employing recombinant DNA (rDNA), are less reliant on provisions of donor blood and provide a solution to the problem of viral contamination. The novel techniques, however, raise new questions. Do rDNA-derived products deviate from or contain contaminants not normally present in their conventional equivalents? In response, many countries have imposed special regulatory procedures for genetically engineered biologics and drugs. In 1985 the FDA issued *Points to Consider in the Production and Testing of New Drugs and Biologicals Produced by Recombinant DNA Technology*, which described the information needed to evaluate the expression system, host cells, and manufacturing procedures for products prepared by rDNA techniques.[17] In 1987 the EU established a new mandatory evaluation procedure for all high-technology medicinal products derived from biotechnology. In 1990 the EU issued two directives on the containment and release of genetically modified organisms. More recently, based on over ten years of experience with biotechnology, the FDA issued a new policy for specified biotechnology and synthetic biological products that can be clearly determined and controlled.[18]

Development of a new chemical entity (NCE) or biological agent, including approval by the regulatory authorities, takes on average seven to ten years and entails a cost of $100 to $250 million. The regulatory process includes initial preclinical studies in animals, three phases of clinical studies in humans, and the submission of the license application to the regulatory authorities. While carrying out its clinical studies, the company operates a pilot manufacturing plant to provide material for the trials. Regulatory authorities closely monitor the company's methodology and test results, demanding proven results in each phase before allowing the company to move on to the next level of investigation. The regulators also request proof of proper operation of the pilot manufacturing plant.

A. Company Y's Recombinant Coagulation Factor

The product is a new antihemophilic factor, administered to hemophiliacs as an important cofactor for the coagulation of human blood. Until recently, the antihemophilic factor was produced from human plasma. Millions of liters of freshly donated blood plasma had to be obtained and processed every year. The new genetically engineered product, however, relies primarily on a constant supply of the cell culture from the manufacturer's cell bank and an ongoing fermentation process.

Manufacture entails three main steps—fermentation, purification, and finishing—each of which requires extremely high levels of purity and process control. The fermenter is operated, under sterile conditions, for up to six months, during which the culture fluid containing the recombinant coagulation factor is removed and fresh culture fluid is added. To assure the exact reproducibility of the recombinant protein, a variety of culture parameters are monitored and controlled.[19] *Purification* entails a number of steps that increase the concentration of the coagulation factor, eliminate impurities, and remove or inactivate any viruses that may have been inadvertently introduced into the manufacturing process.[20] The highly purified coagulation factor is then stabilized for longer shelf life by adding (plasma-derived) albumin. Regulatory authorities are interested in the capacity of the purification process to achieve the desired "clearance" (level of impurities), the manufacturer's *justification* for that level of clearance, and the consistency with which that level can be maintained in long-term production. All control tests, as well as the data from all preclinical and clinical studies, must be described and analyzed in the company's product license application.

B. Why Regulation?

Manufacturers of biologics are part of an industry that has strong incentives for strict quality control. Biologics are easily contaminated, with serious consequences for the patient. No company can afford a widely publicized injury to a patient; the adverse reputational effects of putting an unsafe product on the market may hurt all of a company's products and create shortages for patients. In addition, the industry operates under strict liability law and is susceptible to multiple million dollar lawsuits. The industry competes not only on the basis of price but also on the basis of quality, as the products are paid for primarily by a vast array of health insurance arrangements. Finally, any scandal in the new biotechnology industry will affect the entire industry. In that sense, manufacturers of biological and particularly genetically engineered products are hostages of each other; a public health disaster or panic caused by quality control weakness in one company could conceivably destroy trust in the product and ruin the market for all producers.[21] Hence, even aside from product regulation, corporate quality assurance officials in the manufacturing companies are granted powers to prevent shipment and to demand further testing or process changes.

Nevertheless, government and company officials alike believe that government regulation and product license applications are not redundant. Even if most firms are very conscientious, companies with unreliable safety controls may end up hurting a consumer, and thus the reputation of the entire industry. In addition, company officials point out that regulatory agencies review many applications and are in a position to compare, recommend, or require the most effective quality assurance procedures, pushing the industry toward higher standards. Similarly, cGMP (current Good Manufacturing Practices) compliance inspectors provide an extra set of eyes that help prevent and identify deficiencies in company manufacturing controls. This is particularly important when introducing new technologies with yet unknown risks. Finally, company officials claim that regulation increases consumer confidence and legitimizes the end product.[22]

V. COMPARING U.S. AND EUROPEAN REGULATIONS

A. Clinical Trials

In the United States, the FDA's approval decision for a new drug is based largely on data derived from clinical studies. To test a new chemical compound or biological agent in humans, a company has to file with the FDA an Investigational New Drug (IND) application that includes (1) the results of all preclinical studies and an analysis of their implications for human pharmacology; (2) an analysis of the drug's composition, and the manufacturing and quality control procedures used in its production; (3) the clinical protocols describing the sponsor's plans for the initial-stage clinical studies and the qualifications of the investigators. Generating the data required by the FDA to show that a drug is reasonably safe for use in initial, small-scale studies takes on average 3.5 years.[23]

If the company does not hear from authorities within thirty days, it can legally start its Phase 1 clinical trial as described in the IND. The FDA can put the trial on "clinical hold" until the company has provided further information. Clinical holds are common; thus, in the 1980s many companies conducted their Phase 1 clinical trials in Europe. This is less true today, following the efforts of the International Conference on Harmonization (ICH), but many U.S.-based companies still find it much faster to take their U.S.-discovered drugs straight to Europe and shift drug development back to the United States after completion of the first trials in humans.[24]

In Europe, a company has to meet the regulatory requirements of the particular European country where it intends to conduct its trial. The EU has made some progress toward the harmonization of clinical trial requirements.[25] Nevertheless, differences between member states persist regarding the need for government approval before initiating clinical trials; the status of ethics committees; their structure, function, and legality; the submission requirements; and agency review times prior to trial initiation.[26] Even after the trials have been completed, member states differ in their insistence on inspection of investigational sites for Good Clinical Practice (GCP) compliance.[27]

Phase 2 and 3 clinical trials entail successively larger and better controlled testing protocols, and they are much more expensive. To facilitate the worldwide introduction of new products, companies like to initiate parallel Phase 2 and 3 clinical trials in the United States and Europe, tapping into a U.S. and pan-European network of physicians and health organizations.

B. Manufacturing and Marketing

In order to manufacture and sell a new biological product in the United States, a company must apply for a product license and obtain an establishment license; in Europe, a company must apply for a marketing authorization and obtain a manufacturing permit. In both places the process is burdensome, costly, and at times slow. In America, the federal FDA's CBER[28] monopolizes premarketing regulation of biological products, preempting regulation by the states. CBER's decisions are not reviewable by other agencies and are rarely reviewed by the courts, since applicants do not want further delays and no advocacy groups routinely oppose the granting of licenses.

In Europe, before the establishment of the EU CPMP and the European Medicines Control Agency (EMEA),[29] companies needed a separate product license in every European country in which they sought to sell their product. This was succeeded by a sequence of multistep procedures involving national and EU authorities, described more fully later. In Europe, as in the United States, the permit process rarely involves court proceedings or judicial review, although in Germany advocacy groups on occasion have challenged manufacturing permits for genetically engineered products in the courts, delaying the approval process.[30]

1. COMPANY Y'S U.S. APPLICATION

The company's Product License Application (PLA) contained reports of all prior investigations and other information pertinent to an evaluation of whether the product, as manufactured, will be safe and effective. Applications are often between 50,000 and 250,000 pages, or hundreds of volumes. Company Y's original application for the genetically engineered biologic filled only eight volumes because the company was already marketing an FDA-approved non–genetically engineered coagulation factor and was able to cross-reference a former application. The company's Establishment License Application (ELA), describing its manufacturing facilities for the new product in question, was also eight volumes long. This was in addition to "its standing ELA"—an application of more than twenty volumes that provides detailed and technical descriptions of all the company's manufacturing facilities (including heating, lighting, ventilation, and air conditioning); equipment (fermenters, valves, and pipes, including cleanliness and maintenance routines); and utilities (water, gas, electricity, and compressed air).

Significant changes in the manufacture of a licensed product require prior approval by the FDA. Minor changes to the process or equipment may require only notification of the FDA. Major equipment changes are considered significant process changes and may require the company to file not only an ELA Amendment but also a product license supplement (which may include preclinical testing in animals and clinical testing to prove equivalence). Process changes are not uncommon. Company Y makes on average one to two minor process changes per year, and one major process change every five years.

TABLE 10.1.   Product Licensing Procedures in the EU and U.S.

EU Concertation Procedure	EU Centralized Procedure (1995)	FDA Procedure
Rapporteur	EMEA	CBER
↓	↓	↓
Member States (12)	2 Rapporteurs	Multidisciplinary Review Team
↓	↓	↓
CPMP / Biotech Working Party	CPMP / Biotech Working Party	Advisory Committee
↓	↓	↓
CPMP / Commission Approval	Commission / Member States	Pre-License Inspection
↓	↓	↓
Member State Approval	Draft Approval	FDA Approval
	↓	
	Standing Committee on Medicinal Products for Human Use (qualified majority vote & approved)	
	or ┊	
	↓	
+ Inspection	Council of Ministers	

2. COMPANY Y'S EUROPEAN APPLICATION

Whereas in the United States only the FDA is involved, in Europe the product application process involves both national and community authorities. Five types of regulatory procedures have been used: (1) the original national procedure whereby companies applied separately to each national agency; (2) the multistate procedure (from 1975 to 1995), whereby a company applied in one member state and then sought approval in other member states based on the same application; (3) the concertation procedure (from 1987 to 1995), whereby an EU committee evaluated the application based on prior review by a *national* agency that assumed the role of "rapporteur"; and (4) since 1995, either (a) the centralized procedure, whereby an EU agency reviews the application and its decision is binding on the member states, or (b) the decentralized or mutual recognition procedure, wherein product approval in one country may be extended to other member states.[31] The EU concertation and centralized procedures, along with the FDA procedure, are outlined in Table 10.1.

From 1987 to 1995 the concertation procedure was required for all biotechnology derived medicinal products. Since 1995, all such products must be submitted according to the new centralized procedure, while the mutual recognition procedure is available for all other products. In all cases, after a company obtains a product license, it must obtain a separate manufacturing permit from the state or national authority of the country of manufacture.

In 1990, Company Y applied for a product license for its genetically engineered coagulation factor, using the concertation procedure. For the product license, the company asked the relevant regulatory body of one member state (in this case, Germany) to assume the role of "rapporteur," representing it at the EU's CPMP. After an initial product evaluation, the German regulatory authorities submitted the application to the CPMP, and to all member states for comments. Once comments had been addressed by the company or the rapporteur, it was up to the CPMP to recommend the product for approval, reject the application, or request additional information. After CPMP approval, the company had to obtain a marketing authorization from every country in which it intended to sell its product.[32] Finally, to manufacture the product in Europe, the company would need a manufacturing permit from a local, state, or national authority. Partly for that reason, it chose to manufacture only in the United States and export the product to Europe.

VI. COMPARING OPPORTUNITY COSTS: THE LENGTH OF THE REGULATORY COURSE

The first injection of a recombinant coagulation factor was given to a patient as early as March 1987.[33] Most of Company Y's product development work was carried out before 1988. Building on ten years of experience with its nonrecombinant coagulation product and after numerous tests of its pilot processes, the company determined in 1989 that its product was safe, effective, and ready to market. At that time, its projected market was two hundred million units per year at eighty cents a unit. Each month of delay in the processing of its product and facility license application, therefore, could amount to $13.3 million in lost sales, as well as delays in the availability of the product to hemophiliacs in the United States and Europe.

Cross-national analyses have indicated that European countries tend to approve new drugs more rapidly than the United States.[34] Certain studies suggest that the CPMP is faster than the FDA in its review of rDNA-derived product applications.[35] This is confirmed by Company Y's experience. More regulatory stops did not mean that the regulatory process for the blood coagulation product took longer in the EU than in the United States. The actual review time of the CPMP was seventeen months, as compared with thirty-one months at the FDA. Moreover, most EU member states granted swift marketing authorization following the CPMP approval. Company Y had to wait more than six months for marketing authorization in Italy, however, and still longer in Belgium.

A. *The United States*

In September 1989, Company Y filed its product license application with the CBER office of the FDA. Over the next several years, the company received four sets of questions from the FDA, the first two sets between December 1990 and February 1991, more than a year after filing its application. During that year, however, company officials were in contact with the reviewers and were kept up to date on the review status of their dossier. The first two sets of questions related very generally to the manufacturing process and the characterization of cell lines.[36] Between April 1992 and June 1992, the company received a third set of questions addressing specific aspects of product manufacture such as a particular virus removal step of the purification process. The questions came from four different reviewers and were forwarded to the company independently; leading the company to believe that there was no "single person [at FDA] who coordinated the review consistently."

In November 1992, three years after the original submission, FDA field officers carried out a preapproval inspection of Company Y's manufacturing facilities. Between December 1992 and February 1993, the company received a fourth set of questions, numerous and detailed, to which it responded by fax. The questions focused on details of the Physician Insert and package label, the use of parts per million instead of micrograms per liter for individual parameters, comments on abbreviations, and even punctuation. On February 25, 1993, Company Y was granted approval.

During the application process the company experienced cross-contamination problems that led it to put the approval process on hold for approximately ten months. Subtracting those ten months from the overall review times, the FDA approved the blood coagulation factor in 31 months, just under the average review time (35.5 months) for important new bio-logical products at that time.[37]

Until 1992, CBER did not have time limits imposed on its reviews of the product license and establishment license applications. In the *Prescription Drug User Fee Act* of 1992, however, the FDA made a series of commitments to reduce review times in exchange for additional funding, provided largely through user fees paid by industry.[38] Recent FDA research indicates that, as of 1995, agency approval times were comparable to, if not shorter than, those in other countries. Company experiences described at the 1996 an-nual meeting of the Drug Information Association confirm such findings.[39] In November 1995 the President's Office issued a report, *Reinventing the Regulation of Drugs Made from Biotechnology,* announcing reforms that will "cut drug development time by months." The most prominent of those reforms was the elimination of the requirement of an establishment license application (in addition to a product license) for specified new biotech-nology and biological products.

B. Europe

In May 1990, Company Y filed an application with the German health authorities (Bundesgesundheitsamt, or BGA) based on the one filed with the FDA seven months earlier. The company chose the BGA as its rappor-teur because of previous experience with the German agency. In November 1990, however, the BGA returned the application, stating that "the pack-age was unacceptable," that the dossier was incomplete, and that additional characterization of the process was necessary. Initially discouraged, and still in the laborious process of gaining FDA approval, Company Y decided not to pursue the European application until the fall of 1991.

From November 1991 to October 1992, the company's director for reg-ulatory affairs interacted frequently with the BGA while redesigning the application to fit the European focus. Company Y also generated new data regarding the manufacturing process. Although it was costly and time-consuming to meet the European requirements, the German reviewer co-operated in helping company officials to understand and meet the "new" requirements. Indeed, Company Y officials came to prefer the European to the FDA process, partly because it included not only the voluminous core documentation but also a high-level summary (called Expert Report), a tabular summary, and cross references.

In October 1992, a year after it really began preparing its EU applica-tion, the company officially filed for the second time with the BGA. Six months later, following validation by the German authorities, Company Y submitted the dossier to the appropriate authorities in all EU countries. In September 1993 the BGA submitted its favorable evaluation of the application and forwarded its "assessment report" to all other member states. British regulators announced their intent to inspect Company Y's facilities in the United States.

In October 1993, a year after filing, the company received a first official list of 272 questions from all European authorities, compiled and coordinated by the rapporteur country. This is about the same length of time as the FDA's first response. Company Y responded to all questions within one month. In December 1993 a second set of nine questions was submitted to the company, followed by a third set in February 1994. In March 1994 the company's representatives made a presentation in Brussels to the CPMP Biotechnology Working Party, which remained concerned about three or four issues. On the night before the meeting, BGA representatives met with company officials to discuss and rehearse the presentation. According to Company Y's director for regulatory affairs, rather than creating an extra layer of bureaucracy, the rapporteur provided "a second set of eyes" and guided the company through the complex review process. The Biotechnology Working Party recommended the product to the CPMP, which within thirty days recommended the product for approval to the commission and the member states. The period from the second submission to the rapporteur country and final product approval by the CPMP was clearly shorter than in the United States.

Then, however, the company had to pursue marketing authorization in several member states, which were not automatically bound by CPMP approval under the concertation procedure. The Netherlands granted the authorization within two weeks of the CPMP's recommendation, Germany within one month, the United Kingdom and France within two months, and Luxembourg, Greece, Ireland, and Spain shortly thereafter. Italy, however, did not grant approval until September 1995, almost a year and a half after the CPMP recommendation, and as of March 1996, Company Y was still awaiting authorization in Belgium. Austrian authorities approved sale but stipulated that a sample of every batch of albumin used in the manufacture of the product sold in Austria had to be submitted to Austrian regulators. Because of such member-state variation, some companies apply for marketing authorization only in countries that represent a significant market.[40] Company Y applied for marketing authorization in all twelve member states.

Under the centralized procedure enacted in 1995, a company is automatically granted marketing authorization in all EU member states following recommendation by the CPMP and approval by the Commission. Differences between member states like those described here must be resolved during the EU approval process. Product pricing and reimbursement, however, will remain within the realm of the national authorities and require companies to continue to negotiate on a country-by-country basis.

The length of Company Y's regulatory course in Europe can be calculated several ways. First, if one includes (1) Company Y's first unsuccessful submission (May 1990 to November 1990), but excludes (2) the twelve months in which Company Y put its European application on hold, and then includes (3) the period of redesign of the application (November 1991 to October 1992), (4) the EU review and approval process (November 1992 to April 1994), and (5) approval by most member states (April 1994 to June 1994), the approval time adds up to thirty-seven months, compared with thirty-one months at the FDA. Second, it would not be unreasonable to exclude the twelve-month redesign period, during which the company engaged in some consultation with the German regulatory authorities. Consultations with regulatory authorities prior to submission are common in Europe and the United States, and company officials generally do not include that period in calculating the overall review timeline. In that calculation, the EU approval time adds up to only twenty-five months.

Third, Company Y officials regard both the initial unsuccessful submission and the redesign period as products of their unfamiliarity with European requirements and of European authorities' lack of familiarity with the company's earlier plasma-derived product. The FDA, in contrast, was familiar with Company Y and its earlier product, while Company Y was experienced with the FDA requirements. Thus one might count only the period in which the European regulators and member states actually considered the application—steps 4 and 5. In this calculation, the regulatory course took only twenty months, eleven months less than the FDA's thirty-one. Company Y officials expect the European regulatory regime to be faster with subsequent submissions. On the other hand, the FDA has recently reduced review times to twelve months, as required by the federal User Fee Act for funding the administrative process, so currently it is difficult to determine in which jurisdiction regulatory review imposes larger opportunity costs.

The situation may be different for firms that choose to *manufacture* biotechnology derived products in Europe. The relative efficiency of the EU product approval system does not take into account costs and delays stemming from nation-level manufacturing permits (not necessary in Company Y's case), which certain cases in Germany and Switzerland suggest can be significant for biotechnology products that elicit local or advocacy group opposition.[41]

C. Process Change Reviews

Europe and the United States also differ in review times for new manufacturing process changes (with respect to previously approved products or facilities). In applying to the FDA for a minor process change, companies must give the agency a thirty-day notice. In Europe, authorities require an initial thirty days for all member states to acknowledge receipt of the application, followed by ninety days to grant CPMP approval, and another thirty days to gain approval from member states—a total of at least four to five months. In both the United States and the EU, major process changes take much longer and may require new preclinical and clinical studies.

The delays associated with process changes, even "minor" changes, can be very costly. At Company Y's sales level for the product in question during 1997, a thirty-day delay in the United States could cost $8 million in forgone revenue, compared with $32 million from a four-month delay in the EU. If the market grows threefold, as expected, the same process change in the year 2000 could cost the company $96 million in Europe, as opposed to $24 million in the United States. However, under some circumstances, the company can build up a large inventory before initiating the process change, or it can create a parallel new production process, continuing the old one while the agencies review the new one. But that is not always possible, for sometimes the process change is required because of problems in the existing process. In such cases the company may be seriously affected by lengthy review times.

VII. STYLES OF REGULATION

National "styles of regulation" refer to agencies' regulatory approach, their propensity toward legalistic or flexible modes of enforcement, and the character of the interaction between regulators and industry officials. American regulatory agencies have often been characterized as more inclined toward a legalistic or even an adversarial style of regulatory enforcement than their European counterparts.[42] This section provides some perspective on differences in styles of regulation concerning product licensing for biologics in Europe and the United States.

A. *The Regulatory Approach: Technical versus Process Orientation*

In processing Company Y's product and facilities license application, the U.S. FDA focused primarily on manufacturing facilities and equipment. As Company Y's regulatory affairs official put it, the FDA said essentially; "Tell us how you run your operations on a daily basis and what operations you have in place to monitor the consistency of the process. Include details regarding utilities, equipment, facilities, and procedures for testing the product that you are manufacturing."

As noted earlier, Company Y's U.S. application provides eight volumes of information on the manufacturing establishment for the specific product, complementing the standing establishment license of more than twenty volumes. Multicolored floor plans indicate levels of sterility for each area, where and how people circulate, how contamination is controlled, and how buildings and manufacturing areas are protected from cross-contamination. Of the fourteen pages of the FDA's *Draft Application for License of Recombinant DNA Derived Biological Products,* nine full pages pose manufacturing-related questions, while just one page poses questions regarding the nonclinical and clinical sections, labeling, samples, protocols, records, and environmental impact.[43] The Chemistry, Manufacturing and Controls (CMC) section of the product license application (one volume) must include information pertaining to the validation and reproducibility of the process design. Through "technical validation," it describes each manufacturing step, the piece of equipment and its operations, what is achieved by that particular step, and data from several batches demonstrating that the step meets design criteria.

The European regulator, according to Company Y's officials, has a different approach. He says, in effect, "Tell me *why* you design your process the way you do, which parameters are critical, and how you control those parameters to ensure consistency." Rather than demanding descriptions of specific technical aspects of the manufacturing facilities and equipment, CPMP officials in the EU demand and review the producer's own in-depth analysis of potential risks and justifications for the control measures adopted. Thus, the EU's CPMP was stricter than the FDA in demanding *justifications* of process parameters. For example, when Company Y claimed that it could assure the removal of 80 to 90 percent of a contaminant, the European regulators required proof that the company actually had operated at both 80 percent and 90 percent. The FDA had been satisfied by the company's statement of the range of operation. The European regulators, unlike the FDA, also required an explanation for why Company Y operated at the chosen quality control limits and whether it had knowledge of the consequences of operating above or below those limits. Similarly, for the EU application, Company Y had to supply trend charts concerning critical product characteristics that demonstrated consistency within a relatively tight range, rather than the wider variation permitted by the FDA.

While the U.S.-style technical validation considers all elements of the manufacturing process to be equally important, and sets broad limits across the board, the European approach monitors fewer elements more carefully. Thus, to show consistent operation to EU authorities, Company Y had to differentiate between more important parameters (known as "governing parameters") and less important parameters, and had to establish a statistical relation between the variation in the governing parameters and effective reproduction of the process. Thus, in the long run, company officials said, the EU's emphasis on crucial risk analysis and justification of all steps and specifications may ultimately be beneficial to the company.

The FDA focus on manufacturing facilities and equipment, it should be emphasized, also entails a considerable attention to the manufacturing process. Whereas FDA regulators may be somewhat less fanatical about the consistency of the manufacturing process than their European counterparts, they *were* interested in whether the rDNA coagulation factor consistently compares to the conventional coagulation factor. Conversely, European regulators have become increasingly interested in manufacturing facilities. Nonetheless, the European focus on the manufacturing process, process validation, and consistency, versus the American focus on the manufacturing facilities, equipment, and technical validation, compelled Company Y to provide two different sets of test data for the same product.

B. Regulatory Stringency, Flexibility, and Unreasonableness

Premarketing approval, like other *ex ante* regulatory controls, put the agencies in a powerful position vis-à-vis the company. Failure to meet regulatory demands results in delay or potential denial of the product license. Hence, companies commonly comply even if they disagree with the agency's standards and acceptance limits, or view its demands as overly stringent or unreasonable.[44] Regulatory agencies, however, vary in responsiveness to a regulated company's argument that a particular requirement is unreasonable under the particular circumstances.

European and American regulatory regimes for new biological product applications differ substantially with respect to regulatory "acceptance limits," that is, in the range of product characteristics within which a manufacturer must operate. Given the inherent variability of biologics and biological assays, relatively broad acceptance limits reduce distribution problems, since unnecessarily tight limits make lot failures much more common. If a lot fails to meet a limit, such as the required salt level, the company's Quality Assurance (QA) Group, in conjunction with clinical studies experts, must then determine whether this failure is critical to the overall efficacy, safety, and quality of the product. Depending on the type and number of failures per lot, the QA review may take as long as two months. As a result, the product will not be delivered on time. A lot failure, in the case of the product in question, can amount to a cost of as much as $10 million. Moreover, if delays occur frequently, the company will lose market share to its competitors.

The European regulators, according to Company Y officials, required tighter acceptance limits for some parameters and enforced them more legalistically. In the United States, the company has been allowed to operate within somewhat broader, self-defined acceptance limits for in-process and final container controls. For example, the FDA expressed concern about a host cell contaminant that remains in the final container at the end of the manufacturing process. In 1989, when Company Y had limited experience with the manufacturing process, it proposed to the FDA CBER a level of 500 picograms of host cell contaminant per unit. The agency considered that limit high, considering the company's actual process experience, and Company Y reduced the limit to 100. After the FDA had completed its review of all preclinical, clinical, and manufacturing data, it concluded that Company Y actually operated well within the limit of 100 picograms and suggested that the limit be tightened. The company proposed a limit of 50, which was accepted, and in practice generally operated at 30.

In Europe, regulators from the start required a minimum level of 10 picograms per unit and refused to engage in any discussion on the subject. Company Y submitted data showing that the product was perfectly safe while operating the process at 30 picograms. The EU regulators, however, continued to press for a limit of 10. When asked about the motivation for such a stringent requirement, the CPMP replied that the 10-picogram limit reflected FDA standards. In fact, the FDA had briefly held the industry to such standards in 1991, but it had since reversed this requirement in light of additional scientific data. Nevertheless, EU officials did not relent. Company Y then carried out sophisticated pilot studies that achieved less than 10 picograms per unit and gained product approval from the EU agency. At times, however, the company has been unable to meet these stringent European requirements in full-scale operation. The resulting lot failures create extra work for the QA personnel, make it difficult to plan manufacture and distribution, and may make it difficult consistently to meet the European demand, risking loss of market share to the company's competitors.

The more stringent European approach sometimes has had useful secondary effects. When Company Y found that from time to time it had difficulties meeting the EU's 10-picogram limit, manufacturing personnel (following the more searching European approach) started wondering about the origin of variations in the contaminant in the final container. After a reevaluation of the purification system, Company Y instigated a process change that led to an improvement in the overall manufacturing system.

On the other hand, Company Y officials have found some European requirements unreasonably stringent. In 1994, Germany unilaterally tightened its requirements for the removal of viral particles in biologics. This forced the company to withdraw a plasma-derived product from the German market, develop an additional virus removal step, and eventually reregister the product with the German authority—although company officials do not believe that the additional process control and cost add significantly to the safety or efficacy of the product. Similarly, the EU's CPMP required that Company Y map the gene of its recombinant product before use in manufacture and after fermentation, using a very difficult technique that remains highly contested in the industry. Company experts argued that the required tests would not provide any relevant information. The CPMP insisted on the performance of the test, arguing that Company Y's competitors had employed that test in the context of an earlier application. Ultimately, Company Y performed what from its experience were tests of no value, at a cost of $50,000.

Not that the FDA is always reasonable. Since 1989, the company had been operating a large-scale fermenter for development purposes. In 1994 it decided to add the fermenter to the product license. To evaluate the safety of the product, the company studied in-process results, tested the product in the final container, and carried out preclinical studies. The data showed that the product from the large-scale fermenter was identical to that from the existing fermenter. In spite of such clear scientific evidence, the FDA demanded that Company Y carry out new clinical studies with the product from the large fermenter. The company questioned the FDA's request on scientific grounds, and the agency allowed it to carry out its clinical studies after approval had been granted, but the studies were costly and, to company officials, wholly unnecessary.

In a more troublesome case discussed by Company Y officials, the FDA decreed in 1992 that manufacturers that pooled donated blood plasma from many donors to make their product should exclude any plasma containing antibodies to hepatitis C. Several experienced companies were reluctant to follow the decision because experience showed that the products on the market did not transmit the virus. Hence they saw no value in adding another step to the purification process, and several companies argued that by removing the antibodies, one increases rather than reduces the risk of contamination. One company (not Company Y) did introduce the FDA's antibody clearance step into its blood-screening process, but in 1995 it received reports that its product had infected hundreds of patients with hepatitis C. It pulled the product from the market. Tests revealed that the antibody-free lots were the culprits.[45] The FDA argued that the company should have introduced an *additional* virus removal step. As a result of the FDA's decree, the company faced litigation from infected patients across the world and had to withdraw its product from the market, add an additional virus removal step, carry out animal and clinical studies, and resubmit a new application, with all fees and delays.

Overall, therefore, it seems that both FDA and EU regulators are prone to overregulation. The ethos of the regulatory process provides few incentives for regulators *not* to err on the side of caution. The keys to avoidance of excessive stringency lie (1) in the development and continued maintenance of expertise in the regulatory agencies, so that regulators develop confidence in their knowledge of risks and in the level of expertise and commitment of particular regulated companies; and (2) in the quality of the interaction between regulators and the regulated. As the next section indicates, Company Y's experience provides some basis for comparing American and European regulators on these dimensions.

C. Interaction with Regulators

Since the agency must make discretionary judgments in its implementation of rules and regulations, the requirements imposed on companies are likely to vary according to the "dialogue" between regulators and manufacturers. In the ideal case, for example, if clinical or other studies do not show the expected results, a company that has a good rapport with an expert regulator may benefit from the agency's scientific and technical advice, and avoid triggering a high-profile and costly "clinical hold."

Earlier studies have shown that company-agency interaction tends to be less formal and legalistic in Europe than in the United States. In the current case study, this is only partially true. Once engaged in the review of its EU product license application, Company Y experienced fairly informal interaction with the rapporteur country reviewer. Because of the time difference between Europe and the United States, the reviewer allowed calls in the evening at his home number. At times the same informality also existed between the company and the FDA regulators. However, while Company Y's informal rapport with the European rapporteur grew over the years, company relations with the FDA changed with the arrival of a new group of reviewers. Because of their inexperience, the new reviewers had a more formal, legalistic, and at times stringent regulatory style. Since reviewer turnover is common at the FDA, the risk of legalistic interaction seems to be higher in the United States.

Overall, in Company Y's experience, the EU's system of review operates more through expert dialogue, in contrast with the FDA's more mechanical regulation-applying approach. The European agencies require that the company submit "Expert Reports" summarizing the pharmaceutical, pharmacotoxicological and clinical parts of their application and to designate an expert with formal qualifications and practical experience in the subject matter. Only when the national reviewers discern inconsistencies or analytic weaknesses in the Expert Report do they pursue a detailed statistical analysis of test results and manufacturing procedures. The U.S. CBER, in contrast, typically carries out a broad range of batch release tests at its in-house laboratories and systematically reviews company data at its statistical division.

Yet in some respects, the European regime is more formal. In contrast to the FDA, European authorities require that all applications be submitted in full; they do not allow parts of the data to be submitted after the initiation of the review process, largely because they must consult regulators from many national agencies. Pursuant to the 1997 FDA Modernization Act, a more gradual review process allows for a step-by-step submission for certain products, permitting a company to initiate application procedures before all the data has been generated.

Furthermore, according to Company Y, at least some European inspections are more legalistic than FDA inspections. Under an agreement of mutual recognition of good manufacturing practices, the European authorities rely almost entirely on the FDA to assure the reliability of the facilities for products manufactured in America and exported to Europe. Whereas the FDA inspects foreign facilities producing for the American market with some frequency, European inspectors rarely visit manufacturing facilities in the United States.[46] In the case of Company Y, however, its U.S. facilities were inspected by British authorities, notwithstanding the mutual recognition agreement. The British officials conducted "a very harsh inspection" according to Company Y's regulatory affairs officer, demanding to see everything and requiring immediate corrective action when they discovered anything they regarded as problematic. FDA inspections, though frequent, are often very cursory. In the words of one industry official:

> I think they [the FDA] operate a lot on appearances. I have not seen an inspection yet where they really find something and ask a question about a document and really take it to a conclusion. I don't know how popular these inspections are within the agency, if people consider these to be drudgery or not. It is almost as if they want to get in and get out as fast as they can.

Industry officials suggest several reasons for the contrast in inspection styles. First, British inspectors are on average much better trained than the FDA inspectors, and inspections abroad are carried out by the agency's more senior members. To be a facility inspector in Britain is considered a rather prestigious government career, whereas in the FDA, reviewers as well as inspectors often view their time in government as a stepping-stone to a "more promising" career in the private sector.[47] Hence, FDA inspectors and reviewers are often new on the job and inexperienced with the companies. This can lead to either excessive legalism or excessive leniency. Company Y has experienced both.

Regulatory behavior, in Company Y's experience, varies according to the officials' specific knowledge. When the company submitted its U.S. product license application in 1989, the FDA reviewers were familiar with the company's history, earlier nonrecombinant product, and regulatory affairs personnel. The reviewers, in the opinion of Company Y officials, were not excessively stringent. As discussed earlier, Company Y has experienced what it considers regulatory unreasonableness at the FDA, but these incidents were often tied to a period of frequent reviewer turnover.

The German reviewers, in contrast, had little history with either the company or its earlier product. They were very concerned about proper procedures and documentation. They held Company Y to stringent standards of data analysis and required clear explanations for every manufacturing step. The company considered some of these requirements excessively stringent and unreasonable. Five years later, however, the same German and CPMP regulators are still in place, and Company Y's official says,

> I think that our relationships with Europe are now better than with the United States. Exactly because you have new reviewers [at the FDA] who are not familiar with the product. They are conservative. In Germany, they are knowledgeable about the product. They have been involved with us for over five years, and so, when we make a change, they have all the documentation, they know where to look, and, as a result of their involvement with this product, they are credible to the member states.

VIII. CONCLUSION

This study of the regulatory process for a new biological product does not provide consistent support for the conventional wisdom that American regulatory processes are more legalistic, adversarial, and costly than those of European nations. The European multistep approval process, as compared with the U.S. one-step process, was *more* complex, difficult, and costly. Although Company Y, once it figured out the EU system, gained product approval in Europe in eighteen to twenty months, compared with thirty-one months at the FDA, subsequent manufacturing process changes are faster and therefore less costly in the United States than in Europe. Moreover, the U.S. FDA now consistently reviews license applications within twelve months as the agency strives to meet its performance goals established under the User Fee Act. Europe is now attempting to align its review times for applications as well as process changes for biotechnology-derived products with those of the FDA. Therefore, differences in review times and time to market no longer constitute an obstacle for companies pursuing simultaneous submissions to European and U.S. authorities.

In their interactions with Company Y, European regulatory officials were in some respects more stringent and more legalistic than their U.S. counterparts, although both systems were considered legalistic and unreasonable on some issues. Legalistic inflexibility and its costs appear to be associated with lack of familiarity with the company and its product on the part of the regulatory reviewer. In that regard, the risk of regulatory inflexibility seems in general to be higher in the United States because of greater turn-over of regulatory personnel.

The U.S. FDA's regulatory approach entailed a more mechanical focus on manufacturing facilities, as contrasted with a more searching and useful European-style process control analysis. Yet the FDA recently has sought to emulate the EU method, while European regulators now put more emphasis on the manufacturing facilities, including inspections of U.S. facilities for products marketed in the EU.

Based on this study, both approval systems are costly and burdensome. Neither system is clearly more cost-effective, as savings in one area are undermined by costs in another. In this case, the cost of compliance probably was slightly higher in Europe than in the United States because more tests were required and authorities insisted on tighter tolerances. Yet, in light of the cross-national harmonization of product specifications and more global product planning in the industry, such differences may be eliminated in the future. While differences in regulatory requirements, procedures, and styles persist, and while European regulatory agency officials insist that U.S. approval is not automatically a ticket to the European market, regulatory convergence and harmonization are clearly under way.

NOTES

1. Robert A. Kagan, "Adversarial Legalism and American Government," *Journal of Policy Analysis and Management* 10 (1991): 369–406; Joseph L. Badaracco, *Loading the Dice: A Five-Country Study of Vinyl Chloride Regulation* (Boston: Harvard Business School Press, 1985); David Vogel, *National Styles of Regulation* (Ithaca, N.Y.: Cornell University Press, 1986); Harvey Teff, "Drug Approval in England and the United States," *American Journal of Comparative Law* 33 (1985): 567.

2. Jerry Mashaw, "Regulation, Logic and Ideology," *Regulation* 3 (1979): 44.

3. Eugene Bardach and Robert A. Kagan, *Going by the Book: The Problem of Regulatory Unreasonableness* (Philadelphia: Temple University Press, 1982).

4. David Vogel, *Barriers or Benefits? Regulation in Transatlantic Trade* (Washington, D.C.: Brookings Institution, 1997), 33.

5. David Jordan, "International Regulatory Harmonization: A New Era in Prescription Drug Approval," *Vanderbilt Journal of Transnational Law* 25 (1992): 471–507.

6. PDUFA was reauthorized in 1997 for another five-year period under the FDA Modernization and Accountability Act. Jill Wechsler, "FDA Reform: From Without and Within," *Pharmaceutical Technology*, December 1996, 16–27; Wechsler, "Congress Debates FDA Fees and Funding," *Pharmaceutical Technology*, April 1997, 16–28; David Kessler, "FDA Is Meeting the Performance Goals of the Prescription Drug User Fee Act," *Pharmaceutical Technology*, January 1997, 40.

7."An FDA Panel Urges Approval of AIDS Drug," *Wall Street Journal,* November 8, 1995, B11.

8. CBER was created in 1987 as part of a reorganization of the FDA, separating the reviews of drugs and biologics.

9. I interviewed two directors of worldwide regulatory affairs at two large multinational companies and a director and manager of regulatory affairs at a biotechnology company that does business in Europe, the United States, and Japan.

10. Because of pledges to keep Company Y's identity confidential, I was not able to interview U.S. FDA or EU regulatory officials about the license applications submitted by the company.

11. Since the case study, the FDA has rewritten its policies for the regulation of specified new biotechnology and biological products, but not for vaccines, in vitro diagnostics, and blood products, which are the subject of this case study.

12. U.S. Food and Drug Administration, *Timely Access to New Drugs in the 1990s: An International Comparison* (Washington, D.C.: Food and Drug Administration, December 1995); "FDA's Approval of Drugs Gains Speed," *New York Times,* January 20, 1996, 9.

13. Elimination of Establishment License Application for Specified Biotechnology and Specified Synthetic Biological Products; Final Rule. Federal Register, 14 May 1996.

14. ICH Final Guideline on the Need for Long-Term Rodent Carcinogenicity Study of Pharmaceuticals. Federal Register, 5 April 1996. ICH Guideline on Structure and Content of Clinical Study Reports. Federal Register, 17 July 1996.

15. "Makers of Blood Products Agree to Offer $640 Million to Settle Cases Tied to AIDS," *Wall Street Journal,* April 19, 1996, B5; Dan L. Burk and Barbara A. Boczar, "Symposium: Biotechnology and Tort Liability: A Strategic Industry at Risk," *University of Pittsburgh Law Review* 55 (spring 1994): 791–864.

16. "Blood Stain: A Drug from Baxter Is Said to Have Posed a Risk of Hepatitis," *Wall Street Journal,* July 20, 1995, 1.

17. Robert Kozak, Charles Durfor, and Curtis Scribner, "Regulatory Considerations When Developing Biological Products," *Cytotechnology* 9 (1992): 203–10.

18. Elimination of Establishment License Application for Specified Biotechnology and Specified Synthetic Biological Products; Final Rule. Federal Register, 14 May 1996.

19. The basic fermentation parameters, such as oxygen concentration, temperature, and agitation speed, are continuously monitored on-line. Other parameters, such as glucose concentration (an indicator of the nutrient state of the medium), recombinant coagulation factor concentration, cell density and cell viability, perfusion rate, sterility, and absence of adventitious agents, are monitored off-line from fermenter samples. In addition to these directly measured parameters, there are calculated parameters, such as specific recombinant coagulation factor production, which indicate how the cells perform during the cultivation period. Berthold G. D. Boedeker, "The Manufacture of the Recombinant Factor VIII," *Transfusion Medicine Reviews* 6 (1992): 256–60.

20. In the purification process, the *ion exchange step* binds all cell culture material that has a negative charge, including the coagulation factor itself, to a resin column, thus separating it from the DNA. *Immunoaffinity chromatography* is a key viral removal

step. It consists of an antibody column that binds the recombinant coagulation factor and separates it from all major contaminants. *Gel filtration* is comparable to a tea strainer that removes many high-molecular-weight proteins while letting the coagulation factor sift through. The *heat treatment step* removes rodent retroviruses. Retroviruses produce reverse transcriptase to transfer their own genome into a host's DNA for replication.

21. See, generally, Joseph V. Rees, *Hostages of Each Other* (Chicago: University of Chicago Press, 1994); "Protein Design Labs Inc. AIDS-Related Drug Test Is Halted, and Stock Dives," *Wall Street Journal,* August 16, 1996, B10.

22. When the White House Council on Competitiveness suggested in 1991 that all regulation for biotechnology products be abolished, the chairman of the Biotechnology Industry Organization sent a letter to the council stressing the importance of regulation for the development and commercialization of biotechnology products.

23. Marc Mathieu, *New Drug Development: A Regulatory Overview,* 3d ed. (Waltham, Mass.: Parexel International Corporation, 1994), 6–8.

24. "Pfizer's English Site Is Research Boon," *Wall Street Journal,* September 6, 1996.

25. In 1991, it issued a Note for Guidance on Good Clinical Practice for Trials on Medicinal Products, followed by some twenty guidelines codifying the principles and methodology of clinical trials, and Directive 91/507/EEC on norms and protocols for the conduct of analytical, pharmacotoxicological, and clinical tests.

26. Peter O'Donnell, "View from Brussels: A Directive Takes Shape," *Applied Clinical Trials,* n.s., 5, no. 6 (1996): 80–82. For example, in order to start Phase 1 clinical studies in France, a company is required only to *notify* the authorities and provide all critical trial information to the investigator. Belgium, instead, requires explicit agency approval before testing; the company must submit clinical protocols and chemistry, manufacturing, and control (CMC) data to the regulatory authority, who is obligated to review the information within a time frame of thirty to sixty days. Britain mostly operates on the basis of a Clinical Trials Exemption (CTE) Scheme that allows companies to submit a data summary and initiate the clinical trial unless otherwise notified by the regulatory agency. Clinical trials in healthy volunteers are not covered by the U.K. Medicines Act, and no prior approval or notification is required. C. Legrand et al., "Clinical Trial Initiation Procedures in Europe: The Legal Framework and Practical Aspects," *Drug Information Journal* 29 (1995): 201–59. In Germany, the investigator has to consult with an institutional ethics committee before initiating the trials; agency approval is not required, and the company is entirely responsible for its own action. Toxicology studies and CMC information, however, must be sent to the federal health authorities (to serve as a reference in case of a liability suit), and state authorities must be notified. S. Spitzer et al., "Gute klinische Praxis: Neuorientierung der klinischen Forschung," *Deutsche Medizinische Wissenschaftsschrift* 118 (1993): 838–43.

27. Malcolm VandenBurg and Michael Allen, "European Clinical Trials—Taking a United Approach," *SCRIP Magazine,* May 1997, 22–23.

28. CBER was created in 1987 as part of a reorganization of FDA, separating the reviews of drugs and biologics.

29. The CPMP consists of representatives of all member states and the European

Commission. The committee was set up in 1977 to harmonize product licensing decisions made by the national health authorities. For the approval of conventional pharmaceutics, member states and companies can apply to the CPMP to obtain advisory opinions or recommendations. For products derived from rDNA, the competent authorities are *obliged* to consider the recommendation of the CPMP before deciding to authorize, reject, or withdraw any product from the market.

30. "Next Round in West Germany's Licensing Struggle," *Nature*, September 15, 1988, 199; "Court Blocks German Biotech Plant," *Science*, November 17, 1989, 881.

31. According to the mutual recognition procedure, a company may potentially extend a product license in one country (reference member state, RMS) to other member states (concerned member states, CMS) by filing the same dossier with their respective authorities.

32. Under the new centralized procedure, a company may submit its product license application directly to the newly created EMEA located in London, whose licensing decision is binding on member states. The EMEA arranges for a rapporteur and a co-rapporteur to assess the dossier and circulate the assessment to the CPMP, which then provides an opinion on the product to the EMEA. The EMEA translates this opinion into a licensing decision through a standing committee of the European Commission in Brussels, unless a member state raises important new scientific or technical questions. That licensing decision is then valid throughout the EU, abolishing the need for country-by-country marketing authorizations. D. B. Jefferys and K. H. Jones, "EMEA and the New Pharmaceutical Procedures for Europe," *European Journal of Clinical Pharmacology* 47 (1995): 471–76.

33. Gilbert C. White II, Campbell W. McMillan, Henry S. Kingdon, and Charles B. Shoemaker, "Use of Recombinant Antihemophilic Factor in the Treatment of Two Patients with Classical Hemophilia," *New England Journal of Medicine* 320 (1989): 166 70.

34. "FDA Reform and the European Medicines Evaluation Agency," *Harvard Law Review* 108 (1995): 2009–26.

35. *European Biotech 94: A New Industry Emerges* (Brussels: Ernst and Young European Executive Office, 1994), 8; Zafar Hakim and Suzan Kucukarslan, "Regulation of Biotechnology Products in the Global Pharmaceutical Market: The Case of the European Community and the United States," *Clinical Therapeutics* 15 (1993): 442–58.

36. Cell line characterization includes a description of their history, identity, and testing for adventitious agents.

37. Mark Mathieu, "CBER and the Biological IND Review" in *Biologics Development: A Regulatory Overview*, edited by Mark Mathieu (Waltham, Mass.: Parexel International Corporation, 1993), 79.

38. Mark Mathieu, "The PLA and ELA Review" in *Biologics Development: A Regulatory Overview*, edited by Mark Mathieu (Waltham, Mass.: Paraxel International Corporation, 1993), 224.

39. U.S. Food and Drug Administration, *Timely Access to New Drugs in the 1990s;* Emily Donnelly, "The Second Year in Operation of the EMEA Centralised Procedure" (paper presented at the annual meeting of the Drug Information Association, San Diego, June 1996).

40. In 1988, five countries—France, Germany, Italy, Spain, and the United Kingdom—accounted for 90 percent of total pharmaceutical expenditures within the EU. M. L. Burstall, "Europe after 1992: Implications for Pharmaceuticals," *Health Affairs,* fall 1991, 157–71.

41. The German pharmaceutical company Hoechst AG, when applying in 1986 for a permit to operate its new insulin manufacturing plant in the state of Hesse, became involved in the most costly biotechnology lawsuit in German history. Recently in Basel, Switzerland, local opposition delayed approval of a $150 million biotechnology manufacturing facility for almost two years. "Swiss Stakes: Basel's Drug Giants Are Placing Huge Bets on U.S. Biotech Firms," *Wall Street Journal,* November 29, 1995, A1.

42. Robert A. Kagan, "What Makes Uncle Sammy Sue?" *Law and Society Review* 21 (1988): 718.

43. Al Ghignone, "The Product License Application (PLA)," in *Biologics Development: A Regulatory Overview,* edited by Mark Mathieu (Waltham, Mass.: Paraxel International Corporation, 1993), 145–73.

44. Regulatory unreasonableness can be defined as occurring when an agency demands protective measures whose compliance costs clearly exceed the resulting social benefits, or forbids practices that, under particular circumstances, pose no risk of harm. Eugene Bardach and Robert A. Kagan, *Going by the Book: The Problem of Regulatory Unreasonableness* (Philadelphia: Temple University Press, 1982).

45. "Blood Stain," A1.

46. "Medicines from Afar Raise Safety Concerns," *New York Times,* October 29, 1995, 1.

47. Vogel, *National Styles of Regulation;* James Q. Wilson, *The Politics of Regulation* (New York: Basic Books, 1980).

CHAPTER ELEVEN

New Chemical Notification Laws in Japan, the United States, and the European Union

Lori A. Johnson, Tatsuya Fujie, and Marius Aalders

I. INTRODUCTION

Recently, local fishermen removed the net that for over twenty-three years had enclosed Minamata Bay in southwestern Japan. The net was used to prevent the migration of fish in and out of the bay because methylmercury chloride, discharged from chemical plants in the 1950s, accumulated in the marine life and poisoned 2,261 people in this region. During the 1960s and 1970s, many widely used chemical compounds—from DDT to kepone to chlorofluorocarbons (CFCs)—were judged, belatedly, to be harmful to human health, to ecosystems, and even to the global environment. Meanwhile, chemical companies continued to invent and market new, socially useful chemical substances, and to do so at a high rate. In all economically developed democracies, therefore, government policy makers were called upon to create laws and regulatory systems that would detect and prevent the potential health and environmental risks that might be associated with new chemicals—but without blocking the continued production of socially useful chemical innovations. The challenge was to devise a regulatory "net," not unlike the one in Minamata Bay, that would evaluate chemical products, restrict the harmful ones, and allow the beneficial and safe ones through. Of particular concern was the lack of advance information about the environmental or health effects of the large number of new chemicals introduced each year.[1]

Accordingly, many economically advanced countries adopted regulatory statutes requiring chemical companies to conduct tests for hazardous characteristics before manufacturing or marketing new chemical substances. Government regulators were instructed to assess the adequacy of the testing and to prescribe other precautions (e.g., concerning packaging and warnings) before permitting manufacture or marketing—much as premarket testing and governmental clearance had been required for new pharmaceutical products. In 1974 Japan enacted Kashin-hou, which established legal controls for industrial chemicals, including premarket notice and classification of newly manufactured and imported substances, as well as some existing substances. The United States enacted the Toxic Substances Control Act (TSCA) in 1976. In 1979 the European Economic Community, following the lead of several European countries such as France and Switzerland, adopted the Sixth Amendment to the existing directive on the classification, packaging, and labeling of dangerous substances.

Notwithstanding these convergent trends in law, one would expect significant differences to remain in the ways these laws are designed, implemented, and enforced. Many studies indicate that U.S. regulatory and liability law tends to be designed and implemented in a more adversarial, legalistic, and punitive way than comparable legal regimes in Japan and Europe.[2] A study conducted by Ronald Brickman, Sheila Jasanoff, and Thomas Ilgen compares the development of several chemical regulation schemes in Europe and the United States.[3] Although there is no attempt to systematically compare the impact or effectiveness of the policies, the authors do note that "it appears that U.S. legislative and regulatory policies have created a potential for higher costs than are likely to be imposed on industry in Europe . . . [and] with respect to the administrative costs of complying with regulations . . . there is little question that U.S. industry has to spend considerably greater sums than its European counterparts."[4]

This case study attempts to test these generalizations with respect to the new chemical notification and clearance laws of Japan, the United States, and the European Union (EU). We draw on the experience of multinational chemical companies to examine the *operational differences* and relative burdens among premanufacture and premarket clearance laws, as actually implemented. Our findings partially contradict the conventional wisdom about comparative regulatory style. According to chemical company officials with substantial cross-national regulatory experience, initial compliance with new chemical notification and clearance laws is less costly, more expeditious, and less burdensome in the United States than in Japan and the EU. On the other hand, regulatory officials in the United States, as might be expected, are uniquely legalistic in their response to noncompliance; U.S. officials are much quicker to impose monetary fines, even for violations that are not directly harmful, and they impose much larger fines. Overall, however, the American regulatory system is regarded as more conducive to chemical product innovation than the Japanese and EU systems. Yet we have uncovered no evidence, moreover, that this has led to less protection of the public in the United States.

II. RESEARCH METHOD

The research effort began by arranging interviews with regulatory compliance officials in several multinational chemical companies, selected because they conduct parallel business operations in the United States and either Japan, the European Community, or both. The methodology is best described as a "snowball" sample, beginning with a few informed chemical company officials with cross-national experience. As we talked with these officials, they suggested other persons with broad comparative experience, both within their corporation and in other multinational corporations, who might be helpful in our research. We were particularly interested in talking with officials who have participated in repeat interactions with the different regulatory regimes and discussing the impact of those differences on their corporate practices. Although the interviews are not representative in the statistical sense, we have spoken with some of the most knowledgeable informants within the chemical industry, many of whom know each other through international meetings of industry associations.

Unlike other case studies in this book, this chapter does not focus on the experience of a single company and its compliance with notification requirements for a single product in Japan, the United States, and Europe. This is due, in part, to the practical reality of how our research developed. We were able through referrals and introductions to speak with many chemical company officials in different major multinational corporations. We determined that, for these regulatory programs, entailing large numbers of new chemical substances each year, evaluating compliance efforts in different companies in different countries would be more appropriate. This greater breadth justified any sacrifice in the depth of detail with respect to specific products, companies, and experiences. Although we report several companies' experiences in notifying regulators about particular chemical products, we also report experienced company officials' broader generalizations about cost, delay, enforcement officials' attitudes, and the effectiveness of regulation in the different regimes. We have considerable confidence about the validity of these generalizations for several reasons. First, the company officials we spoke with had extensive cross-national regulatory experience. Although personally based in either Japan, the United States, or Europe, they had either supervised compliance in all regimes or were responsible for informing company officials of the requirements of more than one regime. Second, the company officials had no obvious incentive to disparage any one country's regulations apart from the impact of the regulation on their company, which was specifically what we were interested in exploring. The officials interviewed, regardless of their own country of origin, generally agreed in their characterizations of the

American, Japanese, and European regulatory regimes for new chemicals. In contrast to what some readers might presume to be a corporate incentive to be especially critical of American regulation on grounds of its greater legalism and costliness, the officials we interviewed, while often criticizing some aspects of the American regime, were unanimous in judging it to be generally more flexible, more efficient, and less costly to comply with than the Japanese and the EU regimes.

We conducted in-depth interviews with company officials, government representatives, academics involved in either government or industry, and representatives of industry associations and organizations. In Japan we interviewed company officials from three multinational chemical manufacturing companies (J-1, J-2, and J-3) based in Japan. We also interviewed several research scholars in private institutes dedicated to studying chemical safety; these individuals had retired from major Japanese chemical manufacturing companies but maintain strong influence in the industry and ties to government. We also talked with officials of the Ministry of International Trade and Industry (MITI), the Ministry of Health and Welfare (MHW), the Environment Agency, and a U.S.-based consultant to the Japanese chemical industry. In the United States we have interviewed nine officials in four major multinational chemical manufacturers in the United States (US-1, US-2, US-3, US-4), an Environmental Protection Agency (EPA) official responsible for enforcement of TSCA, and a representative of the chemical industry association. In Europe we conducted interviews with five company officials responsible for product safety and regulatory compliance in five different multinational chemical manufacturers (two in Germany [EU-1, EU-2], two in the Netherlands [EU-3, EU-4], and one in England [EU-5]). Together, these experienced individuals constitute a cluster of "elders" in the international community of chemical risk managers. They are knowledgeable informants concerning the law and practice of chemical risk regulation in the United States, Japan, and Europe.

We conducted some interviews by phone, others in person, and others through written reports prepared by the company. Some interviews used a common questionnaire containing open-ended questions intended to elicit the informants' own descriptions, explanations, and comparisons of the three legal regimes. Other interviews were more casual, with the researcher and the informant meeting or talking on the phone frequently; these "free-ranging" discussions often led to valuable insight and information. The pool of interviewees, including the company and government officials, came from a variety of backgrounds and included chemists, lawyers, professors, private researchers and scholars, government officials, plant managers, laboratory researchers, business consultants, and insurance company officials.

In these interviews we sought the insight of company officials on two primary questions. First, in which system is compliance with premarket regulations most *costly* for their business and *why*? Second, from the standpoint of operating chemical companies, what are the most significant differences between the chemical control laws of the United States, Japan, and the Western European nations with respect to *efficiency* and *effectiveness*?

III. CHEMICAL CONTROL NOTIFICATION LAWS: GENERAL OVERVIEW

The chemical control notification laws of Japan, the United States, and the European Community can be compared with regard to three aspects of the chemical control notification systems: (1) the stringency of the premarket testing and clearance requirements, and the related costs and delays; (2) the cooperativeness of agency decision making regarding compliance and required precautionary measures prior to marketing; and (3) the strictness of regulatory enforcement through inspections and penalties. In each of these categories, we will be considering not only cross-national variation in the substantive requirements of the laws but also the structure and style of enforcement of the law as experienced by regulated enterprises.[5]

One characteristic dilemma associated with government regulation is the effort to strike the appropriate balance between costs and benefits. National regulatory programs for premarket clearance of chemicals arose in the shadow of existing programs for new *pharmaceutical* products in the United States and Europe. Such programs, experience showed, were subject to criticism for two kind of errors. Type I errors are errors of leniency, allowing the marketing of products (such as thalidomide in several European countries and Japan) that turn out to have serious harmful side effects. Type II errors entail excessive stringency. They arise, of course, from the effort to avoid excessive leniency. Thus during the 1970s, the U.S. Food and Drug Administration (FDA), many studies indicated, imposed such stringent and costly testing obligations on pharmaceutical manufactures, and took so long to approve applications, that American citizens were unable to obtain valuable new drugs that their counterparts in Europe benefited from months or even years earlier. Moreover, pharmaceutical companies were reluctant to undergo the cost and delays of developing so-called orphan drugs—therapies for conditions and diseases that are relatively rare, and hence would not generate revenues large enough to cover the costs and delays of the regulatory process.[6] Although industrial chemicals differ from pharmaceuticals in terms of marketing, exposure, and hazard scenarios, premarket clearance regulations on industrial chemicals engender the same dilemma—finding the right balance between excessive leniency (Type I errors) and excessive stringency (Type II).

In designing premarket clearance programs for new chemicals, the

European system leans toward the avoidance of Type I errors by imposing mandatory testing requirements on chemical companies for *all* new chemicals and even for increased production of previously tested chemicals. The U.S. TSCA, in contrast, was crafted in the mid-1970s, at a time in which the FDA "drug lag" had become a serious concern. TSCA seeks to minimize Type II errors by emphasizing company *notification* of regulators regarding the identity of chemicals rather than universal premarket testing. TSCA puts the burden on the EPA to decide which chemicals must be tested by the applicant company and requires the EPA to make that "notification-only or test" decision quickly, within ninety days. Japan's Kashin-hou leans toward avoidance of Type I errors, but errors of a particular kind: the dissemination of nonbiodegradable chemicals that pose a risk of contamination of food sources.[7] To that end, it mandates a step-by-step system of classification under which the results of the initial testing trigger the requirement or waiver of further testing; it falls between the U.S. and European regimes, since full-scale testing is not required for all new chemicals.

A. *Japan: Kashin-hou*

The Japanese chemical control law, as originally formulated, reflects that country's painful experiences with the contamination of marine food resources by pollution in the 1950s and 1960s. Although the law as revised in 1986 addresses broader concerns, the focus remains on risk of harm to humans from chemical substances that enter the marine food chain.[8] Both for chemicals manufactured in Japan and for imported chemicals that are not on an inventory of approved chemicals maintained by MITI and MHW, Kashin-hou requires that the chemical substance be classified according to its level of degradation in water, its accumulation in fish, and its chronic toxicity.[9]

In principle, the notification and testing proceeds on a step-by-step basis:

First, the company must test the degree of *biodegradation* of the chemical using a test called the Ready Biodegradability Test.

If biodegradability is high, the substance is considered safe, and the company is free to manufacture.

If the degree of biodegradation is low, the company must proceed to the next level of testing.

The next level of testing is the bioaccumulation level determination, which measures bioconcentration by means of the Flow-Through Fish Test.

If the level of bioaccumulation is high, the company must conduct full chronic toxicity tests, which include carcinogenicity testing, reproduction tests, teratogenicity tests, as well as toxicokinetics and pharmacological and mutagenicity testing.

> If the results of the full chronic toxicity testing are negative, the company can freely produce the chemical.
> If the results are positive, the substance will be considered a First-Class Specified Substance, and companies are virtually banned from manufacturing it.

If the level of bioaccumulation is low, the company must conduct Screening Toxicity Tests, which include testing of mutagenicity and the Repeated Dose 28-Day Test.

> If the results of the Screening Toxicity Tests are negative, the company can manufacture the chemical without restriction.
> If the results are positive, the chemical will be classified as a Designated Substance. A Designated Substance will be reclassified as a Second-Class Substance if annual environmental monitoring indicates an increase in the substance in the environment. In such cases, further restrictions on production will be imposed.

Although the law requires the preceding tests on a step-by-step basis, according to our interviews, companies often conduct the Biodegradation, Bioaccumulation, and Screening Toxicity Tests together for low-molecular-weight substances, in order to save time and because generally only 15 to 20 percent of new chemicals have high biodegradability.

After testing is completed, there are three stages to the new chemical notification process in Japan. The first step is an informal interview session, referred to as a "hearing," three weeks prior to the date of the formal notification before the Chemical Product Committee, composed of chemists appointed by the two agencies.[10] This hearing is provided independently by MITI and MHW. The next step is the preliminary evaluation, which is another informal session with MITI and MHW a week after the initial hearing.[11] After responding to MITI and MHW comments, the company submits its data to the Chemical Product Committee.[12] MITI is responsible for the biodegradation and accumulation concerns, and MHW for the chronic toxicity issues. After the Chemical Product Committee reviews the submitted data, the company receives a notice classifying the notified substance as safe, designated, or first class specified, which entails restrictions or a prohibition on manufacture or import.[13] For violation of the regulatory requirements, Kashin-hou authorizes imposition of penal servitude of no more than three years, a maximum fine of $10,000, or both, for persons or companies manufacturing or importing First Class Specified Substances.

B. United States: Toxic Substances Control Act

Of the many different aspects of TSCA, the category we are most concerned with is the new chemical review process for manufactured and imported chemicals. The TSCA procedure initially emphasizes providing the information government regulators might need to identify and control possible risks, rather than comprehensive testing.[14] Section 5 of TSCA requires companies to file a premanufacture notice (PMN) with the Office of Pollution Prevention and Toxics of the EPA for any new chemical that is not on the TSCA inventory of existing chemicals.[15] The company must file the PMN ninety days prior to manufacture or import of a new chemical substance, or before the manufacture or processing of an existing chemical for a "significant new use."[16] There are exemptions to the full PMN requirement for test-marketing of chemicals, low-volume release, and polymers, which are not considered chemically active or bioavailable.[17] The PMN submission must include available data on chemical identity, expected production volume, by-products, intended use, expected environmental release, disposal practices, and human exposure.[18]

Although the submitter, in contrast to the submissions in Europe and Japan, is not *required* to conduct new testing, the company must include all existing health and environmental test data in its possession and a description of existing data it knows about. For example, if the company has conducted testing in connection with past or present marketing in Japan or Europe, it must submit that data to the EPA. According to the EPA, less than half of the PMNs submitted include toxicological data.[19] Using the information on chemical identity submitted by the company, computer analysis, and Structure Activity Relationship (SAR) Data, the EPA compares the chemical to structurally similar chemicals to assess the potential risk. The EPA is concerned primarily with whether the chemical is similar to asbestos, radon, lead, or polychlorinated biphenyl (PCB). If the EPA determines that the chemical may pose an *unreasonable* risk to health or the environment, it can request additional testing from the company.

Significantly, TSCA states that the EPA must complete its review process on the PMN within ninety days.[20] For almost 90 percent of the PMNs submitted, the EPA determines that the chemical does not pose an unreasonable risk and places it on the TSCA inventory without restriction.[21] After filing a "notice of commencement," the company is free to manufacture the substance without further restriction. Once any company has filed a PMN regarding a chemical substance, it is placed on the TSCA inventory, and no further notification by any company is necessary for that chemical unless the company plans a "significant new use" of the chemical.[22]

For the other 10 percent of PMNs—those for which the EPA determines that the chemical substance may pose an unreasonable risk to health or the environment—the EPA may request additional toxicological testing, permit manufacture only under conditions specified in a consent order, or prohibit the manufacture of the chemical. If the EPA determines that a chemical presents an unreasonable risk, it has broad discretion under TSCA to require companies to comply with a wide range of possible precautionary measures. These precautions generally are codified into a Significant New Use Rule (SNUR) for that chemical, and other companies that manufacture the chemical will have to adopt the precautions. Unlike the Japanese and European regimes, the EPA is explicitly required by TSCA to consider the economic consequences and to conduct cost-benefit analysis of required precautions.

A company violates TSCA if it manufactures or imports a chemical that is not on the TSCA inventory without filing a PMN, or if it does not comply with requirements of consent orders or SNURs. Fines for TSCA violations, at up to $25,000 per day, are much larger than potential fines in the Japanese or European systems.

C. Europe: Sixth and Seventh Amendments

The EU premarketing directive was adopted in 1979 and took effect in 1981 as Directive 67/548/EEC, the Sixth Amendment to the existing directive on the classification, packaging, and labeling of dangerous substances.[23] Member states adopted implementing legislation and are charged with implementation of the amendments at the national level.[24] In 1992 the EU adopted Directive 92/32/EEC, the Seventh Amendment, further harmonizing the procedure for the notification of new substances, adding a requirement for risk assessment, and modifying some of the requirements of the Sixth Amendment.

The EEC directives contain both notification and quantity-triggered mandatory testing requirements prior to marketing or importing of chemicals that are not on the European Inventory of Existing Chemical Substances (EINECS). The EEC directives require only *premarketing* notification, rather than TSCA's *premanufacture* notification requirement, so that notification is not required for intermediates (substances produced for use in manufacturing other chemicals but not marketed to third parties).[25] A company seeking to market a new chemical substance must notify the competent authority in the member state where the substance is produced sixty days prior to marketing.

In contrast to the TSCA inventory, which expands to include each new chemical notified, the EU inventory (EINECS) has been static as of 1981. No new chemicals are added to the inventory; each company marketing or importing a chemical not on the inventory must notify again, even if the chemical has been notified previously by another company. In order to address duplicative test-marketing that occurs because of a static inventory, the EU allows subsequent notifiers to use test data from earlier notifications, with the written permission of the previous notifier, and publishes a list of substances previously notified called European List of Notified Chemical Substances (ELINCS).

For chemical substances that are marketed in quantities of one ton or more a year (Level 0) per producer,[26] the company must submit to a national administering agency technical information including the identity of the substance, the Chemical Abstract Service (CAS) number, if available, the chemical composition, impurities, the scope of use, production levels for that year, projected production for the future, recommended handling methods and precautions, and proposals for the classification and labeling of the substance. The key distinction from TSCA is that the company must provide, in addition to information on the physicochemical properties of the substance, a base set of toxicological studies, including tests for acute toxicity, mutagenicity, and carcinogenicity, and ecotoxicological studies for acute toxicity for daphnia and fish, and biodegradability.[27] The company submits three separate dossiers containing physicochemical data such as melting point, flash point, flammability, toxicological data such as acute toxicity and carcinogenicity test results, and ecotoxicological data such as biodegradation and fish and algae daphnia tests. There are exemptions in the EU for test-marketing and research and development, which unlike in the United States do not require an application.[28]

Under the EU regime, as the quantity of production of the chemical increases, additional toxicological tests are added, and subsequent notifications must be filed. The focus of the administering agency is on the appropriate classification and labeling of the chemical based on its potential toxicity. The enforcing agency of the member state in which the company filed the notification must decide whether a company's testing, notification, packaging, and labeling of a new chemical are in accord with the directives. If the company meets the paperwork requirements of the regulations and follows any labeling requirements, it is free to market the chemical in any member state. According to our interviewees, the agencies enforcing the Sixth Amendment, unlike the EPA, rarely engage in risk assessment and management of risks through controls on the chemical or use restrictions.

The Seventh Amendment specifies that the administering agency of the member state has the ultimate responsibility for conducting risk assessment of new chemical substances according to principles specified by the EC Commission, but a notifier may choose to conduct and submit its own risk assessment with its notification. Whereas the directive introduces the potential for more comprehensive risk assessment, according to our interviewees it remains unclear what impact this will have on the notification process. Prior to the Seventh Amendment's passage, low-volume substances (less than one ton of production per year/per producer) were regulated only at the national level. The Seventh Amendment harmonizes the regulation of those substances and subjects them to a reduced notification procedure. The Seventh Amendment also, for the first time, formally defined a polymer and considerably narrowed the polymer exemption.

Another change brought by the Seventh Amendment responded to certain importers' practice of marketing a low-volume substance through as many as ten or twenty different European corporations to avoid increased testing requirements for larger quantities. Now, a non–European Community producer must nominate one entity, a sole representative, which is responsible for notification of the aggregate import.

IV. COSTS AND DELAYS IN THE THREE NEW CHEMICAL CLEARANCE SYSTEMS

All company officials interviewed think compliance with the notification requirements generally is cheapest in the United States and most expensive in the EU. Japan, while occasionally the most expensive, is always the most time-consuming, partly because of the staged character of testing, partly because of delays at the agency decision-making level. The primary factors causing these differences are the level of mandatory testing required and the availability of exemptions.

The experience related by a company official in US-2 vividly illustrates the cost impact of the EU and Japanese mandatory testing requirements. US-2 sought to market a monomer that was not on the TSCA inventory, EINECS, or the MITI inventory. In each instance, the company elected not to claim the identity of the specific chemicals as confidential. The official conducted an estimated breakdown of the costs of collecting the necessary scientific data and filing PMNs under TSCA, Kashin-hou, and the EC directive. For Europe, his estimate was $200,000 for the required base set of testing required. In Japan the estimated cost for biodegradation, bioconcentration, and a series of toxicology tests was $140,000. In the United States the company conducted a standard battery of toxicity tests and was able to submit environmental data on chemically similar substances (SAR Data), at a total cost of $20,500 for testing and $2,500 for the filing fee. Thus, the total cost for compliance with the notification process was $200,000 for Europe, $140,000 for Japan, and $23,000 for the United States.[29] As this example illustrates, chemical firms' ability to rely on the EPA's use of structural analogies in evaluating the risk of the chemicals, rather than mandatory testing, provides a significant cost savings compared with other systems.

Further savings arise in the United States because (1) TSCA allows the filing of consolidated PMNs for similar chemicals, unlike the Japanese and European systems, which require a separate notification for each chemical substance; and (2) unlike Europe's static inventory, which requires each company marketing a chemical to notify it, TSCA adds previously notified chemicals to the inventory, so that subsequent companies manufacturing the chemical do not have to file PMNs. Consolidated PMNs and "once and for all" notifications contribute to even more stark cost differentials. For example, US-2 wanted to market a family of surfactants consisting of forty-eight chemicals. In Europe, US-2 estimated that the cost of testing was $200,000 each for almost all of the new chemicals (some were on the EINECS inventory), totaling almost $8 million. In Japan the cost, assuming that the chemicals pass the biodegradability tests and no further testing would be required, was $17,000 per chemical,[30] for a total estimate of $680,000. In the United States the company spent $96,000 in testing for acute environmental harm studies and filed three consolidated PMNs for the forty-eight chemicals, for a total cost of $102,000. Thus the total estimated cost for US-2's compliance with the notification regulations for this family of chemicals was almost $8 million in Europe, $680,000 in Japan, and $102,000 in the United States.

Whereas US-2 reported significant potential cost variation across jurisdictions depending on the testing required, other companies that regularly sell large volumes of chemicals worldwide were less concerned with this type of variation. For example, US-1, a manufacturer of large-volume industrial chemicals, estimated that it spent approximately $500,000 in testing prior to the manufacture or marketing of a typical new product. The standard procedure for US-1 is to conduct the required base set of testing for EU and the bioaccumulation tests for Japan, and then submit the notifications in each region. Because the testing conducted for the other systems is submitted with the TSCA PMN, US-1, in effect, internally harmonizes the regulations for its compliance efforts.

Similarly, EU-5 reported that when it did a worldwide notification, it tended to do the EC directives base set and then add the Japanese protocols. For example the Repeated Dose 28-Day Test of acute toxicity is required for both, but Japan requires additional information, so EU-5 builds on the EU protocol to make it acceptable for Japan. EU-5 sets up one schedule of testing for all regions and designs a whole package of information on the new chemical for use in all of the PMNs. The regulatory manager at EU-5 reported that he tries to convince the businesspeople that "notification is like a building block," and the company should do everything it can to help them in future marketing efforts. If the molecule is not listed in Japan or Korea, EU-5 tries to conduct tests that will meet these countries' requirements or builds tests into the protocol that will address typical EPA concerns.

Although filing PMNs under the U.S. system is almost always less expensive, a company official in charge of product safety and regulatory affairs for EU-1 observed that one can never be completely sure what the cost will be in the United States because of the possibility that the EPA will decide to demand further testing. The flexibility of the system, thus, is accompanied by a degree of uncertainty concerning testing costs. The European system, which requires testing for all chemicals, depending on volume, is very predictable but very costly. The Japanese system, most officials assert, is both unpredictable and costly.

One company official from EU-1 observed that the U.S. regulatory system was preferable in terms of promoting innovation and introduction of new chemicals, largely because of its unlimited exemptions for research and development and for test-marketing of new chemicals.[31] In the United States, a chemical producer can cooperate with a customer on research and development of a new product without having to file a notification; using these exemptions does require a lot of paperwork and record keeping, but the exemptions, if the EPA grants them, have no time or volume restrictions. In Europe, according to the official from EU-1, if a chemical company cooperates with a customer, it is deemed to have placed the product on the market. The only exemptions for research and development in Europe are for process-based research, which comes with a time restriction, and for scientific research, which comes with a volume restriction.

In addition to the direct costs of the new chemical notification systems, company officials reported various indirect costs such as delay, loss of market opportunity, and diminution of innovation. According to a company official with EU-1, the EU system leads to diminished innovation of new substances, a concentration of innovation in bigger companies, and increased cost and time to market. The official supplied us with figures demonstrating that the number of high volume substances notified by EU-1 has been decreasing over the past five years, especially after the promulgation of the Seventh Amendment, implying a slowdown in innovation. He also reported that his company often notifies first in the United States because it can test the market easier there to know whether its product will be accepted. The company still begins with the EU-required base set of tests for marketing one ton of a new chemical. Then it files in the United States (where the EPA says "just submit whatever you have from doing your base set in the EU") and moves some of the substance on the market to determine whether there is commercial potential. Based on these efforts, the company will decide whether to go through with the more stringent EU testing required for larger tonnages. In the same vein, another company official described the EU notification system as a "gamble"—if you want to use a new chemical for the market and the notification flops, as it has for his company on occasion in Germany, then you lose a fortune.

If you fulfill the notification requirements and the market does not want the product, you have also lost.

An official of US-4, a manufacturer of specialty chemicals, also focused on the costly delays associated with mandatory testing requirements in Japan and the EU. Describing US-4's regulatory experience with registering a new chlorofluorocarbon molecule, he said it reflects the company's general rule of thumb that "getting a chemical to market" will take three to six months in the United States, a year in Europe, and two years in Japan. For this particular chemical, US-4 spent ten months conducting the testing for the EU requirements and forty-five days of regulatory review.[32] After the three months of regulatory review in the United States, the EPA required additional testing, but its consent order did not require the testing to be done prior to marketing. The company had not received approval from Japan at the time of the interview, but the official expected that it would take eighteen months, less time than usual, because the company had taken a gamble and started the long-term testing early, rather than waiting for the results of the short-term testing.

Japan-based chemical manufacturing companies reported similar concerns with the cost of testing and the time involved in complying with Kashin-hou. Conducting the biodegradation testing alone costs approximately $17,000; on the other hand, the biodegradation, accumulation, and toxicity screening exams together can cost $200,000, and if full chronic toxicity testing is required, the cost can escalate to $4 million.[33] An official from J-2 discussed an aspect of Kashin-hou it found particularly problematic. During the biodegradation tests, if the new substance degrades into multiple chemicals that have not been tested before, the company must conduct further tests on all these chemicals. Moreover, unlike TSCA and the EC directives, Kashin-hou does not exempt new polymers from notification and requires polymer flow-scheme testing, which costs from $25,000 to $30,000.

A corporate official from J-2 estimated that it takes his company a minimum of one and a half years for testing and collecting data, and at least five more months, including one month for the initial MITI/MHW hearing and three months for evaluation at the Chemical Product Committee and its notification procedure, before it can market the chemical product. Moreover, if the demanding standards for data accuracy applied by the enforcing agencies are not met, then the testing must be repeated until the company "gets it right." Companies also considered compliance with Japanese regulations more burdensome because there are no explicit guidelines on how the results of the chemical testing will be evaluated, which complicates the company's marketing decision. For example, an official from EU-2 reported that although his firm very often files notifications in Japan, they are accepted only some of the time, and he has no clear understanding of why this is so.

V. AGENCY DECISION MAKING

After a chemical company submits its notification to the relevant agency, its ability to proceed with marketing depends on the competence and caseload of the agency officials, the speed with which they assess the information submitted, and their posture in negotiating conditions and precautions concerning production, shipping, packaging, and marketing. To the company officials we interviewed, the regulatory style of the agencies administering the notification system—their cooperativeness, flexibility, technical expertise, and speed of decision making—had as much significance as the stringency of the legal requirements. All the company officials we talked with had some experience with regulatory agencies in the United States, Japan, and Europe, but they had the most experience with the agency in the location where they operated.

Generally speaking, the company officials saw all the agency regulators as cooperative at the "prefiling" stage, while the company is gathering necessary information and preparing to submit the PMN. The EPA was viewed as somewhat less cooperative with respect to determining appropriate precautions for chemicals that it thought might pose an unreasonable risk. Overall, however, the regulated enterprises viewed the EPA as the most flexible, and as having the most expertise. In both respects, this perception runs counter to the dominant view of U.S. regulatory bodies among multinational corporations.

In the EU, company officials characterized member-state agency decision making as generally rapid, although there is variation among the countries. Although the entire notification process in Japan is the slowest, the evaluation procedure by the Chemical Product Committee generally takes place within ninety days, and J-3 reported a thirty-day evaluation process. In the United States, in 90 percent of the notifications the EPA can be relied on to meet its ninety-day deadline. In the 10 percent of cases where the EPA determines there is some risk, several company officials told us that the negotiation of a consent order regarding precautions usually adds three to six additional months.

A. United States

U.S.-based companies and companies in Japan and Europe reported that the EPA's Office of Pollution Prevention and Toxics is helpful, cooperative, and flexible. For example:

- An official from US-4 reported that he could go to the EPA before submitting a PMN and ask: "Do you have any concerns? What do you think?" An EPA official might reply "Well, you're going to have a water discharge here, so you should probably do some fish studies." The company can ask, "Will we get a consent order (requiring precautions or restricting production)?" Though they will not tell you definitively, because they do not have the final authority, they will say, "If you do all of these tests, it will allow us to make a proper risk assessment."

  The same official from US-4 said, "We can negotiate with EPA in a 'scientific way' regarding what testing should be done." He also gave examples of industries and industry associations working with the EPA to correct the TSCA inventory, for example, by eliminating 1,300 isocyanates that actually boil down to about eighty distinct chemicals.
- European-based companies described the EPA as responsive and helpful but sometimes "very nagging" and "terribly specific" about the precise identity of a substance. One official from EU-5 commented, "If you genuinely want advice on a notification and what kind of testing you should do, they will be quite helpful with that." Another from EU-2 said that American regulatory officials are more cooperative: "You can go to them, and they can set up a testing program with the company." An official from EU-3 said he could "phone EPA officials directly, and they respond most kindly."
- An official from J-2 commented on the scientific expertise of the EPA regulators, which enables them to conduct not only safety and risk assessment but also cost-benefit analysis.

Reports were more mixed in cases in which the EPA determined that there was some risk in the production or marketing of the chemical. US-4 reported that although the EPA worked with the company in developing appropriate precautions, the negotiation took a good deal of time although there was no litigation. US-3 reported that in one case the consent order negotiation took so long that the company missed its "market window" for the product and discontinued production. Similarly, European officials referred to the almost incomprehensible text of EPA consent orders and reported that the additional testing protocols required by them can be quite time-consuming.

B. Japan

The most significant difficulty with agency decision making reported by Japan-based companies is that they have to deal with both MITI and MHW. The company official from J-2 described the notification process in a case in which MITI found the chemical to be safe and MHW thought it should be classified as a designated substance. According to this official, the division of labor between MITI and MHW complicates the process enormously. Moreover, in Japan, there is no postfiling communication with the evaluation committee, and this makes J-2's decision whether to conduct the costly testing more difficult. At the same time, company officials described Japanese regulatory officials as very serious about punctuality and strict compliance with regulations, and as sometimes rigid:

- An official from US-3 commented, "In Japan, they are there to help, but they will not change the rules regarding testing." For example, for one chemical marketed, Japanese officials asked the U.S.-based company to perform tests that were physically impossible at room temperature. The protocols are rigid, even if the tests will produce "meaningless results."
- European officials often commented on the need to employ a Japanese intermediary interface with the agencies. "Contacts have to be arranged; they need everything in the Japanese language." Another from EU-2 said, "I wouldn't say they are unhelpful. But you have got to have a good person in Japan, who is comfortable with the authorities and respected by them." He added that EU-2 could conduct a toxicity study that involved a lot of animals for an EU notification, "but if we try to get acceptance of that in Japan we would have to repeat that study to include the Japanese protocols, and use the same number of animals again."
- An official from J-2 said that what chemical manufacturers in Japan are most apprehensive about is unexpected additional testing that the Chemical Product Committee might request without explanation. This kind of uncertainty makes it especially difficult for manufacturers to plan and schedule production.

C. European Union

The implementing agencies of European nations, our respondents agreed, are the speediest decision makers, once the base set of testing has been accomplished. European officials also are said to have less discretion or flexibility than their U.S., and even their Japanese, counterparts. However, the European company officials we talked with complained about differing interpretations of the law and variation in style of regulation among the member states.

- A director of corporate safety for EU-3, a chemical manufacturer in the Netherlands, reported a differing interpretation about whether a particular chemical was on the EINECS inventory. British regulators told a competitor that the company did not have to notify the substances, whereas the EU-3 official was certain that scientifically the chemical was distinct from the one on the inventory, and EU-3 had been required by

Dutch regulators, correctly he believed, to file a notification for the chemical.
* A regulatory manager from EU-5 in England described the difference in dealing with the British and the French authorities. In Britain, after the company submits the dossier, the regulator may have some questions, "but once the 'day one' of your regulatory review begins, you can be fairly certain you will get to produce your product sixty days later, even if you have more testing to do." In France, the company submits the dossier, and only after the sixty-day review period do the regulators begin to ask questions. The manager also described more reasoning and negotiation with British regulators regarding hazard and risk, in contrast to the German and Dutch, who simply say, "Do these tests."
* A company official from EU-2 in Germany discussed his difficulties dealing with the competition among differing German agencies. He described the overall system of regulation as "having no flexibility to speak of."

Although all company officials reported some problems and difficulty with regulatory officials, they all said that ultimately they comply rather than contest decisions. The overall impact of agency decision making in this regulatory arena might best be summed up by a German company official who said, "As far as we are concerned, if the authorities do not accept our arguments, then we have to do what they ask." Even in the United States, where access to courts is not difficult, the delays of litigation make legal challenge infeasible for companies eager to bring the new product to market.

VI. ENFORCEMENT

We asked company officials: What happens if you fail to notify the agency properly about a new chemical, either through oversight or through the belief that it is not really "new"? In Europe and Japan, chemical company officials said, there are fewer inspections of company plants and much less proactive enforcement of the laws. Indeed, the company officials in Europe complained about "commercial injustice," noting that, whereas their companies, large multinational manufacturers, complied fully with the laws, smaller companies and importers, they believed, could get by without doing so. As a demonstration of the problems with enforcement of the EC directives, company officials in Europe pointed to the July 1996 final report of the European inspection project on the Notification of New Substances (NONS). The focus of the study was coordinated company inspections in fourteen member countries, with a concentration on chemical dyestuffs as "an innovative group of substances with the possibility of having inherently hazardous properties and the potential for high risk of exposure to both workers and the environment."[34] The inspection revealed that of the almost four thousand substances that were checked at ninety-six companies, 37 percent were new substances that had not been notified and were thus illegally marketed. The report indicated that of the twenty-nine sample chemical substances analyzed, 31 percent did not conform to the information provided by the company. The project found that the controlling authorities thought that forty-five of the ninety-six companies participating were not working according to the EC directives either because they were marketing non-notified substances or because they lacked sufficient labeling, safety data sheets, registration, or internal control.

In Japan, enforcement is accomplished through cooperation between MITI, MHW, and the chemical manufacturers' association, so that the regulator and representatives of the regulated work together in assessing the appropriateness of the regulation, and there is internal pressure for conformance within the industry association. When a violation is found, company officials told us, the attitude of regulators in Europe and Japan is one of helpfulness and cooperation; the most you get is a "slap on the wrist." As one regulatory compliance official in Europe reported, "If there exists a good, open relationship between company and authority, then it is hardly imaginable that anything can go wrong." Indeed, there have been no reported fines in Japan. Although warnings are issued to companies that do not satisfy the requirements of compliance with Kashin-hou, the most likely consequence is that the company must send a formal apology (Shimatsu-sho).

The United States is a very different story. If a company fails to file a PMN, the EPA can assess a fine of $25,000 per day for every day the non-notified chemical is marketed.[35] The imposition of such penalties is not uncommon. Under TSCA alone, for the fiscal year 1996 the EPA assessed almost $10 million in administrative penalties, collected over $15 million in injunctive relief, and negotiated over $22 million in supplemental environmental projects (SEPs), nonmonetary actions that parties agree to carry out as part of settlements.[36]

Several respondents complained about what they saw as EPA's legalistic and punitive enforcement style. According to an official from US-4, there are three main reasons that violations of the PMN requirements occur despite prenotice consultations with EPA: (1) EPA's strict interpretation of the inventory of existing chemicals; (2) purchase of chemicals from foreign vendors who are unwilling to disclose sufficient information for the purchaser, who might simply produce the chemical itself, to verify full compliance with notification; and (3) simple human error resulting from the administrative burden of tracking and notifying hundreds or thousands of new chemical formulations.

One U.S.-based company we interviewed had the dubious honor of receiving the highest initial penalty, $22 million, ever assessed for a violation of TSCA resulting from a strict interpretation of the TSCA inventory. The company had refined its manufacturing process for an existing chemical substance, changing the number of carbon molecules. Believing the refined chemical substance was already covered by the TSCA inventory, it did not file a premanufacture notification. EPA officials, interpreting the TSCA inventory differently, disagreed and imposed the fine, based on the number of days the company had produced the refined product. The company found the fine especially troubling because the chemical substance in question, it strongly asserted, posed no particular risk.

Although the initial fine was automatically reduced to $17 million for self-reporting, and the final negotiated amount was $375,000, the frightening impact of that kind of initial penalty, not just in monetary terms but also as a "public relations disaster," was noted by all of our interviewees. It seems to be the practice of the EPA to announce huge fines that send a shudder throughout the industry, then negotiate the fines to much smaller amounts. For example, in another recent case, a $3.1 million proposed fine was reduced 99 percent in negotiations to $43,400, primarily because of self-reporting and statute of limitations issues.[37] The negotiations to obtain a reduction, however, involve time, company expertise, and often expensive legal services, all of which are costs to the company. Unlike the notification stage, companies socked with fines can and do challenge EPA administrative actions before administrative law judges and in court.[38] Of course, companies are not always successful in such challenges, as a company that operates a small metal recycling and shredding facility employing fewer than twenty people found recently when an administrative law judge upheld a $1.3 million fine for leaving unattended for ten years a pile of electrical equipment contaminated by polychlorinated biphenyl (PCB).[39] In any case, not only are fines more common in the United States, but litigation is more readily available to force the EPA to justify penalties, or to use as leverage to negotiate down the amount of the fine.

A consultant to chemical companies on TSCA issues told us about discovering that the company from which his client had imported a product had not notified all the chemicals included in the product in order to protect trade secrets. The EPA conducted an inspection of the company, and during the inspection the company realized the discrepancy. That is, violations were found, and the importing company self-reported the problem to the EPA, but still received a large fine.

However, as an official from the EPA we spoke with pointed out, the arguable purpose of statutory fines under TSCA is not to redress harms but to create the incentive for companies to accurately report chemicals so that hazards can be identified and minimized, and to ensure compliance with steps imposed to reduce risk. In the experience of this official, who is charged with enforcement of TSCA, there are few instances of willful violations; the only one she could recall involved a person importing herbal medicines. This was consistent with the EPA official's experience that most of the violations of TSCA occur within small firms, rather than large chemical companies, which have elaborate TSCA compliance programs in place. With regard to EPA enforcement philosophy with respect to TSCA, she stated "it is very much a preventative statute," and the fact that the neglect of a PMN by one firm may pose no actual harm or risk of potential harm to any person or the environment is irrelevant. In her view, if not punished, "the violation, though only technical, would break down the integrity of the system for preventing the bad chemicals, like PCBs, from getting out. TSCA is about *potential* for harm or risk, not the harm or risk of *this* chemical." From the perspective of this EPA enforcement officer, the criteria for evaluating TSCA enforcement should be whether it is "consistent and efficient," not necessarily how much it reduces harm or risk.

The tendency to penalize violations, even if they are unintentional and do not lead to harm, is in keeping with multinational corporations' general perceptions of the distinctive legalism of the U.S. regulatory enforcement agencies. Notwithstanding the EPA officials' justifications, it has an alienating effect in the chemical industry. This alienation is exacerbated by the perception of some in the chemical industry that the EPA is more concerned with symbolic politics than with serious risk reduction. It was not only the initially large amounts of the punitive fines under TSCA that disturbed company officials but also what they described as the "political motivations" of the fines. According to an official from US-1, enforcement at the EPA can change depending on the political winds of the administration, making it difficult for companies to predict what the agency may want in the future. This official characterized the "command and control" approach of the EPA as a "joke," because at the notification stage it required no serious testing yet focused on insignificant minutiae at the enforcement stage. He contrasted this with the certainty and predictability of the European system and the willingness to work with companies that were out of compliance.

VII. EFFECTIVENESS

In each jurisdiction, new chemical notification laws exist alongside laws regulating worker safety, requiring dissemination of material safety data sheets (MSDS), delineating proper waste disposal, regulating air and water emissions, and mandating cleanup of contaminated sites. To the extent that there has been a reduction in exposure to toxic chemicals, it is virtually impossible to sort out the relative contribution of new chemical notification laws, and hence it is impossible to compare the relative effectiveness of TSCA, the EC directives, and Kashin-hou.[40] Incentives to restrict potentially dangerous chemicals and the way in which they are used also are generated by product liability laws and the prospect of costly lawsuits that they can generate. Moreover, there is disagreement among the environmental and scientific communities over what level of toxicity or exposure presents an unreasonable risk,[41] as well as disagreement among regulators and regulated about what positive effects to expect from notification laws. For example, with regard to TSCA there is disagreement over the relative importance of the premanufacture notification goals of toxicity information collection, dissemination of toxicity information to the public, and actual prevention of harm, as well as the focus on new chemicals as contrasted with testing existing chemicals.

The effectiveness question is further complicated by the varying rationales that underlie each new chemical notification system. In Japan the laws are targeted primarily at preventing harm to humans from the consumption of contaminated marine food sources. In Europe the EC directives focus on preventing the potential harm to health and the environment from chemicals manufactured and released in *large volumes*. In the United States the focus seems to be on preventing the marketing of chemicals that are similar in properties to chemicals that are already known to be carcinogenic or harmful to the environment, such as PCBs.

One way to address effectiveness might be to note whether particular chemicals that have been approved and placed on the inventory in one regime (e.g., the United States) have been *not* approved or restricted in another. We did not find such an inquiry feasible, however. There are over seventy thousand chemicals on the TSCA inventory, and the European inventory is static, that is, approved chemicals are not added to the inventory. We did ask our interviewees about any instances in which one country approved a product without restriction while the same chemical was rejected or restricted under another country's regulatory system. Unfortunately, this question did not offer us much helpful information to assess effectiveness. First, the company officials, especially those directly responsible for health and safety issues, noted that their firm had no interest in manufacturing or marketing unsafe chemicals. This was especially true in the United States, where product liability concerns are paramount. Thus, the officials told us, if there was regulatory concern about a chemical in Europe or Japan, often the company never notified it in the United States or withdrew its notification. On the other hand, chemical company officials rejected the implication that more stringent regulatory requirements in a particular jurisdiction necessarily implied greater effectiveness, which they seemed to define in terms of reducing actual risks. Thus they argued that the mechanical application of EU testing rules that focus particularly on the tonnage of the amount of the chemical produced, or of Japanese rules that sought maximum testing of any chemical that was toxic in any degree to marine organisms, did not necessarily make those systems more "effective," in terms of actual risk reduction, than the U.S. regulatory regimes.

Nevertheless, if the U.S. system of notification of new chemicals is cheaper and quicker than that of Europe or Japan, and seeks to avoid Type II errors of overregulation, the obvious question is whether it incurs Type I errors of excessive leniency as a result. Although there are no "dead or maimed bodies" to point to, there has certainly been criticism of TSCA and its effectiveness. A 1994 General Accounting Office (GAO) report commissioned by the U.S. Senate Subcommittee on Toxic Substances, Research and Development and the House Subcommittee on Environment, Energy and Natural Resources argued that (1) the legal standards of TSCA—requiring the EPA to demonstrate unreasonable risk before taking action—were so high that the EPA has been able to issue comprehensive regulations to control only nine chemicals in eighteen years;[42] (2) the EPA review process of new chemicals does not adequately ensure assessment of potential risks and exposure before and after manufacture; and (3) the excessive use of the confidential business information provisions makes the information collected under TSCA less available and useful to state agencies and the public. But the GAO's assessment is not without controversy because it is unclear what criteria EPA *should* have applied or what social benefits "doing more" would have generated.[43]

The most significant factor making TSCA cheaper and quicker than the notification systems of either Europe or Japan is the EPA's use of SAR analysis, rather than mandatory testing, to screen chemicals and determine if there is sufficient risk to warrant additional testing. In 1993 the EPA conducted a study with the EU asking what difference European-style testing would make.[44] The physical properties and hazards identified through SAR for 144 chemicals were compared with properties and hazards identified using test data required under the EC directive. The study found that the accuracy of SAR varied depending on the chemical property tested. SAR was highly effective (93 percent) for assessing biodegradation but only 50 percent and 63 percent effective for predicting boiling point and vapor pressure. EPA officials concluded that SAR was effective in screening new chemicals to determine if there is need of further testing or regulation but less effective in predicting the exact type and level of toxicity, especially for general health effects.[45] EU officials noted the variation in SAR effectiveness in assessing chemical properties and found SAR to be insufficiently developed for determining eye and skin irritation or sensitization, but *more* successful at determining acute lethal toxicity.

When we asked chemical company regulatory compliance officials directly about perceived effectiveness of the different systems, their responses were inconclusive. Whereas company officials consistently described the European system as the most expensive, primarily because of the mandatory base set of testing, some believed that no "added safety" came with the high price tag, and others viewed the European system as the safest and most comprehensive. Some company officials viewed the length of time for the required testing of the Japanese system as a costly delay with possibly no corresponding precautionary benefit in terms of safety. Some company officials believed the U.S. system—with no mandatory testing under TSCA but the possibility of testing if there is potential risk—was as effective, if not more so, at preventing the marketing of harmful chemicals.

Two factors contributed to the interviewed officials' estimation of the benefits of the U.S. system: (1) the EPA's commitment to scientifically appropriate risk assessment, and (2) broad EPA discretion to implement precautions. The EPA conducts risk assessment based on the intended use and volume of the chemical. If the EPA finds an unreasonable risk with a particular chemical, it has the discretion to develop mandatory precautions with the company to protect against that risk. Examples of precautions included mandatory wearing of gloves, warning labels, and use of air respirators. Sometimes the EPA also issues what the company official from US-3 referred to as "killer 5(e)'s"; these include requirements such as labels stating that a substance is a "cancer-causing agent," or precautions, such as mandatory use of an air respirator, either of which might make the customer not want to buy the product. On the other hand, TSCA requires the EPA to consider the economic benefits of the chemical and the costs of the proposed precautions in determining what precautions to impose.

In contrast, testing in the European system is based entirely on tonnage of production per company; the presumption is that increased tonnage increases the risk. The U.S. system considers volume of production, but only as it contributes to the risk of the individual chemical reviewed. In the view of one European official, U.S. regulations are more concerned with the purpose for which the chemical will be used, and they use tonnage as a criterion proportionate to risk. In his estimation, this is a better way of assessing the costs and benefits of additional testing.

The potential fines that the U.S. enforcement system employs made companies more wary of committing violations than did the EU system. In some respects, this may make TSCA more effective by compelling more attention to compliance. Thus, chemical company officials also told us that as a consequence of TSCA's punitive enforcement system, there are increased costs related to more stringent intracorporate review for compliance with TSCA. This seemed especially true for companies exporting chemicals to the United States. For example:

- A European company official reported that whenever a chemical is sent to the United States, the company blocks the export and allows only "authorized people in the firm" to release it. Accordingly, "no chemical that is placed on the market goes to America without compliance with TSCA requirements."
- A regulatory compliance official estimated that assuring compliance with TSCA requires more manpower than the European system, because any product to be sold in the United States that might be composed of new chemicals undergoes a very stringent review procedure in the corporation's regulatory compliance section.

Considering all new chemicals notified under the three regimes, there are clearly more test results collected under the European and Japanese systems than in the United States. But the essential question for assessing effectiveness in preventing harm is not simply whether more data are generated, but what is done with the data that are collected and whether there is sufficient information to assess harmfulness. Whereas more information might always be preferred, there is no indication that the approach of TSCA—screening chemicals before selectively requiring additional testing—has significantly increased the risk to the public from the marketing of toxic chemicals.

VIII. CONCLUSION

Although the U.S. regulatory system in general tends to be designed in a more adversarial and legalistic manner than comparable legal regimes in Japan and Europe, that is not the case with regard to new chemical notification laws, as experienced by numerous officials of multinational chemical companies. They do observe in the United States, however, the characteristic American tendency toward legalistic and punitive responses to violations of the detailed and prescriptive rules, even if the violations are unintentional or not harmful.

The surprising result is the greater flexibility and efficiency of the American regulatory regime. In 1976, when TSCA was enacted, the regulatory regime for premarketing approval and testing of new pharmaceutical products, administered by the FDA, was criticized for unduly delaying provision of valuable new drugs and deterring innovation. One speculative explanation for TSCA's flexibility is that it was a response to this FDA criticism.[46] The TSCA regime deliberately provided more flexibility by (1) making requirements for extensive testing discretionary, according to the judgment of officials in the implementing agency (EPA); (2) stipulating that the EPA must make that judgment within ninety days; (3) providing exemptions for test-marketing and use of new chemicals for research purposes; and (4) providing EPA with flexible powers to impose custom-tailored *postmarketing* restrictions on handling, labeling, and use of those chemicals it determines pose special risks. At the same time, the TSCA regime included some features of the pharmaceutical regulation regime that tend to promote regulatory flexibility: rather than delegating implementation and enforcement to state and local government agencies, which often lack expertise and are thought by some to require federal oversight,[47] implementation is assigned to a centralized cadre of officials in Washington, D.C., who have or acquire significant expertise. The EPA's enforcement system is strict and legalistic partly, perhaps, as an offset to the more pragmatic, less stringent substantive regulatory requirements, and partly as a response to the more open U.S. economy, in which there are many small chemical manufacturers and importers, which are difficult for the U.S. agency to monitor and perhaps cannot be trusted to comply.

In contrast, the European system, which had not experienced the political controversy over product delays in pharmaceutical regulation, became more concerned with promoting harmonization of regulation across member states; hence it sought to restrict member state discretion by imposing mandatory requirements, such as the universal base set of testing. Japan's Kashin-hou, reflecting a political response to a series of environmental and human tragedies stemming from chemical pollution, reflects a stricter and more conservative attitude toward certain risks. Structured to avoid Type I errors (of excessive leniency), it probably makes more Type II errors, delaying dissemination of useful new chemical products. Kashinhou's focus on biodegradation and bioaccumulation, moreover, may make it more tolerant of other, equally troubling risks. In addition, weak enforcement systems in Europe and Japan may well produce more Type I errors in the *manufacturing* process than does the American system.

The impact of the operational differences between the three notification systems, our interviews indicate, is smaller for large, multinational chemical manufacturers that consistently market a smaller number but larger volume of chemicals worldwide. These companies tend to find it most cost-effective to internally harmonize the requirements for notification in different regimes by adopting the highest standard, generally the European. Such internal harmonization efforts are consistent with the efforts of organizations such as the Organization for Economic Cooperation and Development to harmonize testing protocols and good laboratory practices, and to encourage mutual acceptance and sharing of data.

Variation in the cost of testing and the delay associated with the notification of new chemicals has a much more significant impact on manufacturers of specialty chemicals with smaller markets. Moreover, to the extent that costs and delays in the development of new chemicals dampen innovation in the industry at large, they may in fact have an adverse impact on health and environment. As a company official with EU-1 argued, an effective system must balance the need to protect the health and environment through premarket testing with protection gained from the introduction of improved substances in the market. According to this official, the costs and delays under the European system have significantly discouraged innovation by smaller and medium-sized companies that might have led to newer substances with more desirable properties in terms of health and environmental protection than older, existing chemicals.

Comparison of the costs, delays, style of administration and enforcement, and effectiveness of the new chemical notification schemes of Japan, the United States, and Europe has implications for the rest of the world as well. The developed nations' regulatory schemes provide the primary models for the many developing countries implementing similar notification systems. Indeed, we heard a veritable chorus from corporate officials that their companies were *most* concerned about the impact of new notification systems in countries like Korea, China, Australia, and New Zealand. Whereas there is general, and obviously growing, acceptance of the need to address and attempt to prevent the harmful effects of potentially toxic chemicals through some type of premanufacture or premarketing screening device, the means employed, as this chapter illustrates, can have significant negative impacts on multinational chemical companies without necessarily increasing effectiveness.

NOTES

We thank our interviewees for their willingness to speak frankly with us and for their generosity in giving us access to their time, expertise, and experience. Mr. Fujie especially wishes to express his appreciation to the government officials, corporate executives, and scholars in Japan who assisted him in his research there and requested anonymity in order to provide their unreserved opinion.

1. *Legislative History of the Toxic Substances Control Act* (Washington, D.C.: Government Printing Office, 1976).

2. For a list of such studies, see Robert Kagan, "Adversarial Legalism and American Government," in *The New Politics of Public Policy,* edited by Marc Landy and Martin Levin (Baltimore: Johns Hopkins University Press, 1995).

3. Ronald Brickman, Sheila Jasanoff, and Thomas Ilgen, *Controlling Chemicals: The Politics of Regulation in Europe and the United States* (Ithaca, N.Y.: Cornell University Press, 1985). See also Sam Gusman, Konrad von Moltke, Frances Irwin, and Cynthia Whitehead, *Public Policy for Chemicals: National and International Issues* (Washington, D.C.: Conservation Foundation, 1980) (an early substantive overview of TSCA and European directives).

4. Brickman, Jasanoff, and Ilgen, *Controlling Chemicals,* 312.

5. For example, questions we have asked interviewees have included: Are the

agencies enforcing the law cooperative and helpful through the compliance process? Are the precautions determined by "command and control" style orders, or is there negotiation? What is the attitude toward enforcement?

6. Henry Grabowski et al., "Estimating the Effects of Regulation on Innovation: An International Comparative Analysis of the Pharmaceutical Industry," *Journal of Law and Economics* 21 (1978): 133.

7. Other Japanese laws (see next note) target other varieties of risks associated with chemical substances.

8. There are several other Japanese laws, such as the Poisonous and Deleterious Substances Control Law, the Labor Safety and Sanitation Law, and environmental laws that address other specific concerns involving chemical products.

9. When less than one ton of the chemical is marketed in a year, there is simply an application for permission to market, which requires reporting of the structural formula of the chemical and physicochemical data.

10. This "hearing" is encouraged, effectively required, by "government notice" adopted subsequent to the Kashin-hou statute.

11. The time involved for this preliminary evaluation process varies with each case.

12. There are ten formal notice days scheduled throughout the year, one per month with the exception of July and August.

13. According to statistics from the Chemical Safety Division of MITI, between 1974 and 1996:

TOTAL NOTIFICATIONS SUBMITTED

Domestic: 4,619
Imported: 1,580

RESULTS OF NOTIFICATION

Safe: 4,930
Designated: 344
Other: 1,169
(including withdrawn notifications and first class specified substances)

14. For an exhaustive discussion of TSCA, see Carolyne Hathaway, David J. Hayes, and William K. Rawson, "A Practitioner's Guide to the Toxic Substances Control Act: Parts I, II, and III," *Environmental Law Reporter,* May–July 1994.

15. After TSCA's enactment in 1976, the EPA established an inventory of sixty-two thousand chemicals already in U.S. commerce referred to as "existing chemicals." As of 1994, the EPA has added approximately ten thousand new chemicals to this inventory.

TSCA does not regulate pesticides, tobacco, nuclear material, firearms and ammunition, food, food additives, drugs, and cosmetics, all of which are regulated by other laws.

16. If a company seeks to produce a chemical that is already on the TSCA inventory but for a different intended use than what the EPA has approved the chemical for in the past, this is called a "significant new use notice," or SNUN.

17. "Low-volume" chemicals are those produced in volumes less than 10,000 kg per year.

18. The fee for the submission of a PMN is a relatively moderate $2,500, reduced to $100 if the submitter qualifies as a small business. Consolidated PMNs

may be filed for related chemicals with the approval of the EPA pre-notice coordinator.

Protection for confidential business information (CBI) must be claimed and substantiated by the submitting company, but if demonstrated, the EPA will take security measures to protect the specific properties of the chemical from disclosure.

19. General Accounting Office, *Toxic Substances Control Act: Legislative Changes Could Make the Act More Effective* (Washington, D.C.: General Accounting Office, September 1994), 34.

20. During the first thirty to forty-five days of this process, the EPA will notify companies if their requests for test-market, low-volume release, and low-volume/low-exposure exemptions have been granted.

21. According to a report by the General Accounting Office (GAO) published in 1994, of the 23,971 new chemicals reviewed, the EPA took some action to reduce risk on 2,431, or about 10 percent. General Accounting Office, *Toxic Substances Control Act,* 16.

22. New uses include an additional application of the chemical as well as changes in the projected volume or the degree of human exposure.

23. This directive, adopted in 1967, requires that the packaging of every dangerous substance show clearly the name of the substance; the origin of the substance; the danger symbol, where this has been designated, and an indication of the danger involved in the use of the substance; a reference to special risks; and safety advice.

24. EC directives instruct member states to adopt appropriate implementing legislation and are binding only on the national governments of member states. Directives themselves are not directly applicable to companies or individuals who do business in member states.

25. One expert estimated "that approximately 55 percent of the chemicals subject to premanufacture notification under TSCA do not make it to the market in the United States," which illustrates the potential significance of this distinction. Gabrielle Williamson, panel discussant "Chemical Regulation: The U.S. and E.E.C.," in *Understanding US and European Environmental Law: A Practitioner's Guide,* edited by Turner T. Smith and Pascale Kromarek (London: Graham and Trotman/ Martinus Nijhoff, 1989), 93.

26. Chemicals with an annual production volume of 10 kg or less per year require a limited notification and one acute toxicity study; for chemicals with annual production volume of 100 kg or less per year, there is a limited notification and an additional ecotoxicity test.

27. The EC directive was based on Organization for Economic Cooperation and Development (OECD) recommended criteria for determining the minimum data needed for premarket evaluation of chemicals.

28. The exemptions in the EU for scientific and process-oriented research and development are limited to either 100 kg per year and producer, or to one year with unlimited quantities, extendable to one further year.

29. Figures are in U.S. dollars and do not reflect variation in exchange rates over time, and hence inevitably are not precise comparisons. What is important is that they capture the rough proportional differences across jurisdictions.

30. Japanese company officials, however, reported that companies often

conduct biodegradation, bioaccumulation and screening tests together for low-molecular-weight substances. Those tests together cost approximately $200,000. Thus $17,000 would be an extremely low assessment in practice. More than 80 percent of new chemicals notified in Japan required further testing beyond the biodegradation stage.

31. This is the kind of generalization by company officials that we found persuasive. This European official had no incentive to prefer the United States system over the European one, other than the economic interests of his company.

32. The Seventh Amendment changed the waiting period from forty-five to sixty days.

33. These estimates from Japanese company officials were reported in yen, and the exchange rate of 100 yen/U.S. dollar was used for our convenience in this paper to convert to U.S. dollars.

34. Ministry of Housing, Spatial Planning, and Environment (VROM), the Netherlands, "European Inspection Project on the Notification of New Substances (NONS)," final report, July 1996.

35. Penalties are also assessed for violations of the regulations on PCBs, asbestos, inventory updates, and chemical importation regulations.

36. BNA, "Enforcement: Record $76.7 Million in Criminal Fines Assessed by Agency during Fiscal 1996," *Environment Reporter* 27, no. 42 (February 28, 1997): 2174.

37. "Current Report: Enforcement," *Chemical Regulation Reporter* 20, no.11 (June 14, 1996): 351.

38. It was another company's litigation against the EPA that resulted in the statute of limitations protection that has helped companies negotiate reductions in fines. In *3M v. Browner*, 17 F.3d 1453 (D.C. Cir. 1994), the court clarified the application of the statute of limitations for TSCA issues and held that the EPA could not seek penalties for violations that occurred more than five years before the agency complaint was filed.

39. Sara Thurin Rollin, "Toxic Substances: Polychlorinated Biphenyls: ALJ Levies First Million Dollar Fine; Texas Firm to Pay for Improper Disposal," *Chemical Regulation Reporter* 21, no. 29 (October 17, 1997): 813.

40. In its 1996 fiscal year report, the EPA for the first time attempted to quantify the reduction in pollution achieved through its enforcement, but it made no attempt to differentiate the effect of the various environmental laws.

41. The definition of "unreasonable risk" is the subject of ongoing debate among chemists and biologists. For example, many of the toxicological tests required under the notification laws use concentrated or maximum doses to determine hypothetical hazard levels in a shorter time, yet such concentrated levels of exposure are unlikely to occur under ordinary conditions. For further discussion of these issues, see Bruce N. Ames and Lois Swirsky Gold, "Environmental Pollution and Cancer: Some Misconceptions," in *Phantom Risk: Scientific Inference and the Law*, edited by Kenneth R. Foster, David E. Bernstein, and Peter W. Huber (Cambridge, Mass.: MIT Press, 1993).

42. Of these nine chemicals, five were existing chemicals (PCBs, chlorofluorocarbons, dioxin, asbestos, and hexavalent chromium).

In this case study we are focusing on the aspect of TSCA regarding the notification of new chemicals, but the sharpest criticism of TSCA, from organizations like the Natural Resources Defense Council and the Environmental Defense Fund, has generally been targeted at the statute's ineffectiveness at regulating the harm from existing chemicals (i.e., those on the market before the 1976 law).

The example most often cited of TSCA's ineffectiveness is the EPA's ten-year effort to issue regulations to phase out most uses of asbestos. In promulgating such regulations, in addition to determining whether risks are "unreasonable," the EPA must conduct a cost-benefit analysis that considers the economic and societal costs of placing controls on the chemical. The Fifth Circuit Court of Appeals struck down the EPA's regulations banning most uses of asbestos on the grounds that it had not considered sufficient evidence and failed to show that its control actions were the least burdensome reasonable regulation. *Corrosion Proof Fittings v. EPA*, 947 F.2d 1201 (5th Cir. 1991).

43. Others have praised TSCA's potential as a regulatory mechanism for filling what they call the "data gap" by collecting information about toxicity of chemicals, but they contend that the use of such vague terms as "unreasonable risk" and "substantial" have made it more difficult for the EPA to use the statute effectively. See John S. Applegate, "The Perils of Unreasonable Risk: Information, Regulatory Policy and Toxic Substance Control," *Columbia Law Review* 91 (1991): 261; Mary L. Lyndon, "Information Economics and Chemical Toxicity: Designing Laws to Produce and Use Data," *Michigan Law Review* 87 (1989) 1795. See also Milton C. Weinstein, "Decision Making for Toxic Substances Control: Cost-Effective Information Development for the Control of Environmental Carcinogens," *Public Policy* 27 (1979): 334–35; David Hayes, "The Potential for New Life in an 'Old' Statute: The Toxic Substances Control Act in Its 13th Year," *Chemical Regulation Reporter* 13 (April 21, 1989): 58–59.

44. General Accounting Office, *Toxic Substances Control Act*, 34–37; "Changes to U.S./E.C. Chemical Reviews Mulled Based on Results of Pilot Study," *International Environment Reporter* 16, no. 16 (July 28, 1993): 542.

45. The GAO report included an example of the potential impact of inaccurate SAR predictions. As part of a PMN review for a new chemical, the EPA identified potentially adverse health and environmental effects based on SAR data, but it did not make a determination of "unreasonable risk."

Before the chemical was placed on the TSCA inventory, the EPA received and decided to evaluate a PMN for the same chemical. The second PMN contained the results of several toxicity tests indicating that the actual vapor pressure was one hundred times greater than predicted by SAR, considerably increasing potential inhalation exposure and leading the EPA to find an "unreasonable risk" and propose regulations on the use of the chemical. General Accounting Office, *Toxic Substances Control Act*, 36.

46. There is some evidence in the legislative history to support this speculation. Opponents of TSCA pointed out that "similar regulations covering safety and effectiveness of drugs are in effect in the Federal Drug Administration and have served to greatly burden the development and marketing of new drugs and medicines. With passage of this bill, the same type of testing could be required of all new chemicals." *Legislative History of the Toxic Substances Control Act*, 623.

47. See Aoki and Cioffi, chapter 2, this volume; Aoki, Axelrad, and Kagan, chapter 3, this volume.

CHAPTER TWELVE

The Consequences
of Adversarial Legalism

Robert A. Kagan

What conclusions can be drawn from the case studies in this volume? Rich in detail, varied by area of law and regulated industry, often containing stories with contradictory outcomes or implications, they show that the world does not always conform to any parsimonious theory. The lessons of the cases, therefore, must be constructed inductively. Generalizations sometimes must be offered tentatively and with significant qualifications and exceptions. This effort to order the findings is organized in sections that address (1) the effectiveness of law in shaping the behavior of large corporations; (2) trends in economically advanced democracies toward convergence in the substantive norms of regulatory law; (3) the continued persistence, salience, and uniqueness of American adversarial legalism; (4) the substantial social and economic costs of adversarial legalism; and (5) adversarial legalism's relatively minimal compensating social benefits.

I. LAW MATTERS

In the regulation of large business firms in economically advanced democracies, law ways can and do change folkways. That message is conveyed by virtually all the case studies in this volume. All the companies studied relate to the relevant laws and legal controls with great seriousness. They maintain substantial staffs of regulatory compliance specialists and lawyers. With rare exceptions, they comply with those laws. Although the regulatory compliance personnel interviewed occasionally offered criticisms of particular regulatory requirements, they did so surprisingly infrequently. To a considerable degree, one can say that corporate officials in these large, multinational companies have accepted—in some cases even "internalized"—the basic norms of the regulatory programs and legal regimes they encounter in economically advanced democracies, and they take the specific rules and institutions that implement those norms as a fixed constraint, part of a business environment that they must try to adapt to as best they can.

This finding has become commonplace. Commenting on their findings in a recent study of fifty firms subject to the British Integrated Pollution Control (IPC) regulatory regime, Alex Mehta and Keith Hawkins observe:

> It seems reasonable to suggest that the days of companies consciously polluting the environment for purely financial motives (because it is easier to pay a fine than the costs of compliance) may well be disappearing. Indeed, most managers interviewed agreed with the principle of IPC and with the broad aims of pollution control in general. Many also mentioned a strong sense of moral and legal obligation supporting compliant behavior. No manager thought the IPC regime represented an unreasonable or in some sense illegitimate intrusion by the law.[1]

Of course, an attitude that views regulation as legitimate does not mean that corporations, or particular subunits, managers, or employees within a corporation, will attend to or adhere faithfully to every one of the myriad regulations that govern contemporary business behavior. But large corporations have entirely self-serving, profit-oriented reasons to adopt a general policy of full compliance. As Mehta and Hawkins found,

> Big firms were intensely concerned about the public and political consequences of transgression. Being squarely in the public eye they thought that news of their transgressions which would come to light if they were every prosecuted (regardless of whether they were formally punished) would seriously stain their corporate image. This assault on their reputation could have repercussions for sales and income. . . .
> It is immaterial whether such consequences in fact flow from prosecution. What is more important is that managers believe they do. . . . The result is that many big firms feel compelled to comply with IPC requirements because they cannot take the risk of their carefully cultivated (and expensive) consumer image being exposed to the uncompromising stare of the media. The bargaining chips held by environmental regulators are the threat of prosecution coupled with exposure to the glare of harmful publicity, which suggests that they enjoy an effective power that exceeds the fines that might be imposed upon a conviction for a violation of IPC requirements.[2]

With the exception of the Japan-based multinational metal parts manufacturing company studied by Aoki and Cioffi (chapter 2), each of the companies in the other case studies, as well as virtually all of the chemical companies interviewed by Johnson, Fujie, and Aalders (chapter 11), are household names in the United States, Western Europe, or Japan. They all market widely used consumer products or services under their corporate name. Hence, they all appear sensitive to precisely the kind of reputational risk that Mehta and Hawkins write of, and tend to take a "minimax" attitude toward legal or regulatory noncompliance: noncompliance is regarded as risky because it is impossible to predict whether a worst-case scenario—a highly visible environmental problem, or injury to a large number of consumers, or a multi-million-dollar lawsuit—will ensue.

The regulatory risk-aversiveness of large, visible corporations is reflected in many of the case studies. Aoki, Axelrad, and Kagan (chapter 3) report on a prominent Japanese corporation's deep concern that it should never be found to have violated official water pollution standards. Consequently, it established "internal standards" for contaminants in its wastewater that are substantially more stringent than those required by law or regulatory permit; by monitoring compliance with its internal standards, company officials would have an early warning system against violation of the regulatory standard. The multinational pharmaceutical corporation studied by Nielsen (chapter 7) prided itself on having an internal set of rules governing employee discipline and dismissal that would exceed, in terms of due process norms, the legal and regulatory standards of the jurisdictions in which it operated, and on having never lost a lawsuit by a dismissed employee in either the United States or Canada. When the large chemical company studied by Axelrad (chapter 4) became aware of site contamination at one of its manufacturing facilities in Great Britain, it immediately implemented the same set of investigative procedures it uses in the United States, although there are no specific British regulations on the subject. The metal parts manufacturer studied by Aoki and Cioffi (chapter 2) developed a cleaning system in its U.S. plant that dispensed with the use of chlorofluorocarbons (CFCs) well before the deadline called for by the Montreal Protocol and quickly implemented it in its plants in Japan and Asia, although there was no legal requirement there to do so. Thus these case studies provide some evidence for a dynamic toward transnational, "corporation-level" harmonization of regulatory compliance routines in multinational companies, keyed to compliance with the most stringent national standards (sometimes with a margin of error).

Corporate-level "harmonization" of compliance measures, the case studies suggest, is not automatic in every regulatory sector. Although U.S. law required Waste Corp. (chapter 5) to install a "double liner" at its municipal waste facilities in California and Pennsylvania, the company did not volunteer to do so at its facilities in England and the Netherlands, where regulators accepted a different design. Ford Motor Company (chapter 6) moved much more quickly to reduce paint shop odors in the surrounding community (by building a taller exhaust stack) at its plant in Cologne, Germany, than it did in St. Paul, Minnesota. And sometimes "harmonization" is thrust on a company by the extraterritorial reach of national regulatory laws. Kraus (chapter 10) shows that a biologics manufacturing plant in the United States was compelled to adopt tighter tolerances on its processes than had been required by the FDA because it could not market its U.S.-made product in Europe without satisfying the tight tolerance demanded by the European Union (EU) regulatory body. Similarly, as noted by Johnson, Fujie, and Aalders (chapter 11), chemical companies that seek to market new substances in Japan, Europe, and the United States often undertake the expensive toxicity testing required by Japanese and European regulatory agencies, even for products for which the U.S. EPA decides no such testing is necessary.

A disposition toward regulatory and legal compliance by visible multinational corporations does not imply that the meaning of "compliance" is always clear, or that these companies are unwilling to battle agencies or even litigate to obtain favorable interpretations of the law. The U.S. subsidiary of the Japanese metal manufacturing company studied by Aoki and Cioffi (chapter 2) spent thousands of dollars on a legal dispute with state and federal regulators concerning the cleanup of contamination that had been caused by the previous owner of its U.S. plant. A Japanese electronics company (chapter 3) disputed a local agency's method of sampling for water pollution outside the factory. ACME (the chemical company discussed in chapter 9) engaged in extended negotiations and litigation in the United States, Japan, and the EU alike when patent examiners initially did not find its innovation patentable. Ford spent years arguing with New Jersey regulators about the legally required and technically appropriate way of controlling emissions from a paint shop in its assembly plant (Dwyer, Brooks, and Marco; chapter 6). In short, the technical nature of the problem subject to regulation—and the lack of legal specificity about the level of small or remote (but costly to control) risks that can be tolerated—often makes "compliance" a matter of contention. And multinational companies, well armed with experts and money for lawyers and consultants, are formidable actors in the struggle to define legality.

Nevertheless, the dominant impression conveyed by the case studies is that the regulatory officials, not the regulated corporations, had the upper hand in the negotiations about regulatory requirements. In California, Pennsylvania, England, and the Netherlands alike, Waste Corp. was compelled to reformulate its design for a solid waste disposal site to meet regulators' and neighbors' environmental objections, and also to provide costly additional environmental amenities that were only loosely related to the problems the garbage dump created (see chapter 5). Ford Motor Company was forced by regulators and neighbors in both Germany and the United States to build higher exhaust stacks and adopt a more expensive pollution control method (carbon absorption) than it had proposed in its initial permit applications (chapter 6). When regulatory officials at the FDA or the EU agency for regulating biologics demanded more information or tighter tolerances, regulatory affairs personnel in "Company Y" burned the midnight oil to give them what they asked for, whether or not they personally regarded it as reasonable (chapter 10).

The case study method employed does not enable us to assess the other side of the coin. We cannot tell whether or when, in any of the studies, the regulators agreed to a company proposal or permit modification or argument that they "should not have accepted" by some legal or public-regarding standard. But the tone of all the case studies provides no ground for thinking that the corporate officials were able to overwhelm the regulators with argument or expertise, or with political or economic leverage. Above all, it appears that it was the regulatory officials' view of the law that mattered most.

II. SUBSTANTIVE SIMILARITY, SUBSTANTIVE DIVERGENCE

Linked by a global communications system, political elites, advocacy groups, and electorates in all economically advanced democracies lament the same kinds of injustices, environmental harms, and technological hazards. Regulatory officials, scientists, legal scholars, and environmental activists all flit across borders, in person and electronically, sharing knowledge about risks and policy solutions. When the European Union and Japan promulgated legal standards for product liability lawsuits, the standards were remarkably similar to those established by state courts in the United States.[3] A comparative study by scholars at Resources for the Future stated, "Although U.S. environmental regulations are arguably the most stringent in the world, the *differentials* between U.S. standards and those of our major industrialized trading partners are not very great."[4]

In this respect, the case studies in this book contain no big surprises. Most multinational corporate officials and lawyers interviewed in the course of the Comparative Legal Systems Project claimed that the substantive legal and regulatory standards they encounter in the United States and in other Organization for Economic Cooperation and Development (OECD) countries are basically similar. European representatives of an international petrochemical company told us that safety regulations in Europe and the United States concerning the labeling, packaging, and land transportation of hazardous chemicals were fundamentally the same. Project researchers encountered few criticisms of the United States for enacting safety and environmental regulations or other substantive legal rules that are significantly more stringent than the obligations imposed in other economically advanced democracies.

Most (but not all) of the detailed cases studies, therefore, support the "competitive convergence" hypothesis at the level of basic substantive legal policies and norms. At the same time, they highlight more subtle differences at the level of regulations and administrative decisions that implement those norms. Thus Dwyer, Brooks, and Marco (chapter 6) found that both German and American air pollution standards restricting air pollution from motor vehicle plant paint shops are stringent, but they note that Germany's "statutory 'state of the art' requirement" for control technologies "is based on the proportionality principle, under which benefits and costs are balanced," in contrast with the American lowest achievable emission rate (LAER) standard for control technologies in high-pollution "nonattainment areas." The American regulations thus were more stringent in the sense of allowing regulatory officials less discretion in adapting general standards to particular situations and to the economic cost of preventive measures. A similar tendency for U.S. regulations to be more inflexible (and hence more stringent) surfaced in many other case studies, such as Axelrad's comparison of British, Dutch, and American regulations governing investigation and remediation of contaminated industrial sites (chapter 4) and Welles and Engel's comparison of the detailed prescriptions for the liners in American municipal waste disposal sites with the more flexible site-specific standards that are employed in the parallel Dutch and British regulatory regimes (chapter 5).

A few case studies turned up more significant differences in substantive law, but differences that did not seem to be particularly significant in practice. The Canadian law against arbitrary discharge of employees, as described by Nielsen (chapter 7), is more comprehensive in its coverage than the patchwork of targeted antidiscrimination statutes and state common law rules in the United States, and Canadian law provides employees with more protection against sudden firing. But when Nielsen compared actual practices in a pharmaceutical company's Canadian and American operations, she found that these substantive differences were less significant in shaping personnel administration and postdismissal legal conflict than certain *procedural* features of American adversarial legalism, such as the greater risk of a very costly and disruptive civil damage suit in the United States, or the greater likelihood of an investigation by the federal Equal Employment Opportunity Commission (EEOC) or a state antidiscrimination commission. Similarly, according to Aoki and Cioffi (chapter 2), Japanese statutes provide less comprehensive restrictions on industrial waste disposal than does American law, and Aoki, Axelrad, and Kagan (chapter 3) note that the effluent standards under Japan's water pollution control law are, on average, somewhat less stringent than those imposed by federal and state regulations and permits in the United States. Nevertheless, Aoki and his coauthors found that due to informal "administrative guidance" and agreements with local governments, the Japanese factories studied actually controlled industrial wastes and effluents at least as thoroughly as similar factories in the United States that were owned and operated by the same corporation's U.S. subsidiary.

In one case study, substantive legal differences were clearly important in terms of actual impact. Charles Ruhlin (chapter 8) examines a multi-national bank's experience in attempting to collect delinquent consumer credit card debt in Germany and the United States. In both countries, consumer debt obligations are governed primarily by contract law, which is basically similar across countries. But in the United States, the bank encounters laws that grant debtors defenses and rights not available to German consumers: (1) federal and state "fair debt collection practice" laws that regulate creditors' dunning techniques, and (2) federal law that makes it relatively easy for debtors to discharge debts (while preserving some assets) by filing for bankruptcy. In consequence, Ruhlin found, the bank is far more cautious about bringing legal action against defaulting debtors in the United States, and it ends up treating a larger proportion of delinquent debt as uncollectible. Yet the bank's greater reluctance to take debtors to court in the United States also is due in part to the procedural characteristics of American adversarial legalism—which make American courts and collection practices far more inefficient, costly, and unpredictable than the less formal debt collection procedures provided by German courts. Ruhlin tells us, however, that Germany has now enacted a law expanding opportunities for consumer bankruptcy. And as this is written, a law curtailing some credit card debtors' bankruptcy rights is moving through the U.S. Congress.

In summary, the studies suggest a good deal of convergence of substantive regulatory norms and standards in economically advanced democracies, combined with continuing divergence in legal or regulatory style. For even when national laws are substantively *similar,* the chapters indicate, they often are applied and interpreted differently. Japanese and German patent examiners, Deepak Somaya's case study (chapter 9) indicates, are more conservative than their U.S. Patent Office counterparts in agreeing that an application meets the "innovativeness" standard, and the Japanese Patent Office is more insistent that the applicant's claims concerning inventions must be narrowly stated. The chemical company Somaya studied obtained a U.S. patent for a breakthrough process but could not do so in Japan, and it succeeded in Germany only after great difficulty. Similarly, officials in the company studied by Martine Kraus (chapter 10) noted that European regulators adopted a more searching analytic approach than their counterparts at the U.S. Food and Drug Administration (FDA) in evaluating the safety of a process for manufacturing a genetically engineered biological product. EU officials also insisted on tighter tolerances in the manufacturing process. Such differences in what might be called "legal or regulatory" style generally loomed far larger in the experience of the multinational companies studied than did cross-national differences in substantive law.

III. THE SALIENCE AND DISTINCTIVENESS OF ADVERSARIAL LEGALISM IN THE UNITED STATES

According to the chief environmental attorney for a multinational chemical firm, the chief contrast between the legal systems of the United States and other economically advanced democracies is not that the laws or standards are different but that "cultural processes" are different. The salient features of the American process he identified are familiar components of adversarial legalism: more complex and prescriptive bodies of legal rules; a more fragmented system of authority, which means that a company often must satisfy many agencies and respond to scattered claims in different courts; broader provisions for public participation in and influence on administrative decision making; greater uncertainty concerning legal requirements; and longer decision-making delays. For example, this attorney noted that American air pollution permit processes for new or renovated chemical manufacturing facilities, when contrasted with permit systems in other economically advanced democracies, involve more jurisdictional stops, more opportunities for local opponents to appeal to court, and more types of decisions in which approvals must be sought from both federal and state regulators, who often do not agree. This procedural legal maze, in his view, is far more significant than the minor cross-national differences in actual emission standards.[5] Many of the same dimensions of America adversarial legalism are highlighted by the case studies in this book.

A. Public Participation

Welles and Engel (chapter 5) recount the experiences of a multinational waste management company in obtaining permission to develop or expand solid waste disposal landfills in California, Pennsylvania, England, and the Netherlands. In each of these jurisdictions, permits must be obtained both from a local governmental body that regulates land use and from at least one environmental protection agency. In each jurisdiction, the law provides for some form of participation or input from neighbors or from members of the public who object to the location or design of the landfill facility. But the American legal system, particularly in California, gave local objectors far more *legal leverage*. If their concerns were rejected in one forum, there were more agencies to which they could complain, and the law gave them greater capacity to challenge adverse administrative decisions in the courts.

Similarly, in both Germany and the United States, the air pollution control system requires companies to apply for permits for process changes that may increase pollution; it also provides for public comment and objections with respect to permit conditions. But as Dwyer, Brooks, and Marco demonstrate (chapter 6), opportunities for public participation under German law are more limited:

> In the United States, federal and state law requires every permit decision to be preceded by public notification, an opportunity for public comment, and a meeting where members of the public can voice their concerns and demand answers from regulators (and often company officials). Typically, state implementation plans provide an opportunity for contested administrative hearings (as well as judicial review) to resolve factual disputes underlying the permit decision. Entrepreneurial activists can use these procedures to generate publicity, create and energize a political constituency, and force the agency to address their concerns.
>
> Under German law, . . . the *Land* environmental agency has no legal obligation to give public access to the proposed permit and supporting documents . . . so long as the modification does not increase pollutant emissions. . . . Even when a German environmental agency must make the draft permit and supporting documents available to the public, . . . German agencies accept written comments and objections from members of the public, but they are not required to hold a public meeting or initiate a contested administrative hearing.

Thus neighborhood groups and environmental activists in St. Paul, Minnesota, Dwyer and his colleagues report, contested Ford Motor Company's permit application and used public meetings to generate political pressure on the state environmental agency, which created a task force, with citizen group participation, that ultimately resulted in a plant modification to control objectionable odors. In Germany, neighbors filed only *written* objections concerning odors from a Ford assembly plant's paint shop; although this process resulted in similar plant modifications, Ford's German neighbors did not get to sit on a task force like the one created in St. Paul, which got to hire its own consultant, review the options in detail, and help shape the solution.

B. Legalistic Regulatory Enforcement

For years, observers have criticized many regulatory programs in the United States for employing a legalistic enforcement style, that is, for rigidly enforcing detailed regulatory requirements, declining to make exceptions based on the risks and compliance costs peculiar to the particular case, and for measuring success in terms of numbers of prosecutions and amounts of fines. Legalistic enforcement, it has repeatedly been said, often results in unnecessary regulatory requirements and stimulates resistance on the part of regulated entities.[6] The Clinton administration's *Reinventing Environmental Regulation* report of 1995 stated, "The adversarial approach that has often characterized our environmental system precludes opportunities for creative solutions that a more collaborative system might encourage."[7] Thus academic analysts, regulatory officials, and political leaders regularly have called for more flexible methods of regulatory enforcement and for redesigning regulation to encourage industry cooperation.[8] Many efforts to institute such reforms have been reported, especially in the 1990s.[9] It was therefore somewhat surprising that in the Comparative Legal Systems Project, multinational corporation officials repeatedly referred to—and expressed fear of—legalistic, punitive enforcement of environmental and safety regulations in the United States. A pollution control consultant with wide experience said, "In the United States . . . if you screw up, you can have stiff fines. You can readily get sued." In other countries, such as the United Kingdom, "they have fines, but they're peanuts."

Adversarial enforcement is not universal in the United States. It is not difficult to find cases in which state or federal regulatory agencies declined or simply failed to punish detected regulatory violations.[10] In some industries, such as meat and poultry processing, companies have managed to ward off legislation calling for large and more automatically imposed administrative fines for violations of safety regulations.[11] Several corporate officials told us that they enjoyed cooperative, nonlegalistic relations with certain American regulatory agencies. But many corporate regulatory affairs officers told us of incidents in which violations of "prophylactic" regulations (reporting, labeling, design of storage containers, etc.)—violations that entailed no actual harm to workers or to the environment—were met with automatic fines amounting to tens of thousands of dollars. For example, in their study of premarketing regulation of new chemical compounds, Johnson, Fujie, and Aalders (chapter 11) recount the experience of a U.S. chemical firm that had begun marketing a new substance which company chemists believed was essentially identical to others on the long list of substances that had previously been cleared by the U.S. Environmental Protection Agency (EPA) pursuant to the Toxic Substances Control Act (TSCA). Company officials, however, sought confirmation of their action from the EPA. EPA officials, it turned out, disagreed with the company's interpretation of the scope of the prior clearances and found that the company had violated TSCA. Despite the fact that the company had been forthcoming and that it had at least a plausible scientific argument, the EPA assessed a $23 million fine (although it subsequently reduced it to $375,000). Another instance of legalistic, adversarial enforcement, this time by a state environmental agency, is the centerpiece of Aoki and Cioffi's comparison of industrial waste regulation in the United States and Japan (chapter 2).

In contrast, in the experience of the corporate officials interviewed, regulators in Western Europe, the United Kingdom, and Japan rarely respond to regulatory violations with formal enforcement and fines so long as the violations are not willful and the regulated company seems genuinely committed to remediation and improvement. The contrast is conveyed by a story told by a regulatory compliance officer in a U.S. subsidiary of a multinational petrochemical company. It arose in a meeting with her counterparts from corporate subsidiaries in the United Kingdom, Canada, and Australia. These nations all have laws requiring chemical companies to maintain detailed inventories of chemicals in process and in shipment. But given the volume and rapidity of shipments in a large chemical company, said the U.S. official, it is "extremely easy to make a mistake." When a British regulatory compliance official discovered he had made such an error, his attitude, the bemused American official said, was, "Oh dear, I think I'll have to do something about that," indicating that a call to the relevant agency would take care of such a nonwillful, not immediately harmful violation. In contrast, the American official said, if the U.S. subsidiary's compliance office discovered a similar error, "We'd panic. We'd start calculating the fine we owed," because reporting can reduce the statutory fine (up to $25,000 a day) by half.

In other countries, regulators were said to be much more inclined to sit down with company officials to work out agreements on technically appropriate remedial measures. Axelrad (chapter 4) describes how Dutch and British regulators informally worked with the regulated company to determine what steps should be taken to investigate the extent of ground and water contamination at an industrial site and how it should be contained and remedied. Both state and federal regulators in the United States, in contrast, inspected, consulted the detailed official regulations, and subsequently mailed the company orders about what it should do—orders that in significant measure were unrelated to the actual tasks of remediation. "In the United States," company officials told Axelrad, "there's no sitting down with the agency and saying, 'Let's focus on risk.' "

Regulatory inflexibility in the United States reflects the legal structure and political environments within which American regulators work. Legalistic enforcement is rare in the Japanese system for regulating factory waste disposal, Aoki and Cioffi point out, partly because Japanese waste control regulations are more outcome-oriented—in contrast with American regulations under RCRA, which prescribe in the minutest detail what the company must do to prevent environmental contamination. American air and water pollution permits, our respondents repeatedly observed, are more detailed and specific than those in Japan and Europe. As described by Welles and Engel (chapter 5), federal regulations concerning municipal waste sites in the United States are much more prescriptive, technical, and inflexible than the standards in the Netherlands and Great Britain, which Dutch and British officials can tailor to the particular site in light of evolving technologies and the perceived risks at the particular location. Noting that American regulators acted legalistically even when RCRA rules concerning industrial waste cleanup allowed them discretion, officials at one multinational company told Axelrad (chapter 4) that in his experience American regulators want to issue a permit that is "risk-free to themselves" because they operate in an atmosphere in which they are "pilloried and abandoned if it turns out that they have made a mistake."

As that observation suggests, behind the greater specificity of American regulations, and hence behind the propensity toward legalistic enforcement, lie cross-national differences in political culture—particularly the greater mistrust of governmental bureaucracy in the United States, which is expressed in the restriction of bureaucratic discretion by detailed rules and ready access to judicial review. In this political environment, "going by the book" provides regulatory officials with protection from at least some kinds of criticism. In countries that are more trusting of government, regulatory accountability rests less on legal mechanisms and more on professional training. Edward Rubin reports that the German Bundesbank's regulations for assuring bank safety and soundness are bound in a pamphlet less than one hundred pages in length. The U.S. Federal Reserve Board's operative statutes and regulations fill several thick binders. Officials hired by the Fed to work on bank regulation, aside from having a law degree or an adequate grade on a civil service examination, receive a few weeks of on-the-job training. The Bundesbank runs a three-year "college" for its regulatory recruits.[12] When regulatory officials are thoroughly trained professionals, dedicated to a career in the same regulatory program, Rubin notes, authorities can trust them to make programmatically sensible judgments and need not bind their discretion with detailed rules. Repeatedly, officials of multinational corporations whom we interviewed commented on frequency of turnover among the regulatory personnel they deal with in American agencies—which in turn led to variability in American regulators' level of technical knowledge when compared with their counterparts in Europe and Japan. When regulatory personnel are "new on the job," they are more likely to "go by the book," applying rules legalistically, because they do not have the specialized knowledge that enables them to confidently negotiate with professionals in regulated enterprises or to defend discretionary decisions to mistrustful superiors or politicians. Legalistic behavior—demanding strict adherence to the rules, demanding more tests and certifications—is a common response to that lack of confidence.[13]

C. The Distinctiveness of American Liability Law

The case studies in this volume and other exploratory interviews by project researchers also underscore the uniquely threatening character of the American liability law regime, particularly tort suits and civil cases that are brought pursuant to regulatory statutes. The distinctiveness of American liability law arises from (1) the readiness with which the liability system can be and is mobilized; (2) the unpredictability and potential magnitude of damage awards (due to both the vagueness of American legal rules for damages and the use of juries); and (3) the costs of the litigation process itself.

The multinational corporation studied by Nielsen (chapter 7) prescribes identical personnel management and employee termination policies for its American and its Canadian branches. Yet in one recent year, Nielsen found, almost 23 percent of "forced separations" of employees in the United States resulted in a lawsuit against the company, compared with 7 percent of forced separations in Canada—even though Canadian substantive law protecting employees against arbitrary dismissal is more comprehensive than is American law. Nielsen's chapter thus supports the general research literature, which suggests that whereas (and perhaps because) American law provides weaker *statutory* protections against dismissal and less generous postdismissal severance and unemployment benefits than the labor law of Western European states and Canada, American employers are far more likely to be sued for substantial money damages in courts of general jurisdiction on grounds of unjust dismissal or discrimination.[14]

A senior risk manager for a major chemical manufacturer, 55 percent of whose sales are in the United States, told us that for every one hundred product liability claims against his firm in the United States there are about twenty or twenty-five in Western Europe and none in Japan. Claims filed in the United States (which include actions for products marketed and even manufactured abroad) account for 85 percent of the dollars his company expends on product liability claims, the rest of the world, 15 percent.[15]

Officials of multinational chemical companies headquartered in other countries told us that they feel threatened by the sheer cost of defending cases filed in American courts as much as by the fear of potential damage awards. The uncertainty of the American product liability system also is widely regarded as troublesome. A Japanese chemical company official reported that after consulting with American legal counsel, his company decided not to market in the United States a household "air freshener" designed to neutralize the odor of tobacco smoke—a product that it sells in large volumes in Japan—because of the *possibility* of liability suits by individuals harmed by tobacco smoke, whose lawyers might employ a difficult-to-anticipate legal theory.

A legal counsel for a non-American motor vehicle manufacturer (echoing the accounts of some tort scholars)[16] told us that no country in which his firm sells vehicles comes close to the United States in terms of the incidence and cost of product liability litigation. Canada is perhaps the closest, he noted, but it remains a very distant second, for several reasons: (1) Canada requires losing plaintiffs to pay some or all of the defendant's lawyer fees, and in Ontario, the most populous province, contingency fees are prohibited; this, he said, "chills the filing of frivolous cases in Canada"—as opposed to the United States, where he claimed that a significant proportion of cases are filed without much investigation, in hopes of getting a quick "nuisance settlement." (2) In civil cases, most provinces in Canada (like almost all other countries) do not use juries. In the United States, jury trials in auto product liability cases typically involve complex and conflicting expert witness testimony on such issues as "accident reconstruction, body mechanics, and motor vehicle design engineering and decisionmaking," and juries, in this corporate lawyer's view, often are swayed by clever lawyering. (3) Canada (like most other countries) has much more specific damage rules and does not impose punitive damages (which even in the United States are actually imposed in only a small percentage of claims but are important, this lawyer claimed, because 10 percent of the liability cases generate 90 percent of the firm's financial exposure). (4) Canadian law provides that if the injured plaintiff was contributorily negligent as a result of alcohol or drug abuse, no recovery is permitted. (5) Canada (like other countries) does not have the highly organized litigation machine that American entrepreneurial lawyers have created—in which plaintiffs' lawyers draw on (and help fund) databases, "litigation kits," workshops on particular vehicles, and expert witnesses provided by the American Trial Lawyers Association and the Center for Automotive Safety.

IV. EXCEPTIONS TO THE RULE: ADVERSARIAL LEGALISM ABROAD, SUBDUED ADVERSARIAL LEGALISM AT HOME

If the case studies as a whole confirm both the prevalence and the distinctiveness of American adversarial legalism, some of the case studies and exploratory interviews provide three kinds of counterexamples: (1) instances in which a multinational encountered equal levels or more adversarial legalism in other countries, (2) instances in which there were low levels of adversarial legalism in the United States (and abroad), and (3) regional variation within the United States in the amount or intensity of adversarial legalism.

A. Adversarial Legalism Abroad?

Somaya's account of ACME chemical company's efforts to patent its innovations in Japan, Europe, and the United States (chapter 9) provides a muted counterexample of the first kind. ACME experienced a great deal of costly, time-consuming, and legally unpredictable legal contestation in all three places. American procedures for *granting* a patent, in fact, are *less* adversarial. In contrast to the Japanese and European patent offices, the U.S. Patent Office does not provide for pre-grant "opposition" proceedings by competing companies. In ACME's case, oppositions in Japan and the EU were contentious and costly, and resulted in appeals to court.

On the other hand, Somaya's chapter does not suggest that American-style adversarial legalism is spreading abroad, for the American patent system structures legal contestation of patents quite differently, using a more distinctly American mode of adjudication. Instead of centralizing adversarial opposition to patents in a pre-grant or immediately post-grant *administrative* procedure, as in Japan and the EU, inventors or companies that wish to challenge a U.S. patent usually do so via post-grant litigation (often as defenses to the patent holders' lawsuits for infringement). Thus the American system pushes adversarial disputes over patents out of a specialized administrative tribunal into a decentralized, somewhat unpredictable court system, in which juries play a significant role. Since an alleged infringer can challenge the patent in court at any time during its term, the legal uncertainty over a patent's validity can linger much longer in the United States. And the courts themselves provide relatively little certainty. Twice, when ACME sued another company for infringement, a U.S. District Court invalidated the company's patent. Twice, the company appealed to the Court of Appeals, which reversed the District Court and sustained the patent. In addition to this characteristic legal uncertainty, Somaya reports that American legal processes for *enforcing* a patent against infringers are much more adversarial and costly than such actions in other countries. American patent litigation is unique in the extent of its party-driven pretrial discovery, in its reliance on privately hired expert witnesses, and in its threat of imposing treble damages.[17]

B. Centralization of Authority and Subdued Adversarial Legalism

More interesting, perhaps, are the spheres of law in which adversarial legalism did *not* appear to be a salient aspect of the multinational corporations' experience in the United States. The common ingredient in these low-adversarialism policy areas is that legal authority is centralized and difficult to challenge in court, either legally or practically; that is, governmental legal authority is exercised more hierarchically and with more finality than is the American norm (and hence more like most parliamentary democracies).

For example, shipping officials in a multinational petrochemical company described as generally nonadversarial and nonlegalistic their relationship with the tank car safety section of the Federal Railroad Administration (FRA), which regulates the design of tank cars and inspects existing cars for safety. In this policy arena, company officials interact repeatedly with a single federal agency, rather than with a multiplicity of federal, state, and local agencies. It is an area of law that has not attracted many lawsuits (against the FRA or the company) by advocacy organizations. In addition, because the FRA has summary powers to suspend the use of equipment it finds dangerous, the company is not inclined to mount legal resistance even to citations or orders it considers unreasonable; the company's primary interest is to keep the trains rolling, even if the FRA requirements are costly to comply with.

Similarly, the regulatory affairs official in the biotech company studied by Kraus (chapter 10) described the biological products office of the U.S. FDA as somewhat legalistic (in the sense that it is a stickler for strict compliance with highly detailed rules) but not adversarial. Disputes over company applications for an FDA facilities license or new product license rarely end up in court. Here, too, regulatory power is concentrated in a single regulatory office in Washington, and that office that has crucial powers: it can delay the marketing of products in which the company has invested huge amounts of money, and it can publicly question the safety practices of a health care products company, which has an enormously important economic stake in a reputation for absolute safety. In these circumstances, the regulated entity has strong incentives not to appeal even those agency decisions that it considers unreasonable. It is for similar reasons that banks tend not to litigate against the Federal Reserve Board.[18] Such agencies have strong hierarchical powers; that is, they rarely are subject to challenge and reversal in court, or by other agencies. And to refer to the typology of decision-making methods set forth in chapter 1, hierarchical authority structures push policy implementation or dispute resolution into the cell labeled "expert or political judgment" or "bureaucratic legalism," rather than adversarial legalism.

Consider, too, the report by Johnson, Fujie, and Aalders that numerous multinational chemical company officials view the U.S. TSCA regime, as administered by the EPA, as *less* legalistic and more economically efficient in screening new chemical substances than comparable regulatory systems in Japan and the European Union. This surprising finding stems partly from the distinctive political climate in which TSCA was enacted, which resulted in a statute that focuses analysis only on high-risk new chemicals, so as to avoid regulatory delays that would slow the movement of well-understood, beneficial new chemicals into the marketplace. But it is also noteworthy that TSCA concentrated decision-making authority for new chemicals in one agency in Washington, D.C. Chemical company executives regard the EPA officials who administer TSCA as having a reasonably high level of scientific expertise. Chemical companies rarely appeal to court the EPA's decisions pursuant to TSCA (for that would only prolong delays in getting products to the market); nor do pro-regulation advocacy groups. Hence, the TSCA process is dominated not by lawyers but by scientific experts.

The TSCA exception must be tempered, on the other hand, by Johnson Fujie, and Aalders's report that in the experience of multinational chemical companies, the EPA is far more likely than its Japanese and European counterparts to take formal legal action, including the imposition of substantial fines, if a company is found to have violated any of the highly technical filing and testing regulations. This reflects the general tendency of American agencies to respond to detected violations with legal sanctions, in order to emphasize their authority and protect themselves from political criticism.

C. State-by-State Variation in the United States

In their account of the permitting process for municipal waste disposal facilities in California, Pennsylvania, Great Britain, and the Netherlands, Welles and Engel (chapter 5) highlight the prevalence of state-level variation in adversarial legalism within the United States. Whereas Waste Corp. encountered extremely costly litigation in California, it did not encounter lawsuits in Pennsylvania. The state of Pennsylvania has constructed a much more hierarchical decision-making process—and, in that respect, one that more closely resembles the British and Dutch systems. In California the project proponent had to obtain separate permits, certifications of compliance, or agreements from *sixteen* local, regional, and state agencies, each imposing different legal and analytical requirements. In Pennsylvania a single state-level environmental agency issued the facility's solid waste permit and coordinated the issuance of permits (a total of six) required from other state agencies. In Pennsylvania, appeals by local opponents and environmental groups were channeled into a state-level administrative hearing process. But in California, local opponents (with help from a rival waste disposal company) hauled Waste Corp. into court more than once, challenging both the environmental impact report and permit conditions that had been approved by the local agency.[19] Thus the Pennsylvania case, too, suggests that adversarial legalism is less common when regulatory authority is more centralized or hierarchically organized.

Dwyer, Brooks, and Marco (chapter 6) describe two kinds of legal conflict that Ford Motor Company encountered in seeking to expand or change production patterns in two of its automobile assembly plant paint shops, one in Minnesota and one in New Jersey. Referring to the air pollution permitting process at its Minnesota plant, Ford officials describe the Minnesota Pollution Control Agency (MPCA) as cooperative, constructive, and nonlegalistic. Also, when Ford sought a formal "innovative technology waiver" from the U.S. EPA "new source performance standards," based on its plan to develop new low-volatile-organic-compound (low-VOC) paints, the federal agency announced its intention to grant the exception. Legal conflict arose as a result of opposition from local community groups and environmental advocates who had long been unhappy about odors emanating from Ford's plant. These local opponents challenged and then appealed the EPA waiver, politically pressured MPCA to ask Ford to undertake an odor abatement study, and requested a contested hearing before an independent administrative law judge with respect to the MPCA-issued permit—all of which resulted in the creation of a citizens task force that ultimately worked out a cooperative solution. In New Jersey, it also took several years for Ford to obtain a permit. There the conflict arose not because of adversarial opposition from neighbors and environmentalists but because of resistance by officials in the New Jersey Department of Environmental Protection (NJDEP), whom Ford officials characterized as legalistic, distant, and noncooperative—although NJDEP officials blame Ford for failing to provide adequate information to evaluate the permit and predict the consequences for air quality. Conceivably, the difference between the MPCA and the NJDEP regulatory behavior reflects the fact that New Jersey, unlike Minnesota, is in a "nonattainment area" under the Clean Air Act, which puts regulatory officials under some pressure to bring about measurable *reductions* in pollutants even in expanding factories.

V. THE COSTS OF ADVERSARIAL LEGALISM

Notwithstanding the exceptions mentioned, the dominant message of the case studies in this book, along with project researchers' exploratory interviews with a wider number of business executives, lawyers, and consultants, is that adversarial legalism is predominantly an American phenomenon and that it is rather pervasive across business sectors and legal policy areas. Moreover, multinational enterprises generally regarded the "friction costs" associated with American adversarial legalism as both substantial and troublesome. The precise magnitude of those "extra" legal-procedural costs is difficult to specify. The financial statements and accounting schemes of the corporations studied were not designed to identify those costs, which tend to be buried in a variety of other categories. Nevertheless, qualitative information about the friction costs, especially when viewed in the light shed by the explicit cross-national comparisons, provides some useful insight into the consequences of adversarial legalism. The following subsections organize this qualitative information in terms of various kinds of costs.

A. *Legal Services*

All modern societies need lawyers to help communicate the requirements of complex and changing legal rules, to structure contracts, and to defend the accused. But the United States seems to spend much more on them than comparable countries. In 1991 aggregate expenditures on legal services in the United States amounted to more than $100 billion, perhaps 2 percent of the gross national product.[20] Ordinary observation leaves little doubt that when American business executives are engaged in negotiating sales franchises, seeking approval for real estate projects, issuing stock, and launching new products, they are surrounded by larger phalanxes of expensive attorneys than their counterparts in Europe or Japan—where the *legal* risks corporations face are less problematic.

In this project's interviews of officials in multinational enterprises, respondents often mentioned that their company spends far more money on legal services in its American operations than in its parallel operations in other countries. American subsidiaries consult lawyers more often and longer on a wider range of matters, ranging from selecting pollution control equipment to managing problem personnel and conducting sales transactions. They do so, project researchers repeatedly were told, because (1) American law is generally more complex, changeable, and difficult to master, and (2) the legal sanctions for being wrong are generally much higher.[21]

The U.S. subsidiary of PREMCO, the Japan-based manufacturing company studied by Aoki and Cioffi (chapter 2), has spent more money on lawyering—both in-house and outside counsel—than PREMCO has in all its much larger worldwide operations. Nielsen (chapter 7) found that when the pharmaceutical company she studied decided to terminate individual employees in the United States, it consulted its attorneys earlier, more frequently, and in more depth than when terminating employees in Canada. Ruhlin (chapter 8) observes that because German law concerning debt collection is much simpler and more uniform than American law, the German credit card division of Credit Co., a multinational bank, contrasts sharply with Credit Co.'s American operations: the German division does not have to maintain separate in-house counsel's offices to deal with litigation management, consumer bankruptcy, and debtors' counterclaims.

And unlike its U.S. counterpart, the German division does not feel obliged to provide ongoing, intensive legal training for collection agents.

Similarly, in one of the project's exploratory interviews, a corporate general counsel in the U.S. office of a multinational chemical firm said that in the company's U.S. subsidiary—in contrast to its European corporate parent—a wide variety of documents are routinely reviewed by the legal department. One stimulus to this procedure was a lawsuit for breach of contract in which a drawing made by a company sales representative was held, much to the company's surprise, to have been evidence of a contract. The suit cost the company roughly $500,000 in damages and $500,000 in disputing and lawyering costs. Now, the lawyer said, "Half of our salesmen are scared to death to do anything without consulting a lawyer." The U.S. subsidiary employs six specially trained nonlawyers who spend at least half their time fielding legal questions that salespeople routinely ask about sales contracts. To further avoid legal problems, the corporate attorney added, "When European people [from the parent firm] come over here, we have to forbid them from talking or writing letters to anyone."

Most shockingly, Welles and Engel found that Waste Corp. (chapter 5) spent a staggering $15 million on legal services in the course of its efforts to obtain approval for a municipal solid waste landfill in California; for over ten years, the company had approximately seven lawyers on retainer, busy addressing, inter alia, two major administrative appeals and three extended lawsuits. In Pennsylvania, the same company retained seven lawyers (but only part-time) for the five years it took to get a permit there, a process that entailed two administrative appeals but no lawsuits and "only" $1.45 million in lawyering costs. In England, by contrast, the company retained two lawyers, part-time, for an eight-year process that also included at least one administrative appeal; its legal costs there were about $137,000. And in the Netherlands, despite having undergone two administrative appeals, the company did not have to retain lawyers at all (since lawyers are not required in administrative appeals) and spent "less than $50,000" on legal services.

B. Accountability Costs

Viewed in cross-national perspective, American regulatory regimes generally impose more extensive and specific requirements concerning reporting, record keeping, testing, employee education, certifications, and so on.[22] In addition to the costs of complying with substantive regulatory standards, therefore, regulated firms in the United States usually must spend more than in their overseas operations in *proving* that they are complying.

Consider, for example, Dwyer, Brooks, and Marco's comparison between the air pollution permits that German and U.S. regulators issued to Ford Motor Company, when Ford sought to expand production or use new paints on its vehicles (chapter 6). In both countries the regulatory authorities required Ford to install similar VOC-reducing technologies, such as carbon adsorption units. But the American permits, the authors observe, impose much more detailed record-keeping and reporting requirements, designed to ensure that Ford does not exceed the planned level of emissions. Ford's New Jersey permit, these authors tell us, tell us, set hourly, daily, and annual VOC emission limits for each separate step of the painting process; included limits on the amount of volatile organic solvent (VOS) for each of the several coatings; specified the type of fuel and fuel usage rates for afterburners; and specified "destruction efficiency" and operating temperature for the afterburners. The permit also required Ford to install a continuous VOC monitor and recorder after each carbon adsorber; and to seek agency approval for type and calibration of the monitors and recorders; to conduct three types of tests on the efficacy of the controls; to test the solvent content of the paint monthly, and get prior agency approval for its testing methods; to maintain all records—including daily production rates, colors, paint and solvent usage, VOC content of the paint, natural gas consumption (for the thermal oxidizers), and monitoring data—onsite for at least five years, to be made available to regulatory officials on demand; and to submit a quarterly report to the agency covering daily use of coatings and solvents for each stage of the painting processes and daily emission levels.

The German permit for Ford's Cologne plant was also detailed, but basically it set an overall annual limit for VOC emissions, rather than specific step-by-step limits. It required Ford to engage in continuous monitoring of certain parameters, to conduct certain tests, and to keep records of solvent use. But with respect to the number and specificity of the testing, monitoring, and reporting procedures, the German permit was far less demanding—one might say it "displayed much less mistrust"—than the New Jersey permit. For example, after initial tests to be sure the system was operating, the German permit required Ford to undertake performance testing only every three years.

Another telling comparison of regulatory accountability regimes emerged from the visit of two project researchers (Kagan and Marco) to a U.S. plastic products plant in Texas. The plant is closely modeled on its corporate owner's Japanese factory for making the same products. Japanese engineers working at the Texas plant stated that the relevant air pollution control standards in the two nations are roughly the same, as are the basic pollution control systems in the two installations. Thus the Texas and Japanese factories use similar methods to control fugitive emissions from the complex system of pipes and ducts. But in the United States, firms are required to keep more detailed records of emissions and to file much lengthier reports to the state agency that enforces federal regulatory standards. In the Texas factory, for example, there are at least four thousand points in the manufacturing process at which emissions can leak out. Each one must be tagged, monitored, and recorded with time and date, and total emissions must be estimated on a quarterly basis. The Texas plant hires outside consultants to perform this time-consuming task. In Japan, we were told by corporate officials, government audits are less frequent, and fines for detected noncompliance are issued only in instances of continued noncompliance. Once a company has acquired a good reputation for compliance, as this firm's Japanese plant has, it need not invest in the extra layer of monitoring required in the Texas plant. The Japanese engineers did not think fugitive emissions in their Japanese plant were any worse than those in the Texas plant.

One consequence of the more demanding regulatory accountability regimes in the United States, several studies in this book indicate, is that American branches of multinational corporations maintain substantially larger *intracorporate regulatory compliance staffs* than do similar business operations abroad. Thus Nielsen (chapter 7) shows that in addition to its "human resources department," the American division of a pharmaceutical company created a special Affirmative Action Office—an additional layer of bureaucracy that must be consulted in all probation and dismissal cases involving female employees, racial minorities, and employees over forty years of age. The company does not have such an office in its branch in Canada, where litigation and regulatory agency intervention are less frequent and less threatening. Moreover, the character of corporate compliance staffs often differs. In Aoki and Cioffi's study of waste regulation (chapter 2) and in Aoki, Axelrad, and Kagan's study of water pollution control (chapter 3), a multinational manufacturer's U.S. subsidiary confronted a more legally complex and potentially punitive regulatory regime than its sister operations in Japan. In the U.S. subsidiaries, regulatory affairs departments concentrated much more on acquiring *legal* expertise, whereas regulatory compliance specialists in the Japanese factories concentrated much more fully on technical or engineering issues. Similarly, the more threatening and costly American litigation system often induces companies in the United States to spend more on what might be called "defensive legal medicine."[23]

1. WHEN ACCOUNTABILITY DISPLACES RESPONSIBILITY

The cross-national differences in accountability costs are symbolized most strikingly by the huge volume of *supporting evidence* companies must supply to regulators in the United States to demonstrate that the firm has met legal standards. Axelrad (chapter 4) recounts the experience of B

Corporation when it notified regulatory authorities in the United States, England, and the Netherlands that it had discovered solvents which had leaked from deteriorating underground tanks and pipes. In each jurisdiction, B Corporation embarked on discussions with regulators concerning further soil and groundwater testing and remediation. The American regulators, however, demanded far more comprehensive analysis, more voluminous documentation, and more costly reports. B Corporation's corporate regulatory compliance group officials said that documents submitted to American regulators for such contaminated sites typically fill a four-drawer filing cabinet, compared with one foot of depth in a single file drawer for the documents submitted to the other countries. And behind each additional ten pages of documentation, they emphasized, lie scores of hours which company officers must devote to research, testing, measurement, analysis, and preparation and checking of draft reports. All in all, B Corporation officials estimated that "extra" studies, submissions, and negotiations with U.S. regulators added $8 to $10 million to the costs of designing the cleanup plan for the two sites in the United States (out of total costs per site of an estimated $22 million), whereas the "extra" regulatory accountability costs for comparable site investigations and cleanup planning in the United Kingdom and the Netherlands were negligible.[24] As of the time of Axelrad's interviews, remediation efforts in England and the Netherlands were well under way. But in the American sites, action remained on hold while the firm waited to learn if officials considered the company's analysis sufficient. In this case, therefore, the additional demands of the U.S. regulatory regime confirmed the maxim that when pushed too far, *accountability* (proving one has done the right thing) can displace *responsibility* (doing the right thing).[25]

2. TWO EXCEPTIONS TO THE PATTERN

Two case studies highlight policy spheres in which regulatory accountability requirements in the United States appear to be *less* demanding than those imposed by agencies in other countries. Johnson, Fujie, and Aalders (chapter 11) point out that the American regime for premarketing clearance of new chemicals (under TSCA) does not require extensive toxicity testing for all new products, but only for 25 percent or so—those for which the EPA, based on the company's submissions, concludes that the potential risks justify the costs and delays of testing. European Union regulations, in contrast, require extensive testing for all new chemical products produced in volume, regardless of resemblance to previously tested chemicals and regardless of levels of risk. In Japan, too, an innovative company must establish biodegradability characteristics for all new chemicals, and toxicity levels for most; hence obtaining approval for marketing new products in Japan is much more costly than in the United States. Kraus (chapter 10) shows that a multinational manufacturer of genetically engineered biologics found that EU demands for information concerning the company's manufacturing methods were more analytically searching than the U.S. FDA's regulatory requirements. The EU regulators compelled the company to undertake additional testing and quality assurance analyses for a production process already approved by the FDA.

In these two regulatory arenas, American regulatory authority is concentrated in a single federal bureau in Washington, D.C. (rather than, as is often the case, scattered in an overlapping welter of federal, state, and local agencies), and those regulators have considerable technical expertise. It is noteworthy, too, that in these two spheres of regulated activity—genetically engineered health products and production of new chemical substances— the United States seems to have a competitive advantage in launching useful new products.

C. Opportunity Costs

One characteristic regulatory tool, prominent in a number of the regulatory programs described in this book, is prior governmental review and approval of new construction projects, new health care products, and changes in industrial production, all with the purpose of ensuring compliance with safety and environmental standards. Such permitting systems are consciously designed to slow the headlong rush of development and technological change, to force consideration of their potential adverse side effects. This prior regulatory scrutiny, however, may also impose opportunity costs on society, as well as on the businesses that suffer regulatory delays. The community must wait longer for improved goods and services and for the jobs that accompany the new ventures. Kraus (chapter 10) tells us that for every month that an FDA manufacturing process review kept a new genetically engineered blood product off the market, the manufacturer had to forgo serving a market that may be worth more than $13 million in monthly sales, and individuals who were eager for the new genetically engineered (and probably safer) version of the product had to wait longer to obtain it.

The regulatory review systems of other nations sometimes impose even greater delays—and higher opportunity costs—than American procedures. A U.S. General Accounting Office study found that it took six to seven years, on average, to win approval for a patent in Japan, compared with about nineteen months in the United States.[26] When "Company Y" (chapter 10) sought regulatory approval of its facility for manufacturing a genetically engineered biological product, it took more than two years to obtain a license from the European Union's Committee for Proprietary Medicinal Products plus the relevant agencies in certain member states, almost as long as the FDA process in the United States. Johnson, Fujie, and Aalders (chapter 11) found that premarketing clearance procedures for new chemicals typically took longer in the EU and Japan than in the United States. TSCA provides a uniquely rapid, no-testing "track"—unless EPA officials decide (which they must do within a ninety-day period) that the chemical requires more in-depth analysis. Also, the United States provides a faster clearance system for new chemicals produced in small volumes for experimental or "market-testing" purposes, which apparently makes it advantageous to market new chemicals first in the United States.

Nevertheless, this project's research as a whole suggests that American legal and regulatory regimes more often impose *longer* delays and *larger* opportunity costs than comparable regimes abroad. In contrast to the FDA and TSCA regimes, decision-making authority in the United States generally is more institutionally fragmented than in parallel regulatory processes abroad, requiring more applications and administrative reviews, and hence more possibility of costly delay. Moreover, American opponents of new projects generally have more opportunities to challenge regulatory approvals in court, which can result in substantial opportunity costs. The greater prospect of judicial review, moreover, often seems to make American regulatory officials more cautious and legalistic in reviewing proposals than their counterparts abroad. According to an environmental consultant with a great deal of cross-national experience, because the regulatory permitting process for an industrial project in the United States entails a great deal more legal formality, organizational complexity, and documentation than in Western Europe, "It takes less time overseas. The cost for initial studies is less. We are not required to accumulate as much information. In Europe [the time from application to permit averages] one third less."[27]

Consider, for example, Dwyer, Brooks, and Marco's comparison of the American and German permit systems for ensuring that changes in motor vehicle factory production and painting processes do not result in increased air pollution or obnoxious odors. Regulatory officials in both countries required Ford Motor Company to install similar pollution control technologies and to build higher exhaust stacks to diffuse odors. But for two factories in western Germany, the time from permit application to approval was five months and seventeen months, respectively; for Ford's plants in Minnesota and New Jersey alike, it was over four years. The opportunity costs for Ford's American operations were tempered because the state agencies allowed Ford to continue production during the permitting process, albeit at a reduced volume. But the way the American permit process operated, that chapter indicates, suggests that its inherent potential for imposing costly delays is much greater than the German process. In fact, American automakers have complained that the greater prescriptiveness of American air pollution rules concerning paint shop emissions often leads to more regulatory inflexibility and delay than they encounter abroad, sometimes throwing tightly coordinated major model changes off schedule. In another study, Richard Brooks describes how a vehicle manufacturer, frustrated by regulatory delays and resistance in seeking to modify its air pollution permit, ended up contracting out the painting of small truck bodies to a distant firm—and shipping them hundreds of miles by rail back to the assembly plant.[28]

Axelrad (chapter 4) shows that in seeking regulatory approval of methods for investigating contamination and remediation of industrial sites, it took B Corporation scarcely more than a year in Great Britain. In the Netherlands, the regulatory process took slightly over five years. But in the United States (at two different sites) it took fifteen and eleven years, respectively. As noted earlier, this involved substantial opportunity costs: the actual remediation efforts moved forward much more rapidly in the United Kingdom and the Netherlands, while that crucial step remained delayed by regulatory red tape in the United States.

Similarly, as noted earlier, Welles and Engel (chapter 5) report that it took Waste Corp. eleven years to complete the permitting process for a municipal waste disposal site in California, which delayed the opening of the landfill for five years. The process for comparable facilities in the United Kingdom took eight years, despite similarly intense local objections. In Pennsylvania and the Netherlands the permit process took about five years, including the processing of local objections and administrative appeals. A company with lesser financial resources and staying power than Waste Corp. might have given up, especially in California—which is precisely what project opponents (and competitors) often hope to achieve by initiating litigation. But although the opponents of Waste Corp.'s California project did not succeed in stopping the project, by constructing consecutive legal obstacles they did compel a sharp reduction in the size of the planned landfill.

D. Divisiveness and Delegitimation

One of the more intangible costs of adversarial legalism is its corrosive effect on personal and institutional relationships. When a regulatory inspector and a regulated enterprise become locked in a legalistic, adversarial posture, the exchange of information and cooperation that are essential to effective regulation often are reduced.[29] When regulatory rule making is only a prelude to litigation, a National Academy of Sciences analysis of EPA policy making observed, contending interests are more likely to resist compromise.[30] In an excellent comparative study, John Braithwaite found that American regulations concerning quality of care in nursing homes are enforced more legalistically (complete with monetary fines and the threat of court orders) than the Australian regulatory regime. Nevertheless, Braithwaite observed, quality of care in American facilities is on average worse. While there may be multiple reasons for that disparity, Braithwaite argues that legalistic enforcement has played a significant role, encouraging the development of large corporate-run homes (that can better afford to comply with costly regulations concerning facilities) and to a ritualistic, penalty-avoiding attitude toward compliance, rather than to a more caring attitude.[31] As Steven Kelman puts it, "Adversary institutions fail to create any relationship among the parties to a policy disagreement. Participants in adversary institutions remain separate individuals, physically proximate only in order to argue before a third party. They do not talk to each other."[32]

Some of these effects were evident in the case studies in this book and were mentioned in the exploratory interviews that led to them. Environmental compliance officials in B Corporation, a multinational chemical manufacturer, contrasted the quality of the company's communications with British and American regulators. In British manufacturing plants, they told Axelrad, regulatory restrictions concerning control of industrial water pollution, air pollution, and other wastes are combined in a single "unified permit." British regulators, in consequence, can trade off special efforts by the firm or more costly restrictions in one area for greater leeway in another area. B Corporation officials plausibly argued that this give-and-take led to more efficient overall remediation plans than in the fragmented American regulatory system, in which the company typically must deal with a multiplicity of state and federal regulatory offices, each operating under its own specific and highly detailed statutory instructions.[33]

Nielsen (chapter 7) describes a pharmaceutical company that has institutionalized a probation process to deal with allegedly problematic employees and, if dismissal is decided upon, procedures for negotiating a termination settlement. Nevertheless, as noted earlier, Nielsen found that 23 percent of employees dismissed by the company's American operations in a typical year subsequently brought a lawsuit against the company—compared with 7 percent in Canada. The disparity arises, it seems likely, from features of the American legal system that provide stronger incentives to sue rather than to negotiate—much higher money damages for unjust or discriminatory dismissals, contingency fee arrangements for compensating lawyers, and the law's failure to compel losing plaintiffs to pay winning defendants' counsel fees.

California's complex permitting scheme for municipal waste disposal, as described by Welles and Engel (chapter 5), seems to discourage initial compromise by project opponents because they gain a great deal of bargaining power by initiating litigation, which can impose costly delays on the community and the waste disposal company. To settle the third of the costly lawsuits designed to block its project, Waste Corp. agreed to pay the objecting city government $3.5 million for public works unrelated to environmental risks associated with the landfill—such as the remediation of environmental problems elsewhere in the city that had been caused by entirely different enterprises. In contrast, Welles and Engel's chapter suggests, legal objections to a proposed landfill in England and the Netherlands are directed to a single administrative body or administrative court (rather than into courts of general jurisdiction), and higher-level governmental bodies can override a local government's objections. Hence, local opponents have more incentive to engage in dialogue and to reach a compromise. In California, the leverage provided by adversarial legalism gave objectors incentives to hold firm.

Aoki and Cioffi (chapter 2) and Aoki, Axelrad, and Kagan (chapter 3) show how American adversarial legalism can erode regulated entities' respect for the law and incentives to internalize regulatory norms. The American subsidiary of PREMCO, a large metal products manufacturer, was battered by heavy fines for violations of RCRA waste product collection and storage regulations. One consequence was that the subsidiary made significant changes in environmental management, policies, and practices. Nevertheless, both environmental and line managers continued to view a visit from regulatory officials with trepidation. They continued to resent the detailed, complex character of the RCRA rules. In PREMCO's parallel Japanese factory, no citation or fine for waste disposal rules has ever been imposed. Japanese law gives the company more discretion in solving the collection and disposal problem. There, regulators' visits are viewed as neither annoying nor threatening. Compared with their counterparts in PREMCO-USA, shop-floor workers in PREMCO-JAPAN seem to have more fully internalized waste control norms—which are perceived as a matter of company policy, not governmental regulation. Similarly, among the subsidiaries of Q Corp, a large manufacturer of electronic components, only Q USA has dragged its feet in developing an environmental management and auditing plan that would pass muster with an international standards body. The American officials have all they can handle, they say, simply trying to keep abreast of and in compliance with the more detailed, complex, and potentially punitive American regulatory regime.

Thus, by making legal and regulatory processes costly, complex, frustrating, and threatening, adversarial legalism tends to alienate citizens and business executives from the law and from the state, eroding respect for bureaucrats, courts, and active government. A national business and professional elite that trades jokes which demean regulatory bureaucrats and lawyers, I suspect, also is more likely to support reforms that diminish regulatory obligations and rights to litigate—without providing alternative mechanisms to ensure accountability, sensible regulatory protections, and justice itself.

VI. COMPENSATING SOCIAL BENEFITS?

The costs that flow from American adversarial legalism—"defensive medicine," larger expenditures on lawyers and consultants and paperwork, opportunity costs, the defensiveness it often stimulates—might be justifiable if adversarial legalism, by virtue of the legal threats it generates, also stimulated higher levels of legal compliance and correspondingly greater social benefits. Lyle Scruggs's study of comparative environmental performance in rich democracies (measured as rates of reduction of major sources of pollution) suggests the opposite. Using OECD data, Scruggs found that notwithstanding (or perhaps because of) its more prescriptive, fiercer environmental laws and enforcement style, the United States made *less* progress in the 1970–90 period than Germany, the Netherlands, Japan, Sweden, and the United Kingdom, where regulatory policy is forged and implemented in a more consensual manner.[34] And although it cannot be claimed that the case studies in this book are fully representative, the representatives of multinational corporations studied generally could not point to significant public-regarding precautions taken in their American operations that were not also taken in their installations abroad. More specifically:

- PREMCO, a metals manufacturing company (Aoki and Cioffi; chapter 2), encountered much more legalistic enforcement of industrial waste disposal regulations in its U.S. plant (replete with large financial penalties and heavy legal expenses) than in comparable factories in Japan. In consequence, the American operations beefed up their environmental management system. Yet officials with experience in both countries assert that waste collection and disposal practices in the Japanese plant are identical, and are implemented by the company with much more care.
- Aoki, Axelrad, and Kagan (chapter 3) found that in "Q Corp's" Japanese electronic parts factory, control of industrial effluent has been more consistently effective than in the corporation's similar U.S. factory, notwithstanding the fact that statutory standards in the United States are more stringent and prescriptive and that "Q USA" (unlike "Q Japan") has been subjected to costly regulatory penalties.
- Nielsen (chapter 7) indicates that the American legal system encourages dismissed employees to sue their former bosses more often than their counterparts in Canada. But the American branch of the company Niel-

sen studied does not respond by being more solicitous of workers' claims than the Canadian branch; if anything, the American branch is more aggressive in firing employees who are initially tagged as unsatisfactory, for it uses the company-prescribed probation process less often than the Canadian branch.

- The multinational company discussed by Kraus (chapter 10) makes genetically engineered biological products; its officials are quite cognizant of the enormous liability risks that would arise in the United States from the sale of contaminated product, and they design their quality control system accordingly. Yet when the company sought manufacturing licenses, the European Union's regulatory body insisted on more probing analyses of quality control than did the U.S. FDA. The EU's standards led the company to establish certain controls that had not been stimulated by the more legalistic American legal and regulatory system.

- Axelrad (chapter 4) finds that U.S. regulations concerning the study and remediation of contaminated industrial sites are significantly more detailed and prescriptive than Dutch and British regulations. A multinational chemical company that dealt with all three jurisdictions described both federal and state regulators in the United States as much more demanding, in terms of required investigatory data. But the "extra" research and reviews required in the United States, company officials convincingly assert, did not result in any additional protections for the public because much of that work was demanded as a matter of regulatory routine and produced information that was irrelevant to the risks posed by the contamination at the particular sites. Indeed, as noted earlier, American regulatory legalism delayed the actual cleanup efforts enormously, while in England and the Netherlands the company moved forward much more quickly to contain any remaining risks to human health.

In three other case studies, it is more uncertain whether American adversarial legalism led to "extra" public protections that might be thought to outweigh its higher costs:

- Credit Co., a multinational bank with credit card operations in the United States and Germany, encounters more adversarial legalism in seeking to collect unpaid debts in the United States (Ruhlin, chapter 8). Because of differences in the law and in the efficiency of the court system, American debtors are much more likely than German debtors to raise legal defenses based on the complex regulations governing direct collection efforts, and much more likely to use the bankruptcy law to block collection efforts. Credit Co., accordingly, "writes off" a larger proportion of delinquent consumer debt in the United States; this might be considered a social cost, since the bank's losses are presumably passed on to other customers in one way or another. But the American system arguably provides certain benefits as well—greater legal protection from overly aggressive or manipulative collection efforts; the "fresh start" that bankruptcy provides debtors who encountered sudden, crushing financial reversals (as a result of serious illness, for example, or divorce or job loss). At the same time, one could argue that Germany's more generous unemployment and public health care systems do a more consistent job of providing for victims of economic reversals of fortune, and that it is precisely the greater difficulty and expense of collecting debts through the courts that lead credit card companies in the United States to resort to extended and aggressive dunning methods.

- Dwyer, Brooks, and Marco (chapter 6) show that in seeking permits from air pollution control authorities, Ford Motor Company encountered more adversarial legal conflict in Minnesota and legalistic resistance in New Jersey than it experienced in its applications for two sites in Germany. It took far longer to obtain the permits in the United States than in Germany. Yet Ford was obliged to install similar pollution control and odor reduction technologies in its assembly plant paint shops in Germany and the United States. However, Dwyer, Brooks, and Marco indicate that the controls on the U.S. plants are tighter, that the permits more demanding, and that Ford may have done more to incinerate odors (as opposed to merely diffusing them) in its Minnesota plant than in Cologne. Although one could argue that those "extra" benefits provided by the U.S. regulations do not outweigh the far greater "friction costs" in the United States, others might disagree. Moreover, it appears that the adversarial proceedings in Minnesota seem to have been the primary precipitant of the odor control plan eventually adopted.
- Welles and Engel (chapter 5) found that in seeking permission to construct solid waste disposal facilities in the United States, the United Kingdom, and the Netherlands, Waste Corp. encountered in all jurisdictions a complicated set of regulatory controls and procedures that provided an opening for public and local concerns or opposition. In each jurisdiction, the regulatory process was effective in that it compelled Waste Corp. to modify its original plans to build in more extensive protections against pollution, odors, traffic, monitoring, and the like. In California and Pennsylvania, however, the permitting process required the corporation to expend vastly more money on lawyers and studies than in England or Holland; and in California, lawsuits and other adversarial challenges resulted in extra multiyear delays in obtaining a final permit. Did adversarial legalism produce protections or benefits for the public in the United States, over and above those provided by the British and Dutch regulatory systems?

Welles and Engel note that Waste Corp. was required to install a thicker, double lining at its California and Pennsylvania sites than was required in the United Kingdom and the Netherlands, and they are uncertain whether the Netherlands site includes a comparable leachate collection system. On the other hand, the designs of the liners and the leachate systems in the United States are products of the detailed, nationwide legal standards in the federal RCRA law; they were not the products of the local regulatory process described in the case studies.

However, in order to curtail the delays of adversarial legalism in California, Waste Corp. agreed to extensive "exactions." It "donated" lands (well removed from the waste site) for parks and recreation. It paid for revegetation research, offside tree planting, and cleanup of hazardous waste facilities (totally unrelated to Waste Corp.'s wastes) in other parts of the county. It also agreed to pay for governmental inspection vehicles, county staff members, and "road access fees." Together, Waste Corp. estimated, these exactions cost $10 million—compared with the roughly $3 million in exactions in connection with obtaining a permit in Pennsylvania, just under $2 million in the United Kingdom, and some noncostly modifications of the waste facility itself in the Netherlands. The much more costly and extensive amenities and "side payments" Waste Corp. provided in California might be considered "extra" social benefits that were generated by adversarial legalism. Perhaps they could be considered, as Welles and Engel suggest, compensation to the community for negative externalities of the waste disposal operation that could not be directly mitigated—compensation that communities in Pennsylvania, England, and the Netherlands did not receive because their regulatory system did not provide local objectors with the weapons of adversarial legalism. From another perspective, however, the costly California exactions might also be considered the product of legal extortion—social benefits that in fairness ought to be publicly debated in a legislative forum and paid for by the taxpaying public.

In sum, in a number of case studies, American adversarial legalism generated extra costs and no extra social benefits; in a few case studies, the balance of costs and benefits is more difficult to assess. Of course, the balance may be different with respect to other spheres of regulation, other industries, and other kinds of regulated companies. In some areas of American environmental regulation, some of our interviewees pointed out, technology forcing and tough enforcement have compelled American firms to take the lead in developing and implementing control technologies that firms overseas employ later, at lower cost and with less need for governmental coercion. As mentioned earlier, Richard Wokutch found that despite OSHA's legalistic regulatory style, large automobile manufacturers in

Japan, where regulators are far less legalistic, have better occupational safety and health practices than comparable American plants, but working conditions in small Japanese subcontractors were comparatively worse than those in small American parts suppliers.[35] At the same time, the *costs* of American adversarial legalism undoubtedly bear more heavily on smaller firms, which can less easily afford to hire lawyers and consultants and to bear the delays that the larger multinationals described to us.[36]

Some might argue that even if adversarial legalism does not yield better precautionary measures than less legalistic controls abroad, things would be worse without it because the United States is different. American business firms, some have argued, are less deferential to governmental authority than are Japanese and European firms.[37] Perhaps Waste Corp.'s extended adversarial legal struggles in California and Ford Motor Company's lengthy permit processes in Minnesota and New Jersey reflect a tendency of American corporate officials to *resist* regulatory demands. The more rambunctious American business style, the argument goes, is one reason that American tort and regulatory law are—and ought to be—more adversarial, legalistic, and deterrence-oriented. Others would disagree, arguing that there is no empirical basis for concluding that American business firms, overall, are more resistant to regulation than British, Dutch, or German enterprises. The case studies in this book cannot resolve that issue. But they provide no hint that American corporate subsidiaries acted rambunctiously in other countries, resisting reasonable regulatory demands. Indeed, in most other countries, U.S. multinationals have a reputation for being especially good regulatory citizens. That weakens the argument that adversarial legalism is needed in the United States to tame a cowboy business culture, but it does not resolve it, since multinationals may not be representative of the American business culture as a whole.

More fundamentally, even if one assumes that adversarial legalism adds *something* to the deterrence equation, the overall size and distribution of those social benefits are highly uncertain. Nor is it at all clear that the presumed deterrent regulatory effects of adversarial legalism are large enough to offset the substantial social costs—defensiveness, litigation and lawyering expense, accountability costs, opportunity costs, and alienation—highlighted by the studies in this book. Perhaps most important, as suggested in the discussion of "divisiveness and delegitimation" in the preceding subsection, adversarial legalism may *discourage* the kind of business-government cooperation that is essential to the full achievement of regulatory goals. In analyzing national rates of pollution reduction, Scruggs found that "neocorporatist" governmental systems (such as Germany, the Netherlands, Sweden, and Japan), where strong industrial associations participate in consensus-seeking methods of policy making and implementation, exhibited stronger environmental performance than more "pluralist" countries such as the United States, where policy making and implementation are more conflictual[38]—and hence conducive to a prescriptive, legalistic, adversarial, and costly style of regulation that generates further mutual mistrust.

Finally, it might be argued that given American political culture, adversarial legalism is necessary to maintain the legitimacy of legal and regulatory processes. In a nation that mistrusts political authority and corporate power, adversarial legalism is valued, perhaps, not because it is efficient or effective but because it supports civic values such as governmental accountability and transparency, checks and balances, responsiveness to minority and local interests, and equal protection of the law. Several case studies in this book underscore the role of adversarial legalism in giving citizens a larger and more powerful voice in the regulatory permitting process than is enjoyed by their counterparts abroad. Adversarial legalism thus democratizes regulation to a certain extent. In some ways, this may add to its legitimacy. Moreover, some multinational corporate officials we spoke with suggested that despite its additional costs and inefficiencies, adversarial legalism helps ensure the integrity and evenhandedness of American regulatory and legal processes. Compared with the closed-door corporatist decision making of many other nations, American adversarial legalism provides both domestic and foreign companies greater assurance that they are competing on a level regulatory playing field and that all business firms enjoy legal recourse against official arbitrariness or favoritism. The American court system, some corporate executives note, is very expensive, but its powerful tools of legal discovery engender confidence that contracts can be enforced, trade secrets protected, and extortive demands repulsed. After all, viewed in comparison with other economically advanced democracies, the United States has been remarkably successful in fostering vibrant financial and venture capital markets, promoting innovation and entrepreneurial activity, and facilitating industrial restructuring; this, too, suggests that in some respects the American legal system has favorable effects on economic growth and competitiveness, at least in cross-national comparative terms.

That said, it does not follow that all aspects of American adversarial legalism are necessary or desirable. The studies in this volume suggest that in many particular spheres of legal activity, adversarial legalism is economically wasteful and sometimes counterproductive, imposing costs that other nations do not, without producing compensating social benefits. Even in a successful economy, wasteful legally imposed expenditures and legally created delays and uncertainties are worth worrying about.

VII. CONCLUSION

Governance in the United States is pervaded by adversarial legalism. Compared with other economically advanced democracies, American processes for policy implementation and dispute resolution generally involve more formal legal contestation, of a particularly adversarial and costly kind. American regulatory programs involve more detailed and complex bodies of rules, harsher penalties, a more legalistic enforcement style, more fragmented institutional structures, and more frequent recourse to courts to challenge administrative decisions. Liability law and civil litigation are more frequently employed in the United States than in Western Europe, Japan, and British Commonwealth nations, and those processes are more punitive, more expensive, and more unpredictable. In consequence, besides the direct costs of complying with federal and state laws and regulations, productive enterprises operating in the United States bear the additional costs of coping with adversarial legalism. These costs, we have seen, often are considerable.

Of course, no legal or regulatory system is free of exasperating "transaction costs." When Shakespeare's Hamlet soliloquized about reasons for shuffling off this mortal coil, he cited "the law's delay" in the same breath as "the insolence of office" and "the pangs of dispriz'd love." Nevertheless, in contemporary Denmark (or England), the law's delay is far less burdensome than in the United States, and its processes are significantly less costly. Comparative studies in numerous policy areas, as well as the studies of multinational corporations reported in this book, indicate that businesses in the United States usually face much higher dispute-resolution and regulatory "process costs" than do parallel business operations in other economically advanced democracies. These costs include:

1. Larger expenditures on lawyers, specialized regulatory affairs personnel, consultants, documentation of compliance, and other formal accountability mechanisms.
2. Longer delays in gaining regulatory approval for new projects and products.
3. More frequent legal conflict, higher monetary penalties, more diversion of managerial time, and more frequent public embarrassment—all of which stem from the more legalistic, unforgiving, and punitive American style of regulatory enforcement.
4. Much larger expenditures on liability insurance, litigation-related legal services, litigation avoidance, and compromise of legally justified claims and defenses—all of which stem from the more adversarial, expensive, and unpredictable American methods for adjudicating

civil cases, paying lawyers, and covering accident victims' lost wages and medical needs.

Indeed, according to the studies in this book and additional exploratory interviews that did not result in case studies, the costs, uncertainties, and delays associated with the American legal and regulatory style generally are more salient and significant to multinational enterprises than are cross-national differences in substantive law and regulatory standards.

At the same time, despite adversarial legalism's demanding processes and despite the deterrent threat of its harsher legal sanctions, multinational enterprises, the studies in this book tentatively suggest, often achieve levels of environmental protection and safety in their European and Japanese operations that are similar to those in their more legally threatened American facilities. This accords with numerous cross-national studies of environmental and safety regulation.

Finally, adversarial legalism, because it more often subjects productive enterprises to wasteful expenditures and unpredictable risks, has certain alienating effects. Multinational enterprises, comparing their experience in the United States and in other countries, often come to regard American legal and regulatory processes as arbitrary, threatening, and counterproductive.

These generalizations have been painted with a rather broad brush, however. American governments project an immense, constantly shifting array of rules into hundreds of different industries and thousands of individual enterprises. The policy areas covered by existing studies and by the case studies in this book represent only a sample of all the existing areas of law and commerce. It will not be difficult for knowledgeable readers to point to instances in which substantive differences in national regulatory or legal rules—such as American restrictions on banking activity, or German restrictions on employee layoffs—are much more important than differences in legal and regulatory style, or in which the fierceness of American law or regulation produces higher levels of protection than the legal regimes of comparable countries. The legalistic American approach to water pollution control, according to a study by Kathryn Harrison, has been more effective than Canada's cooperative style in producing compliance with certain regulatory standards on the part of pulp and paper mills.[39] Japan's nonlegalistic mode of legal control, it appears, is far less effective than American adversarial legalism when the regulatory goal is to change established social norms and practices, such as promoting equal opportunity for women in employment or protecting workers and other nonsmokers from exposure to "secondhand" cigarette smoke.[40] Moreover, some multinational companies we have studied pointed to instances in which legal processes in

Japan (e.g., in obtaining patents, in gaining approval for new chemical products) or in Europe (e.g., in obtaining licenses for genetically engineered products) were as slow, complicated, and unpredictable as in the United States, or even a little more so.

Nevertheless, the overwhelming weight of the existing literature and of our current research supports our generalizations concerning the greater pervasiveness, salience, and economic significance of American adversarial legalism. Thus far, the exceptions we have encountered do not come close to obviating the rule.

By and large, the case studies in this volume were not able to provide meaningful quantitative estimates of the "extra" costs specifically attributable to American adversarial legalism, either at the level of the whole economy or at the level of particular firms or industrial sectors. Since our research focused on large multinational enterprises that do have operations in the United States, we encountered no direct evidence that the burdens and risks associated with adversarial legalism scared away foreign businesses or drove out American firms. The United States benefits in this regard from the enormous size of the market it offers both American and foreign businesses, which appear to treat adversarial legalism as a price to be paid to gain access to this market. It does seem clear, however, that the costs of American adversarial legalism, as distinct from the costs of complying with substantive regulatory standards, rise to an economically significant level and often are very significant to individual enterprises. These costs detract from the economic efficiency of the American economy, saddling it with costs of a kind that are not borne by other national economies.

That does not exactly prove that the costs of American adversarial legalism outweigh its social benefits. The United States is a particularly diverse, undeferential society. Multinational enterprises operating in America undoubtedly pay more for security guards, employee drug testing, and the like than they do in parallel facilities in Japan or Germany; such extra security costs, in comparative terms, operate as a drag on the American economy. Still, given the social conditions in the United States, it would be foolish not to invest in the extra protection. Similarly, American regulators work in a more diverse, less deferential, and difficult-to-regulate business environment than their Japanese, Canadian, and European counterparts. Sprawling and decentralized, the United States does not have the strong trade associations, respected national bureaucracies, and comprehensive social welfare systems that characterize Western European states. Thus, to maintain similar levels of protection for its citizens, it might be argued, the United States has little choice but to employ the shock troops of adversarial legalism—legal rights and penalties, lawyers, and litigation. Adversarial legalism may be a costly, inefficient method, but without it, conceivably, substantive legal and regulatory policies would be evaded more often.

Moreover, the same legal arrangements that lead to high litigation costs, unpredictability, and defensiveness—easy access to courts, entrepreneurial lawyering, extensive pretrial discovery, strong legal remedies, a politically responsive (rather than a narrowly professional) judiciary, institutional fragmentation (checks and balances)—also are used to attack and deter governmental unresponsiveness, bureaucratic arbitrariness, abuse of economic power, discrimination, and negligence. Adversarial legalism makes the American political and legal system more responsive to new ideas and justice claims often generating regulatory ideas and norms that other countries later emulate. Thus, despite its failings and inefficiencies, some would argue, adversarial legalism makes a positive contribution to social welfare.

Adversarial legalism's admirable functions, however, do not justify ignoring its costly excesses. Some defenders of American adversarial legalism, afraid that conservative reformers will throw the baby out with the bathwater, tend to dismiss attacks on the system's costs and inefficiencies as unrepresentative exaggerations. They act as if any diminution of adversarial legalism in any sphere of law or any regulatory program would have adverse effects. That surely is not the case. Although the techniques of adversarial legalism apply across a broad range of American policy arenas, they were institutionalized and are now invoked on a program-by-program, case-by-case basis. They can be reassessed and moderated in the same way.

NOTES

1. Alex Mehta and Keith Hawkins, "Integrated Pollution Control and Its Impact: Perspectives From Industry," *Journal of Environmental Law* 10 (1998):65.

2. Ibid., 66–67

3. Gary Schwartz, "Product Liability and Medical Malpractice in Comparative Context," in *The Liability Maze*, edited by Peter Huber and Robert Litan (Washington, D.C.: Brookings Institution, 1991).

4. Karen Palmer, Wallace Oates, and Paul Portney, "Tightening Environmental Standards: The Benefit-Cost or the No-Cost Paradigm?" *Journal of Economic Perspectives* 9 (1995): 129–30 (emphasis added).

5. Interview with chief attorney, environmental affairs, chemical company, September 29, 1995.

6. Eugene Bardach and Robert A. Kagan, *Going by the Book: The Problem of Regulatory Unreasonableness* (Philadelphia: Temple University Press, 1982); John Braithwaite, *To Punish or Persuade: Enforcement of Coal Mine Safety* (Albany: State University of New York Press, 1985).

7. See Jonathan Adler, "Bean Counting for a Better Earth: Environmental Enforcement at the EPA," *Regulation* 21 (Spring 1998): 43.

8. Ian Ayres and John Braithwaite, *Responsive Regulation* (New York: Oxford University Press, 1992).

9. See Daniel Fiorino, "Toward a New System of Environmental Regulation: The

Case for An Industry Sector Approach," *Environmental Law* 26 (1996): 457; Douglas Michael, "Cooperative Implementation of Federal Regulations," *Yale Journal on Regulation* 13 (1996): 535; Jody Freeman, "Collaborative Governance in the Administrative State," *UCLA Law Review* 45 (1997): 1–98; Joseph Rees, *Reforming the Workplace: A Study of Self-Regulation in Occupational Safety* (Philadelphia: University of Pennsylvania Press, 1988); Eugene Weber, *Pluralism by the Rules: Conflict and Cooperation in Environmental Regulation* (Washington, D.C.: Georgetown University Press, 1998).

10. See, e.g., Mark Lifsher, "EPA Urged to Move against Firm," *Wall Street Journal,* June 17, 1998, CA1, 4.

11. David Rogers, "Meat and Poultry Packers Defeat Move to Allow Civil Penalties in the Industry," *Wall Street Journal,* June 17, 1998, A5.

12. Edward Rubin, "Discretion and Its Discontents," *Chicago Kent Law Review* 72 (1997): 1299.

13. Bardach and Kagan, *Going by the Book,* chap. 6.

14. For a polemical but compelling account of employment-related litigation in the United States, see Walter Olson, *The Excuse Factory: How Employment Law Is Paralyzing the American Workplace* (New York: Free Press, 1997). In the mid-1980s, some nine thousand employment discrimination cases were filed annually in federal courts (double the rate of a decade earlier); most of these involved allegations of wrongful termination. John Donohue and Peter Siegelman, "The Changing Nature of Employment Discrimination Litigation" *Stanford Law Review* 43 (1991): 983. In California (with about 11 percent of the nation's population), researchers estimated that one thousand common law wrongful termination cases were filed in 1986; nationwide in that year, wrongful termination jury awards averaged final payments of $208,000 and defense fees of $81,000. James Dertouzos, Elaine Holland, and Patricia Ebener, *The Legal and Economic Consequences of Wrongful Termination* (Santa Monica, Calif.: RAND Institute for Civil Justice, 1992).

15. Similar observations are recounted by Schwartz, "Product Liability and Medical Malpractice in Comparative Context," 47–51.

16. Ibid.

17. See James Maxeiner, "The Expert in U.S. and German Patent Litigation," *International Review of Industrial Property and Copyright Law* 22 (1991): 595. Maxeiner explains nicely why the intensely adversarial American approach to patent litigation is much more expensive than similar litigation in Europe. See also Andrea Gerlin, "Patent Lawyers Forgo Sure Fees on a Bet," *Wall Street Journal,* June 24, 1994, B1

18. In a study of Australian regulatory agencies, Braithwaite and Graboski refer to bank regulators and others with equivalent power to impose harsh reputational sanctions or long delays on regulated companies as "benign big guns," referring to their ability to regulate effectively without resorting to legal sanctions. Peter Graboski and John Braithwaite, *Of Manners Gentle: Enforcement Strategies of Australian Business Regulatory Agencies (*Melbourne: Oxford University Press, 1986).

19. Confirming the prevalence of cross-state variation in adversarial legalism concerning land use projects, a survey concluded that between 1986 and 1990, two to three hundred lawsuits were filed under the California Environmental Quality Act, objecting to local government decisions. While New York approached California's levels of litigation, respondents estimated that in most states fewer than ten

environmental-analysis-related lawsuits were decided in the previous five years. J. D. Landes et al., *Fixing CEQA: Options and Opportunities for Reforming the California Environmental Quality Act* (Berkeley: California Policy Seminar, University of California, 1995). The multinational waste management company (Waste Corp.) studied by Welles and Engel conducted an internal study comparing its costs for obtaining a permit for a few recent California projects with ten other landfills for which it had sought permits in other states. Waste Corp.'s average permitting cost in California was $25 million, compared with an average of $1.6 million in the other states.

20. Richard Sander, "Elevating the Debate on Lawyers and Economic Growth," *Law and Social Inquiry* 17 (1992): 665.

21. One could imagine other reasons for the greater use of lawyers in the United States. It is conceivable that the American business culture is more aggressively competitive and more tolerant of business efforts to evade or bend the law than the business culture of some European countries and Japan. See David Vogel, *National Styles of Regulation* (Ithaca, N.Y.: Cornell University Press, 1986). Thus American firms, and subsidiaries of foreign-based multinationals that are staffed by American executives, may be more defiant, more willing to engage in legal conflict with regulators, or more inclined "to see what they can get away with," than are firms operating in other countries—in short, American companies are more adversarial, and thus induce more adversarial legalism on the part of regulators. Another possibility, however, is that the more detailed and prescriptive nature of American law makes business managers in the United States feel that the governmental demands are unreasonable, and hence deserving of an aggressive response, than the more flexible regulations of other countries. See Robert A. Kagan, "What Makes Uncle Sammy Sue?" *Law and Society Review* 21 (1988): 734. In some of the case studies in this book—PREMCO in the United States (chapter 2), Waste Corp. in California (chapter 5), Ford Motor Company in New Jersey (chapter 6), there are intimations that those kinds of corporate attitudes, as well as the behavior of regulators and citizen-complainants, played some role in stimulating legal conflict and the need to consult lawyers. But by and large, the case studies tend to support the notion that the complexity, unpredictability, and potential punitiveness of American law are the more important explanatory factors.

22. For an exception, see Johnson, Fujie, and Aalders, chapter 11, this volume.

23. William T. Barker, "Managing the Discovery Process: Some Thoughts for In-House Counsel," *Corporate Practice Commentator* (1990–91): 604–14. Barker suggests that firms with no current litigation under way take the following steps to prepare for discovery requests that may arise in conceivable future litigation: (1) systematically and consistently retain documents reaching back as long as any pertinent statutes of limitations (fifteen years or longer in some cases); and (2) "instill a bias toward documentation" among company employees. Litigation against insurance companies often involves discovery inquiries into documents and routine firm practices dating back many years, and in many instances no longer in use. This is a burdensome inquiry for defendants "and one likely to justify significant prophylactic actions to minimize both defense costs and liability." Ibid., 604–5.

24. Axelrad, chapter 4, this volume, Figure 4.2.

25. Eugene Bardach and Robert A. Kagan, eds., *Social Regulation: Strategies for Reform* (San Francisco: Institute of Contemporary Studies Press, 1982), pp. 347–48.

26. U.S. General Accounting Office, *Intellectual Property Rights: U.S. Companies' Patent Experiences in Japan* (Washington, D.C.: General Accounting Office, 1993). Recently, the Japanese government has instituted a number of changes to speed up the process.

27. "In Western Europe," this experienced environmental consultant continued, "there are several levels of implementation where you sit with them and work through the process. U.S. bureaucrats are overly cautious and want to attach too much cost to impact assessments. Furthermore, they never want to make a real decision. I think the problem is that they always want more information." This presumably reflects the fact that American regulators, operating under more specific statutes, enjoy less administrative discretion and are more susceptible to court challenge and judicial review.

28. Richard Rexford Wayne Brooks, "The Role of Law and Regulation in Contracts and Organizations" (Ph.D. diss., University of California, Berkeley, 1998).

29. Bardach and Kagan, *Going by the Book.*

30. National Academy of Sciences, *Decisionmaking at the U.S. Environmental Protection Agency* (Washington, D.C.: National Academy Press, 1977), 79–81.

31. John Braithwaite, "The Nursing Home Industry," in *Beyond the Law: Crime in Complex Organizations*, vol. 18, *Crime and Justice*, edited by Michael Tonry and Albert J. Reiss Jr. (Chicago: University of Chicago Press, 1993), 11–54.

32. Steven Kelman, "Adversary and Cooperationist Institutions for Conflict Resolution in Public Policymaking," *Journal of Policy Analysis and Management* 11 (1992): 186.

33. A striking illustration of the inefficiency associated with fragmented, legally prescriptive environmental regulation characteristic of the United States was provided by the often-cited 1994 Yorktown Project. Amoco was invited by the U.S. EPA to devise its own least-cost means of achieving environmental improvements at its Yorktown refinery, free from highly prescriptive regulation under separate air, water, and waste disposal legal regimes. The company demonstrated the possibility of dramatic improvements in environmental performance at far less than the cost of conforming with existing, uncoordinated regulatory requirements. Marc Landy and Loren Cass, "U.S. Environmental Regulation in a More Competitive World," in *Comparative Disadvantages? Social Regulations and the Global Economy*, edited by P. Nivola (Washington, D.C.: Brookings Institution, 1997), 210–12.

34. Lyle Scruggs, "Sustaining Abundance: Environmental Performance in Advanced Societies" (Ph.D. diss., Duke University, 1998). Scruggs used OECD's *Environmental Data Compendium* to create measures for member states' rates of improvement (pollution reduction, waste reduction) over five- and ten-year periods between 1970 (or 1975) and 1990 with respect to a number of key indicators—air pollution (reductions in sulfur dioxide and nitrous oxide emissions); solid waste (reductions in municipal waste, recycling rates for paper and glass); and water pollution (reductions in untreated wastewater and in pesticide use per unit of arable land). Only with respect to nitrous oxide reduction rate did the United States rank near the top of the seventeen nations, and it did comparatively well in reductions in pesticide use in the 1980–90 period. See also Scruggs, "Institutions and Environmental Performance in Seventeen Western Democracies," *British Journal of Political Science* 29 (1999): 1–31.

35. Richard E. Wokutch, *Worker Protection, Japanese Style: Occupational Safety and Health in the Auto Industry* (Ithaca, N.Y.: ILR Press, 1992), 8, 223, 225, 228.

36. One study has indicated that to comply with federal regulations, it costs firms with fewer than twenty employees almost twice as much per worker as it does firms with over five hundred employees. Small firms, too, are less able to afford the legal costs and uncertainties of fighting lawsuits. "Behind America's Small-Business Success Story," *The Economist*, December 13, 1997, 51–52. In a study of pollution control regulation in the United Kingdom, Mehta and Hawkins also found that compliance costs were especially large, in relation to sales volume, for small companies, although compliance costs also were high for very large companies. Mehta and Hawkins also found that small companies were especially fearful of the costs that would stem from official prosecution of regulatory violations, whereas very large firms were more concerned about the prospect of adverse publicity. Mehta and Hawkins, "Integrated Pollution Control and Its Impact."

37. For a discussion of American business culture in this context, see Vogel, *National Styles of Regulation*.

38. Scruggs, "Sustaining Abundance," 23, 26–27, 163, 286–87.

39. Kathryn Harrison, "Is Cooperation the Answer? Canadian Environmental Enforcement in Comparative Context," *Journal of Policy Analysis and Management* 14 (1995): 221. See also Benoit LaPlante and Paul Rilstone, "Environmental Inspections and Emissions of the Pulp and Paper Industry in Quebec," *Journal of Environmental Economics and Management* 31 (1996): 19, indicating that it is the frequency of inspections, and not necessarily the punitiveness of regulatory sanctions, that significantly affects compliance levels.

40. Joyce Gelb, "Equal Employment Opportunity Law: A Decade of Change for Japanese Women?" *Yale Asia Pacific Review* 1 (1998): 40; Mark Levin, "Smoke around the Rising Sun: An American Look at Tobacco Regulation in Japan," *Stanford Law and Policy Review* 8 (1997): 99; David Vogel, Robert A. Kagan, and Timothy Kessler, "Political Culture and Tobacco Control: An International Comparison," *Tobacco Control* 2 (1993): 317.

CONTRIBUTORS

Marius Aalders is an associate professor of environmental law and policy at the Centre for Environmental Law, University of Amsterdam, the Netherlands.

Kazumasu Aoki, LL.M., the University of Chicago Law School, is a doctoral candidate at Keio University and was a visiting scholar at the Center for the Study of Law and Society, University of California, Berkeley, from 1994 to 1997.

Lee Axelrad, J.D., M.C.P., University of California, Berkeley, is an attorney with the Resources Law Group, LLP, Sacramento, California.

Richard W. Brooks, J.D., University of Chicago, and Ph.D. (economics), University of California, Berkeley, is an assistant professor of law at Northwestern University.

John W. Cioffi is a doctoral candidate in the Department of Political Science, University of California, Berkeley, and a member of the bar in New York and New Jersey.

John P. Dwyer is the Dean and John H. Boalt Professor of Law, University of California, Berkeley.

Kirsten H. Engel is an associate professor of law at Tulane Law School.

Tatsuya Fujie is a doctoral student in the Graduate School of International Cooperation Study at Kobe University.

Lori A. Johnson is an attorney and a doctoral candidate in the Department of Political Science, University of California, Berkeley.

Robert A. Kagan is a professor of political science and law, University of California, Berkeley.

Martine Kraus, Ph.D. (economic geography), University of California, Berkeley, is Associate Director of Regulatory Affairs at Gilead Sciences, Inc.

Alan C. Marco, Ph.D. (economics), University of California, Berkeley, is an assistant professor at Vassar College.

Laura Beth Nielsen, J.D. (Boalt Hall), and Ph.D. (jurisprudence and social policy), University of California, Berkeley, is a research fellow at the American Bar Foundation.

Charles Ruhlin is a doctoral candidate in economics at the University of California, Berkeley, and a medical student at the University of California, San Francisco.

Deepak Somaya, Ph.D., Haas School of Business, University of California, Berkeley, is an assistant professor at the Robert H. Smith School of Business at the University of Maryland, College Park.

Holly Welles is a doctoral candidate in the Department of City and Regional Planning, University of California, Berkeley.

INDEX

Note: Page numbers in italics indicate tables and figures.

abatement notices (U.K.), 120n41
Abraham, Steven E., 233
acceptance limits, 330–33
accountability: costs of, 391–95; displacing responsibility, 394; record-keeping requirements for, 76–78, 196–97, 201, 203–4, 219n164, 220n203
Ackerman, Bruce, 26n14
ACME (pseud., chemical company): basic invention of, 275, 289–92, *296;* as case study, 276–77; compliance issues and, 375; context of, 275–76, 386; differences in patent regimes and, 297–99, 304n2; enforcing patent rights and, 276, 283–85, *286–87,* 288, 289–90, 303, 310n73, 386; European patent experiences of, 291–92; harmonization and, 276, 278, 299–300, *301–2,* 303, 378; Japanese patent experiences of, 290–91; lamination technology of, 293–94, *296;* medical devices of, 292, *296;* opportunity costs and, 395; overview of, 277–78, 294–95, *296,* 297, 303–4; polymer coating of, 293, *296;* product commercialization by, 276, 288; U.S. patent experiences of, 289–90
ADEA (1988, Age Discrimination in Employment Act, U.S.), 246, *247,* 248–49n4
administrative guidance (Japan): areas covered by, 48, 69–70, 78; concept of,

44, 61n49, 69; LEOPC and, 59n39; penalties vs., 79, 94n49; as predictive of future trend, 49, 70; prevalence of, 58n27
adversarial legalism: agency personnel continuity and, 333–35; in air pollution permit process, 207–8; automobile paint shops and, 23, 24, 380, 389, 411n21; as bias in case studies, 20–21; chemical notification laws and, 24, 342, 365–66, 387–88; concept of, 3–4, 8–11, *10;* consequences of, 1, 13–14; costs of, 13, 23, 25, 389–400, 406–9, 411n21; distinctiveness of, 379–85; divisiveness/delegitimation and, 397–400; economic impact of, 405, 408; in employee termination process, 247–48; evaluation of, 406–9; exceptions to, 385–89; legalistic enforcement and, 380–83; patent protection and, 276; political sources of, 11–13, 51; public participation and, 379–80; questions about, 14–15; social benefit issues and, 400–405, 409; solid waste management and, 42–44; Superfund site and, 36–37; support for, 22–23; variability in, 23–24, 385–88
Affirmative Action Office (PCO, Canada), 238, 239–41, 243, 246–47, 393
Age Discrimination in Employment Act (1988, ADEA, U.S.), 246, *247,* 248–49n4